The Ultimate Experience

The Ultimate Experience

Battlefield Revelations and the Making of Modern War Culture, 1450–2000

Yuval Noah Harari

Department of History
Hebrew University of Jerusalem

First published 2008 by
PALGRAVE MACMILLAN
Houndmills, Basingstoke, Hampshire RG21 6XS and
175 Fifth Avenue, New York, N.Y. 10010
Companies and representatives throughout the world

PALGRAVE MACMILLAN is the global academic imprint of the Palgrave Macmillan division of St. Martin's Press, LLC and of Palgrave Macmillan Ltd. Macmillan® is a registered trademark in the United States, United Kingdom and other countries. Palgrave is a registered trademark in the European Union and other countries.

ISBN-13: 978–0–230–53692–0 hardback
ISBN-10: 0–230–53692–1 hardback

This book is printed on paper suitable for recycling and made from fully managed and sustained forest sources. Logging, pulping and manufacturing processes are expected to conform to the environmental regulations of the country of origin.

A catalogue record for this book is available from the British Library.

Library of Congress Cataloging-In-Publication Data
Harari, Yuval N.
   The ultimate experience:battlefield revelations and the making of modern war culture, 1450–2000/Yuval Noah Harari.
       p. cm.
   Includes index.
   ISBN 0–230–53692–1 (alk. paper)
   1. Combat—Psychological aspects—History.   2. War (Philosophy)
   3. Experience—History.   4. Experience (Religion)—History.
   5. Combat in literature.   6. Military history, Modern.   I. Title.
   U21.2.H357 2008
   355.001—dc22   2007052972

10   9   8   7   6   5   4   3   2   1
17   16   15   14   13   12   11   10   09   08

Transferred to digital printing in 2009.

To Itzik.
Anicca vata sankhara.

Contents

vii

List of Figures

On the Cover. A detail from John Singleton Copley, *The Death of Major Peirson, 6 January 1781* (1783). © Tate Gallery, London. Image N00733/118.

Preface

This book is the product of a lifetime of impressions and experiences. Writing it was an act of closing a very personal account with the study of military history and with the experience of war. Luckily, most readers do not know me. Consequently, they can read the book without being disturbed by its autobiographical aspects. In contrast to many of the people about whom I write, I have no intention of basing my arguments on the authority of personal experience.

However, the personal nature of this book makes it difficult to thank those who helped me write it. Singling out the people most deserving of gratitude is a tricky and misleading enterprise. A partial and biased list should begin with my university teachers. An academic history book is a very peculiar way of observing and arranging human reality. No matter what personal input there is in this book, it is the mold that holds it together and gives it power. The book's biggest debt is therefore to the epistemic framework that gave it shape and authority, and to the academic community that taught me how to produce such an artifact. Above all I would like to thank my teacher and mentor at the Hebrew University, Prof. Benjamin Z. Kedar. I also owe a huge debt to Prof. Martin Van Creveld and to Dr Steven J. Gunn, and important debts to Prof. Gabriel Motzkin and Alon Klebanoff.

In contrast to the book's form, its contents were shaped to a far smaller degree by the academic world. Leaving aside structural influences and concentrating on personal ones, I would like to express my gratitude first and foremost to Sarai Aharoni, my friend of many years, who time and again has provided me with crucial intellectual stimuli. Many thanks are also due to my friends and colleagues, Tom Gal, Diego Olstein, Yaron Toren, Amir Fink, and Yossi Maurey. I am also grateful to the writings of many scholars whom I have never met, but who influenced my thinking and opened new intellectual vistas for me, including Charles Taylor, John A. Lynn, John Keegan, Barbara Ehrenreich, Jared Diamond, and Elaine Scarry.

My students at the Hebrew University have a significant share in this book. Many of its ideas took shape – and others took a severe knocking – in classroom discussions.

I would like to thank my research assistants Ilya Berkovic, Eyal Katz, and Eva Sperschneider.

I am greatly indebted to the Yad Hanadiv Fellowship Trust for their generous support of this research project, and in particular to Natania Isaak, who made it a pleasure as well as a privilege to enjoy the Trust's generosity.

Last but not least, I would like to thank my family for its emotional and material support, and in particular to Itzik, my spouse and life-companion.

As noted, this is a very partial and biased list. Many of the true influences that shaped this book can hardly be acknowledged in a respectable academic format, from a good-looking paratrooper I dated for several weeks, to Saddam Hussein and Hassan Nasrallah who made me think about war even when I preferred to occupy myself differently.

Other influences remain unknown and unacknowledged even in my own mind.

Please note that throughout the book, the use of *italics* within quotation marks indicates that the words were italicized in the original. ***Bold italics*** indicates that the emphasis is my own.

Acknowledgments

The author and publishers wish to thank the following for permission to reproduce copyright material:

Photo Scala, Florence for *Saint Martin Renouncing Arms* by Simone Martini (1312–17).

The British Library for plates 2 and 4 from *A series of 80 engraved plates, illustrating the life of St. Ignatius Loyola* (Rome, 1609–22); p. 1503 from Foxe's *Book of Martyrs* (1563); and pp. 14–15 from Henry Hexham's *The Principles of the Art Militarie* (1637).

Time magazine for the magazine's cover of October 2, 2006.

The Bildarchiv Preussischer Kulturbesitz for *The Fortunes of War* by Niklaus Manuel (c.1514/15); and for *Prince Maurice of Nassau* by Jan Saenredam (c.1600).

Stedelijk Museum De Lakenhal, Leiden, The Netherlands for *Allegory on the Death of Admiral Tromp* by Pieter Steenwyck (1653?).

Mount Holyoke College Art Museum, South Hadley, Massachusetts for *Vanitas Still-life* by Henrdick Andriessen (c.1650).

The Bibliothèque nationale de France for folios 4 and 36 from *La Danse Macabre* (1510?), fonds français, 995.

Kunstmuseum Basel, Kupferstichkabinett for *Battlefield* (*Schlachtfeld*) by Urs Graf (1521).

Visual Photos for *Soldier Glances Sideways at Dead Comrade* (1967).

Rome, Galleria Borghese, Photo Scala, Florence and the Ministero Beni e Att. Culturali for *Deposition* (*Deposizione*) by Raphael (1507).

Fine Arts Museums of San Francisco for *After the Battle* by Jacques Courtois (le Bourguignon) (c.1660); and for *The Dead Soldier* by Joseph Wright (1789).

Szépművészeti Múzeum, Budapest for *Mucius Scaevola before Porsina* by Peter Paul Rubens and Anthony van Dyck (1620).

Museo del Prado, Madrid for *The Defense of Cadiz* by Francisco de Zurbarán (1634).

The United States Army for US Army Recruitment Poster 553-RP-SKILL TRAINING-RPI-217 U.S.G.P.O. 547-121 (2003).

Réunion des musées nationaux, Paris and châteaux de Malmaison et Bois-Préau for *Napoleon Crossing the St. Bernard* by Jacques-Louis David (1800).

The Metropolitan Museum of Art for *Washington Crossing the Delaware* by Emanuel Gottlieb Leutze (1851).

The National Gallery of Canada for *The Death of General Wolfe* by Benjamin West (1770).

The Tate Gallery, London, for *The Death of Major Peirson, 6 January 1781* by John Singleton Copley (1783).

Réunion des musées nationaux, Paris and the musée de Louvre, Paris for *Napoleon on the Battlefield of Eylau* by Antoine-Jean Gros (1808).

The Anne S. K. Brown Military Collection, Brown University Library for Plate 89 from Christian Wilhelm Faber du Faur, *Pictures from my Portfolio, Collected in situ during the 1812 Campaign in Russia* (1831).

Every effort has been made to trace rights holders, but if any have been inadvertently overlooked the publishers would be pleased to make the necessary arrangements at the first opportunity.

Part I

Introduction: War as Revelation, 1865–2000

'Every man thinks meanly of himself for not having been a soldier,' said Samuel Johnson in 1778. 'Were Socrates and Charles the Twelfth of Sweden both present in any company, and Socrates to say, "Follow me, and hear a lecture on philosophy;" and Charles, laying his hand on his sword, to say, "Follow me, and dethrone the Czar;" a man would be ashamed to follow Socrates.'[1]

In fact, at the time Johnson spoke these famous words, a link was forged between war and philosophy, which made the choice between Charles the Twelfth and Socrates redundant. Under the influence of the Enlightenment and Romanticism, Western war culture was being transformed, and the battlefield was becoming a privileged site for learning the truth. Consequently, no matter whether one was interested in proving one's manliness or in acquiring wisdom, it was in both cases better to follow Charles the Twelfth.[2]

John Malcolm, a young British officer fresh to the Peninsular War, was told by his fellow officers before his first battle in 1813 that 'in less than twenty-four hours hence, I might be wiser than all the sages and philosophers that ever wrote.'[3] Count Pierre Bezuhov, the hero of Tolstoy's *War and Peace*, met dozens of philosophers, sages, and princes in his search for truth. Ultimately, he found 'the eternal personification of truth' in the shape of Platon Karatayev, an old common soldier who spent almost his entire life in the army.[4]

The quintessential late modern Western war story that Malcolm and Tolstoy helped to develop describes the experience of war as an experience of learning the truth about oneself and about the world.[5] The hero of the story is most often an ignorant youth whom war turns into a wise veteran. Combat is depicted as a quasi-mystical experience of revelation.

An American soldier wrote about his first kill in Vietnam: 'I looked into my enemy's face. He had stopped jerking and all at once his eyes stopped blinking and at that moment I think I learned the secret of life.'[6] A British paratrooper in the Falklands shouted to a journalist in the midst of combat: 'I've just learnt more about myself in the last ten minutes than I knew in my whole life before.'[7] An American World War II veteran wrote about his first combat: 'Everything my life had been before and has been after pales in the light of that awesome moment when my amtrac started in amid a thunderous bombardment toward the flaming, smoke-shrouded beach for the assault on Peleliu.'[8] A German World War II veteran said about a particularly difficult battle that in the course of combat 'reality touched the deepest recesses of my being.'[9] A character in an Israeli semi-autobiographical war novel says about his experiences in Lebanon:

> If peace does not come first, I would like my kid too to go through what I went through there, the challenges, the pains and fears. They made me look differently at the world, to discover myself, the things that are really important to me, the love to my family, the love to life, the brittleness of life.... I matured there, for better or worse.[10]

Like religious conversion, combat is often compared to birth (a baptism of fire). Another Israeli veteran titled his military memoirs *Three Births in September*, referring to his two combat injuries as rebirths. 'I was born in September 1948,' he wrote, 'I was injured and reborn in September 1969, and I was born once again in September 1984.'[11]

When veterans try to give a detailed description of combat, they often describe it as an epiphany. The flow of time changes, slows down, or stops altogether. Unfamiliar sensations appear, and familiar sensations mutate. Awareness becomes completely absorbed in the present moment, and combatants feel more alive ever before. As the most basic laws of physics seem to bend and change, combatants are exposed to hitherto unknown layers of reality.[12] In *Der Kampf als inneres Erlebnis* (*Battle as an Inner Experience* [1922]) Ernst Jünger described combat in the following terms:

> Once again: the ecstasy. The condition of the holy man, of great poets and of great love is also granted to those of great courage. The enthusiasm of manliness bursts beyond itself to such an extent that the blood boils as it surges through the veins and glows as it foams through the heart... it is an intoxication beyond all intoxication, an

unleashing that breaks all bonds.... There [in combat] the individual is like a raging storm, the tossing sea and the roaring thunder. He has melted into everything.[13]

Shawn Nelson, an American soldier, described his combat experience in Mogadishu (1993) in more concrete terms:

> It was hard to describe how he felt...it was like an epiphany. Close to death, he had never felt so completely alive. There had been split seconds in his life when he'd felt death brush past, like when another fast-moving car veered from around a sharp curve and just missed hitting him head-on. On this day he had lived with that feeling, with death breathing right in his face [...] for moment after moment, for three hours or more. [...] Combat was [...] a state of complete mental and physical awareness. In those hours on the street he had not been Shawn Nelson, he had no connection to the larger world, no bills to pay, no emotional ties, nothing. He had just been a human being staying alive from one nano-second to the next, drawing one breath after another, fully aware that each one might be his last. He felt he would never be the same.[14]

What truths are revealed to combatants during such epiphanies, and what veterans actually learn in war, differs widely. Many veterans say that war revealed to them the positive truths of masculine heroism, patriotism, and camaraderie, which remain obscure in the deadening monotony of peacetime. Henry Paul Mainwaring Jones, a 21-years-old lieutenant in the British army, wrote to his brother three days before he was killed (1917):

> Have you ever reflected on the fact that, despite the horrors of war, it is at least a big thing? I mean to say that in it one is brought face to face with realities. The follies, selfishness, luxury and general pettiness of the vile commercial sort of existence led by nine-tenths of the people of the world in peacetime are replaced in war by a savagery that is at least more honest and outspoken. Look at it this way: in peacetime one just lives one's own little life, engaged in trivialities, worrying about one's own comfort, about money matters, and all that sort of thing – just living for one's own self. What a sordid life it is! In war, on the other hand, even if you do get killed you only anticipate the inevitable by a few years in any case, and you have the satisfaction of knowing that you have 'pegged out' in the attempt to

help your country. You have, in fact, realized an ideal, which, as far as I can see, you very rarely do in ordinary life. The reason is that ordinary life runs on a commercial and selfish basis; if you want to 'get on,' as the saying is, you can't keep your hands clean.

Personally, I often rejoice that the War has come my way. It has made me realize what a petty thing life is. I think that the War has given to everyone a chance to 'get out of himself,' as I might say.... Certainly, speaking for myself, I can say that I have never in all my life experienced such a wild exhilaration as on the commencement of a big stunt, like the last April one for example. The excitement for the last half-hour or so before it is like nothing on earth.[15]

Fascist authors such as Ernst Jünger celebrated this type of militaristic revelation in the 1920s and 1930s,[16] and though it has since been challenged many times, it is far from extinct.[17] Indeed, even avowed pacifist writers often praise war for revealing to them the previously unimaginable joys of male comradeship.

An alternative war story equates revelation with disillusionment. In this version of the story, the ignorant youth enters war with expectations of glory, but combat teaches him not to believe the false promises of heroism and patriotism, and never again to trust powerful establishments. Jean Norton Cru, a French World War I veteran, wrote that 'on the score of courage, patriotism, sacrifice and death, we had been deceived and with the first bullets we recognized at once the falsity of anecdote, history, literature, art, the gossip of veterans, and public speeches.'[18]

The disillusioned narrative easily merges with another dominant narrative, which draws on psychological theories and which views war as "trauma."[19] The widespread expectation that veterans must suffer at least some degree of Post-Traumatic Stress Disorder (PTSD) is often just another twist on the basic theme of martial revelation. The story of PTSD is frequently narrated as a story of negative revelation, in which the horrible truths exposed by war transform the innocent "boy next door" into a war criminal, a social misfit, or a madman. PTSD harps upon the age-old *topos* of the holy fool: a man who saw too much of the truth for his own good, and is consequently shunned and ridiculed by a society unable to stomach that truth. As in the traditional holy fool tales, so also in numerous PTSD tales, the "madman" who knows the unwanted truth is of course wiser than the society that tries to suppress that truth.[20]

Political movements of all parts of the political spectrum have also learned the value of military revelation narratives. The *Vietnam Veterans Against the War* and the Israeli *Peace Now* movements often brought forth veterans who explained how war opened their eyes about the correct political stance. Similarly, gay "coming out" stories have occasionally been grafted unto the military revelation story to produce "coming out under fire" stories. In these narratives, war experiences break open the doors of the closet, revealing a previously suppressed sexual truth.[21]

Last but not least, the military revelation story has been successfully combined with the spiritual conversion narrative. Numerous late modern war narratives tell the story of people who thanks to the shock of combat, and often in efforts to overcome the traumas it involved, discovered a spiritual path.[22] The archetypical example, and the most famous combat conversion story of the late modern era, is the conversion of Prince Andrei Bolkonsky in Tolstoy's *War and Peace*. Prince Andrei arrived on the field of Austerlitz (1805) burning with desire to win glory and worldly success for himself, taking Napoleon as his model. He was, however, critically injured. As he lay wounded on the battlefield, Napoleon passed by, noticed the wounded Russian officer, and commented: 'That's a fine death!' Andrei heard the words, yet,

he saw far above him the remote, eternal heavens. He knew it was Napoleon – his hero – but at that moment Napoleon seemed to him such a small, insignificant creature compared with what was passing now between his own soul and that lofty, limitless firmament with the clouds flying over it. ... So trivial seemed to him at that moment all the interests that engrossed Napoleon, so petty did his hero with his paltry vanity and delight in victory appear, compared to that lofty, righteous and kindly sky which he had seen and comprehended ... Everything did indeed seem so futile and insignificant in comparison with the stern and solemn train of thought induced in him by his lapsing consciousness, as his life-blood ebbed away, by his suffering and the nearness of death. Gazing into Napoleon's eyes, Prince Andrei mused on the unimportance of greatness, the unimportance of life which no one could understand, and the still greater unimportance of death, the meaning of which no one alive could understand or explain.[23]

Andrei emerged from Austerlitz a completely changed man.

The connection between war and the revelation of truth has been forged so successfully, that it often leads to a general association of peacetime and peace with illusion, and the association of wartime and war with reality and truth. In the pacifist-leaning contemporary West, this association is one of the most potent arguments left in the militaristic arsenal. There is no shortage of Cassandras warning that peace is drawing a curtain of illusion over the West's eyes, and that the awakening may be extremely rude and painful (a recent alarmist book about the supposed Muslim threat to Europe is titled *While Europe Slept*).[24] Mark Bowden summarizes this approach in relation to the American intervention in Somalia (1993):

> War was ugly and evil, for sure, but it was still the way things got done on most of the planet. Civilized states had nonviolent ways of resolving disputes, but that depended on the willingness of everyone involved to *back down*. Here in the raw Third World, people hadn't learned to back down, at least not until after a lot of blood flowed. Victory was for those willing to fight and die. Intellectuals could theorize until they sucked their thumbs right of their hands, but in the real world, power still flowed from the barrel of a gun. If you wanted the starving masses in Somalia to eat, then you had to outmuscle men like this Aidid, for whom starvation *worked*. You could send in your bleeding-heart do-gooders, you could hold hands and pray and sing hootenanny songs and invoke the great gods CNN and BBC, but the only way to finally open the roads to the big-eyed babies was to show up with more guns. And in this real world, nobody had more or better guns than America. If the good-hearted ideals of humankind were to prevail, then they needed men who could make it happen.[25]

Late modern men who regret missing war[26] feel disappointed for missing its hard won wisdom as much as for missing its authoritative stamp of manliness.[27] One of the best books written on this premise is Anthony Loyd's *My War Gone By, I Miss It So* (1999). Loyd, a British civilian, went first to Bosnia and then to Chechnya to experience war at first-hand. 'I wanted to know what it was like to shoot people. I felt it was the key to understanding so much more. I had to find out.'[28] In Bosnia he met other men who 'were even more vitriolic than me, and came right out with it: "We want to know what killing is like." ' [29] His wishes were largely fulfilled. The experience of war 'was as if a door had opened, slowly at first, to a new understanding.'[30] When he got back home, he became an attraction. 'My friends in London were eager to know "what war was like." ' [31]

A hundred and fifty years earlier, Tolstoy wrote in *War and Peace* about one's thoughts before one's first battle: 'One step beyond that line, which is like the bourne dividing the living from the dead, lies the Unknown of suffering and death. And what is there? Who is there? . . . No one knows, but who does not long to know?'[32]

What is it about war that reveals truth? Most late modern veterans point to the extreme bodily conditions of war: hunger, cold, exhaustion, injury, the presence of death – and occasionally the thrill of killing and the exhilarating adrenalin rush of combat.[33] Eschewing the rationalist authority of logical thinking, and the scientific authority of objective eye-witnessing, veterans lay claim to the visceral authority of "flesh-witnessing." They are neither thinkers nor mere eyewitnesses. Rather, they are men (and occasionally women) who have learned their wisdom with their flesh.

In order to establish their authority as flesh-witnesses, late modern veterans first have to create the idea of flesh-witnessing in the minds of their audience. This is done by repeating two basic formulas when describing extreme war experiences: "It is impossible to describe it" and "Those who were not there cannot understand it." These formulas create a fundamental difference between flesh-witnessing and eyewitnessing or scientific observation. The knowledge gained through eyewitnessing and scientific observation is factual, and can be quiet easily transmitted to other people. A scientist would never say that it is impossible to describe the experiment she has conducted, or that other people cannot hope to understand it. The whole point of Baconian science is to conduct experiments that *can* be reported in such a way, so that other scientists could subsequently rely on their results without repeating them. In the judicial system, an eyewitness often squanders her authority by using it, for once she tells other people what she saw, they come to know as much as she knows. A witness in a murder trial tells what she saw to the judge, and once her story is told, the judge knows everything the witness knows, and it is the judge rather than the witness who would pass judgment on the case.

In contrast, a flesh-witness can never really transmit her knowledge to other people – she cannot really describe what she witnessed, and the audience cannot really understand. Consequently even after repeated usage of her authority, a flesh-witness continues to enjoy a privileged authority to speak about *and judge* what she witnessed. The differentiation between eyewitnessing and flesh-witnessing is doubly important today, when so many people eyewitness war via live television broadcasts, without ever flesh-witnessing it.

After creating the unique authority of flesh-witnessing, veterans take possession of it by repeatedly narrating incidents when they underwent extreme bodily experiences, and in particular extreme experiences of suffering, which are unknown to peaceful civilians. For example, Guy Sajer, who served in the German army during World War II, wrote that

> Too many people learn about war with no inconvenience to themselves. They read about Verdun or Stalingrad without comprehension, sitting in a comfortable armchair, with their feet beside the fire, preparing to go about their business the next day, as usual. One should really read such accounts under compulsion, in discomfort, considering oneself fortunate not to be describing the events in a letter home, writing from a hole in the mud. One should read about war in the worst circumstances, when everything is going badly, remembering that the torments of peace are trivial, and not worth any white hairs. Nothing is really serious in the tranquility of peace; only an idiot could be really disturbed by the question of salary. [...] Those who read about Verdun or Stalingrad, and expound theories later to friends, over a cup of coffee, haven't understood anything.[34]

The message to Sajer's civilian audience is that simply by reading Sajer's narrative – sitting in our comfortable armchairs and drinking coffee – we can't really know what Sajer knows. Consequently the only knowledge we gain from reading Sajer's narrative is that we do not and cannot understand war, and that we should have confidence in Sajer's knowledge and judgment about that matter.

Netiva Ben-Yehuda often writes in a similar vein. Addressing the politicians and philosophers who formulated Zionism, she tells them about her experiences in the Israeli War of Independence:

> If you sit in committees, and congresses, and conventions, and argue, and discuss, and formulate visions – this is a charade. And even if all the Jews in the 'General Debate' sit with frocks and cylinder hats, and even if the chairman, the visionary-of-visionaries, the king of visionaries [i.e., Theodor Herzl], has a big beard.... [War] is what you wanted? Right? So here you are – take it! And goodbye. I'm going home. You have nothing to worry, we are doing it, and we will do

it, exactly what you want, but you should know, just know, that you know absolutely nothing. You don't know what you have done to us. You don't know what you wanted. You have no idea what it is. Not the flimsiest idea. You can talk about it from morning till night, and get up in the morning, and talk about it again from morning till night, every day, every day, your entire life – and you won't have a clue what you are talking about. We – we have a clue. And we are going to tell you. So that you know. At least know. We will come from here [the battlefield], and we will tell you exactly, exactly-exactly, what all your talking was about. What was it, the things you wanted. We will tell you. Because we – we know.[35]

Elsewhere Ben-Yehuda tells her civilian friends: 'You can't imagine the edge of the edge of what we are going through here. You can't grasp anything. From the stories and the newspapers – you will never understand anything. Only if you be inside – you'll understand.'[36]

Militaristic veterans argue along exactly the same lines. Like Ben-Yehuda, Adolf Hitler wrote in *Mein Kampf* scathingly about the politicians who "talk big" but send others to do the fighting.[37] Concerning his World War I experiences he wrote that

It often seemed to me almost a sin to shout hurrah without having the inner right to do so; for who had the right to use this word without having proved it in the place where all playing is at an end and the inexorable hand of the Goddess of Destiny begins to weigh peoples and men according to the truth and steadfastness of their convictions?[38]

Ernst Jünger, though an extreme German patriot, writes sarcastically that he and his comrades went to war in 1914

to carry forward the German ideals of 1870 [...] We had set out in a rain of flowers to seek the death of heroes. The war was our dream of greatness, power, and glory. It was a man's work, a duel on fields whose flowers would be stained with blood. There is no lovelier death in the world [...] Our fevered thoughts cooled down as we marched through the heavy chalk loam of Champagne. Pack and ammunition and rifle weighed on us like lead.[39]

Soon after they witnessed their first bombardment and sustained their first casualties, and the disillusionment deepened:

> A feeling of unreality oppressed me as I stared at a figure streaming with blood whose limbs hung loose and who unceasingly gave a hoarse cry for help, as though death had him already by the throat [...] What was all this, then? The war had shown its claws and torn off its pleasant mask [...] I could tell from talking to my companions that this episode had somewhat damped their martial ardour. It had affected me too.[40]

The bodily discomfort of carrying a leaden weight in fatiguing marches was enough to unburden their minds from its patriotic fantasies, and these fantasies were completely cast away at the sight of a torn human body.

Thus veterans from throughout the political spectrum condemn mere intellectual musing, depict themselves as flesh-witnesses, and stress that only harsh bodily conditions produce authentic and reliable truth by separating the mental chaff accumulated in peacetime from the wheat. The intellect may toy with these truths, commenting on them, inventing theories about them, thinking up arguments to contradict them – yet this is all delusive, because the intellect can have no idea what it is talking about.

Veterans who employ this kind of arguments are actually walking along a well-trodden path, marked and utilized by generations of religious visionaries. Mystics throughout the eras have argued that no one can understand and judge their experiences except those who shared them, and that consequently the knowledge and authority conferred by these experiences are above criticism.[41] For instance, the Lutheran pastor Johann Arndt tried to describe in his *True Christianity* (1605) the joys of mystical union with God, but commented that 'No one, I say, can know this except the person who has experienced it. To feel and to experience this is possible for a man but to express it is impossible.'[42]

It is vital to realize, however, that the term "revelation" – which I shall be using throughout the book – has no essential connection to religion. Revelation denotes a particular *method* for gaining knowledge rather than a particular type of knowledge. People usually discover new knowledge – religious, historical, scientific, personal – thanks to a controlled process of inquiry, observation, study, and analysis. In contrast, we say that people "had a revelation," when new knowledge is thrust upon them by some external force, often against their will. Frequently, the knowledge gained by revelation cannot be gained by any "controlled" means. The external force that brings the revelation about could be God, but it could also be a natural phenomenon or a man-made experience such as war. The contents of the revelation could be religious, but they could also be political, artistic, psychological, and so forth.

Revelation is not merely a method for gaining knowledge, but like all other such methods it is also a basis for authority. Religious revelatory experiences were an extremely important source of authority in the Middle Ages and early modern period, particularly for disempowered persons. For instance, a peasant girl such as Jeanne d'Arc, standing at the bottom of the medieval social pyramid, could hope to become a military and political leader almost only through religious revelations.[43] Late modern common soldiers have similarly sought to challenge the established powers and claim political authority by an appeal to martial revelatory experiences. Common soldiers everywhere, from Hitler to the *Vietnam Veterans Against the War*, have argued that the truths revealed to them on the battlefield through the extreme experiences of war allow and impel them to wield political power. These truths have a message for all humanity rather than only for the veterans, and like religious visionaries, the veterans now have a sacred mission to disseminate that message.

The political dividends this line of reasoning may produce can be gleaned from a letter sent by a civilian with no military experience to *Time* magazine. The civilian, John Riley, responded to a story about an American Marine who at the battle of Fallujah (2004) apparently shot and killed an unarmed wounded Iraqi in a mosque. Riley writes that

> I hold no ill will toward the Marine, because I cannot begin to fathom what he and others endure in Iraq every day – car bombs, roadside rockets, booby-trapped bodies and Iraqi civilians who act like your friend one day and shoot at you the next. To all the armchair generals who criticize what happened at the mosque, I say grab a gun and try living a Marine's life for a few weeks and see how you would react.[44]

The Turkish prime minister, Recep Tayyip Erdogan, concurs. When Turkish security forces opened fire on Kurdish demonstrators in April 2006, killing 16 civilians, European Union parliamentarians sent a severe letter of criticism to the Turkish government. Erdogan fumed: 'Those who write such letters should first come and experience what [the security forces] have been going through.'[45]

But how exactly do extreme bodily conditions produce truth? How exactly does walking with a heavy knapsack or seeing a dead body dispel patriotic ideals or set up new truths of comradeship? This has best been explained by Elaine Scarry's seminal *The Body in Pain*. Though Scarry herself is not a veteran, and though she did not directly rely on veteran war stories, her book largely parallels their arguments, presenting them with unprecedented clarity and depth.

Leaving aside the joys of war, Scarry's basic insight is that bodily pain distorts and ultimately annihilates the contents of the mind. In analyzing torture, she argues that when a human being suffers extreme pain, 'in the most literal way possible, the created world of thought and feeling, all the psychological and mental content that constitute both one's self and one's world, and that gives rise to and is in turn made possible by language, ceases to exist.'[46] Suffering thus functions as a Darwinian test for reality. While people are at ease, their minds generate countless thoughts, ideas, and fantasies, and they may become attached to these mental products, thinking that they are real. As long as they continue to be at ease, they cannot differentiate their minds' fantasies from reality. But when suffering comes, the unrealistic and inessential fantasies of the mind vanish, leaving behind only what is in the final analysis real and essential.

Scarry applies the same logic when analyzing war as a collective phenomenon. She argues that before war erupts, each side generates a collective identity containing many ideals and fantasies, and it is these ideals and fantasies that often provoke wars in the first place. In the course of the war, the suffering it involves causes at least one side to 'undergo a perceptual reversal [...] in which claims or issues or elements of self-understanding that had previously seemed integral and essential to national identity will gradually come to seem dispensable or alterable, without seeming (as it once would have) to cancel out, dissolve, or irreparably compromise the national identity.'[47] For instance, two horrible world wars have convinced most Germans that the possession of Alsace-Lorrain is dispensable to German identity. On the other hand, whatever ideals manage to retain their hold on the belligerents emerge from the war much strengthened, because they have passed the test of reality, and were proven to be real and worthy even under the worst circumstances.[48]

How different ideals will survive the test of war cannot be foretold merely by intellectual meditations, because these intellectual meditations are precisely the problem. It is the intellectual visionaries sitting in frock coats at conferences that generate the very ideals that must then be tested by people like Ben Yehuda and Hitler on the battlefield.

This is exactly the logic at work in twentieth-century military memoirs. Before the war, the author's mind is a storehouse full of ideals imbibed from literature, art, history books, oral stories, and propaganda. Ideals such as comradeship, patriotism, humanism. Before the war, the author is unable to tell which of these ideals is true to reality, and which a groundless fantasy. When war comes, the suffering the combatant undergoes differentiates the two. Some ideals – for instance, patriotism – disappear from the mind on contact with bodily discomfort, and are thereby revealed as fantasies. Other ideals – for instance, comradeship – persist through the worst difficulties, and are thereby revealed as far more real than one imagined beforehand.

It should only be stressed that unlike Scarry, veterans occasionally argue that the extreme bodily experiences of war may include experiences of unequaled joy as well as unequaled suffering. For instance, Philip Caputo describes how he led a platoon in Vietnam during some jungle skirmish.

> I felt a drunken elation. Not only the sudden release from danger made me feel it, but the thrill of having seen the platoon perform perfectly under heavy fire and under my command. I had never experienced anything like it before. When the line wheeled and charged across the clearing, the enemy bullets whining past them, wheeled and charged almost with drill-field precision, an ache as profound as the ache of orgasm passed through me.[49]

We can, however, press our question further, and ask what actually happens at moments of such extreme joy or suffering? How can the body take control over the thought process? Ariel Glucklich takes this extra step in *Sacred Pain*. He tries to give a biological answer to this question, and show how 'pain produces states of consciousness, and cognitive-emotional changes, that affect the identity of the individual subject and her sense of belonging to a larger community or to a more fundamental state of being.'[50] He argues that 'When the organism is bombarded with incoming signals moving afferently (from periphery to center),' it can result in 'the minimization of *all* mental phenomena.' For example, when the skin is

> assaulted with unpleasant sensory stimulation, the phenomenal field becomes radically simplified and free of mental images; in fact, it becomes reduced to simple embodiment.... An extreme bombardment of incoming signals, in whatever sensory modality, can produce

a virtual shutdown of outgoing signals, resulting in dissociative states, either trance or psychotic breakdown.[51]

Elsewhere Glucklich writes that

the more irritation one applies to the body in the form of pain, the less output the central nervous system generates from the areas that regulate the signals on which a sense of self relies. Modulated pain weakens the individual's feeling of being a discrete agent; it makes the 'body-self' transparent and facilitates the emergence of a new identity.[52]

It is questionable how applicable this biological model is for understanding the connections between body and mind, because the dichotomy mind/body, so precious to Western culture, may very well lack any biological sense. However, from a cultural and historical perspective, Glucklich's model closely corresponds to the explanation late modern Western combatants have for bodily takeovers. Heirs to a long Western tradition of seeing body and mind at odds with one another, and of seeing both body and mind as militarily "assaulted" and "bombarded" by the external world and by each other, late modern Western combatants tend to depict the relations between body and mind in the following way: At normal times, the body sends the mind sensory data, which humbly waits to be interpreted by the mind. But at a moment of great suffering (or joy), this sensory data cannot wait. It overwhelms the mind, forcefully obliterates some of the mind's contents, and installs other contents in their place. If urgent pain signals race from the hand to inform the mind that one has been hit by a bullet, and they find the mind occupied by thoughts such as "it is glorious to die for my sacred motherland," the pain signals barge in by force, shoving out in the process the patriotic fantasy.[53]

This cultural image has been used by memoirists not only for describing the happenings underneath their skin, but also to offer a political manifesto. Just as, according to this image, the body somehow revolts and seizes the power to think and create ideas from the mind, so also many common soldiers have fantasized that the nation's muscles and bones – that is, the common soldiers – may somehow revolt and seize the power to think and make decisions from the nation's mind – that is, from the politicians, priests, and philosophers.

What happens once the body has seized control and purified the mind of the enervating luggage it acquired in peacetime? Veterans disagree.

Here two schools of thought vehemently oppose each other: idealists versus materialists.

The idealists, represented in particular by fascist writers, claim that ultimately mind (or soul) is superior to the body. During peacetime decadent ideas contaminate and clog the mind, and it is only these decadent ideas that are swept away in war by the body. Once these ideas are swept away, the purest core of the mind can resurface and regain control from the body. Some new positive ideals – either forged in war or at least purified by war – emerge triumphant from the ordeal, and for the sake of these positive ideals the purest core of the mind can withstand any amount of bodily suffering. Idealists accordingly tend to view war as a positive regenerating experience, in which body has an indispensable part to play, but which ultimately results in "the triumph of the will."

Hitler's description of the process he underwent in World War I is a good example. During his first encounters with combat 'the romance of battle had been replaced by horror. The enthusiasm gradually cooled and the exuberant joy was stifled by mortal fear.'[54] He was then tormented by his imagination, which appealed to his 'weak body' in the mask of 'reason,' and tried to frighten him and make him run away. But the voice of inner duty was up to the challenge and

> By the winter of 1915–16, this struggle had for me been decided. At last my will was undisputed master. If in the first days I went over the top with rejoicing and laughter, I was now calm and determined. And this was enduring. Now Fate could bring on the ultimate tests without my nerves shattering or my reason failing. The young volunteer had become an old soldier.[55]

Ernst Jünger spells out the idealist way of thinking in even clearer terms. Reflecting on his service in World War I, he writes that

> I had set out to the war gaily enough, thinking we were to hold a festival on which all the pride of youth was lavished, and I had thought little, once I was in the thick of it, about the ideal that I had to stand for. Now I looked back: four years of development in the midst of a generation predestined to death, spent in caves, smoke-filled trenches, and shell-illumined wastes ... And almost without any thought of mine, the idea of the Fatherland had been distilled from all these afflictions in a clearer and brighter essence. That was the final winnings in a game on which so often all had been staked:

the nation was no longer for me an empty thought veiled in symbols; and how could it have been otherwise when I had seen so many die for its sake, and been schooled myself to stake my life for its credit every minute, day and night, without a thought? And so, strange as it may sound, I learned from this very four years' schooling in force and in all the fantastic extravagance of material warfare that life has no depth of meaning except when it is pledged for an ideal, and that there are ideals in comparison with which the life of an individual and even of a people has no weight. And though the aim for which I fought as an individual, as an atom in the whole body of the army, was not to be achieved, though material force cast us, apparently, to the earth, yet we learned once and for all to stand for a cause and if necessary to fall as befitted men.[56]

Religious writers tend to adopt similarly idealist stances. In a journal of a Jewish *Yeshiva* which was sent to frontline soldiers in the 1973 Arab–Israeli war, one letter stated that

The time of war is a time of crisis. In the fire of war material structures dissolve, and even mental structures, ways and methods of thought and behavior. In the soul of the fighting human being the outer shell is peeled, and then, sometimes, the person comes in direct contact with the depths of his soul, with his inner parts, with old and solid truths that day-to-day life has covered up. One observes things more penetratingly, more widely, more deeply, more truly.[57]

In contrast to the idealists, materialistic veterans believe that there is nowhere to proceed beyond the body. Once the body takes over it remains in control, and no "purer mind" is thereby liberated. According to the materialists, the deepest and most important truth revealed by war is simply that man is matter. A good example of this school is Joseph Heller's *Catch-22*. Authored by a World War II veteran, this book has become one of the cornerstones of late twentieth-century war culture.

The novel harshly criticizes and ridicules almost every military convention. The power of its devastating criticism is drawn from an appeal to some deeper strata of military reality. These deeper strata are encapsulated in one particular "primal scene," to which the novel repeatedly refers. From hints dropped here and there throughout the novel, it becomes clear that this scene involves the death of an American soldier, Snowden, in a bombing mission over Italy sometime toward the end of World War II. Apparently, while dying, Snowden disclosed some secret to Yossarian, the novel's hero, which shaped Yossarian worldview. What this secret is, and what exactly happened in the plane, is hidden from the readers.

Only at the very end of the novel the secret is disclosed and the scene spelled out fully. After the plane was hit by German anti-aircraft fire, Yossarian was trying to help the wounded Snowden and bind his wounds.

> Yossarian bent forward to peer and saw a strangely colored stain seeping through the coveralls just above the armhole of Snowden's flak suit. Yossarian felt his heart stop, then pound so violently he found it difficult to breathe. Snowden was wounded inside his flak suit. Yossarian ripped open the snaps of Snowden's flat suit and heard himself scream wildly as Snowden's insides slithered down to the floor in a soggy pile and just kept dripping out. A chunk of flak more than three inches big had shot into his other side just underneath the arm and blasted all the way through, drawing whole mottled quarts of Snowden along with it through the gigantic hole in his ribs it made as it blasted out. Yossarian screamed a second time and squeezed both hands over his eyes. His teeth were chattering in horror. He forced himself to look again. Here was God's plenty, all right, he thought bitterly as he stared – liver, lungs, kidneys, ribs, stomach and bits of the stewed tomatoes Snowden had eaten that day for lunch. [...] Yossarian was cold, too, and shivering uncontrollably. He felt goose pimples cracking all over him as he gazed down despondently at the grim secret Snowden had spilled all over the messy floor. It was easy to read the message in his entrails. Man was matter, that was Snowden's secret. Drop him out a window and he'll fall. Set fire to him and he'll burn. Bury him and he'll rot, like other kinds of garbage. The spirit gone, man is garbage. That was Snowden's secret.[58]

The secret that stands at the basis of *Catch-22*, and which war reveals, is that man is matter; that Snowden – rather than just Snowden's body – is a thing that can be ripped open, can be measured in quarts, can be drawn and spread over the floor. Snowden is so material, that it is impossible to tell where the stewed tomatoes end and Snowden begins.

Similar "primal scenes" form the foundation of numerous other twentieth-century war memoirs, war novels, war poems, war paintings, and war films. Again and again authors describe death and injury scenes in pornographic detail, reading the secrets of war and of the world in the displayed intestines, learning from them that man is matter.

Netiva Ben-Yehuda describes how two recruits found an unexploded shell, which burst when they tried to make a souvenir out of it. The force of the explosion smashed the head of one recruit right inside the stomach of the other, killing both. When Ben-Yehuda rushed to one of them and tried to check his pulse, she discovered to her horror that the man had no hands left. The two bodies were taken away, but a shock victim was left screaming behind, untended.

> Regarding the one who screamed and screamed, who laid on the side wallowing in the dust, who was in shock from the whole business – the doctors were unwilling to move a finger for him, and one had already tried to calm him with a slap. So I walked over to him, grabbed his chin forcefully, so that he would look me in the eyes, and I said to him: 'Wait a minute! Wait! Let me tell you something!' And in his ear, quietly, so that no one hears what I say to him, I let him have it: 'So what? So you have seen death with your eyes, eh? That's the terrible thing – yes? What good would it do if you wail? You – are not dead! They – died! You are alive – right? They would love to wail now, like you, but they can no longer wail. You – can. So stop it! Stop wailing, do you hear?' And I hugged him, and shook his hand, so that he stop shaking, and I continued, whispering, a kind of secret, just of us two: 'Suddenly you realize that you too can be a meat-ball, eh? Suddenly – they [the dead] can't control any more, they are – meat, only meat, and suddenly – you too can't control any more, right? It isn't you who is screaming, it's your flesh that is screaming, right?'[59]

Ben-Yehuda reads the same message in the spread human intestines as Heller. What they reveal is again that humans are mere flesh and blood, mere matter. When war puts humans to the test, it reveals to them that it is really their material flesh who is in control, rather than their cherished, conscious, mental "I."

Contemporary war movies have tended to adopt this materialistic vision wholeheartedly (in part because it films better than the idealist vision). Movies such as *Platoon, Full Metal Jacket, Saving Private Ryan,* and *Black Hawk Down* present the horrors of war in pornographic details, focusing on the fragile materiality of combatants' bodies. In the opening scene of *Saving Private Ryan* bullets and shells rip open the human body, spilling and spraying human intestines all over the screen, letting the audience see for themselves the same message that Heller and Ben-Yehuda tried to convey in their writings.

* * *

Though the idealist and materialistic schools ultimately diverge in their conclusions from war, they proceed together most of the way. Both see war above all as a revelatory experience, both see the bodily experiences of war as superior to the intellectual meditations of peacetime, and both equate war experience with truth and peacetime thinking with illusion.

The present book argues that this revelatory view of war represents an unprecedented revolution in Western war culture. For millennia, stories of war in the West had emphasized the complete and unwavering supremacy of mind over body, and of lofty ideals over tangible experiences. Martyrs and heroes from the Bible and the *Iliad* onward suffered and died, affirming their *pre-war* ideals even in their last agonized moments. Since ancient times the model war story was the one told by Titus Livius about Gaius Mucius Scaevola. When Rome was besieged by the superior forces of the Etruscan King Porsina, Scaevola infiltrated the Etruscan camp to assassinate Porsina, but was caught and threatened with torture and death if he did not disclose his accomplices. Livius writes that Scaevola said to Porsina:

> 'See here, that you may understand of how little account the body is to those who have great glory in view'; and immediately thrust his right hand into the fire that was lighted for sacrifice. When he allowed it to burn as if his spirit were quite insensible to any feeling of pain, the king, well-nigh astounded at this surprising sight, leaped from his seat and commanded the young man to be removed from the altar.

According to Livius, Porsina was so impressed and frightened by this display of Roman courage that he not only allowed Scaevola to go back to Rome safely, but also made peace with the Romans.[60] Contrary to Scarry's theory, Scaevola's mind retained full control even as his body was in agonizing pain, and his immense pain strongly affirmed what every Roman already knew from childhood: *dulce et decorum est pro patria mori*.[61] Scaevola did not acquire any new knowledge, either of himself or of the world, at the altar.

The present book aims to trace the origins of the revelatory interpretation of war. When did people begin to expect the Scaevolas to discover anything *new* at the altar? When did some Scaevolas begin to say that when they thrust their hand into the fire, they realized that it was sense-less to die for one's country? When did others begin to say that when their hand was slowly roasting, they acquired a completely new under-standing of what patriotism is all about, which stay-at-homes such as Titus Livius cannot possibly understand?

It should be stressed that the book traces only narratives and cultural constructs. It does not try to trace the actual experience of the combatants. Postmodernist scholarship habitually argues that lived experience is itself culturally constructed. Images precede and shape "reality." We cannot experience anything unless we have first of all constructed and gave meaning to that experience, and this is something we can accomplish only with the help of prior narratives and cultural models.[62] This book is greatly indebted to this line of thinking, but it strives to keep it at a critical distance. This critical distance is vital because the combatants' idea of flesh-witnessing is the exact opposite of this postmodernist idea of cultural construction. Combatants argue that the experience of war is completely independent of all previous cultural constructions. They agree that the tame experiences of peace are culturally constructed, but not so the wild experiences of war. War experiences reveal the truth precisely by blowing apart all cultural constructions.

Mystics would not like the idea that their angelic visions and their divine revelations are culturally constructed. If a postmodernist scholar would point out that their vision of the Virgin Mary is influenced by previously seen paintings, they would retort that – if true – the paint-ings in question must have been modeled on some previous authentic visions. Similarly, combatants would not like the idea that their war experiences are culturally constructed. If a scholar would point out that their experience of injury or of a comrade's death is influenced by Holly-wood war movies, they would retort that – if true – the war movies in question must have been modeled on authentic war experiences.

The present book takes a skeptical middle stance. On the one hand, I believe that cultural expectations shape people's experiences to a far larger degree than they are aware. Moreover, cultures are very complex things. Even when experiences smash one set of cultural expectations, people almost never break free into a primeval sphere of pure experience, unshaped by culture. For there are always competing sets of cultural expectations waiting on the sidelines for just such an opportunity, and most people – when their previously chosen set is broken – quickly adopt another, which is more suited for the experience they confront.

Indeed, precisely when people are confronted by extreme and bewildering experiences, they tend to hold ever more tightly to their cultural cipher, like storm-tossed sailors clutching frantically at their compass.

On the other hand, it would be rash to argue that if no narratives of disillusionment have survived from the seventeenth century, it proves that seventeenth-century combatants never had experiences of disillusionment. To avoid reaching such extreme and ill-founded conclusions, the present book is not defined as a book about the history of military experience, and it does not attempt to reach any firm conclusions on what past combatants *actually* experienced. Instead, the book studies the history of war culture and in particular the role of military experience in war culture. If no seventeenth-century narratives of disillusionment have survived, I believe we can conclude that seventeenth-century war culture had no place in it for experiences of disillusionment. Real-life combatants might still have had such experiences, but they were not given any cultural visibility, and they were most probably of little social and political significance.[63]

The rise of the revelatory interpretation of war in the twentieth century has received a lot of academic attention, and particular parts of this story have been described at length (e.g., the transformation of the image of war following World War I and Vietnam).[64] In contrast, the earlier history of this interpretation has been left largely unstudied. Though there are numerous books about pre-1900 military experience, they either ignore the revelatory interpretation or take it for granted.[65] The present book tries to fill the gap and put the twentieth-century developments in a much wider historical and cultural context, by charting the history of the revelatory interpretation of war from the late Middle Ages. In so doing, the book hopes to offer a critical and contextualized overview of the late modern revolution in the culture and image of war.

In order to trace the origins of the revelatory interpretation of war the book looks at war as a cultural and mental phenomenon, and places the culture of war within a wider cultural context, examining in particular its links to Western understandings of the mind–body problem, to Western ideals of selfhood, and to Western conceptions of authority.

This investigation relies partly on an examination of theoretical and philosophical writings and of literary and artistic representations of war. Yet the book focuses primarily on one type of war account, namely combatants' military memoirs. As explained in the following pages, the fortunes of this genre have been closely linked with those of the revelatory interpretation of war, and over the last two centuries, the rise in the importance of the revelatory interpretation and the rise in the importance of combatants' military memoirs facilitated and manifested each other.

The book has one overarching argument: War became a revelatory experience in the period 1740–1865. Before the eighteenth century combatants almost never interpreted war as a revelatory experience. To understand this one should remember that "revelation" indicates only a method for gaining knowledge, and has no essential connection with religion. Prior to 1740 combatants often interpreted war in religious terms, utilizing religious doctrines to understand military events. Defeat in battle was proof of God's displeasure; a miraculous escape from death was proof of God's grace. Yet combatants never saw war as an experience that reveals new knowledge. For example, in Crusader memoirs it is often said that the launching of the crusade was inspired by revelation. However, Crusader memoirists such as Jehan de Joinville never argued *à la* Ben Yehuda that their experiences in the East thrust upon them new knowledge that people back home (say, the Pope) cannot comprehend.

It was during the second half of the eighteenth century and through the nineteenth century that the Enlightenment, the culture of sensibility, and Romanticism led soldiers to begin seeing war as an agent of revelation. Of particular importance was the Romantic idea of "the sublime." Romanticism highlighted "sublime" experiences as privileged sources for knowledge and authority, and war experience fitted perfectly to the Romantic definition of the sublime.

It should be stressed though that the book does not attempt to offer an exhaustive causal explanation for the rise of the revelatory interpretation of war. It maps its rise, explaining what changed and how things changed, but without delving too deeply into the question of *why* things changed. For example, the book emphasizes the importance of the adoption of the culture of sensibility by eighteenth-century armies and soldiers, but without attempting to explain *why* armies and soldiers adopted it. I wrote the book on the assumption that explaining what happened is more important than explaining why it happened.[66]

* * *

This book stands at the intersection of several disciplines and its writing required me to engage with very different kinds of material. Three fields of study were especially pertinent to this book. First and foremost, since this is a book about war and military history, writing it necessitated a thorough understanding of strategy, tactics, weaponry, recruitment methods, training methods, supply arrangements, and so forth in armies from the fifteenth century to the present.

Since the book's source material is largely military memoirs, writing it also necessitated a good understanding of the history of autobiography and of the novel, of religious writings, of printing, and of much literary theory.

One of the book's main arguments is that the culture of war has been intimately related to the understanding of mind and body. Up to the eighteenth century war was interpreted as a primary model for the victory of mind over body, whereas from then onward the tables began to turn, and by the twentieth century war became a primary model for the victory of body over mind. Consequently, writing the book required some understanding of Western philosophy, of the history of the mind–body problem, and of the history of the body.

It was impossible for me to dedicate equal attention to all these fields, either during my research or when allocating the limited space of the finished book. After much deliberation, I decided to give preference to the military field. I have spent most of my career as a military historian, and I have become quite jealous of the rights of this sub-discipline. While writing this book, I was often annoyed to find that scholars whose main interest is in literature, or cultural history, or the history of the body, write about war without a deep understanding of the subject, and often make the most elementary mistakes. I then realized that this is most probably how literary historians, say, would look upon my own foray into their fiefdom. I particularly dread the result of my mentioning the term "body." So much has been written about the history of the body in recent decades, that I hoped I could somehow write this book without ever mentioning the human body. This proved impossible, but it proved equally impossible to read all the latest studies that touch upon the history of the body from the viewpoint of half a dozen disciplines.

I was similarly forced to give up a gendered discussion of my subject. It seems almost ridiculous to write about the experience of war without a gendered angle, but given the limitations of time, space, and energy – and given the amount of literature in existence about gender and war – that proved to be the only manageable course of action. If I had 20 more years, and if my publisher allowed me 200,000 more words, this book would have been very different, and would have engaged more seriously not only histories of the body and of the role of gender in war, but also anthropological studies of rites of passage, psychological studies of trauma and its history, and biological studies of the influence of sensation on cognitive processes.

So I ask forgiveness in advance from all other disciplines and sub-disciplines, and excuse myself by positioning this book within the sub-discipline of military history. It belongs specifically to the trend known as "cultural military history," and is in dialogue primarily with the works of such military historians as Michael Howard, John Keegan, John A. Lynn, and Armstrong Starkey. This book's revered ancestor – for better or worse – is Carl von Clausewitz rather than Marx or Foucault.

I must similarly ask forgiveness for focusing my attention solely on the experiences of combatants. There is hardly a word in this book about non-combatants and their war experiences. Today, there is a growing circular convergence between the war stories of combatants and non-combatants. Combatants are increasingly seen as victims of war, which blurs the difference between them and non-combatants. On the other hand, the discourse of trauma and of military revelation, which originated with combatants, has subsequently been adopted by non-combatants as well. Yet this is a peculiarity of the last few decades. In earlier centuries, even if there was a similarity in experiences, the differences between the war stories of combatants and non-combatants remained huge, and I could not do justice to both in a single book. I chose to focus on the stories of combatants, because historically, they were of far greater importance, and the late modern revolution in the culture of war started with the stories of combatants, and spilled over to the stories of non-combatants much later.

This book also stands at the intersection of several historical periods, and is very "Presentist" in its approach. It aims to answer a popular contemporary question: "When people go to war, do they learn anything profound about themselves and the world? Do they gain authority that other people lack?" It examines military memoirs from previous centuries in light of this question even when these texts show absolutely no interest in it.

In answering this question, I constantly had in mind my typical B.A. student. He or she understands perfectly well that war five hundred years ago was different in its technology, tactics, and so forth from present-day conflicts. But were the people different? Did they really think differently from us? Though historians are supposed to take it for granted that the answer is yes, my experiences in the classroom taught me that it is extremely difficult to explain to intelligent students that this is indeed the case. Moreover, after ten years of reading medieval and early modern memoirs, I myself still find it hard to believe that human beings with the same biological framework as myself really managed to think and behave in such strange ways.

The reason it is so difficult to believe that other people thought differently is that it requires us to disengage from our own worldview, and accept in a deep sense that our worldview is just one possibility out of many. If past people have managed to view the world radically different from us, then perhaps the world is "really" radically different from what we believe it to be.

In order to make it easier for us to disengage from our worldview, the book runs back and forth between the fifteenth century and the twenty-first century, continuously measuring and mapping the distance that separates the two. This accounts for its complex structure. The introduction has presented an overview of the revelatory interpretation of war as it became familiar in the West since 1865. (The year 1865 was chosen to represent the moment when this interpretation has received its canonical form, for in that year Tolstoy published the first volume of *War and Peace*.)

The book's second part then makes an abrupt jump back to the early modern period. The sharp contrast with the twentieth century is meant to draw the readers' attention to the unfamiliar features of early modern stories of war, and thereby open the necessary critical distance. Without this sharp contrast, readers may well fail to notice the peculiarities of either early modern or twentieth-century war stories.

The book's third part then re-familiarizes readers with the late modern interpretation of war from a new angle, examining the creation of this interpretation in the "long" Romantic period of 1740–1865.

In order to preserve the necessary critical distance between readers and war stories throughout the book, examples drawn from the twentieth century are frequently referred to when discussing early modern developments. Thus a sixteenth-century battle painting is analyzed by comparing it to a twentieth-century battle photograph. Many scholars may view this as a glaring case of anachronism. However, in almost all cases when I juxtapose supposedly similar descriptions from the early modern and late modern periods, the aim is to uncover their deep *differences*. I assume that we cannot really perceive early modern war descriptions except through the lens of twentieth-century descriptions, so it is best to flesh out this anachronistic tendency and explain its errors in detail. Furthermore, I hope that the danger of anachronism is more than compensated for by the creation of a fruitful intellectual tension, which should enable readers to gain a far better understanding of the revelatory interpretation of war and its underlying assumptions.

Part II

The Supremacy of Mind: 1450–1740

1
Suffering, Death, and Revelation in Early Modern Culture

The idea that encountering suffering and death may reveal deep truths and may confer unique authority was very popular in the early modern period. Pre-modern Christianity, early modern Catholicism, and early modern Protestantism all provided ample models for interpreting death, injury, and suffering as sites of truth and revelation. The central mystery of this culture involved a man being pierced with a spear by soldiers and dying after suffering extreme bodily pain.[1] This image was reproduced countless times in oral narratives, written texts, music, drama, sculpture, and painting, so that '[t]he tortured male body on the Cross stood as a religious paradigm for truth' and, by extension, the figure of a bloody male body came to be a paradigmatic representation of truth in Western culture.[2] This image also inspired innumerable secondary narratives, of various saints and martyrs who likewise enlightened mankind by suffering torture and death (often at the hand of soldiers), and whose suffering was reproduced in myriad oral, written, and artistic representations.[3]

These various narratives and images, and above all the image of Christ on the Cross, were the most important objects of religious devotion and meditation. The late Middle Ages witnessed an increasing devotion to Christ's bodily suffering, a tendency which was formulated by early modern Catholicism in the cults of the Sacred Heart, the Five Wounds, and the Stations of the Cross, and popularized through Passion plays and Pieta images.[4]

Other favorite objects of meditation were dead bodies, images of death, and macabre images. The macabre was one of the most vibrant and lively currents of early modern European culture. Images of Death, the *Danse Macabre*, putrefied bodies, skeletons, death's heads, bones, and hourglasses were ubiquitous not only in churches, but also in palaces and private houses, where they even decorated furniture, house utensils, and jewelry. Artists incorporated skulls and hourglasses into almost any picture. *Memento Mori* was the catchword of the day, and many religious teachers recommended a constant meditation on death as the best way for realizing the vanities of earthly life and for seeing the Truth.[5]

It was extremely common to interpret the death and suffering of even ordinary people as sites of potential revelation and conversion. Suffering was seen as opening one's eyes and enabling the believer to imitate Christ (*Imitatio Christi*) and thereby get closer to Christ and his Truth. Numerous oral and written narratives from the Bible onwards recounted how an ordinary and even impious person who just lost his loved ones, or who himself suffered from illness or injury, or who was about to die, was made aware by these calamities of the vanity of this world and of the ultimate Truth, and was thereby converted from sin to piety.[6]

The Puritan Vavasor Powell describes how he suffered from such a strong toothache, that 'I thought I should have been deprived of my senses, or life.' A book he read led him to think how much greater the pain of hell must be compared with a mere toothache. This caused such a great terror in his mind that it actually eclipsed the toothache itself, and 'put me upon crying out to *God* with greater sense than before, and between fear and pain, a troubled muddy spirit of prayer began to spring up.'[7] Desiderius Erasmus called the kidney stones that tormented him "his teachers."[8] Certain types of bodily suffering were particularly favorable teachers, as, for example, blindness. From classical and biblical times it became clichéd to argue that physical blindness opens one's spiritual eyes.[9]

Since suffering was a privileged medium of revelation, sufferers often enjoyed substantial religious authority.[10] Bodily sufferings were such a valuable means for getting closer to Christ, for understanding his Truth, and for empowerment that when they did not come naturally through illness and injury, medieval and early modern Christians of all sects indulged in various practices of asceticism and self-mortification as a means for gaining spiritual revelation and authority.[11]

Similarly, numerous oral and written narratives depicted the moment of death as a moment of truth, when a person revealed his true measure of faith and understanding. Dying was an art taught to people of all backgrounds in the shape of various *artes moriendi*. A saintly person invariably had a good death, even under the worst circumstances, whereas hypocrites who deceived people during their lifetime were exposed as ignorant sinners by having a bad death. Even such sinners often had Truth revealed to them on their deathbed, so that the last words of the worst sinners were sometimes thought to bear deep truths.[12] The connection between revelation and experiences of death and suffering was burnt deep into the consciousness of medieval and early modern people.

Even the connection between revelation and the particular circumstances of wartime suffering was of common currency. In the Old Testament numerous sin–punishment–conversion cycles portray war as God's rod, threatening or forcing people to mend their ways. Later on, millions were converted to Christianity at the edge of the sword, and war was recognized as one of the foremost tools in the missionary's kit.[13]

Christian authors of all eras, sects, and backgrounds were in the habit of describing spiritual struggles in military terms, comparing Christ with a military commander; comparing Christian believers with soldiers (*Miles Christi*); comparing sin and the Devil with military enemies; comparing the life of a Christian with war; comparing spiritual difficulties encountered in life with battles, sieges, and campaigns; and comparing conversion and martyrdom with victory.[14] Religious treatises were often given martial titles such as *The Christian Warfare* (1604) or *The Bible-Battal, or the Sacred Art Military* (1629).[15] Erasmus's *Enchiridion Militis Christiani* (1503), which was written in order to recall a soldier-courtier to piety, is one long comparison of spiritual life and earthly warfare. Even today, searching at *Amazon.com* for the keywords "Spiritual Warfare" brings up dozens of Christian self-help books with titles such as *Spiritual Warfare for Every Christian* (1989), *A Woman's Guide to Spiritual Warfare* (1991), and *The Warrior's Heart: Rules of Engagement for the Spiritual War Zone* (2004).[16]

It was common not only to describe religious experiences in military terms, but also to interpret military events in religious terms. Medieval and early modern narratives of war very often tried to read divine messages in the events of war, or to understand war as part of some divine plan. It was common to interpret defeat as a sign of divine wrath, and victory or a deliverance from danger as a sign of divine grace. It was also common to look for – and find – divine omens and revelations concerning the events of war and the outcome of battles.[17]

Moreover, it was often claimed in medieval and early modern Europe that a combatant can attain salvation by fighting and dying for the true religion. The Crusades and the orders of warrior-monks are obvious examples. Some literary narratives such as the Grail Cycle described "the way of the warrior" as a true spiritual path, whereas the mercenary captain Jean de Bueil wrote in the late fifteenth century that 'we poor soldiers will save our souls by arms, just as well as we would by living in contemplation upon a diet of roots.'[18]

Hence, if contemporaries described religious experiences as life-changing battles, described battles as manifestations of divine will, and sometimes even described combatants as spiritual seekers, it should have been an easy step to describe real battles as life-changing revelatory experiences.

The connection between bodily suffering and revelation was not confined to spiritual contexts. It was also familiar in judicial contexts, where torturing the body was a dominant method for extracting truth. As Lisa Silverman argues in *Tortured Subjects*, judicial thinking in early modern Europe closely paralleled the logic of Scarry and twentieth-century military memoirists. It distrusted people's minds and wills, and the utterances made freely by the mind, since these were liable to be lies. Truth could be extracted only through bypassing the mind and the will. By torturing the bodies of suspects and witnesses, unwilled testimony was elicited. 'Torture,' writes Silverman, 'inflicted pain as a means of achieving the spontaneous truth of the body rather than the composed truth of the mind.' [19] The dominant judicial view was that

> truth is lodged in the matter of the body: judges were required to draw it out or extract it from the body, just as tears and teeth are drawn. Truth resides in the flesh itself and must be torn out of that flesh piece by piece. It is a physical as much as a metaphysical property. As a result, any attempt to reach the truth must occur through a physical process of discovery. Because of its physical location, truth must be discovered by physical means. No amount of discussion will achieve it; although the truth has a language, it is the revealing and unwilled language of the body. Only torture can satisfy the demand for the real truth, hidden in the flesh, perhaps unknown even to its possessor. Pain is, then, the vehicle of truth-telling, a distillation of the pure substance lodged in the impure flesh. Pain betrays the truth in the sense of exposing it to view through the sounds and gestures it produces.[20]

Not only pain, but blood too was a vehicle of truth. In duels, which were often fought until blood was drawn, the spilling of blood confirmed the participants' honor and the truthfulness of their word of honor. Unsolved murder cases – at least according to popular images – were occasionally solved when the victims' blood began flowing in the presence of their murderers. Such cases strengthened the tie between blood and the revelation of truth which the Christian mysteries created.[21]

In the scientific context, Baconian principles encouraged people to learn the truth from direct experience, and several branches of medicine tried to read truth from direct observation of people's bodies. One's character and even one's virtues and sins were often thought to be located in bodily innards or in 'the Galenic regime of humoral physiology.'[22] In particular, the new science of anatomy, which was immensely influential not only on the medical sciences but also on the public conception of human nature, claimed that truth can be read in human intestines, and displayed this truth through public anatomical dissections.[23] This attitude is most famously represented in Caravaggio's *Incredulity of St Thomas* (1601/2). The doubting saint tries to find out the truth of Christ's divinity and resurrection by inserting his finger into Christ's wound and pocking around inside Christ's body.[24]

In 1669 Thomas Watson in his *Christian Soldier* conflated together his basic military metaphor with an anatomical one. His Christian Soldier was called upon to dissect himself: 'As a Chirurgeon, when he makes a dissection of the body, discovers the *intenstina*, the inward parts, the heart, liver, arteries; so a Christian anatomizeth himself; he searcheth what is flesh, and what is spirit; what is sin, and what is grace.'[25]

The availability of this anatomical model for real soldiers is evident in the case of John Gwyn, a royalist company commander in the British Civil War. Gwyn writes that during the retreat from Farrington (1645), a corporal and another person called Mr Jewell were killed when jumping over a ditch, and 'I jumped just after them, and quite over, or I might have been anatomized as Mr Jewell was.'[26]

Leaving aside these particular currents of late medieval and early modern European culture, it has often been claimed that the connection between suffering, death, and revelation is universal and inherent in human nature, as evidenced by the fact that initiation rites in all human cultures involve bodily suffering and images of death.[27] Particularly important is the fact that 'for so much of human history and in the vast majority of human cultures [war] has been the prime place to define oneself as a man,'[28] and that in numerous cultures across the world, the main masculine rite of passage has involved killing and war. Among different cultures from the Masai of Africa to the Kaoka of Guadalcanal, a boy becomes a man, and a male is considered a real man eligible for marriage, only after he has killed a man in war, or at least taken part in a military expedition.[29] In hunting cultures such as the !Kung, a male is considered eligible for marriage only after he has hunted a large animal.[30] In the late modern West war has continued to be a prime masculine rite of passage, and in many countries various civilian and political rights have been reserved for combatants.[31] These rites of passage all assume that taking part in killing changes a man in profound ways, revealing to him some particularly masculine truth about himself and the world.

In explaining the connection between suffering and revelation in initiation rites, Alan Morinis has argued along very similar lines to Scarry. He writes that pain – like any 'extreme experience' – has the potential to 'directly assault the established patterns of cognition of self and others' and lead to 'new patterns of insight into self and object. Pain serves to initiate the subject into a reality that remains closed to those who remain in innocence.' Morinis emphasizes the disillusioning quality of pain, writing that pain has particular 'potential to mature consciousness by wasting the innocence of childhood and giving birth to the heightened self-awareness and greater consciousness of adulthood [...] ordeals of initiation are meant to induce a more mature, self-aware, adult consciousness in the minds of initiands.'[32]

Hence it seems that early modern combatants had all the cultural models and resources they needed in order to think that war should reveal to them some deep truths, and in order to argue that by personally experiencing war they have gained some special knowledge and authority. They experienced far worse bodily sufferings than many a monk; they heard more tortured screams than many a judge; and they saw more human entrails than many an anatomist. Indeed, they occasionally heard their own tortured screams and saw their own entrails.

It is obvious that combatants also had a lot to gain from arguing along such lines. As twentieth-century examples show, describing war as revelation grants combatants a privileged political authority, both in wartime and in peacetime. They could have used it, for example, in their struggles against the civilian nobility of the robe.

Some scholars have argued that this is exactly what happened. In particular, Jonathan Dewald has contended that according to the early modern nobility of the sword, 'War [...] created forms of knowledge inaccessible to others,'[33] and that 'Violence defined a special knowledge of the world; it gave the military noble access to realities that were closed to others.'[34] However, as we shall see below, early modern memoirists hardly ever thought along such lines. Despite the favorable cultural conditions, and despite the political dividends they could have earned, early modern military memoirists did not interpret war as a revelatory experience.

2

The Absence of Revelation from Early Modern Military Memoirs

The conversion narratives of Christian soldiers

Early modern religious culture sought to interpret *everything* as revealing some divinely ordained truth. In particular, it saw death and sufferings as privileged sites of truth and authority. Hence the failure to interpret war as a revelatory experience is most glaring in the case of early modern narratives combining military and religious agendas. These include hagiographies of soldier-saints, spiritual autobiographies and conversion narratives written by veterans, and military memoirs written by soldiers-turned-clerics.

Though there were numerous saints with combat experience, and though hagiographies often ascribed conversion to experiences of suffering, the hagiographical tradition systematically downplayed the importance of *military* experiences as a source for revelation and conversion. Hagiographies that were first composed in the classical and medieval periods, and that continued to dominate early modern spirituality, provided only two models for dealing with the combat experiences of converts. Both models ignored the revelatory potential of such experiences.

(1) The New Testament and classical martyrology contain numerous stories of soldier conversions, but most of them simply do not mention combat experiences. The conversion of the first soldier-convert, the faithful Roman centurion, is brought about by the illness of his servant. It is nowhere mentioned whether the centurion ever fought in battle, and what impact it might have had on him.[1] Instead of combat, conversion is usually attributed to the impact of preaching, miracles, visions, or witnessing martyrdom scenes, as in the cases of Saint Longinus (the centurion who pierced Christ's side on the cross),[2] Saint Sebastian,[3] Saint

Eusctache,[4] Saint Florian, Saint Acacius, Saint Hadrian of Nicomedia, and Saint Theodore Stratelates.[5]

Later stories of soldier-converts did mention the converts' combat experiences, primarily in order to appeal to a secular warrior aristocracy. However, the combat experience was not instrumental in bringing about the conversion. Such is the case of the conversion of Saint Guthlac, the model soldier-saint of Anglo-Saxon England. According to the *Vita Sancti Guthlaci*, Guthlac spent nine years as a leader of a roving war band, inspired by the valiant deeds of past heroes. He devastated villages, towns and fortresses with fire and sword, and amassed much booty, though he took care, writes his hagiographer, 'to return to the owners a third part of the treasure collected.'[6]

One night, as he lay down to sleep thinking over mortal affairs, 'a spiritual flame' began to burn in his heart. He contemplated the vanity of the world and

> then in imagination the form of his own death revealed itself to him; and, trembling with anxiety at the inevitable finish of this brief life, he perceived that its course daily moved to that end ... [S]uddenly by prompting of the divine majesty, he vowed that, if he lived until the next day, he himself would become a servant of Christ.[7]

The image of death that revealed itself to Guthlac was not death in combat, and his *Vita* does not give any place to Guthlac's earlier combat experiences in this conversion.

Much the same is true of the conversion story of Saint Francis of Assisi. Saint Francis's lifestory has occasionally been cited as the primary medieval example of "combat conversion." In 1202 Francis was about 20 years old, the pampered son of a rich cloth merchant. Dreaming of martial glory, he joined the army of Assisi in its war against Perugia. The subsequent battle was a disaster; the Assisians were massacred, and the young Francis spent several months in captivity. In 1205 Francis again marched to war, hoping to join the papal troops fighting in Apulia under Walter of Brienne. On his way to Apulia he dreamt that an angel was showing him a palace full of glittering arms, telling him that these arms would belong to Francis and his knights. He interpreted this dream as indication of his coming military success.

However, a short time afterward he fell sick at Spoleto and became apprehensive of the coming journey and war. He then had another vision, in which the same angelic voice told him that he had misinterpreted his previous dream. The arms he saw in his dream were spiritual, and his vocation was to be a *miles Christi* rather than an earthly soldier. Upon awakening, Francis abandoned his military plans, turned back to Assisi, and embarked on a spectacular spiritual career.

Some modern commentators have described Francis's experience as similar to that of the enthusiastic bourgeois volunteers of 1914, and have ascribed his turning away from the world in favor of a spiritual vocation to his disillusionment.[8] Niza Yarom even argued that after the campaign of 1202 Francis suffered from PTSD. On his way to Apulia in 1205 his suppressed trauma resurfaced. The flashback caused Francis to abandon the path of war, and he adopted a spiritual path as a means to recover from the trauma and to justify his otherwise "cowardly" flight to himself and to his family.[9] Such an interpretation comes easily to modern readers. If we heard about, say, an American soldier who on his way to a second tour of duty in Vietnam had a breakdown, fled the army, abandoned his family, joined some esoteric sect, and began talking with birds, who would not be tempted to think that war and trauma must have had something to do with it?

Yet tempting as this idea may be to modern commentators, medieval hagiographies of Francis present things very differently. They hardly mention his combat experience at all. Thomas of Celano in his *Second Life* writes only that 'once there was a bloody battle between the citizens of Perugia and those of Assisi, Francis was made captive with several others and endured the squalors of a prison.' The *Legend of the Three Companions* is similarly terse, reporting only that 'During a year of war between Perugia and Assisi Francis was captured together with many of his fellow citizens and was taken to prison in Perugia.' Voragine's *Golden Legend* says that

> Once he and a number of companions were captured by the Perugians and confined in a horrid prison, where the others bemoaned their fate while Francis alone rejoiced. When his fellow prisoners rebuked him, he answered: "Know that I rejoice now because in time the whole world will worship me as a saint!"

No hagiography gives this combat experience any importance in Francis's subsequent conversion and spiritual career. Needless to say, no hagiography ascribes his conversion to suppressed combat trauma or fear of future combat.[10] During his subsequent spiritual career, Francis often spoke against war and even against the attempt to convert heathens by military force. Yet he never tried to rely on his potential authority as a flesh-witness.

Saint Martin of Tours was perhaps the best-known soldier-saint of Christianity. Martin aspired to serve God already from childhood, and his hagiographer writes that at the age of twelve he 'converted entirely to the work of God.'[11] He enlisted in the Roman army against his will due to the pressure of the authorities and his own family. In the army he resisted all the vices common to 'men of such a type' (i.e., soldiers), and displayed instead his Christian virtues. He was eventually baptized, but remained in the army, wishing to complete his term of service as required.

His term of service had nearly expired without Martin ever seeing combat. But then the barbarians invaded Gaul, and Emperor Julian assembled the army to give them battle. On the eve of the expected encounter, Martin asked Julian to be discharged from the service, for he was a 'miles Christi' and wished to fight only in Christ's service. Julian naturally accused Martin of cowardice. Martin offered to prove his mettle by advancing during the coming battle unarmed in front of the army's battle-line. Luckily, thanks to divine intervention the barbarians surrendered without battle and Saint Martin was spared any combat experience.[12]

In Martin's case neither combat nor even the prospect of combat had any impact on his conversion. Rather, the story highlights how inconsequential combat experience was. No matter what horrors Martin could have expected to see and undergo on the field of battle, he was sure they would have no bearing on his faith. This message was echoed in the medieval iconography of Saint Martin. Though the saint was often shown in military garb, the context is usually civilian. He is most often shown dividing his cloak with a beggar.

Tellingly, one of the sole paintings showing Martin in the context of battle is a fresco by Simone Martini, painted for an Assisi church dedicated to Saint Francis in 1312–17. In the background of the fresco we can see the barbarian host approaching in battle array. Saint Martin is advancing toward them with a cross in his hand. However, instead of looking toward the barbarians and the battlefield, Martin is looking toward the Emperor Julian. The message is clear: The typical martyrology conflict between convert and emperor is all important, whereas combat is of no importance. Martin does not look toward the battlefield, because there is nothing there that could be of any importance.[13]

John France has identified at least 50 other medieval saints who had previously been soldiers, and more saints who as bishops and lay rulers led armed forces in combat. Yet France nowhere cites a case of a soldier who was converted *by combat* to piety, and according to him hardly any

Figure 1 Simone Martini, *Saint Martin Renouncing Arms* (1312–17)

of these saintly men became hostile to war or war culture due to their military experiences.[14]

Stephen Scrope, a fifteenth-century squire, wrote that many knights turned in their old age from deeds of arms to 'dedes of armes spirituall, as in contemplacion of morall wysdome and exercisying gostly werkys.' Yet for him this was a natural part of the life cycle rather than a reaction to the horrors of war. It is only because they were physically incapable of fighting in earthly battles that the knights turned to spiritual warfare.[15] In fictional narratives too, though the figure of the combatant-turned-monk was very popular, the conversion of these figures was not attributed to the horrors of war, but rather to general weariness with this world or simply to old age.[16]

It should finally be noted that throughout the late Middle Ages and the early modern period monasteries were often used as houses for invalid veterans, and at least the king of France was able from 1516 to force monasteries to accept military invalids as lay brothers. In this case war injuries were directly responsible for turning soldiers into hermits, but only in a very literal sense. What the soldiers themselves thought of their enforced new vocation is attested by the fact that many abused the system and sold their place as lay brothers in monasteries to the highest bidder.[17]

(2) As Christianity gained power and became a fighting religion, another hagiographical model arose which linked combat and religious conversion very tightly, but presented combat as the *outcome* rather than the cause of conversion. Thus in the famous story of Saint George, first comes the conversion, and only afterward the fight with the dragon.[18] Jeanne d'Arc found herself leading a French army at Orleans due to earlier mystical experiences. Neither her subsequent hagiographies nor her own testimony presented her battle experiences as revelatory occasions.[19] Crusader chronicles and Crusader memoirs often narrate how a man was divinely inspired to join the holy war. Yet I could not locate any model story of a sinner who joined the crusade for base purposes and was converted to piety through combat experiences.

Hence the hagiographical legacy bequeathed to early modern Christianity did not provide any models of military experiences revealing the truth and converting combatants. The same is true of the new autobiographical texts that began to be composed in ever greater numbers from the sixteenth century onward.

In the early modern period, Christianity became a more experiential religion, focusing on inner experience rather than outer behavior.[20] Both the Reformation and the Counter-Reformation encouraged or even obliged the faithful to scrutinize and record their inner spiritual life with ever-growing zeal. Spiritual autobiography consequently became an extremely popular genre in large parts of Europe and North America, particularly but not exclusively amongst Protestants.[21]

These spiritual autobiographies usually focused on two main themes: How the author was converted from sin to piety; and how the author faced various trials and tribulations after his initial conversion. Revelation played a prominent part in the description of both themes. Conversion was frequently ascribed to some kind of revelatory experience. Further steps on the spiritual way were usually marked by other revelatory experiences, which taught the author deeper and more subtle levels of the Truth.[22]

The experiences giving rise to such revelations were varied. Almost any incident could result in revelation. Robert Blair had a spiritual awakening when he one day saw ' "the sun brightly shining, and a cow with a full udder": he remembered that the sun was made to give light and the cow to give milk, but began to realize how little he understood the purpose of his own life.'[23] Jacob Boehme had such a deep experience of enlightenment at the sight of a pewter dish, that 'in one-quarter of an hour I saw and knew more than if I had been many years together at a University.'[24] For our purposes it is important that in accord with prevailing religious ideas, experiences of suffering or witnessing suffering were particularly useful in revealing hidden truths.

It is also of great importance that the authority that spiritual autobiographers claimed for themselves emanated from the personal experience of ordinary people. Though few outside the circles of radical Protestant groups argued that this experiential authority was superior to that of Church teachings and Scripture, most did view it as an *independent* and complementary source of authority.[25] Combatants therefore had in spiritual autobiography a model for claiming authority on the basis of personal experiences, particularly experiences of suffering.

Moreover, the assumption underlying and justifying the writing of most early modern spiritual autobiographies was that the religious experiences of all people are essentially similar, and that consequently it was worthwhile for even the most humble person living the most ordinary life to record and publish his or her experiences. For in recording them, the person was really recording a universal experience, and other people could benefit by reading his or her autobiography.[26] Such line of thinking could have empowered early modern combatants of even the humblest ranks to write their experiences.

A considerable number of combatants indeed utilized the new opportunities and composed spiritual autobiographies. These narratives, like most contemporary narratives, certainly interpret war in religious terms and try to read divine messages in the events of war. They commonly interpret defeat and injury as a sign of divine wrath, and victory or a deliverance from danger as a sign of divine grace. For instance, Colonel Blackader marked in his spiritual journal a large number of *Ebenezers* – providential deliverances from imminent danger. In his view, at the siege of Lille (1708) God even took the trouble of directing two bullets to pierce his body in such a way that they only wounded him slightly, so as 'to make me a greater monument of mercy and kindness.'[27]

Yet such lessons were always learned from the external *facts* of war. In contrast, these narratives hardly ever tried to extract divine messages – or any messages whatsoever – from personal *experiences* of war. In particular, the autobiographers – like the hagiographers before them – never ascribed conversion to combat experiences.

Many of them simply copied the two aforesaid hagiographical models. Their conversion either antedated their military experiences, or was unrelated to them. For example, the spiritual autobiography of the Puritan Richard Norwood passes in almost complete silence over Norwood's military service in the Netherlands in 1608/9.[28] Alonso de Contreras had a far lengthier military career in the late sixteenth century, fighting mainly against the Turks in the Mediterranean. In the midst of his stormy adventures he retired from the world to become a hermit, though after seven months he abandoned the spiritual path and returned to the earthly fray. Contreras attributes his decision to retire from the world to his mistreatment at court, rather than to anything he had seen in war. It is noteworthy that when he prepared himself for his retreat from the world, he purchased all the necessary hermit paraphernalia, including a hair shirt, a whip of chains, plenty of penitential books, and a skull.[29] Whereas now Contreras found the skull an object of meditation, previously he saw countless skulls without getting any religious inspiration from them. For example, he jokingly tells how he once saw a Dutch gunner who was hit in the face by a cannonball. His head was blown to pieces, and the men around him were splattered with the pulp of his brain and pieces of bone. One such bone hit a sailor on the nose. The nose was crooked from birth, but the blow now straightened it, to the happiness of the sailor and to the astonishment and mirth of all.[30]

The Lorrainer Nicolas Herman was a contemporary of Contreras. He fought as a soldier in the Thirty Years War, until he was wounded and went back home to recuperate. According to his seventeenth-century hagiography – which was based on Herman's own testimony – during this period of enforced inactivity Herman's innate religious tendencies were allowed to blossom. He became a monk, and 'It was by meditating on the engagements of his baptism, on the disorders of his youth, on the mysteries of Christianity, and especially on the passion of Jesus Christ, that he was changed into another man' – not by meditating on war.[31]

No other reference is made to Herman's military experiences in this hagiography, and Herman himself – better known as Brother Lawrence –

makes absolutely no reference to them in the best-selling meditation manual he dictated. In this manual Herman often refers to suffering, illness, and various calamities – but not to war and its horrors. As for his own conversion, he does not attribute it to anything he witnessed in war, and instead singles out a revelation he had at the age of 18, when

> in the winter, seeing a tree stripped of its leaves, and considering that within a little time, the leaves would be renewed, and after that the flowers and fruit appear, he received a high view of the Providence and Power of GOD, which has never since been effaced from his soul.[32]

Donald Lupton, who served as a minister in an English regiment that fought in the Thirty Years War, composed in 1634 a meditation manual aimed to inspire Christian sentiments and convert men from sin to piety. This manual was clearly influenced by his military background. For instance, in his meditation on the sight of a grasshopper he describes the insect as a *'Summer singing* Souldier', not knowing where he should take his winter quarters.[33] He includes meditations on a sword, on a frontier garrison, and on a soldier – in which he compares an army of soldiers to the spiritual army of humanity.[34] Despite this martial inclination, and though he includes meditations on such trivial things as the sight of a door turning upon its hinges,[35] Lupton nowhere includes a meditation on the *experiences* of war.

Like Lupton, the divine Thomas Fuller rarely alluded to his military experiences in his spiritual writings, whereas the theologian Jeremy Taylor, who barely survived the brutal storming of Cardigan Castle (1645), mentioned his military experiences only once, when he needed to compare a sea-storm to something. In his *Divine Meditation up Several Occasion* (1680) General William Waller – the veteran Parliamentarian commander – made absolutely no reference to his military experiences.[36]

Nevertheless, the rising emphasis in early modern religion on the revelatory potential of the most mundane experiences resulted in the appearance of one new model for treating war experiences. This model linked military experiences with religious conversion by way of contrast; that is, soldier-converts began writing spiritual autobiographies which highlighted the fact that, unlike many other mundane experiences, combat *cannot* convert soldiers. Having a toothache, seeing a cow with a full udder, or looking upon a barren tree in winter may open one's eyes to the truth. Killing people, seeing friends killed, and getting injured in combat cannot.

This model is apparent, for example, in the spiritual autobiography of the most famous Catholic soldier-convert of the era: Saint Ignatius Loyola. Born Iñigo Lopez de Loyola to a noble Basque family, the future saint played a key role in the 1521 siege of Pampeluna. When an invading French army of superior strength approached the city, the local Spanish commander decided to go plead for reinforcements in person, conveniently absenting himself from the scene of danger. Before leaving, he appointed the 29-years-old Loyola to raise a force of volunteers to help in the defense.[37]

When Loyola returned to Pampeluna with his volunteers, the city was already as good as lost. The local population wished to surrender rather than fight, fearing the dreadful fate reserved for cities stormed by force. The defeatist atmosphere infected the soldiers, who had as much to fear from such a prospect as the civilians. They abandoned the city and retreated to the citadel, and then convened a war-council to decide whether to surrender the citadel as well.

Thirty-four years later, when he was head and founder of the Jesuit Order, Loyola dictated his lifestory for posterity, and chose to open the account of his life with this council of war. Speaking about himself in the third person, Loyola recounts that 'all the others saw clearly that they could not defend themselves and were of the opinion that they should surrender provided their lives were spared.' However, he himself, who was then 'a men given over to vanities of the world,' possessing 'a great and vain desire to win fame' and delighting 'in the exercise of arms,' had a different opinion. The young Loyola, speaking of honor and glory, managed to convince the garrison's commander to defend the citadel. Though 'this was contrary to the views of all the knights [...] they were encouraged by his valor and energy.'[38]

And so the siege began. The French invested the citadel, erected powerful batteries, and opened a devastating fire. It took the French artillery only six hours to breach the walls, and then the infantry stormed forward. At that moment, Loyola recounts that 'a shot hit him in the leg, breaking it completely; since the ball passed through both legs, the other one was also badly damaged.'[39] Upon the fall of the young hero, the defenders lost heart and immediately surrendered. The French infantrymen paid little attention to the surrender, and began massacring the garrison, until they were stopped by the French cavalrymen. Loyola, on the other hand, was treated magnanimously by the French. French officers, impressed by his courage, took care of him, and had their doctors treat him. After a fortnight they sent him home.[40]

Doctors and surgeons were summoned from many places to the family castle. After examining the patient, they reported that the bones healed badly, and hence the leg ought to be broken again and the bones reset. 'This butchery,' recounts Loyola, 'was done again; during it, as in all the others he suffered before or since, he never spoke a word nor showed any sign of pain other than to clench his fists. Yet he continued to get worse, not being able to eat and showing the other inclinations that are usually signs of death.' He recovered almost by a miracle, but the bones again healed badly, one leg being shorter than the other, with the bone protruding so much 'that it was an ugly sight.' Loyola was greatly displeased, 'because he was determined to follow the world and he thought that it would deform him.' He asked the surgeons to cut it again.

> They said that indeed it could be cut away, but that the pain would be greater than all those that he had suffered [...] Yet he was determined to make himself a martyr to his own pleasure. His older brother was astounded and said that he himself would not dare to suffer such pain, but the wounded man endured it with his customary patience. After the flesh and excess bone were cut away, means were taken so the leg would not be so short; many ointments were applied to it, and, as it was stretched continually with instruments, he suffered martyrdom for many days.[41]

This was the turning point of Loyola's life. For it was during this 'martyrdom' that Loyola's eyes were opened to the vanities of the world and of his earlier ideals, and he was set on the road that led him to sainthood. But it was neither the injury, nor the pain, nor the horrific sights at the storming of Pampeluna that opened his eyes. As he lay on his sick bed recuperating from his ordeal, he asked for some books to pass the time with. Which books did he ask for? Loyola explains that he was still 'much given to reading worldly and fictitious books, usually called books of chivalry,' and it is for these books that he asked.[42]

Contrary to what the revelatory paradigm of war would have us expect, the cannonball that shattered Loyola's body left his mental fantasies intact. These fantasies of honor and glory, gleaned from chivalric romances and chivalric culture in general, were the direct cause of all his physical misery. First, it was these that caused him to convince his commanders and comrades to defend Pampeluna against overwhelming odds, which led to their death and to his own crippling injury. Secondly, it was these very same fantasies that led him to insist on cutting and re-cutting his legs. Still, all the resulting pain did not shake Loyola's belief in chivalry.

Yet something more powerful than bodily pain now intervened. To the disappointment of the young Loyola – but to the fortune of the Counter-Reformation – there were no chivalric romances in the house. Loyola had to satisfy himself instead with two devotional texts: Ludolph of Saxony's *Life of Christ* and Jacopo de Voragine's *The Golden Legend* (a collection of saints' lives).[43] It was reading these texts and reflecting on them that first opened his eyes. He began to see how vain was his previous way of life, and resolved to mend himself and imitate the lives of the saints.[44] Soon after, Loyola had his first mystical vision, which was followed by many others. These visions revealed to him the Truth, step by step. For instance, Loyola describes how one time while praying on the steps of a monastery, he had a vision of the Trinity in the form of three musical keys, and at other times during prayer the nature of Christ and the manner in which God created the world were revealed to him.[45]

The autobiographical text Loyola dictated in 1555 comprises mainly descriptions of these visions and revelations. There is hardly an event narrated that did not reveal some deep truth to Loyola. The main exception is the siege of Pampeluna and his own injury. Nowhere in the text does Loyola reflect on these events or draw any lessons from them. Though he repeatedly attacks and undermines the chivalric view of the world and the vanity of the secular nobility, and though he often does so on the basis of his personal revelations, he never utilizes his experiences at Pampeluna for that sake. The sole importance of his injury was that it gave him the time and opportunity to read the aforementioned books and reflect on them. If it was not for these books, Loyola would have gone on believing in the chivalric ideals of honor and glory, and would probably have become a combatant and courtier rather than a saint.

Equally surprising from a present-day perspective is Loyola's lack of guilt. According to his autobiography, during the initial stages of his spiritual career one of Loyola's biggest hindrances was an obsession with sin and confession, and a recurring doubt that he has not confessed all his sins. Loyola pestered any available priest, confessing and re-confessing the most trivial of sins.[46] Yet Loyola never considers the unfortunate men killed and injured at Pampeluna due to his inflated sense of honor and to his craving for glory, and gives no indication that they troubled his conscience. Similarly, though throughout the narrative Loyola repeatedly describes various mistaken ideas and views that came to his mind in order to warn his audience against making similar mistakes, he never warns his audience about the dangers of mistaken views of war.

It cannot be argued that perhaps upon becoming a monk Loyola just forgot all about war. For his Society of Jesus was first named *Compania Jesu Christi*, purporting to be a military company headed by Jesus as company commander. Even after the name was changed to *Societas Jesu*, the military trappings remained. The society was organized along military lines, with a hierarchical command structure headed by a General. (The veteran of Pampeluna thus had the satisfaction of becoming a general after all.)

Apart from his spiritual autobiography, Loyola also composed one of the most popular Christian meditation manuals: the famed *Spiritual Exercises*. One of the main exercises Loyola recommends in this manual and in other writings is to think about one's death, and to imagine how a human body looks in death and as it decomposes. These images are supposed to make the believer realize the vanity of earthly being and of the human body. Loyola also recommends that the believer asks God for 'pain, tears, and suffering' in order to understand Christ's suffering.[47] Yet Loyola never refers in these exercises to the real suffering he experienced at Pampeluna or to the real bodies he saw there. Whereas the *mental image* of dead and wounded human bodies was a central source for revelation, the real dead bodies he personally saw at Pampeluna, and his own shattered legs, revealed nothing to him.

In 1609, a year after Loyola was beatified, the Jesuits produced a pictorial biography of their founder for the benefit of illiterate devotees. The illustrations, drawn by Peter Paul Rubens, made it absolutely clear what was war's role in the saint's life, and how Loyola was converted.

The battle scene at the siege of Pampeluna contains no indication of the saint's spiritual vocation and his coming conversion, or of war's revelatory potential. Instead, the moment of revelation and conversion shows Loyola in a domestic setting, laying peacefully in his bed and reading a book. Note in particular the contrast between the cloud of smoke emanating from the cannon at the foreground of the siege scene and the heavenly cloud in the bedroom scene. They look the same, but whereas the former is spiritually empty, sending forth a mere cannonball to shatter the future saint's leg, the latter is spiritually full, sending forth a ray of light that opens the saint's eyes and heart.

Loyola's story is paradigmatic of the early modern period. In the spiritual autobiographies of veterans even the harshest bodily experiences do not reveal any deep truths about oneself or about the world, and war

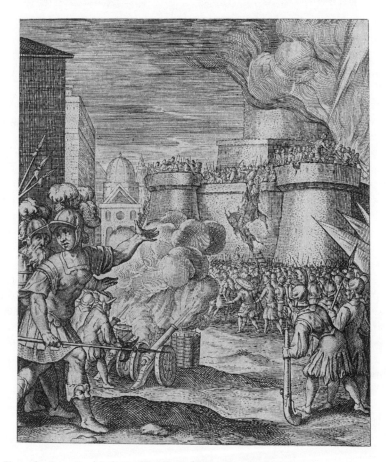

Figure 2   Peter Paul Rubens, *The Siege of Pampeluna* (1609)

is not interpreted as revelatory. If any revelations are mentioned, they are almost always due to either direct divine intervention or reading books. Ink and paper speak far more convincingly than blood and intestines, and the thinkers in the ivory towers have a clearer vision than the combatants on the battlefield.[48]

Louis de Pontis was a French nobleman and officer who took far more time than Loyola to abandon the path of arms, but eventually entered the Jansenist monastery of Port-Royal and spent the last 18 years of his life in solitude and meditation. While there, he told his lifestory to Pierre Thomas du Fossé, who wrote it down and published it in 1676. The book was a great success, re-appearing in numerous French and

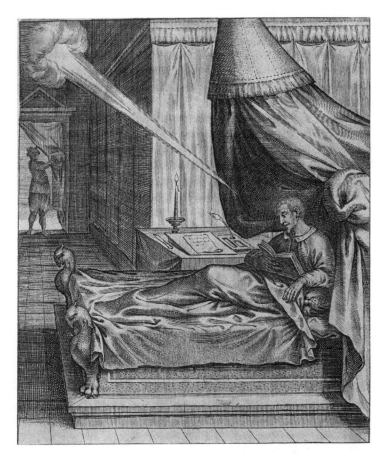

Figure 3 Peter Paul Rubens, *The Conversion of Saint Ignatius Loyola* (1609)

foreign editions during the seventeenth and eighteenth centuries, and influencing a large number of other memoirists.[49]

During his career Pontis killed dozens of men, and saw thousands of others die. He was in mortal danger countless times, was severely injured several times, and lost many close friends and relatives in combat. None of these experiences, writes Pontis, ever caused him to doubt his chosen vocation. Particularly interesting in this respect is Pontis's injury at the siege of Montpellier (1622). During the siege Pontis's close friend, the lord of Zamet, was mortally wounded. In revenge, Pontis killed some Huguenot prisoners in cold blood.[50] God, says Pontis, punished him for this crime. As he was leading an attack on an enemy fortification, 'I felt myself wounded with two musket balls, one in the body, which did not enter very far, and which only passed by the flesh and the skin, the other in the ankle, the bone of which it broke into several splinters, making me fall at the same time into the ditch.' He encouraged his men to leave him and continue the attack, and was satisfied when the fortification was taken.

He was carried back to camp, where his wound soon became infected with gangrene. The doctors recommended an amputation, but Pontis refused, preferring like Loyola to die than to live as a cripple and give up his military career. The doctors resolved to use violence to force him to undergo the operation. When they approached his tent with all their instruments and balms, Pontis was so frightened that his hair stood on end. He shouted and fought with all his power, and finally had his way. A country doctor he knew managed to cure his gangrene and save his leg, though it took 7–8 months till the leg healed and he could walk and ride again. In the midst of all this, the lord of Zamet died, and when he was told of it, Pontis writes that 'I received it with a grief not possible to express.'[51]

What it felt like to suffer from gangrene can be inferred from the description given by *Mercurius Rusticus*, the royalist newspaper in the British Civil War, of the wound Colonel Sandys suffered at Powick Bridge:

> In his thigh the flesh did daily rot and putrefy, and was cut away by degrees even to bearing the bone naked, and stunk in so loathsome a manner that as he was a burden to himself so to his friends, too, and those that were about him were hardly able, for the noisomeness of the smell, either to come near him, or to do the office of necessary attendance, or so much as to endure the room where he lay, so intolerable was the stench, and so offensive.[52]

Yet except for a few dry comments, Pontis does not describe the emotional or sensory misery of his own ordeal. Neither does he say that he learned anything from it, nor was changed by it. Despite his sadness over his cruel behavior toward the Huguenot prisoners, the narrative describes Pontis as largely the same person before and after Montpellier. It is notable that he was certainly not disillusioned with his martial ideals. All his sufferings in war never led him to criticize the ideal of honor. When in 1637 he was appointed to the cushy job of governor of Abbeville, he soon quit it, because it threatened to 'reduce him to a bourgeois,' and prevented him from having the 'unique pleasure' which he found in commanding combatants in the field and doing battle against the enemies of his state.[53] Even at Port-Royal, when Pontis reflected on his lifestory, though he is sometimes critical of the pursuit of worldly honor, on the whole he is still very proud of his martial exploits.[54]

With hindsight Pontis attributes his many escapes from death to divine mercy. God saved him so that he could spend his last days in God's service.[55] Yet this is something Pontis did not know at the time. Throughout his career he remained an ignorant sinner, who thought only of worldly honor and worldly friendships.[56]

The death that finally converted Pontis was a bloodless civilian death at home. In February 1651 Pontis visited the home of his friend, Saint-Ange. While staying there, Saint-Ange suddenly died, without any clear reason. According to late modern views, this is the perfect death – sudden and painless.[57] Yet this death had a crushing impact on Pontis.

> It pleased God at last to bring me out of the wretched condition in which I had lived so long... Utilizing the surprising death of one of my best friends in order to frighten me for my own good, and to make me think of myself. The infinite deaths of my friends, which up till then I had been an eyewitness of in the army, made no deeper impression upon my spirit, than to make me cry over those whom I loved. But this death pierced me to the very heart, and made me think of crying for myself, and of making a serious reflection on the fate that was likely to befall me too as well as him.[58]

Pontis explains that Saint-Ange's death made him for the first time reflect seriously on the uncertainty of this life, and on the inconstancy of the things of this world. He reasoned with himself that

> This man was well but a quarter of an hour ago, and yet he is dead in an instant. I may die in an instant just like him. I am presently alive, and I may be gone a quarter of an hour hence. Ah poor wretch, what will become of you then? It is time you think about this. It is perhaps to you, that God speaks through this death.[59]

Another friend of Pontis seized the occasion to lecture Pontis further on the vanity and nothingness of the world, and since God already touched Pontis's heart through that accident, he resolved to quit the world.[60] After some more adventures he carried out this resolution, and retired to Port-Royal, where his sole occupation was to thank God for his past graces, and to prepare himself for death, 'of which I have thought very little until now, even though in the armies I had it presented to my eyes very often.'[61]

Why should witnessing a calm civilian death at home so shake a soldier who remained unmoved by seeing so many of his friends and enemies die gruesome deaths on the battlefield? Pontis does not give us an answer. What he does make clear is that war – in contrast to the death of Saint-Ange – reveals no truths. Even though he became a changed man, spending his remaining years in prayer and meditation on death, when he reflected back on his military experiences he could not find even with the help of hindsight any revelations there except two: that God saved him from death because he had plans for him; and that God decides the fortunes of war.[62] Apart from that, his reflections on war are just a list of battles, sieges, and brave exploits, focusing on matters of worldly honor and virtue. The only thing they could inspire in readers is a desire to imitate Pontis's martial career, go to war, and gain there honor and earthly glory.

If we move from the Catholic to the Protestant camp, we shall encounter the same basic attitudes. John Bunyan, the most famous Protestant soldier-convert of the era, was in full agreement with Ignatius Loyola, the Jesuit saint. Bunyan served for several years as a common soldier in the Parliamentarian army during the British Civil Wars. Though in *Grace Abounding* he often compares spiritual struggles to warfare, Bunyan makes only one passing reference to his own military career. While recounting various incidents of his youthful days of sin when God saved him from death, he writes that

> When I was a Soldier, I, with others, were drawn out to go to such a place to besiege it; but when I was just ready to go, one of the Company desired to go in my Room; to which when I had consented, he took my Place; and coming to the Siege, as he stood Sentinel, he was shot into the head with a Musket bullet, and died.[63]

Just as Loyola learned nothing from the siege of Pampeluna, so Bunyan learned nothing from this incident. He comments that this experience did not 'awaken my Soul to Righteousness; wherefore I sinned still, and grew more and more Rebellious against God, and careless of mine own Salvation.'[64] Nowhere else throughout his writing does Bunyan say he learned any truths from his military experiences.

Instead of blood and intestines, it was books and sermons which set Bunyan on the path of righteousness. His first nudge in the right direction was given by two books his wife brought him: *The Plain Man's*

Pathway to Heaven and *The Practice of Piety*.[65] Later on, reading the Bible opened his eyes to deeper and deeper truths.[66] In direct opposition to Ben-Yehuda and Sajer, Bunyan writes that

> Oh! one sentence of the Scripture did more afflict and terrify my mind, I mean those Sentences that stood against me, (as sometimes I thought they every one did,) more I say, than an Army of forty thousand men that might have come against me.[67]

Bunyan's other great work, *The Pilgrim's Progress*, was destined to become the model tale of spiritual revelation in Anglo-Saxon Protestantism. In World War I it was extremely popular amongst British soldiers, and greatly influenced how many of them constructed their understanding of war and their memoirs.[68] Yet the author of this work, though he had ample military experience of his own, makes no apparent use of it.

Adam Martindale, a Nonconformist minister who in his youth was the clerk of a Parliamentarian regiment, writes a little more about his military experiences. He has nothing positive to say about 'the hated life I had lived about two years among souldiers; though mine office was all along to employ my penne, not my sword, and to spend inke, not spill blood.'[69] He describes in some details the suffering he, his family, and Lancashire civilians underwent during the war. In particular, he describes how God saved him once,

> When Leverpoole was surrendered upon terms of free-quarter, though prince Rupert's men, upon their first entrance, did (notwithstanding these termes) slay almost all they met with, to the number of three hundred and sixty, and, among others, diverse of their owne friends, and some artificers that never bore armes in their lives, yea, one poore blind man; yet the first that I met with offered my quarter before I asked.[70]

Nevertheless, according to his narrative, the only thing which enlightened Martindale about the nature of the world during the war years was a sermon he heard.[71] In his autobiography Martindale ends each chapter with a list of reflections and lessons drawn from the incidents described. At the end of the chapter devoted to the war period Martindale reflects about various incidents, but none of these reflections concerns military experiences, and the only lesson he draws from the war itself is 'Let us pray to be delivered from unreasonable men that want common humanity, as soldiers too oft doe.'[72]

A more complex example is the spiritual journal of Lieutenant-Colonel J. Blackader. On several occasions Blackader writes that the horrors of war and, in particular, death in combat revealed to him the vanity of worldly ambitions. After the battle of Schelenberg (1704), 'I went alone into the field of battle, and there got a preaching from the dead.'[73] After the battle of Oudenarde (1708) 'I went again through the field of battle, getting a lecture on mortality from the dead.'[74] After Malplaquet (1709) 'I went to view the field of battle to get a preaching from the dead, which might have been very edifying, for in all my life, I have not seen the dead bodies lie so thick.'[75]

After another engagement he spent the day 'going through and visiting the wounded and dying officers. I see the vanity and emptiness of all things here below. Many who last week thought themselves brave and healthy men, are groaning and sinking down to the dust again.'[76] About the death of his commanding officer he writes that 'I got the surprising account of our Brigadier's death, with which I was greatly affected. *Man's breath goeth out, to earth he turns, that day his thoughts perish.* O the vanity of human grandeur! He was just come from court, where he was sent for that he might be raised a step higher for his services.'[77]

Though these lessons are exactly what we would expect to read in the memoirs of spiritually inclined early modern combatants, Blackader is quite unique amongst contemporary memoirists in noting them at all. And even he goes on to stress how ephemeral the impact of these lessons is, and how utterly incapable war is of truly changing people. Regarding the preaching he got from the dead on the battlefield of Schelenberg, Blackader writes that

> When we see what an uncertain thing our life is – now in health, and the next moment in eternity, it is wonderful we are not more affected by it [...] In the evening I went alone into the field of battle, and there got a preaching from the dead. The carcases were very thick strewed upon the ground, naked and corrupting; yet all this works no impression or reformation upon us, seeing the bodies of our comrades and friends lying as dung upon the face of the earth.[78]

After Blenheim he bemoans: 'shall nothing work upon us – shall nothing be blest to reform us, when so many of us are cut off – shall not the rest bethink themselves and turn unto thee.'[79] Another time he writes,

> Taken up all day in the house of mourning, burying a friend. O, I wonder at the sottish stupidity of men of our trade. They see their

comrades with whom they used to drink and debauch, plucked out of the world in a moment, yet they have not so much as a thought that they have a soul, or what will become of it when they die. I look upon this impiety as the greatest madness a rational creature can be guilty of. The longer I live, I see the greater necessity for holiness. To see a poor creature on a death-bed, on the brink of eternity – forced to quit the hold of all earthly comforts, – nothing but horror – nothing comfortable to look to in the other world, surrounded with jolly companions, miserable comforters, is very affecting.[80]

Instead of war, Blackader normally attributes revelation to direct divine intervention or to books. Blackader quite often mentions various divine visions,[81] whereas the Bible is by far the most important source of knowledge according to his text, including knowledge about war. Blackader often describes how he read the Bible on campaign,[82] and how he meditated on various passages during battle.[83] More importantly, like many of his contemporaries, when he tries to make sense of military events, he invariably turns to the Bible for guidance. It is very common for him to describe military events to which he himself was an eyewitness by means of biblical quotations.[84]

The Quaker Thomas Symonds is even more damning in his verdict on war's revelatory potential. In his spiritual autobiography Symonds wrote that he enlisted as a soldier in the British Civil War as a means to find relief from his inner spiritual war. The only significance of the outer war was that it indeed calmed down Symonds's inner war. Instead of combat leading to revelation, in Symonds's case it provided a convenient screen of ignorance.[85]

The ineffectiveness of combat as a means for revelation was reflected in the early modern *topos* of describing combatants as the worst of ignorant sinners, the ones least able to behold and understand the Truth. Erasmus described soldiers as 'the dregs of mankind' and as 'parasites, panders, bandits, assassins, peasants, sots [and] bankrupts.'[86] Tales and pictures of the Thirty Years War, of which Jacob Christoph von Grimmelshausen's *Simplicissimus* and Jacques Callot's *Miseres et malheurs de la guerre* are only the most famous examples, habitually focused on the image of the impious soldier who loots, rapes, and murders.[87] Painters used Biblical scenes such as the Massacre of the Innocents to express the extremely negative image of contemporary soldiers.[88] Even when painters depicted soldiers engaged in peaceful activities on garrison, these were most often gambling, card-playing, drinking, and whoring.[89]

In Farquhar's *The Recruiting Officer* (1706) Sergeant Kite explains the qualities of a sergeant like himself. '[I]f your worship pleases to cast up the whole sum, *viz.* canting, lying, impudence, pimping, bullying, swearing, whoring, drinking, and a halberd, you will find the sum total will amount to a recruiting sergeant.' Later on when Kite recruits someone who is said to be 'a very honest man,' Captain Plume, Kite's company commander, says: 'Pray, gentlemen, let me have one honest man in my company for the novelty's sake.'[90] Other early modern writers were even less kind to the soldiers.[91] Blackader sees his association with his comrades as a deadly threat to his salvation, writing that 'I am not afraid of the dangers or battle; through grace I shall do valiantly. I am more afraid of the snares and sin of the wretched company I must be chained to.' He was speaking of his fellow officers.[92]

To conclude, authors who had both military and religious agendas utilized religious knowledge in order to interpret military events, and utilized military events to demonstrate religious knowledge, but they almost never claimed to have gained any new knowledge from their military experiences. Though they often spoke of revelation, the idea that *war* could reveal anything was foreign to them. Blackader was the only one who got a preaching on mortality in battle, and even he concluded that such preachings went into one ear and immediately exited from the other.

Hence, though they very often made the comparison between spiritual struggles and war, and between Christians and combatants, memoirists somehow failed to read this comparison backward, and did not interpret death and suffering on the battlefield as containing any spiritual knowledge. After reading Blackader's text, or Loyola's, no one would be inclined to view combatants as possessing a privileged authority of flesh-witnesses.

Secular military memoirs[93]

Military memoirs were the most popular secular autobiographical genre of the early modern period. They were not a novel invention, and had a considerable number of precursors and models both in the classical era and in the Middle Ages. They were most probably a direct continuation of late medieval written and oral war narratives, rather than a product of some early modern individualist revolution.[94]

Early modern military memoirs were written mainly – though not exclusively – by noblemen who served as commanders of medium and senior ranks. These white male aristocratic officers occupy today the lowest rung in the politically correct Great Chain of Beings. Their writings too have fallen from grace. Whereas in the nineteenth century they were collected and printed in their dozens, today the fruits of this immense scholarly labor lay like so many white elephants on the library shelves, doing nothing except collecting dust and taking up valuable space. As a researcher, I was lucky enough to find the memoirs of numerous early modern counts, dukes, and marquises on the shelves of even the most impoverished libraries of provincial Israeli universities. Despite the growing interest in ego-documents, in most cases I was the first reader to open these tomes since they were purchased, and often had to use a paper-knife to separate their pages.

The fate of these books testifies not only to the inability of librarians to anticipate future research interest, but also to the power of the revelatory interpretation of war. The success of this interpretation has drawn a curtain of boredom over early modern military memoirs, and silenced the voice of their authors far more effectively than any censorship. The reason no one has opened these books for many decades is that they seem to be completely irrelevant. Though they discuss war – a fairly interesting topic – they are interested in all the wrong questions, and fail to address what late modern discussions and audiences of war find most interesting. They do not give us any idea of "how it felt like."

I beg the readers not to be misled by the extracts quoted in the following pages. I have naturally quoted those extracts which I thought present readers would find interesting and relevant, and which tend to address, however circumspectly, the experience of war. In fact, out of a typical 300-pages-long volume of memoirs, there are perhaps 5 pages worth of experiential descriptions, but it is from these 5 pages that I normally quote.

I nevertheless hope the following chapters will do a small service to these texts, and show that they are still relevant. The curtain of boredom that shields these texts from today's readers hides the fact that their ideas still permeate current understandings of war, if only as the dreaded "Other." The understanding of war as a revelatory experience was born in opposition to the memoirs of these early modern noble officers, and takes much of its life from this opposition. Soldiers to this day write their memoirs with these aristocrats in mind, as if they are still a powerful menace – which indicates that they probably still are.

War revealed nothing

Early modern war was as terrifying and awe-inspiring as late modern war. In particular, it should be noted that the mortality rates were even higher than in most twentieth-century wars. Though in absolute terms fewer soldiers were killed – because armies were considerably smaller – the soldiers' chances of survival were actually worse. In major battles – which lasted only a few hours – victorious armies often lost more than a quarter of their men, and the defeated side might lose up to two-thirds. It was common for ten or twenty thousand men to lose their lives in the space of two to three hours within an area of a few square kilometers.[95] Disease and hunger killed many more soldiers than battles, so that a few years of campaigning, even without a major battle, could completely wipe out an army. A study of one village in northern Sweden has shown that of 230 men who were recruited for military service in 1621–39, 215 died. The number of adult males in the village fell during these years from 468 to 288. Another study has shown that of 20 men who joined the royalist forces in the British Civil War from 3 Shropshire villages, 13 died in action.[96]

Early modern memoirists did not try to hide the extreme experiences of war. Death, injury, hunger, and disease, as well as the frenzy of killing and the joys of victory, fill page after page of their narratives. Nevertheless, memoirists almost never describe war as an experience of revelation, they almost never describe themselves as flesh-witnesses, and as a rule, they do not lay claim to the authority of flesh-witnessing. The overriding impression one gets from reading these texts is that their authors passed through war without learning anything new and without being changed in any profound manner.

In particular, it is notable that though early modern military memoirs contain thousands of combat descriptions, many of them lengthy and detailed, I could not find a single description of "combat epiphany" comparable to that of Shawn Nelson in Mogadishu. The memoirists could be describing the most harrowing or most exhilarating moments of their life, yet mundane reality keeps flowing on as usual. Time does not stop, the laws of physical reality function normally, and the combatants report neither extraordinary sensations and emotions nor heightened states of awareness.

It is difficult to illustrate what a text does *not* contain. The following pages survey a number of experiences that in late modern memoirs are often described as epiphanic and revelatory, illustrating that in early modern memoirs their revelatory potential was seldom exploited. For each experience, I have selected one or two representative examples. Some of these examples represent the typical early modern description, and I hope readers would trust me that there are dozens or hundreds of similar descriptions in other memoirs. Other examples represent the extreme point of the early modern spectrum, and I hope readers would trust me that the vast majority of similar early modern descriptions are even less revelatory than the one I have chosen to quote.

Baptism of fire

Perhaps the clearest example of the memoirists' disregard for war's revelatory potential is their treatment of the baptism of fire. As we shall see, Romantic memoirs often make a great deal of one's first combat. Even if it was only a minor skirmish, and even if the memoirist did not perform there any remarkable deed, the narrative still contains lengthy descriptions of his thoughts on the eve of action, and of the novel sensations and emotions he encountered during it. By the twentieth century, Westerners came to believe that one's first military action is a universal masculine rite of passage. Ernst Jünger rhapsodized about one's first combat: 'Oh, the baptism of fire! The air was so laden with an overflowing manliness that every breath was intoxicating. One could cry without knowing why. Oh hearts of men that could feel this!'[97]

Philip Caputo wrote in a similar vein about the men in his company after their first few skirmishes in Vietnam:

> Having received that primary sacrament of war, baptism of fire, their boyhoods were behind them. Neither they nor I thought of it in those terms at the time. We didn't say to ourselves, We've been under fire, we've shed blood, now we're men. We were simply aware, in a way we could not express, that something significant had happened to us.[98]

Some historians have claimed that this attitude was shared by early modern combatants as well. For instance, Charles Carlton argues that for the British Civil War soldiers whose first taste of battle was the skirmish at Marshall's Elm, this little fracas was a decisive personal experience.[99]

There certainly were initiation rites in medieval and early modern martial cultures. The knighting ceremony is an obvious example.[100] A few texts even describe one's first combat as involving various discoveries. For example, Grimmelshausen's Mother Courage discovered during her first battle how much she liked to fight.[101] Philippe de Commynes describes in great length his own baptism of fire – the battle of Montlhéry (1465) – and reports that his lord, Duke Charles of Burgundy, had a kind of revelation in that battle. Whereas previously he disliked war, henceforth he loved it more than anything else.[102]

Yet in the vast majority of cases, early modern memoirists did not view their first campaigns and battles as possessing unique personal importance. Some describe these events without specifying what they personally did and experienced. Most neglect to mention these occasions altogether, or do so off-handedly, while devoting far more attention to later campaigns and battles.

A typical example comes from the memoirs of the marquis de Chouppes, a French officer of medium rank, who lived in the mid-seventeenth century. Chouppes wrote a fairly lengthy tome of memoirs, and he occasionally describes his campaigns and battles in great detail (e.g., he dedicates ten pages to describing the battle of Freiburg (1644)).[103] Chouppes begins the account of his life at the age of 13, when he joined King Louis XIII as a page.[104] He then mentions that he was transferred to the royal guards, and from there jumps straight to his first campaigns, about which he writes as follows:

> I stayed [in the guards] two years; and I found myself [je me trouvai] at the siege of la Rochelle [1628], at the barricades of Suze [1629], at the siege of Privas [1629] and at other captures of places from those of the pretended reform religion in Languedoc [the Huguenots], at the taking of Pignerol in Piedmont [1630], at the combat of Veillane [1630], where I was wounded dangerously, and at the succor of Casal [1630]. Peace having been made, the king transferred me from the regiment of guards, and gave me a cornetship of light-cavalry in the company of La Frézelière. I served for seven years in the cavalry, during which I found myself [je me trouvai] in many events, both in Lorraine and in Germany, amongst others the defeat of Colloredo.[105]

Chouppes has nothing else to write about these nine years. His first campaign, his first encounter with the enemy, his first big battle, the first cannonade he heard, the first enemy he killed, the first comrade he saw killed, and his first injury – all these, and all that they revealed to him, are passed over in almost complete silence. There is certainly no indication that Chouppes thought – à la Caputo – that something significant had happened to him. Unlike late modern memoirists, when he writes that he "found himself" at the siege of La Rochelle, he does not mean that he found his self there.[106]

The duke of Navailles, another seventeenth-century French noblemen, describes his own debut into the military world in a little more detail. Following the family tradition, Navailles began his military career at the age of 15 or 16, when he joined a marine regiment serving on the Flanders front (1636). He was keen to do his duty, and he writes that despite his youth, 'I searched for occasions where I could acquire esteem.'[107] Like Chouppes, he passes over his very first campaign in almost complete silence, writing only that 'I found myself [Je me trouvai], on my first campaign, at the siege of Saint-Omer, which we were forced to raise, and at the battle of Polincove where we had the advantage [1638]. I saw during my second campaign the siege of Hesdin [1639], where the king was in person.'[108]

Navailles describes the difficult storming of Rantzau (1640), in which operation he was wounded for the first time, in a single sentence, commenting that 'one hundred officers of the three corps [that stormed the fort] were killed or dangerously wounded there. I too have received there a slight wound.'[109]

In his description of the siege of Tortone (1642) Navailles comments that the army was in danger of perishing from hunger, but without describing the actual experience of starvation.[110] When the commanders thought to lift the siege, the young Navailles objected, and eager for honor, volunteered his company for a difficult operation against part of the enemy fortification. He succeeded in taking the fortification, which resulted in the fall of the town and in much honor for himself. About the actual combat he writes only that the fortification was disputed for a long time, 'but in the end I made myself the master of it.' As for the price of his honor, he tersely informs the readers that 'I have lost on that occasion many soldiers, sixteen sergeants and many officers of merit.'[111]

It should be noted that Navailles wrote his memoirs after his only son was killed 'under my eyes.' Navailles laments that he had great hopes of that son, and that God took him just as Navailles began to feel 'sentiments of glory by the good success I had' in war. Yet, though Navailles learned the divine lesson that one should not glorify in one's power too much, he was not disillusioned with war itself.[112]

The duke of Saint-Simon is the last person who could be accused of being laconic. In the Boislisle edition, his memoirs comprise 45 thick volumes. Nevertheless Saint-Simon dismisses the first military action in which he participated – the siege of the city of Nemur (1692) – in the words 'Nothing of much importance happened during the ten days that this siege lasted.'[113]

During the same campaign Saint-Simon had a close brush with death. He once went to visit his friend, the count of Coëtquen, who was serving with him as a volunteer in the king's Musketeers.

> I went to his tent early, where I found him stretched upon his bed, from which I dislodged him playfully and laid myself down in his place... Coëtquen, sporting with me in return, took his fusil, which he thought to be unloaded, and pointed it at me. The surprise was

great when it went off. Fortunately for me, I was at that moment lying flat upon the bed. Three balls passed just three fingers above my head, and because the gun was a little elevated, the same balls passed above the head ... of our two tutors, who were walking outside the tent. Coëtquen fainted at the thought of the mischief he might have done; we had all the pains in the world to bring him to himself again: indeed he did not thoroughly recover for several days.

Saint-Simon does not explain how the incident affected himself. He informs the readers that he related this incident only as 'a lesson which ought to teach us never to play with firearms.'[114]

Saint-Simon had much more to say about the battle of Neerwinden (1693), the first major field battle in which he participated. Yet, though he devotes 20 pages to this battle, he is extremely reticent about his own experiences. He focuses on the tactical maneuvers of the two armies, and only once interrupts this in order to tell something about himself. After giving his exact position in the order of battle, and explaining that he was accompanied by his governor and by a squire of his mother, Saint-Simon says that 'I charged three times on an excellent light-brown horse, from whose back I did not descend since four in the morning. When I felt he was slackening, I turned around [to my squire] and demanded another. Then I noticed that these two gentlemen where not there anymore.' He turned to some other men of his, who gave him a very pretty gray horse, 'on which I charged two more times. I came out of all [the five charges] with the loss of the saddle-tie of the light-brown horse, which was cut, and of a gold ornament of my blue uniform, which was torn.'[115]

Some may argue that Saint-Simon was a dull soldier who was interested only in uniforms and horses, and who lacked either an interest in human psychology or the means to write about it. Yet from other passages we know that the duke was an extremely keen observer of psychology, and he is rightly judged to be one of the brightest stars of eighteenth-century French literature. For some reason, this gifted writer and astute observer, who left us subtle psychological analyses of every courtier in Louis XIV's court, and who brings to life the pettiest of court intrigues, had no interest in the experience of his first major field battle.

It is true that many memoirists thought of their enlistment and their first campaign as a kind of second birth, and as the beginning of their real life.[116] This is why many chose – like Chouppes – to begin their memoirs not with their biological birth, but with their entry into the martial world.[117] However, by beginning the story with their enlistment, without describing their childhood, these memoirists again ignored war's revelatory potential. For a revelation has meaning only if it is preceded by ignorance. Birth is a revelation and an initiation rite for the mother, but not for the baby. Similarly, religious conversion narratives always describe the initial period of ignorance. If the first words of Augustine's *Confessions* were 'tole, lege,' or if the New Testament introduced Saint Paul to us on the way to Damascus, the whole point of the conversion story would have been lost.

Basic training

In the late modern period, not only one's baptism of fire, but also the very first encounter with military reality – basic training – is often portrayed as a shattering and life-changing revelation. Many agree with Erich Maria Remarque who wrote about World War I that 'We were trained in the army for ten weeks and in this time more profoundly influenced than by ten years at school.'[118] Numerous twentieth-century military memoirs and war films devote as much time and attention to boot camp as to combat (e.g., the entire first half of *Full Metal Jacket*).

In contrast, no early modern memoirist gave much thought to basic training. At a time when military reformers such as Maurice of Nassau brought about the celebrated Military Revolution by instituting elaborate new methods of training, military memoirists seemed to be oblivious to its importance.

This is true not only of noblemen such as Chouppes and Saint-Simon, but also of common soldiers, who where at the receiving end of these new training methods. Thomas Raymond enlisted in the Dutch army in 1633. He writes nothing about his "boot camp" experiences except that 'I put my selfe into the company of Collonel Sir Philip Pakenham ... a person of gallant stature and personage and courage. In his company I traild a pike, and besides had the care and inspection of his family and expenses, he being a bachelour.'[119]

At that time the training methods of the Dutch army were the marvel and model of Europe. Harsh discipline and complex drill were imposed upon recruits to produce the first "military machine" of modern times. All the clichés of twentieth-century boot camp – from the sadistic drill-sergeant to the dreaded kit inspections – go back to the early seventeenth-century Dutch army. Moreover, many scholars, most notably Michel Foucault, see the training methods of the Dutch army as the cradle of numerous other modern disciplinary regimes.[120] The sociologist M. D. Feld even spoke of the reform of the Dutch army as the 'earliest of industrial revolutions, the industrialization of military behaviour in the Netherlands.'[121]

Whereas in the twentieth-century recruits at least arrived to boot camp with ample experience of such disciplinary systems – from school, from mines and factories, from life in a late-modern metropolis with its timetables and ubiquitous supervision – for Thomas Raymond the encounter with military drill and discipline must have been alien in the extreme. Yet Raymond could not care less about his supposedly revolutionary experience. The birth of modern discipline passed him by.

Killing

In many warrior cultures throughout history, killing enemies, and in particular one's first kill, was the pinnacle of existence. It was the single most important experience in a warrior's life, which defined his masculine identity and his social status just as the act of giving birth defined the identity and status of a woman.[122] In contrast, early modern memoirists, members of one of the most warlike elites in human history, treated killing very casually in their memoirs. Many never mention their killings at all – including their first killing. Others do so in passing. For example, Sydnam Poyntz writes about the battle of the Lech (1632) that 'my hand was in blood as other souldiers were.'[123]

Even in the rare cases when a more detailed description was given, killing was not described as a turning point in one's life. For instance, Jean de Mergey remembered his first killing as a joke. He was just 18 then, serving as a page of the Lord Deschenetz. He proudly writes that he looked 'like a little Mars.' In a skirmish in 1554 he killed an enemy soldier with a lance belonging to Deschenetz's equipment, and he describes how the soldier 'uttered a great cry with an ugly grimace, and fell dead under his horse.'

Mergey did not discover the secret of life at that moment. Rather, he was busy trying to retrieve Deschenetz's lance from the body, but he could not, because the lance was barbed and got stuck in the corpse. Mergey humorously remembers how fearful he became that Deschenetz would punish him for losing the lance, but was reassured by the lord Paul Baptiste who laughingly told him that he saw 'how the lance was lost,' and would explain the matter to Deschenetz.[124] Mergey nowhere says that at that day he truly became a man, or that he started seeing the world with different eyes, or that he was henceforth treated differently by his family members, his friends, or society in general.[125]

A handful of early modern memoirs do describe killing as the climax of their life, but all these cases involve staged combats and duels. Thus the climax of Jörg von Ehingen's memoirs is his single combat against a Muslim champion at Ceuta (1458),[126] whereas Richard Peeke titled his memoirs of the 1625 expedition to Cadiz *Three to One*, in memory of the staged combat he fought against three Spanish champions – whom he defeated.[127] Even in these cases, the single combat served only to affirm the memoirists' identity as worthy warriors, without bringing about any change in their personality or worldview. Ehingen gives a lengthy blow-by-blow account of how he defeated the Muslim Goliath, and relates how he was later fêted in the various courts of Europe, but he does not say that he discovered anything new about himself or the world thanks to this experience.

Mortal danger

Moshe Givati titled his military memoirs *Three Births in September*, referring to his biological birth in 1948 and his two near fatal injuries in 1969 and 1984. If Andrew Melville had thought along similar lines, he could have titled his memoirs *Four Births*. In 1648 Melville and a few of his comrades from the French army were taken captive by Imperialist troops. The enemy commander ordered the captives to be executed outright. They were ranged against a wall, and a Croat firing squad was detailed to shoot them. As the Croats began to shoot,

> The musket of the soldier who aimed at me missed fire, which so enraged him that he struck me in the chest with the butt-end, and knocked me over on to my side. Whilst he was putting a fresh priming to his gun I got up and espied one of the soldiers [...] making his escape. I had imagined myself quite indifferent to death, and had even taken off the shirt they had left on me, thinking that the ball would find less resistance.

> Nevertheless, as soon as I saw my comrade escape and jump into a moat full of water which surrounded the house, the desire seized me to follow his example. I did not wait until my executioner was ready to fire again, but ran with all my might, jumped into the moat and crossed it in spite of several shots which were fired but which did not reach me.

Melville hid himself inside a cornfield, and miraculously made his escape.[128] Melville does not say that he experienced anything unusual at the moment when the Croat's musket misfired, or at any other subsequent moment. Time did not slow down, his life did not pass before his eyes, and he certainly did not emerge from the fusillade as a changed man.

Melville was again captured after the battle of Worcester (1651). This time his captor shot him in the stomach right away, so that 'I fell weltering in blood, which flowed in great gushes from my wound, but I did not lose consciousness.' He lay there, tormented by thirst, throughout the night, and the next morning he was stripped naked by pillagers, and eventually thrown into a trench. 'My miseries did not end there; for they threw a dead body into the same place, with its legs right over me, which absolutely prevented my moving.'[129]

Contrary to Colonel Blackader's preaching dead, this corpse was silent on the topic of mortality, and Melville does not record any insight he had gained from this ordeal. He somehow survived to tell the tale, escaped from England, and happily reenlisted into various armies, continuing in his quest for glory and riches. Later on he was accidentally mistaken for a deserter and almost executed by his own side. Melville laments that this was 'the most terrible peril to which I had ever in my life been exposed. Up till now Death had appeared to me under several aspects, **all of which had been glorious.**'[130] Melville was certainly correct to say that in those days he was 'not of a reflective turn of mind.'[131]

Injury

In the late modern era, a distinct genre of invalid memoirs appeared, in which crippling injury leads not only to physical debilitation but also to disillusionment with old ideals, regeneration, and a better understanding of oneself and the world. The cover story of *Time* magazine of October 2, 2006 contains excerpts from reporter Michael Weisskopf's memoirs of his combat injury in Iraq (*Blood Brothers*). The story's headline is 'How I lost my hand but found myself,' and the magazine's cover sports Weisskopf hook, with his face in the background.

In the excerpts Weisskopf says that 'The loss of my writing hand launched an assault on my self-image. If I couldn't be a reporter, then who was I? What would I do?' He then narrates in detail the agonizing period he spent in hospital, and his relationship with the several different artificial arms he tried (one is nicknamed "Ralph," another "Pretty Boy"). He explains the physical and psychological impact of the different devices. He candidly writes how much he 'lost in penmanship, tennis, home repair, lovemaking.' He explains the most mundane realities of having an artificial arm, down to the fact that the rigid shell of the arm chafed his forearm and made him sweat heavily in summer. Eventually he adopted a hook, which 'became my trademark. It was brash, straightforward and pragmatic, virtues I cherished.' The experience completely changed his understanding of himself as a father, a

Figure 4   The Cover of *Time* Magazine, 2 October 2006

husband, a human being. 'It had taken a major loss for me to understand what I meant to others... I resolved to return the love by being
less self-absorbed. I promised my kids I would stay out of war zones.'[132]

Early modern reactions to serious injury are best represented by the
memoirs of Götz von Berlichingen. When Berlichingen was 23, his hand
was cut off in battle by a cannonball (1504). After the battle he became
despondent and prayed God to end his life, for 'I was finished as a

man of war.'[133] At this point it seems as if his injury is about to force Berlichingen to undertake a soul-searching quest similar to Weisskopf's, for his old identity as a warrior was clearly in jeopardy.

However, Berlichingen avoided the soul-searching (either as a protagonist or as a narrator). His old identity was instantly and conclusively reaffirmed, apparently without too much trouble. Just as he thought that his military life was finished, Berlichingen remembered a squire called Kochle, who also lost his arm but nevertheless went on campaigns and fought battles. This example consoled him, and he resolved to imitate Kochle. He replaced his lost arm with an iron one, and continued with his rather infamous martial career as if nothing happened. Berlichingen, the narrator, remarks here that it had now been close to 60 years that he has lived with a single arm, and during that time he took part in many wars and adventures without any difficulty.[134]

It is perhaps understandable why this incident did not cause Berlichingen to question his chosen identity or become disillusioned with war. What is much more remarkable is that Berlichingen does not use it even in order to highlight and strengthen his chosen identity. Despite Kochle's example, one-armed knights were not a common phenomenon. Mounting a horse, putting on one's armor, or swinging a sword were that much more difficult when one had only one arm (not to mention house repairs or lovemaking). Berlichingen overcame all the difficulties, and not only continued to lead an active military life, but managed to become one of the most famous, or infamous, knights of his day. If he were a twentieth-century memoirist, he would probably have made his injury and his reaction to it a central pillar of the text, so that the main storyline would be something like: "How I lost my hand, but nevertheless became a famous and successful knight." Yet Berlichingen does not write such a narrative. Instead of capitalizing on his loss to manifest his unique resolve and prowess, Berlichingen ignores it. Throughout the rest of the narrative, he mentions the fact that he had just one hand only twice (!). Once he mentions in passing that he had the iron-hand repaired.[135] Another time, when narrating how he and Jean de Selbiz defeated the forces of Nuremberg, he quotes Emperor Maximilian who said: 'Holy God, holy God, what is this? The one [Berlichingen] has but one hand, the other [Selbiz] has but one leg. If they both had two hands and two legs, what would you have done?'[136]

Nowhere else throughout the narrative is there the slightest reference to Berlichingen's condition. Berlichingen never describes how it felt to have an iron-hand – physically or psychologically – and certainly does not describe any kind of relationship with his iron-hand.[137] In contrast to Emperor Maximilian, Berlichingen never makes it a point to say that "I managed to perform this or that exploit even though I had only one hand." Moreover, though Berlichingen was eventually made famous by Goethe as "Iron-Hand," and though 'Iron-hand' was quite a flattering name, hinting at the strength and resolve of its bearer, in the memoirs Berlichingen does not make his iron-hand a part of his identity, let alone his trademark.

The crippling injury Berlichingen sustained was not seen as a turning point in his life or as a gateway to self-discovery. It was just one more incident that happened to him. According to the memoirs, after his injury Berlichingen remained exactly the same person, believing the same things, aspiring to the same things, behaving in the same way. If the handful of pages describing his injury were lost, modern readers could never have guessed that there was anything of particular importance in those pages, or that all the following exploits were performed by a one-armed knight.[138]

Captivity and ravages of war

In 1660, Hieronymus Christian von Holsten was captured in battle by the Muscovites, and was held a prisoner in their camp for several months. During that time the Muscovite camp was blockaded so that the Muscovite soldiers themselves were perishing from hunger. Holsten and his fellow prisoners were given neither firewood nor food, except when some merciful guard threw them a piece of raw horse-flesh or moldy bread. So many corpses of men and animals lay about that the camp stunk terribly.

In late modern times, ex-POWs have composed lengthy memoirs detailing their period of captivity, the things it revealed to them, and the changes it wrought in them. Already in early modern times a distinct genre of prisoners' memoirs had flourished, most famously Indian captivity narratives.[139] Yet in military memoirs, captivity and its attending miseries were given little importance. The harrowing months in Muscovite captivity are condensed in Holsten's memoirs into a single paragraph which tells the story of all the prisoners in general terms, without giving particulars of Holsten's personal fate, and without drawing any conclusions about war, about human nature, or about Holsten's personality.[140]

It should be stressed that Holsten and most other early modern memoirists were noblemen, who enjoyed the best living conditions during peacetime. Yet the move from the family chateau to the field or even the prison pen rarely opened their eyes, and never gave them second thoughts about their chosen vocation. For instance, the Chevalier de Quincy writes about his first night on campaign (1697) that he and 12 other musketeers had to lodge together in the granary of a peasant. Their host was amazed, and could not stop murmuring ' "What! The brother of the seigneur de Quincy is obliged to sleep on the hay! And where would I have to sleep, me who am a poor peasant, if I went to war?" ' But Quincy was untroubled. 'I never slept so well,' he writes, 'and I was never so content.'[141]

Comradeship and the death of friends

According to twentieth-century memoirists of all camps and opinions, comradeship is the best thing revealed by war and experienced in war. Even the most pacifistic memoirists usually redeem a bit of war's horrors by thanking it for revealing to them the depths of love that one man can have for another man.

Comradeship certainly existed in late medieval and early modern armies. Indeed, it was more important then than it became in the late modern period, because in early modern armies comradeship had to take care of many things which later became the responsibility of the army. Early modern combatants often organized themselves in formal "families" of comrades called *cameradas* (*Kameratschafft* in German), which contained half-a-dozen to a dozen men. The *camerada* was the real center of a combatant's life. While living in a *camerada*, combatants often pooled their money and possessions together. They typically slept together not merely in the same quarters, but in the same bed. The *camerada* arranged food and lodging for its members, it took care of the sick, and sometimes even took care of widows and orphans, and saw to the execution of wills. Not infrequently, comrades remained together when the war was over.[142]

Yet, despite the claims of several late modern scholars,[143] comradeship did not seem important to early modern memoirists. Though they often used the word comrade, very few of them praised the ideal of comradeship.[144] Robert Monro is the sole early modern memoirist who foreshadows the late modern practice of dedicating one's memoirs to one's dead comrades, saying that he is writing 'to expresse my love, and thankfulnesse to my country, and to my deare Camerades ... eternizing their memory,'[145] and 'because I loved my Camerades.'[146] He compares the sorrow of separating from one's comrades to the sorrow of Christ's separation from his disciples.[147] It is telling that after he returned from Germany he attempted to found a hospital and gain pensions for old soldiers.[148]

No other memoirist thanks war for revealing to him the joys of comradeship, which remain unknown to civilians, and most memoirists never even mention the names of their particular chums. Fery de Guyon is the only memoirist who takes pain to name the seven other members of his *camerada* in the 1541 Algiers campaign.[149] Yet, though their ties were probably very close (he later went with two of them on a pilgrimage to Compostella),[150] he does not describe their relations, and his description of the death of one of them says only that 'in that skirmish died my good friend and companion monsieur de Chassez.'[151]

Guyon's indifference to his friend's death is characteristic. Most memoirists, if they bother to narrate the death of close friends and cherished commanders, do so matter-of-factly, without consecrating it to any high ideals, without redeeming it by patriotic and heroic slogans such as "he died gloriously for king and country," without lamenting war's cruelty, and apparently without learning anything from it. To quote one example out of a myriad, the duke of Navailles records the death of his friend the marquis de Trémoulet at Candia (1669) in the following words: 'among the [dead] was the lord of Trémoulet, captain of the regiment of Montpezat, who was a man of merit.'[152]

A few memoirists describe such death scenes in a more emotional manner, yet even then they do not give them any deeper meaning. For instance, Edmund Ludlow describes in very emphatic terms the death of his cousin, Gabriel Ludlow, at the second battle of Newbury (1644). Gabriel was hit by a cannonball, and was removed to the back. Ludlow

> procured a chirurgeon to search his wounds, he found his belly broken, and bowels torn, his hipe-bone broken all to shivers, and the bullet lodged in it; notwithstanding which he recovered some sense, tho the chirurgeon refused to dress him, looking on him as a dead man. In this condition he desired me to kiss him, and I not presently doing it, thinking he had talked lightly, he pressed me again to do him that favour; whereby observing him to be sensible, I kissed him; and soon after having recommended his mother, brothers and sisters to my care, he died.

Ludlow admits that 'This accident troubled me exceedingly, he being one who had expressed great affection to me, and of whom I had great hopes that he would be useful to the publick.' Yet aside from the loss to the 'publick,' no further comment is made about Ludlow's emotions or of the impact this death had on him.[153]

Up till now we have discussed mainly isolated incidents. Revelation, however, could be a gradual affair, brought about by an accumulation of experiences. In many late modern memoirs, the authors do not interpret every incident as revelatory, but allow the general flow of the narrative to illustrate the way war changed them. The first battles are often described through the eyes of an eager and deluded youth, exhilarated by the adventure, or through the eyes of a frightened rookie, unsure of his step; whereas the last battles are described through the eyes of a grizzled and perhaps disillusioned veteran.

Early modern memoirs seldom indicate change in such a way. The personality of the memoirists is usually depicted as constant from the first to the last page, and this lack of personal change in the memoirists is mirrored by the lack of change in the memoirs' mode of narration. All actions from start to finish are normally described in exactly the same way. Hardly any memoirist begins by describing the first battles through the eyes of a rookie, only in order to describe the last battles through the eyes of a veteran. Memoirists were of course aware of the difference between green recruits and veterans, and were aware that it is experience that makes the difference, but the difference consisted in their eyes in technical skills, knowledge of strategy, tactics or weapon handling, and ability to cope with difficulties.[154]

For late modern readers, particularly glaring is the almost complete absence of disillusionment from these texts.[155] Let us begin with an exception that proves the rule. When Thomas Raymond joined the Dutch army in the spring of 1633, he did so out of a desire to have a 'brave life.' He begins the account of his life in the army bravely enough, writing that 'to the campe I went, and soe now *Arma virumque cano.*'[156] However, after taking part in several sieges and engagements, by October he was very happy to come back to the Hague. He writes that

> I observed how briske and fyne some English gallants were at the beginning of this campagne, but at the latter end ther briskenes and gallantry soe faded and clowdy that I could not but be mynded of the vanity of this world with the uneasines of this profession. And truly, by what I have seene and felt, I cannott but thinck that the life of a private or comon soldier is the most miserable in the world; and that not soe much because his life is always in danger – that is little or nothing – but for the terrible miseries he endures in hunger and nakednes, in hard marches and bad quarters.[157]

This short passage is as close as early modern combatants got to the disillusionment narratives of Erich Maria Remarque or Wilfred Owen. And note that even in Raymond's autobiography his stint as a soldier occupies only a few pages whose relevance to subsequent events is extremely limited. He did not live the rest of his life in the shadow of those grim months.

Youthful expectations of living "a brave life" abounded in other early modern narratives,[158] but they were seldom if ever shattered. Not that these expectations were fulfilled. Many memoirists actually wrote after they fell from grace – or before they ever gained grace – and their narratives were an attempt to defend their name, to regain lost status, or to solicit missing rewards. The authors were occasionally very bitter, lamenting that they were unjustly treated, and that honor and rewards only too often go in this world to the wrong people. Yet the memoirists never lose faith in the ideal of honor and glory. The fault always lay with particular persons or events – not with the ideals or with the essential nature of war. Regarding the horrors of war, memoirists were simply not concerned about them. As we already saw in the memoirs of the duke de Navailles, these horrors were described in a matter-of-fact way, with little comment and without any bitter conclusions being drawn from them.

Even the few common soldiers who wrote memoirs in the early modern era, and who suffered "the most miserable life" to which Raymond referred, seldom expressed disillusionment with war. Alonso de Ercilla y Zúñiga served as a common soldier during the war between the Spanish conquistadors and the Arauco Indians of Chile. Ercilla y Zúñiga subsequently composed the *Araucana* (1569), an autobiographical epic that recounts the events of this fierce war. The epic describes war in more graphic terms than any other early modern text, almost equaling the poetic descriptions produced in the wake of World War I. Ercilla y Zúñiga describes the climactic battle between Spaniards and Araucos in the following terms:

> ... Who can describe the great damage,
> The dreadful and tremendous artillery,
> The turbulent cloud of shots
> Launched of a sudden in a moment
>
> Some were seen shot through
> Others, the head and arm taken off
> Others smashed into a shapeless form
> And many drilled through with lances;
> Members without body, bodies dismembered
> Raining away bits and pieces
> Livers, intestines, broken bones
> Live entrails and still quivering brains

> ...I would like to describe that here
> And to describe the shapes of the dead;
> Some trampled by horses,
> Others with open breast and head
> Others that it was pitiful to see,
> With bare entrails and brains;
> You should see others torn apart into pieces
> Others, entire bodies without a head.
>
> The voices, the lamentations, the groans,
> The miserable and pitiful mourning,
> The clash of the weapons and the howls
> Fill out the air and the vault of heaven.
> The fallen struggling against death
> Making efforts and rolling on the ground,
> So many lives going off at the same time
> By various places and wounds.[159]

Ercilla y Zúñiga is equally graphic when describing massacres of civilians. In his description of one massacre he does not forget to mention that

> ... They have no compassion for those with child,
> Rather direct the blows to the belly
> And it happened that through the wound came out
> The tender unborn legs.[160]

Of his own living conditions during the campaign, Ercilla y Zúñiga writes that

> ...a blackish and moldy biscuit
> Given with stingy hand
> And rainwater without taste
> Was the sustenance of my life.
> And sometimes the ration
> Became two measured handfuls of barley
> Which was cooked with herbs, and we used
> Salt water for the lack of salt.
> The luxurious bed on which I slept
> Was the humid swampy ground
> Always armed and always on the alert
> The hand holding either the pen or the spear.[161]

Like late modern memoirists, Ercilla y Zúñiga says on many occasions that he is afraid his literary skills are not up to the job of describing war.[162] Yet Ercilla y Zúñiga is not disillusioned, and does not try to disillusion his readers. As the *Iliad*, the *Chanson de Roland*, and many other war epics throughout history prove, open and elaborate narration of the horrors of war can co-exist with toleration and even admiration of war.[163] Twentieth-century pacifist memoirists are simply wrong in their belief that war was never reported realistically in the past, and that a realistic report of war is enough to destroy its heroic allure.[164]

It is vital to understand the long-term historical dynamic underlying this erroneous view. That war involves immense physical and mental suffering was obvious to cultures and societies throughout history. In order to express their gratitude for people who endured this suffering, and to compensate them, most societies offered combatants "prizes" in the shape of material rewards and enhanced cultural status. The prizes were inherently connected with the suffering of war, but occasionally, as happened in Europe in the nineteenth century and early twentieth century, the prizes got all the attention, while the suffering was increasingly ignored or denied. This widening gap gave rise in some circles to an unrealistic perception of war as an opportunity to win prizes (such as glory) without paying any price. Twentieth-century "anti-war" culture reminded people of the price, but this was only a correction for nineteenth-century excesses. Most heroic cultures throughout history took the price of suffering as the essential basis of heroism.

Ercilla y Zúñiga did not write his poem to disillusion his readers, and he repeatedly lauds the ideals of honor and glory, describing his heroes as holding on to these ideals till their last breath, and urging his audience to imitate these heroes. His epic was certainly not received as a pacifist manifesto. Rather, it was avidly heard by noble audiences and inspired many imitations. It has since become the national epic of Chile.

In his concluding remarks Ercilla y Zúñiga does offer several arguments against war, but after a nuanced discussion he concludes that war is necessary, glorious, and serves many useful purposes in the world. 'Warfare is the right of nation,' he writes, and maintains the law. Soldiers can 'like angels without sin,' take up arms and defend public causes, and any who 'softens his arms' on such occasions 'offends the public right.'[165] Regarding his own involvement in war, Ercilla y Zúñiga bitterly complains that he did not receive his due rewards and his due honor for the services he performed, and that he is now destitute.[166] The publication of the epic and the public acclamation it received soon rectified that.

The absence of disillusionment narratives cannot be ascribed to censorship or to the rising tide of early modern nationalism. In fact, early modern memoirists were much freer from both censorship and national sentiments than their late modern successors. It is telling that a large percentage of early modern memoirists deserted from the army at one point or the other, and they were usually not ashamed to report this in their texts.[167] In contrast, though late modern memoirists often contemplated or fantasized about making such a move, hardly any of them actually deserted.

In the very rare cases when memoirists describe themselves as being hostile toward war and martial ideals, they have held this attitude from the very beginning, and their hostility is not ascribed to any encounters with death and the horrors of war. This is true in particular of Estebanillo Gonzalez, the semi-fictional hero of a memoirs-cum-picaresque-novel written by an unknown Spanish veteran of the Thirty Years War. Estebanillo is a seventeenth-century precursor of the *Good Soldier Švejk*: a buffoon and good-for-nothing common soldier. He takes pride in his cowardice, and repeatedly explains that he never sought to endanger his person in war, but merely to fill his belly and purse.

For example, Estebanillo gives a unique description of the battle of Nördlingen (1634), the most celebrated Habsburg victory of the Thirty Years War. He describes it at great length and in minute details, but from the viewpoint of a cowardly common soldier, who sneaks to the back and hides while the going is rough, and moves forward only to rob the corpses when victory seems assured. During the crisis of the battle, he hides himself inside the carcass of a dead horse, and when his captain urges him to stop his cowardly behavior and gain some honor, he finds a field full of dead bodies, and attacks and mangles them in order to bloody his sword. At the end of the battle he meets his captain, who now lies dying on the field of honor. When the captain upbraids him again for his cowardice, and asks him why he behaved so dishonorably, Estebanillo answers 'because I had no mind to be in the same condition you are in, Sir; for though it be true that I am both a soldier and a cook, I always play the soldier in the kitchen, and the cook in the time of service.' He adds that soon the captain ended his days, 'for want of being as discreet as I.'[168]

Later on during the siege of Gros-Glogau, Estebanillo runs away at the first sound of artillery fire, explaining that he preferred people to say 'Here he fled, than Here he fell.' When his commander upbraids him for his cowardice, Estebanillo answers 'Pray, Sir, who ever told your

Excellency that I had any courage, or when was I in any danger, and did not behave my self much worse than I have done to day?'[169] And indeed, Estebanillo's total disregard for honor and courage and his cynical view of war were not the result of anything he had experienced in war. Rather, they have characterized him from the outset of the narrative. In his first campaign – a naval campaign against the Turks – Estebanillo writes that

> For my own particular, I stood absolutely neuter during all this war, for I never concerned my self with any thing but filling my belly; my post was in the cook-room, my ladle was my weapon, and my pot my cannon; and so I always told them, when any enemy appeared, or other work was to be done. My chief care was to secure the best place at the fire for my pot.[170]

Hence, even Estebanillo Gonzalez did not learn anything from war. He brought his cynicism with him from home.

Another semi-fictional narrative of great importance and interest is Jacob Christoph von Grimmelashuasen's *Simplicissimus* (1668).[171] At first sight, *Simplicissimus* seems to resemble twentieth-century narratives more closely than any other contemporary memoirs. The narrative describes how the most naïve and innocent of youths, who does not even know his name, loses his illusions and acquires much knowledge of himself and the world through various military experiences. A closer look, however, reveals that *Simplicissimus* too was a child of his times.

The narrative opens with a horrendous scene, in which Simplicissimus's home is destroyed by marauding soldiers, and his family raped and murdered in front of his eyes. The traumatic event brings about no change in Simplicissimus. He remains naïve and innocent as ever. He runs, however, to the forest where he joins a hermit, and it is the hermit who in his peaceful forest retreat reveals to Simplicissimus the eternal truths of Christianity and teaches him to read the Bible.[172] As in the case of Ignatius Loyola and Brother Lawrence, war provides only the circumstances for a revelation that must come from preaching and reading.

When Simplicissimus eventually leaves the forest hermitage, he immediately reencounters the atrocious scenes of war. The narrative describes these scenes with interest and humor, but without saying that they had any impact on Simplicissimus, who remains extremely naïve regarding the ways of the world. Eventually, some turns of fate cause Simplicissimus himself to enlist as a soldier. His real transformation and his loss of innocence result from his military successes rather than from any horrendous scenes he witnessed. As success goes up to his head, he forgets the hermit's good lessons, and sinks into the depths of corruption, until misfortune overtakes him. It is a classical moral tale of Fortune's Wheel, which is set in military circumstances, but in which war fails to teach anything of value. It only corrupts and makes one ignorant.

For the present research, particularly noteworthy is the fact that Simplicissimus compresses the descriptions of the first actions in which he fought as a soldier, together with the descriptions of the first actions in which he commanded, into a single paragraph, which says nothing about his inner experiences. Just like Chouppes, Navailles, and Saint Simon, the garrulous Simplicissimus becomes almost mute when it comes to the matter of his first combat experiences.[173] Similarly, when Simplicissimus suffers his first major reverse and falls captive to the enemy, he says almost nothing about his feelings, and gives the impression that the event had no significant impact on him.[174] Hence, even Grimmelshausen's *Simplicissimus* presents war as a phenomenon that reveals nothing, and corrupts soldiers instead of enlightening them.

The Macabre – Early modern culture could have provided combatants with at least one model for writing disillusionment narratives, namely the macabre. The basic idea underlying early modern macabre culture was that observing dead bodies and symbols of death and decay may remind people of their own mortality, and thereby put in perspective their transient ambitions, habits, worries, and joys. Early modern culture was filled with stories of men who pursued riches and honors, came across death, and were disenchanted of these worldly vanities.

In principle, the macabre could very easily lend itself to war descriptions. In the nineteenth- and twentieth-century military memoirs made extensive use of the macabre, despite its cultural demise within civilian culture. For example, Philip Caputo writes in his memoirs of Vietnam that he once saw the face of a dead comrade transformed into his own image,[175] and later he watched two fellow officers talking, and saw them 'prefigured in death. I saw their living faces across from me and, superimposed on those, a vision of their faces as they would look in death... I saw their living mouths moving in conversation and their dead mouths grinning the taut-drawn grins of corpses.'[176] It is as if Caputo lifted this description straight out of a sixteenth-century meditation manual or macabre painting. (See, for example, the macabre image of an officer drawn by Niklaus Manuel in 1514/15. Manuel superimposed upon the image of the officer in the bloom and glory of his youth an image of the same officer as an impoverished and sick beggar.)

Figure 5 Niklaus Manuel, *The Fortunes of War* (*c.* 1514/15)

Yet early modern military memoirists, who lived in a culture satur-
ated with macabre imagery, almost never use macabre images nor lay
any claim to macabre revelations. We saw above that except for Blackader, none of the more religious-minded memoirists presented war as
a macabre revelation. Amongst lay memoirists, only Robert Monro had

macabre revelations in war. Several war experiences lead him to reflect on the transience of life,[177] and he writes, for example, about the siege of Stralsund (1628):

> Here our enemies were our pedagogues teaching us vertue, every moment minding us of our duety to God and man: yea minding us both of Death, and of Judgement: here we needed no dead mans pawe before us, to minde us of Death, when Death itselfe never went night or day with his horror from our eyes, sparing none, making no difference of persons, or quality, but *equo pede*, reading alike on all came in his way.[178]

However, even Monro hardly digests the message of the macabre. In his general observations on war Monro still believes that there is nothing more glorious than 'lasting fame' acquired through the dangers of war,[179] and he is adamant that 'The bloud is not to be accounted lost, which is shed for a Noble Master.'[180] He further urges readers that they should prefer to be brave and if necessary die with honor than to live shamefully, for

> thou must resolve to shew thy selfe resolute, couragious, and valiant, going before others in good example, choosing rather to dye with credit standing, serving the publique, than ignominiously to live in shame, disgracing both thy selfe and Countrie. Who would not then at such times choose vertue before vice; glorie, honour and immortall fame, before an ignominious, shamefull, and detestable life?[181]

It is also interesting to note that Monro does not believe that the experience of war gives soldiers any privileged knowledge. He writes that 'reading and discourse of warres, inable the minde more with perfect knowledge, than the bare practise of a few yeares.'[182]

Apart from Monro, hardly any lay military memoirist described the horrors of war as a *memento mori* or wrote that he got "a preaching on mortality" in war. We already noted how Melville spent an entire night in close embrace with a corpse, while himself hovering on the brink of death, without learning anything about man's mortal nature or about the vanity of military ambitions. The vast majority of memoirists who describe battlefields in the wake of battle were similarly immune to the macabre. Johann Dietz writes how he and a friend went to visit a battlefield outside Ofen (1686), but instead of listening to the preaching of the dead, they robbed the corpses and even killed a wounded Turk in cold blood.[183] After the battle of Neerwinden the duke of Saint-Simon 'took some old officers with me and went to visit all the field of battle, and particularly the entrenchments of the enemy.' He gives a description of the enemy works, but is silent regarding the dead and wounded who covered the ground (by Saint-Simon's own reckoning, the allies lost more then 20,000 men there, and the French about half that number).[184] Richard Kane describes how he passed over the battle-field of Blenheim (1704) the morning after the battle, riding through the fallen French bodies, 'as they lay dead in rank and file,' without making any further comments on the mortality of man or the price of war.[185]

Robert Parker notes after a battle in 1691 that 'our army halted here the day after the battle, until our tents and baggage came up; and we obliged the prisoners to bury the dead.' He leaves the images of carnage to the reader's imagination.[186] Regarding the battle of Blenheim, Parker assures the reader that his account of the battle is most trustworthy, because 'The next morning I made it my business to ride over the field of battle, and had very particular information of the several transactions I have mentioned, from the parties immediately engaged in them.' He then gives a detailed breakdown of the losses sustained by both sides, but without a single word about any macabre or pathetic scenes he might have encountered during his investigations.[187] Parker was also present on the battlefield of Malplaquet in the wake of that massacre. It was probably the bloodiest scene of carnage in eighteenth-century European warfare, with more than 10,000 dead and 22,000 wounded crammed into a few square kilometers. Yet whatever Parker saw and heard was left out of his narrative.[188]

At the battle of Eckeren (1703) the Count of Mérode-Westerloo stormed a cemetery and turned it into a strongpoint. Though he gives a detailed description of the carnage in the cemetery, he never utilizes the opportunity to make some macabre comment.[189] (In contrast, one of the most famous scenes of Erich Maria Remarque's *All Quiet on the Western Front* is the macabre scene that enfolds when the hero's squad is bombarded when taking shelter in a cemetery.[190]) Somehow, a culture that decorated its living rooms and cutlery with skeletons, cadavers, and death's-head to remind itself of death, became blind to them when looking at its battlefields.

On stage too, the macabre was a civilian theme, and its revelations were kept away from combatants. For instance, in Shakespeare's *Hamlet* the character who investigates the meaning of life and death is a peaceful prince. The furthest this prince goes in his explorations is to the nearby graveyard, where, following the dictates of macabre culture, he medit-ates upon a "civilian" skull. In contrast, the warrior prince Fortinbras, who spends his days campaigning under sun and rain, and who sees thousands die miserably for a few acres of land, learns nothing from his travails, and is the symbol of the non-contemplative man of action.

This is even more apparent in contemporary military paintings. Artists such as Niklaus Manuel occasionally incorporated macabre images into paintings of soldiers, armies, and wars.[191] No *Danse Macabre* was complete without the knight and the soldier,[192] and within the popular seventeenth-century genre of *Vanitas*, a distinct sub-genre focused on images of arms, war trophies, and war emblems.[193] However, the macabre symbols of death that appeared in military paintings, military *Danse Macabre* scenes, and military *Vanitas* were always "unwarlike" symbols. They were the same skeletons, death's-heads, half-burned-out candles, and hourglasses familiar from civilian settings.[194] The unique experiences of war were not seen as having any revelatory power, and soldiers were depicted as ignorant of macabre knowledge.[195]

For example, Pieter Steenwyck's *Allegory on the Death of Admiral Tromp* (1653?), which juxtaposes the admiral's war trophies alongside a skull and a half-burned-out candle, should not be seen as a comment on the horrors of war or on war's revelatory powers. Rather, it was part of a very widespread artistic tradition that juxtaposed the symbols of worldly success alongside reminders of the vanity and transience of this world. There is no difference between this painting and similar paintings depicting the transient glory of statesmen, scholars, merchants, and so forth (compare, for example, Henrdick Andriessen's *Vanitas Still-life* (c.1650)).[196] Things would have been different if Steenwyck had placed Admiral Tromp's war trophies alongside the mangled body of a sailor whose head was blown apart. Yet all my searches failed to uncover such early modern *militarized* macabre images.

The estrangement between the macabre and war is even more evident in the *Danse Macabre*. Consider, for example, the illustrations of the knight and the peasant woman from a c.1510 French *Danse Macabre*.

The typical *Danse Macabre* contained illustrations of death coming to take representatives of various estates and professions: knights and peasant women, queens and monks, merchants and popes. Its message was that everyone, no matter what position he or she occupies in society and what profession he or she follows, would one day be taken by death. A secondary message was that everyone is attached to worldly vanities, and that everyone is consequently surprised by death and frightened by him. No group of people – not even popes and monks – can boast that they are free of worldly attachments and that they can face death serenely.

Figure 6 Pieter Steenwyck, *Allegory on the Death of Admiral Tromp* (1653?)

Figure 7 Henrdick Andriessen, *Vanitas Still-life* (c. 1650)

Figure 8   La Danse Macabre. Death and the Knight (1510?)

Soldiers too were subject to this law. In the *Danse Macabre* they are surprised and frightened by death just like the peasant women, the merchants, and the monks. This is made clear by the captions that usually accompany these illustrations. For example, a *Danse Macabre* image painted by Niklaus Manuel around 1517 for the Dominican church in Berne shows a halberdier in his martial outfit led away by death. The halberdier says, 'In combats I have always been in the front rank, comporting myself like a faithful soldier. I have never retreated a single step. Now I would happily flee; but I cannot.'[197] This statement seems paradoxical. If the halberdier fears death, how could he have missed death's presence on the battlefield? And if the halberdier learned to face death bravely on the battlefield, why should he want to flee now? We have already seen this paradox in Pontis's memoirs. Pontis

Figure 9   La Danse Macabre. Death and the Peasant Woman (1510?)

cannot explain why, after calmly meeting death hundreds of times on the field of battle, an encounter with death in a civilian context shook him to his roots and caused him to abandon the world.

This paradox can perhaps be solved when we compare the *Danse Macabre* to late modern pictures showing death with a soldier, such as the central panel of Otto Dix's *Der Krieg* (1929–32). The *Danse Macabre* was a favorite topic of World War I artists. Several of them – including Dix – created paintings named *Danse Macabre*, and personified images of Death were ubiquitous in numerous other paintings. Almost all these paintings showed Death in a clearly military context. In Dix's *Krieg*, a skeleton dominates the scene, hovering over the battlefield like an angel. Underneath him there are numerous bodies in tormented postures, a war-torn countryside, and a single living soldier with a gas mask.

It is obvious to modern viewers who see Dix's painting hanging in the *Staatliche Kunstsammlungen* in Dresden that the soldier's encounter with Death is taking place under the unique conditions of war, away from themselves, as part of the unimaginable experience of combat. They themselves are unlikely to have a similar encounter right now, in the quiet Museum or as they return home through the peaceful city. In contrast, in the 1510 *Danse Macabre* the encounter between Death and the soldier takes place in a non-military context, which represents "anytime, anywhere." The fact that there is nothing uniquely military about this encounter is further emphasized by the fact that the illustration is part of a much larger cycle of illustrations, in which peaceful civilians meet Death under very similar circumstances.

The message of the late modern painting is that whatever goes on between Death and the soldier is inaccessible to the civilian Museum goers. By looking at the painting we learn that we cannot even begin to understand what soldiers experience in war. In contrast, the message of the early modern *Danse Macabre* is that no matter what soldiers experience in war, on the matter of death they remain in the same boat with the rest of us. Even though they supposedly encounter death in war many times, these encounters cannot really enlighten them and prepare them for the real thing.

It is not easy to explain why the macabre remained divorced from the realities of war. It would be naïve to argue that since the macabre exposed mundane interests and worldly honors as ephemeral vanities, the state and the military aristocracy were interested to suppress it in the context of war. After all, the fact that the macabre exposed commercial interests as ephemeral vanities did not stop rich Dutch merchants from commissioning *Vanitas* in their thousands. On the contrary, the macabre catered exactly for people who were keenly aware of the discrepancy between their actual behavior and their religious beliefs. The tension between what one believed in theory and how one actually lived, represented by the *Vanitas*, was a source for introspection and pleasing self-irony.

The reason that nobody commissioned a painting of Admiral Tromp's war trophies juxtaposed alongside the mangled corpse of a sailor is different. Rich Dutch burghers could be counted upon to draw the correct lessons from macabre paintings. They were good Christians, who were well aware of Christianity's positive truths: the truths of resurrection and salvation. Their worldly success made them over-attached to worldly pleasures and vanities, and made them momentarily forget about the far more precious promises of salvation. The macabre was aimed to remind them of death, wean them from the worldly vanities, and redirect them to seek refuge in salvation. The macabre, however, could not teach them the truths of resurrection and salvation. There was nothing in the human body, alive or dead, that even hinted at resurrection.

Whereas the rich but pious burghers could be counted upon to draw the correct lessons from macabre images, with soldiers – who were considered the worst of ignorant sinners – one faced the danger that they would draw the wrong lessons. If the macabre was imported to a battlefield setting, it would have collided there head-on with the martial cult of honor, which mocked death. One possible outcome of this collision was that soldiers may become cowards on the battlefield or brave-hearted in church – equally disastrous consequences for early modern European culture.

An even worse outcome was that soldiers might lose whatever faith they had to begin with. If these impious rogues looked too hard at dead bodies on the battlefield, they were more likely to follow the path of materialism and atheism than that of religion. For the dead bodies on the battlefields preached the truth of mortality in very convincing terms, but they were dangerously silent on the matter of resurrection and salvation. (In the writings and paintings of late modern soldiers macabre images are most often used to emphasize the utter materiality of human beings, and are utilized to attack a variety of idealistic and other-worldly philosophies.)

Early modern European culture preferred to sidestep these difficulties by reserving the macabre for churches and for the private houses of pious civilians, while ignoring it on the battlefield. Military memoirists towed the line and displayed an amazing ignorance of the macabre nature of war.

Though the macabre was kept away from war culture, medieval and early modern military art did depict the unique horrors of war in great detail, and placed them in a decidedly warlike context. From the Bayeux Tapestry, through medieval chronicle illustrations, to war pamphlets of the Thirty Years War, war paintings often showed lopped off heads and body parts; bright red blood sprouting from wounds; lances, arrows, and swords piercing men in the face, genitals, and other "unheroic" body parts; explosions ripping bodies apart; and people being tortured and killed in the most gruesome manner.[198] Artists such as Urs Graf, Jacque Callot, Romeyn de Hooghe, Pieter Snayers, and Hans Ulrich Franck not only depicted the horrors of war in graphic and shocking ways, but might have had a conscious intention of undermining the heroic image of war, and condemning the phenomenon of war as such.[199]

However, in these cases too the horrific experiences of war were not presented as enlightening the soldiers. In such paintings, it is only the

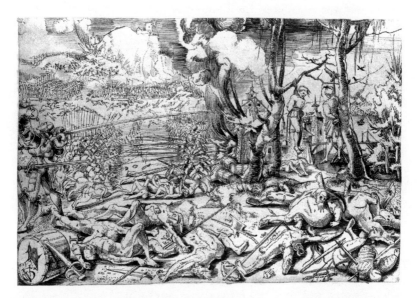

Figure 10   Urs Graf, *Battlefield* (*Schlachtfeld*), (1521)

Figure 11   *Soldier Glances Sideways at Dead Comrade* (1967)

viewers who gain wisdom by looking at the artistic reproduction of war's horrors. The people who were there, and who are depicted in the painting, are depicted as ignorant.

We can understand this by comparing an early modern painting with a late modern photograph. Above is Urs Graf's *Battlefield* (1521), followed by a representative photograph from the Vietnam War.

Urs Graf was both a Swiss mercenary soldier and a gifted artist. He fought as a common soldier in several campaigns of the early sixteenth century,[200] and was one of the few veteran artists who chose to paint war scenes based on his personal experience, without restricting himself to the conventions of his day.[201] Indeed, he drew so many war images as to comprise a visual tome of military memoirs.[202] Graf's *Battlefield* is his best known picture, and has often been hailed as *the* anti-war drawing of the Renaissance, a precursor of Goya and Dix.[203]

As far as the horrors of war go, *Battlefield* is far more detailed and graphic than the Vietnam photograph. Whereas the photograph shows a single dead body, without visible marks of violence, *Battlefield* depicts a field covered with body parts and mutilated corpses in tormented postures. In the background one can see two other men hanging from a tree, a village in flames, and further away a battle rages on.[204] Many present-day viewers would nevertheless find the photograph more haunting, due largely to the stares of the two live soldiers. These stares register the impact of the experience on the soldiers. As viewers, we are not sure what the stares mean: Pity? Apathy? Sadness? Fear? Anger? We cannot understand the stares, because we cannot understand the soldiers' experience. How can we know what soldiers in the midst of combat feel upon seeing a dead comrade? What this photograph tells us is that war is an extremely deep experience, which cannot be understood simply by looking at photographs. The soldiers' stares put us in our place, telling us that we are ignorant, and should back off respectfully. By revealing the deep experience of war, and our own ignorance, the stares shock us more than Graf's mutilated bodies.

Graf's *Battlefield* does not register the impact of the combat experience on any of the painted figures. Looking at the painting may cause viewers to draw various conclusions about war and life, but the combatants depicted in it seem to learn nothing. Indeed, they are not even aware of what is going on around them. Surprisingly, not a single person in the painting notices the carnage. The combatants engaged in the thick of the fighting are the depersonalized horde of pin-men characteristic of contemporary art, and they are all fighting heartily on. The only other living combatant – who forms the drawing's center of attention and who is the only one that might be identified with Graf himself – is a virile figure standing amongst the corpses in a warlike pose. He ignores the scene of devastation around him, lustily drinking from his canteen as his sword and pike point in the direction of the battle – into which he will most probably plunge back in a moment. He does not spare a glance for his dead comrades, nor does he seem to have gained any wisdom from what he has just gone through. War does not reveal to him either hitherto unknown depths of patriotism and comradeship, or the emptiness of these ideals and the transience of all earthly vanities. Because nobody in Graf's picture is aware of the experience, we viewers are left in a comfortable position to speculate on the meaning of the slaughter without feeling that we intrude into someone else's territory.

Technically speaking, it should have been easy for early modern painters to paint deep and forbidding stares on the faces of living

Figure 12   Raphael, *Deposition* (*Deposizione*) (1507)

soldiers, and to make these stares dominate the entire battle scene. Contemporary religious paintings often concentrated on the stare of the painted figures as the key to the action, and used them to register the revelatory power of death scenes. In particular, Pieta and entombment images such as Raphael's *Deposition* (1507) showed people staring at a dead body in a deep and knowing way, as if they just had a revelation.

Paintings of battle scenes did so only very rarely. One exception that proves the rule is Jacques Courtois's *After the Battle* (c.1660). The main action in this painting is the stare that passing soldiers direct at the body of a dead comrade. As in the Vietnam photograph, or the Pieta images, here too it is not easy for viewers to decipher the soldiers' stare. Though David Kunzle writes that the soldiers in *After the Battle* stare at the dead soldier 'surely, in admiration for an exemplary death,'[205] it is hard to be so certain. The impact of this painting is therefore quite similar to that of the Vietnam photograph. The soldiers' stares seem to be beyond our powers of understanding, and the result is a sense of humility and awe before the experience of war.

Figure 13 Jacques Courtois (le Bourguignon), *After the Battle* (c. 1660)

Courtois drew numerous other battle paintings, but rarely gave such attention to the experience of war. Other painters occasionally incorporated similar scenes into their paintings, but they were almost always sideshows within a much larger canvas. Artists usually concentrated their efforts not on making war seem a deep and inaccessible experience, but rather on making war *more* accessible and more easily understandable to viewers. Courtois himself gained his fame from his ability to use elaborate geometric schemes to paint grand battle scenes in a comprehensible way, reducing combat to the collision of lines and squares. If it was still difficult to understand battle in many early modern paintings, it was due to the overabundance of details rather than due to the forbidding stare of the combatants. As we shall see, only in the late eighteenth century did mainstream battle images begin to focus on the soldiers' knowing stare, resulting in the creation of military Pietas.

The absence of flesh-witnessing

Since war was not seen as a revelatory experience, there was no basis for combatants to claim the authority of flesh-witnesses. As evidenced by the examples of both twentieth-century common soldiers and early modern religious visionaries, there is a political fortune to be made from flesh-witnessing. Yet, though early modern aristocratic memoirists were in a better political position to lay claim to that fortune than late modern common soldiers, they neglected to do so.

Whereas early modern spiritual autobiographers and mystics quite often complained of their inability to describe their experiences in words,[206] military memoirists only rarely used formulas such as "it is impossible to describe it" or "those who were not there cannot understand it."[207] They more often used opposite formulas, assuming that their readers can easily understand the described events. For example, Götz von Berlichingen writes that 'everyone can well imagine' the pain he suffered when a cannonball cut off his hand.[208]

Memoirists occasionally ridiculed and attacked inexperienced civilians, politicians, and scholars who spoke about war without understanding. However, in almost all cases they argued that civilians and scholars did not know the correct *facts*, or were guilty of favoritism – not that they failed to understand the experience of war.[209] A good example is the attack Bernal Díaz del Castillo – one of the common soldiers who took part in the conquest of Mexico (1519–21) – mounted on the professional historian Francisco López de Gómara. Díaz began writing a history of the conquest because he thought nobody else had undertaken the task. However, in the midst of his travails,

> While I was writing this chronicle, I saw by chance, what had been written by Gómara, Yllescas and Jovio, about the conquest of Mexico and New Spain, and when I had read their accounts and saw and appreciated their polished style, and thought how rudely and lamely my story was told, I stopped writing it, seeing that such good histories already existed.

The fact that Díaz thought to abandon his own project upon seeing Gómara's history clearly proves that Díaz was not interested in recounting his personal *experience* of the war – for it was obvious to Díaz that Gómara could not and did not narrate the personal experiences of the common soldiers.

Díaz eventually resumed his work when he saw 'that from beginning to end they did not tell correctly what took place in New Spain.' The trouble with Gómara and the other historians was that they got their facts wrong. For example, 'When they begin to write about the great cities, and the great number of the inhabitants, they are as ready to write eighty thousand as eight thousand.' Díaz then expounds his views about how history should be written. Truth should be valued above style, and the facts should be based as far as possible on eyewitness accounts. He says about himself and the other soldiers who took part in the conquest that 'we, who were eye witnesses, will certify when [the stories of historians] are true.'[210]

Throughout the rest of his narrative Díaz then takes every possible opportunity to criticize Gómara and ridicule him. Yet he complains about only two things. One recurrent complaint is that Gómara gave all honor and credit to Cortés while neglecting the other captains and soldiers. The other recurrent complaint is that Gómara made factual errors in his account of the conquest.[211] Only once does Díaz express concern that Gómara misunderstood the *experience* of war.[212] As for his own credentials, throughout the narrative Díaz repeatedly emphasizes his superior authority as an eyewitness; almost never as a flesh-witness. Hence, despite the superficial similarity between Díaz's criticism of Gómara and twentieth-century common soldiers who criticize scholarly histories, the gap between them is huge.[213]

Early modern combatants certainly claimed – and received – unique social and political privileges, including a privileged authority to speak. But this authority was conferred on them directly by the fact that they had fought and risked their lives, without the mediation of revelation. This is plainly explained in the most famous early modern battle speech, the speech Shakespeare puts into the mouth of Henry V before the battle of Agincourt (1415): Henry tells his soldiers that any of them who survives the battle will commemorate it forever after. Every year he will 'strip his sleeve and show his scars,' and remind his neighbors that he received these wounds at the battle of Agincourt, 'on Crispian's day.' Henry promises that these scars would 'gentle the condition' of even the vilest commoner, whereas 'gentlemen in England now-a-bed / Shall think themselves accurs'd they were not here. / And hold their manhoods cheap whiles any speaks / That fought with us upon Saint Crispin's day.'[214]

The veteran's authority to speak and to silence stay-at-home gentlemen is etched in the scars on his arms and in the honorable deeds he performed, rather than in any special knowledge he may have gained in battle. How exactly do scars produce authority without revealing any new knowledge is something we shall investigate in the following chapters.

3
Why War Revealed Nothing

In the previous chapters we saw that early modern combatants did not write stories of revelation in war, and did not view themselves as flesh-witnesses. We also saw that this was not because early modern Europe lacked the necessary cultural resources. In fact, quite a few cultural resources – such as religious conversion narratives, the macabre and Pieta images – could potentially have been employed to portray war as a revelatory experience. It is impossible to give an exhaustive causal explanation why early modern combatants "missed" that potential. The present chapter tries to clarify matters a bit by explaining what alternative stories early modern combatants chose to tell about war.

Three main stories were told about war in early modern military memoirs:

1. The story of war as an honorable way of life.
2. The story of war as an instrument for personal advancement.
3. The story of war as an instrument for achieving collective aims.

These three stories were often combined within the same personal narrative. This could be done with relative ease because they all shared two basic assumptions:

1. Knowledge of military ideals and of the essence of war was the prerogative of the mind. Bodily experiences were vital for learning the practical know-how of war, but nothing else. Hence at all times minds had to preserve absolute mastery over bodies.
2. The quality of a mind could be judged by its ability to master bodies and direct them in the right way. It was consequently enough to describe bodily movements in order to evaluate mind. The ethics of

intention – arguing that intention counted for more than result, and that therefore mind could not be judged by external actions – was rejected by military culture.

This accounts for the fact that despite their exaltation of the mind/soul, early modern stories of war seldom described the inner experiences of combatants, and usually narrated only the movement of bodies in space. Just as judging the qualities of a puppeteer could normally be done by looking at the movements of the puppet, judging the qualities of a soldier's mind could be done by looking at his body, and judging the qualities of a general's mind could be done by looking at the movements of his soldiers.

Bodies should not think

Military culture received the idea that mind or soul has a monopoly of thought and knowledge from general culture. In Christian theology, man was seen as a combination of two elements, soul and body, though often a third element was added – spirit. The exact relations between these two or three elements were constantly debated by theologians, and what crude soldiers thought of them was not always in accord with the latest doctrine. It seems safe to generalize that the soul was thought to be the immaterial essence of the person, a divine spark which goes through the world on its way to salvation or damnation. The body was the material shell of that divine spark. Some believed it to be a mere earthly abode, which only hinders the soul, while according to others it was as much a part of the person as the soul, and was supposed to rejoin the soul in the afterlife. The spirit – or spirits – served as a go between, connecting immaterial soul and material body. The spirit was usually believed to be in charge of movements, appetites, and various emotions, whereas man's spiritual and rational faculties were the province of the soul. It was never clear, especially to the ordinary believers, where the borders of the spirit passed, and many found it easier to dispense with this notion altogether. No matter what role was given to the spirit, it was clear that the soul was supposed to retain full control over body and spirit alike, and to guide them in order to attain salvation.[1]

Not only was the body subordinate, but it was also unreliable. Though the sense organs provided information about the world, they themselves belonged to the material realm and therefore the data they provided was suspect. Following St. Augustine, Christian theologians emphasized that only 'the human intellect, the rational constituent of the soul of man,'[2] which was created by God as superior to the material realm, could arrive at true knowledge, and that too only with the help of Scripture. The Bible was the highway to knowledge, and even those who wished to travel along the byways had at least to start their journey with biblical revelations.[3]

In the *Enchiridion Militis Christiani* (1503) Erasmus writes that man is 'composed of several contending parts: a soul, which may be likened to a sort of divine will, and a body, comparable to a dumb beast.' Though God united the two in harmony, Satan 'has split them in unhappy discord. Now they [cannot] live together without constant war.' Before Satan's intervention, 'the soul commanded the body without trouble, and the body obeyed freely and willingly. Now, with the natural order of things disturbed, the passions of the body seek to override reason.' Erasmus compares the state of man to that of a civil war, in which the 'dregs of the lower classes' – that is, the body – seek to overthrow the rightful king – the soul.[4] Erasmus insists that in a good Christian the soul must rule supreme, and recommends various ways by which the soul might subdue the body to its will.[5]

In his meditation manual the military chaplain Donald Lupton uses a similar martial image. He instructs Christians to meditate on the situation of a frontier garrison, which they should compare to themselves. The soul is compared to the garrison, whereas the body is compared to the fortress walls. The bodily senses are like the fortress gateways, through which temptation may penetrate. Good Christians, like good garrisons, must fortify themselves against such external dangers and always be on their guard.[6]

Colonel Blackader's diary is a day-to-day account of the struggle between his soul and his body. 'My life,' he writes, 'is a struggle, as it were, between faith and corrupt nature – a combat, in which sometimes strengthening grace prevails, sometimes earthly affections and sensual appetites gain ground.'[7] Further on he writes that 'I am surprised at the odd composition of my own heart: Heaven, earth, and hell, seem to make up the mixture. In the renewed part, I delight in holiness; but I find another law in my members, warring against the law of my mind, and bringing me into captivity to sin.'[8]

Raimondo Montecuccoli, one of the foremost Habsburg generals, gives us in his *Sulle Battaglie* (c.1640) a general's view of the soul/body dichotomy. Advising commanders on how they should inspire courage in their men, he instructs them what to say to soldiers of different creeds. Surprisingly, he begins with the atheists. 'If the soul dies with the body,' one should say to atheist soldiers, 'death is desirable, for all suffering will end, and man will be freed from all evil.'

To true believers (i.e., Catholics) one should say that the human soul has arisen from God's breath, that it lives more freely and easily when it is separated from the body, as in sleep, and that it can be preserved for eternity only by total separation from the body and reunification with the Ultimate Principle from which it came. Salvation is assured to he who truly believes and repents, 'Hence most cowardly is the soul which flees peril because of the fear of death, which becomes distressed at the thought of leaving a fleeting and transitory existence for a full and perfect attainment of all the benefits of eternity.' Only the wicked have reason to fear death. As for those who believe in predestination (Protestants), they should fear death in battle least of all, for they can do nothing to escape it.[9]

Montecuccoli also uses the soul/body dichotomy as a metaphor for military arrangements, writing that '[t]he diligence of the generalissimo with regard to his followers must be as the relationship of the soul to the body.' He recommends that the general should control and direct the army as firmly as a soul controls and directs the body.[10]

For Montecuccoli and his contemporaries, man is soul, and in the tug-of-war between soul and flesh, the former is vastly more important, and is hopefully also the stronger. When push comes to shove and the Christian soldier is besieged by bodily temptations (in the shape of pleasant and painful sensations), the soul can and must retain full control of the situation. If the body takes over and starts to think and make decisions, the person is on the highway to perdition rather than to revelation.

When the modern mind/body dichotomy overshadowed the traditional soul/body dichotomy, the body's position remained subordinate. In the summer of 1618 a young French nobleman enlisted into Maurice of Nassau's Dutch army as a gentleman volunteer. A temporary truce reigned in the Low Countries, and the Frenchman soon found daily life as an officer cadet in a peacetime army 'idle.' In 1619 he therefore quit the Dutch service, and left for Germany. 'I was,' he remembered years later, 'attracted thither by the wars.' The Thirty Years War has just erupted, and the young fire-eater happily enlisted as an officer in the Bavarian army, which was setting out to put down the Bohemian rebellion. On November 11, 1619, St. Martin's Day, the officer was caught on his way to the Bavarians' winter quarters by a spell of bad weather. Taking shelter in a stove-heated chamber, he had nothing much to do, so he began to think. The officer's name was René Descartes, and his thoughts that day laid the foundation of modern philosophy.[11]

Searching for some secure basis in the world, Descartes' mind gradually doubted the entire world, and was left with nothing secure except for the thinking itself. Descartes identified his self with this thinking. He abandoned the trinitary division of soul, spirit, and body, and replaced it with a clear-cut dualistic division between body and mind. The body absorbed all the functions of the old spirit and some of the functions of the old soul, and was understood as a self-regulating machine. The mind was defined as 'the thinking soul.' Its only function was to think and formulate ideas, but this was also its absolute prerogative. The idea that the body might take over and start doing the thinking was an even worse heresy from a Cartesian viewpoint than it was from a Christian viewpoint.

It is interesting that Descartes' logic is the exact opposite of Elaine Scarry's. Whereas Scarry argues that the ultimate reality is painful sensations, and that painful sensations can make everything else evaporate, Descartes argues that the ultimate reality is abstract thinking – unrelated to any bodily phenomena – and that this abstract thinking can make everything else doubtful and unreal.[12]

When the weather allowed, Descartes left the warm chamber and rejoined the Bavarian army. His subsequent military career is shrouded in mystery. He certainly took part in some military operations, but the best efforts of dozens of scholars who sifted through thousands of documents over the past three centuries could not establish whether Descartes participated in the decisive battle of the White Mountain (1620).[13] This silence is itself very telling – like so many contemporary memoirists, though Descartes left a vast number of treatises and letters behind him, he too left no record of his first military campaign. His war experiences were considered completely irrelevant to his worldview.

Even if Descartes did take part in that battle, the thousands of bodies strewn on the field of carnage, just like all the subsequent horrors of the Thirty Years War, did not cause Descartes to doubt his insights from the warm chamber. In 1637, as Europe went up in flames, he published his thoughts in the famous *Discours de la Méthode*, followed by the *Meditationes de Prima Philosophia* in 1641.[14]

It is questionable to what extent fellow soldiers absorbed the full intent of Descartes' thoughts. In military memoirs of the period, the terms "mind," "soul," and "spirit" are used interchangeably. But it matters little. For whether one accepted the body–spirit–soul division, or the simpler body–soul division, or Descartes's new body–mind division, according to all three schemes the formulation of ideas and ideals was not something that should be done by the body. Sense-data provided by the body could obviously influence one's thinking, and new sense-data may result in the abandonment of old ideas and the formulation of new ones. However, the body's job was merely to submit the sense-data, which were then coolly analyzed by the soul or the mind. It was this analysis by the mind/soul that was supposed to result in the abandonment, adoption or formulation of ideas. Moreover, this analysis was ultimately based on innate ideas – such as the idea of God – which were independent of all bodily sense-data. Hence, in the final analysis, the thinking process was independent of sense-data.

The process which Scarry and twentieth-century memoirists describe – in which bodily sense-data completely overwhelm the mind, forcefully obliterating some of its contents while introducing new contents – was either impossible or extremely dangerous from an early modern perspective. Even if it could, the body should never be allowed to do the thinking, and if the body did think and did produce some kind of knowledge, this knowledge was extremely suspect. It should not be believed, should not be followed, and certainly was not a source for cultural and political authority.

Even in such cases as Vavasor Powell's toothache, the pain did not impinge on the prerogative of the mind or the soul. The pain was not supposed to overwhelm Powell's mind and start doing the thinking. Rather, the pain was simply a reminder that Powell should beware of hell. After Powell began to experience the pain, a book he read made him realize that the pain of hell must be far worse. This conclusion was drawn by Powell's mind, not by the aching tooth. It was the mind that realized by logical analysis that if the pain of toothache is so frightful, Powell had better do everything in his power to escape the much worse pain of hell. As for the pain of hell itself, this fundamental idea was based on Scriptures rather than on experience, and ultimately on innate ideas placed in the human mind directly by God. It is very telling that once Powell's mind became focused on the pain of hell – a mere phantom conjured up by the mind – this purely mental anguish completely eclipsed the tangible pain of the toothache.

As a story of early modern perceptions of mind and body, the preceding paragraphs are far from complete. In particular, we saw in Chapter 1 that there were important currents within early modern culture that modified the above views, and that gave the body an important place in the production of knowledge. This is true especially for Christianity. After all, the basic idea of Christianity was that of the

Word made Flesh. Yet, whatever the importance these countercurrents had in religious thought and civilian life, their influence on the military sphere was slight. Military culture seized upon those ideas that exalted the position of the mind/soul and denigrated that of the body, while ignoring any opposite ideas. In the early modern era, war was the ultimate model for the superiority of mind/soul over body.

The difference between war culture and general culture in the attitude toward the body can best be appreciated by examining the issue of burial. In civilian Christian culture, due to the belief in the resurrection of the flesh, the burial of dead bodies was an important religious act, accompanied by elaborate rites, and preferably taking place in consecrated ground. In the late modern era, the bodies of fallen soldiers of all social strata were similarly placed at the center of national cults of mourning and glory, and were buried in nationally sacred ground with even more pomp and ceremony than that of normal religious burials.

In contrast, during the early modern period soldiers were obsessed only with the need to immortalize their immaterial name and honor. What happened to their bodies was considered irrelevant.[15] The bodies of the vast majority of soldiers who fell in battle were not given much thought. With very few exceptions, the bodies of friend and foe, of privates and officers, of commoners and noblemen, were thrown together with little ceremony into mass unmarked pits, dug on or near the battlefield. There were no military cemeteries, and only very few monuments to dead soldiers.[16] Montecuccoli assured soldiers that 'If one is buried upon the battlefield, one feels nothing thereby. The glory of one's name is not impaired. Rather, the historical accounts that describe battles will preserve the memory of a person's life far more durably than will all the marble monuments that could be erected on a tomb.'[17]

Let us now turn to these historical accounts, and to the three types of stories that dominated early modern military memoirs, and examine in greater detail how and why they portrayed the body as completely subservient to the mind/soul and as utterly incapable of revealing new knowledge.

War as an honorable way of life

Late modern people tend to rationalize honor. When looking at the actions of early modern noblemen, we only too easily assume that they tried to build a reputation for honor so that they could obtain lucrative posts, boss around their social inferiors, or captivate rich heiresses. This assumption makes honor a mere means, something equivalent to money – something that can be earned, possessed, and then exchanged. There is of course some truth in this line of thought, and many early modern soldiers were influenced by such a way of thinking, but it goes against the grain of the cult of honor and of the honorary story of war.[18]

In essence, the honorary story of war viewed honor as the ultimate good. It was the most important thing in the world, and in particular it was the most important ingredient of noble masculine identity. The terms "name" and "honor" were synonymous, as in the expression "he made a name to himself." A man who lost his honor lost his identity, and a man who never had honor had no identity whatsoever.[19] A popular late medieval maxim said that 'it is better to die with honor, than to live in dishonor.'[20]

Unlike money, honor was not a possession. One could not act honorably for some time, accumulate a stock of honor, and later utilize that stock in order to gain credit as an honorable person. Rather, honor was a moment-to-moment way of life. One was an honorable man by living and acting honorably *all the time*. This could best be done by becoming a combatant and being constantly at war, because fighting was the most honorable activity in the world. According to the honorary story of war, men went to war not in order to gain anything, but simply because it was the most fitting way of life for real men. Such honorable men were naturally appreciated by society and often enjoyed authority, power, and lucrative positions, but this was merely a by-product. It was not the aim of war.[21]

The honorary story narrated and evaluated the events of war according to their bearing on matters of honor. Actions that were honorable – for example, fighting bravely against the odds – were good. Actions that were dishonorable – for example, using a dirty trick to win an engagement – were bad.[22] Actions that were irrelevant to matters of honor – such as supply arrangements – were ignored.

What exactly constituted honorable behavior was a matter for endless debates, but in its purer forms the cult of honor was adamant that military success was not important. It was far better to fight honorably and lose, than to fight dishonorably and win.[23] A good medieval example of this way of thinking is the conduct of Admiral Roger de Luria, the commander of the Aragonese fleet at the battle of Malta (1283). The Aragonese surprised the rival Provençal fleet when the latter was anchoring in Malta harbor. The memoirist Ramon Muntaner recounts that when the Aragonese approached their unsuspecting prey, Luria suddenly halted them. It was the first battle in which Luria commanded a fleet, and he wanted to win it without the help of any stratagem. 'God forbid,' he told his men, 'he should attack them in their sleep, rather did he wish the trumpets and nakers to be sounded in the galleys to wake them up, and he would let them prepare. He did not wish that any man could say to him that he would not have defeated them if he had not found them asleep.'[24] And so the Aragonese halted and made all the noise they could until the Provençals woke up and prepared themselves for battle. Only then did the Aragonese continue their movement, to attack their fully awake and prepared enemy.

The Aragonese still won the battle. But it was a hard fought affair, and they lost 300 men killed and 200 wounded.[25] Luria gained much prestige and honor by his conduct, and apparently none thought to condemn him for risking defeat or for sacrificing 300 of his men for his personal honor. He went on to become the foremost Aragonese admiral of the Middle Ages.[26]

Luria's act was not the act of a lone madman. Although chivalric culture never defined such behavior as mandatory, it certainly depicted it as laudable. The *Chanson de Roland*, the greatest of chivalric epics, revolves around Roland's refusal to blow his horn and summon the Frankish main army to his help. This refusal led to the total annihilation of the Frankish rearguard, yet immortalized Roland as the most honorable of knights. The Nibelungens' suicidal march to Atilla's palace was the Teutonic counterpart of such honorable pigheadedness.

This chivalric ideal was far from dead in the early modern age. Perhaps the most famous early modern expression of the honorary paradigm was King François I's exclamation upon his defeat at Pavia (1525): 'All is lost, save honor.' The king indeed gained much honor from this defeat. Though his army was defeated, François refused to run away and kept on fighting. He was duly captured – with disastrous consequences for France. An early modern kingdom whose king was a captive in enemy hands was sure to face internal turmoil and external catastrophe. Yet, instead of criticizing François for his foolhardiness, noblemen throughout Europe lauded his bravery.[27]

In terms of mind and body, the man-of-honor was defined by two supremely important qualities:

1. His mind was completely devoted to honorable ideals.
2. His mind was strong, and was able to compel his body to always act in accordance with the dictates of honor even if it meant undergoing suffering or death.

In his *Book of Chivalry* the fourteenth-century knight Geoffroi de Charny explained that 'you must in no way indulge in too great fondness for pampering your body, for love of that is the worst kind of love there is. But instead direct your love toward the preservation of your soul and your honor, which last longer than does the body, which dies just as soon, whether it is fat or lean.'[28]

In the economy of honor the body had absolutely nothing to teach the mind. Consequently, there was little to be gained from experiencing fear and bodily weaknesses. Someone who felt fear and managed to suppress it had a strong mind, but someone who felt no fear at all had an even stronger mind. The latter did not miss anything by not knowing fear. As for someone who succumbed to fear even for a minute, he gained no wisdom from the experience, and if others had learned about it, he could expect to be branded a coward. In chivalric culture, a momentary slippage was enough to ruin a man's name forever.

Accordingly, most men preferred to present themselves as completely fearless, and did not admit even to successful inner struggles against fear.[29] The lord of Bayard, the role model of sixteenth-century chivalry, was known as the *chevalier sans peur et sans reproche* – no fear, no reproach.[30] Asking too many questions about inner feelings of fear could easily lead to a duel, and military culture sidestepped this dangerous ground by focusing on external actions. Despite the importance attached to the mind, combatants tended to ignore inner reality, and judge mental qualities by the yardstick of bodily actions. If one fought well, particularly in the face of danger, it proved that one was an honorable man possessing a strong mind. If one ran away, it proved that one was a dishonorable wretch possessing a weak mind. What one felt inwardly while fighting bravely or running away was not probed too deeply. For instance, nobody asked what King François felt during the battle of Pavia. It mattered only that he did not run away.

Montecuccoli advised commanders to post an old incorruptible soldier for every thousand men, whose task would be to watch their behavior, and report acts of cowardice and bravery. Montecuccoli argued that this would cause the soldiers, who would know somebody is always watching them, to act bravely and renounce cowardice. Montecuccoli was probably aware that some of these soldiers may act bravely just because they are being watched, and may suppress inner feelings of fear. However, Montecuccoli was interested only in their outwardly discernable actions. Their inner feelings were irrelevant.[31] Blaise de Monluc similarly recommended to novice soldiers who want to distinguish themselves that

Those who want to gain honor by arms must resolve to shut their eyes to all dangers in the first battles they find themselves. For everyone will be watching, ***to see what they've got inside.*** If at the beginning they carry out some striking action, to show their courage and toughness, they'll be marked and known forever after.[32]

What they have got inside, à la Monluc, is really how they act outside.[33]

The honorable relations between mind and body in war were epitomized by the story of Mucius Scaevola.[34] Peter Paul Rubens and Anthony van Dyck's *Mucius Scaevola before Porsina* (1620) lauds the supremacy of

Figure 14   Peter Paul Rubens and Anthony van Dyck, *Mucius Scaevola before Porsina* (1620)

mind over body, and simultaneously illustrates how mental qualities were evaluated by bodily actions. Scaevola's superior mind manifests itself through the contrast between the roasting hand and the calm features of the body. Conversely, Porsina's moral inferiority is manifested by the frightened facial features and by the involuntary movement of his body, which shrinks as far back from Scaevola as the throne allows it.[35]

Scaevola's action was reenacted in 1556 during the execution of Archbishop Thomas Cranmer. Cranmer – a reformer leader – had previously signed a recantation of his "heretical" views, which he sourly regretted at the stake. According to Foxe's *Book of Martyrs*,

> when the wood was kindled, and the fire began to burn near him, stretching out his arm, [Cranmer] put his right hand into the flame, which he held so steadfast and immovable [...] that all men might see his hand burned before his body was touched. His body did abide the burning with such steadfastness, that he seemed to move no more than the stake to which he was bound; his eyes were lifted up into heaven, and he repeated 'his unworthy right hand,' so long as his voice would suffer him.[36]

Figure 15   The Martyrdom of Thomas Cranmer from Foxe's *Book of Martyrs* (1563)

Note Cranmer's serene features – he is in complete control of his body. In contrast, his executioners involuntarily flinch away, disclosing their lack of mental control.

Contemporaries were well aware that not everyone possesses mental control such as that of Scaevola, Cranmer, or Bayard. The tests of war were difficult, and many who were attracted by the ideals of war in peacetime found the real thing much harder to stomach. For example, in the late seventeenth century the earl of Rochester composed a poem about premature ejaculation, titled *The Imperfect Enjoyment*. In it he compared his penis to 'a rude, roaring hector' who boasts of his bravery and 'justles all he meets' in peacetime, but runs away and hides when war comes.[37] However, such cases were always interpreted as failures of the men rather than of the ideals. If the combatant's body took over and caused him to doubt or abandon his ideals, this was weakness rather than revelation. When memoirists reported acts of cowardice – as they very often did – it was criticism of weak men rather than criticism of the ideals of war.[38] And when Blackader writes that many soldiers became cynical and materialistic due to their war experience, this was a sign of their personal depravity and weak character, not a sign that Christianity might be a false doctrine, incapable of standing war's test of reality.

People admired steadfastness in the face of suffering even when it was displayed by criminals, heretics, and enemies.[39] In contrast, people such as the Jewish *Maranos* who converted to the true faith due to torture or threat of death gained very little admiration – even though they were letting go of false ideals in favor of true ones. Changing one's mind due to bodily suffering was almost always associated with weakness and falsehood, not with revelation.

Early modern duels were based on a similar logic. The duel was a device to test and prove mental qualities,[40] by means of bodily actions. In some duels, the participants' honor was proven by the first drop of blood. In others, only death was considered a satisfactory proof.[41] That the main thing in duels was mental control rather than physical qualities is evidenced by the fact that during the early modern period, pistols increasingly replaced swords as the favorite dueling weapon.[42] The use of swords, despite its traditional halo, had the disadvantage that it gave too much importance to bodily qualities such as strength and menial dexterity.[43] The use of the inaccurate pistols was much preferable, because it allowed purely mental qualities to shine through. A man could not bolster his courage by relying on menial proficiencies. If at all, the only physical skill that counted was the ability to keep the hand from shaking, which obviously depended on mental control far more than on muscular power and dexterity.[44]

The same logic also governed the attitude to combat injuries. As in many other martial cultures in history, in early modern European martial culture injuries and scars were badges of honor, and thus important constituents of a combatant's identity. A fifteenth-century Castillian maxim said that 'The wounds a man sustains in noble battles are signs of nobility.'[45] Don Quixote explained to Sancho Panza that 'Wounds received in battle confer honor.'[46] John Gwyn refers to his injuries as 'those marks of honour I have got with bloud and wounds and broken bones.'[47] However, the honor was gained by the external fact of being injured. What one experienced internally was seldom examined.

Pierre de Bourdeille de Brantôme mentions a Spanish common soldier who, like Shakespeare's Agincourt veteran, rolled up his clothes and showed him half a dozen scars he had, explaining at which battle he got each.[48] These scars were an essential part of that soldier's identity, and entitled him to speak. The stories he told others about who he was, and most probably the stories he told himself about who he was, were woven around these scars. Yet it was only the external fact of having been injured and having a scar that mattered. Like most contemporary memoirists, the soldier did not tell Brantôme what he felt inwardly when he was injured.

Brantôme tells of another Spanish soldier, a commoner, who in a certain battle was shot in the stomach. He went aside, opened his stomach with his knife, and took out the ball. He then sewed the wound, and returned to the battle, as if nothing happened. He was again wounded and lost an eye. When the Emperor heard of his valor, he gave him a pension for life. Unfortunately, writes Brantôme, his story was then cast into oblivion. Brantôme determined to immortalize that soldier, and therefore recounted his brave deed in details, but he wrote not a word about what the soldier *felt* during or after this ordeal.[49]

The only aspect of injuries to which contemporary memoirists gave great importance was the number of wounds they received. Late modern memoirists often devote several pages to describing how injury feels, but they seldom bother to count the number of their wounds. In contrast, early modern memoirists gave no importance to the inner experience of injury, but they cite the number of their wounds with pedantic exactness.

In his chronicle of the conquest of Mexico Bernal Díaz often notes the exact number of wounds each of the conquistadors and their horses received at particular battles.[50] After finishing the first draft, Díaz made corrections to the manuscript, and in several cases changed the number of wounds attributed to different combatants. For instance, in the sentence 'they killed four soldiers and Diego de Ordas received two wounds,' he changed the number of killed to 'eight or ten' and the number of Ordas's wounds was increased to three.[51]

Ramon Muntaner writes that at a battle in Gallipoli he received five wounds. He also mentions that 'a woman was found there who had five wounds in her face from quarrels and still continued the defense as if she had no hurt.'[52] During a particular incident at the battle of Mansourah (1250), Jehan de Joinville 'was only wounded by the enemy's darts in five places, and my horse in fifteen places.'[53] Garcia de Paredes received in a fight against some robbers six wounds.[54] Sebastian Schertlin got seven holes in his foot when a dog bit him.[55] During the attack on Pondicherry (1748) Hannah Snell allegedly 'fired 37 rounds of shot, and received a shot in the groin, six shots in one leg, and five in the other.'[56] Pedro de Baeça received altogether 15 or 16 wounds during his military career.[57] Pontis received throughout his career a total of 17 wounds.[58] Alonso Enriquez de Guzmán received 17 wounds at a battle on Ibiza.[59] Andrew Melville received at Treves (1675) 18 wounds.[60] The Arauco hero Gracolano received 'thirty-six wounds exactly' in his last battle.[61] The lord of Florange received at the battle of Novara (1513) precisely 46 wounds.[62]

One wonders how they counted. How does one count 46 wounds over a single body? Where does one wound end and another begins? Would any bruise count? Such questions would seem to twentieth-century combatants totally beside the point. Philip Caputo, for example, spent part of his Vietnam tour as the officer in charge of reporting casualties. This unpleasant job, which 'had the beneficial effect of cauterizing whatever silly, abstract, romantic ideas I still had about war,'[63] involved filling in forms about dead and injured soldiers, listing the number and nature of their injuries. Caputo ridicules this procedure, presenting it as the epitome of the military machine's insensitivity to the true experience of war. When Lieutenant-Colonel Meyers stepped on a mine, 'They did not find enough of him to fill [...] a shopping bag. In effect, Colonel Meyers had been disintegrated, but the official report read something like "traumatic amputation, both feet; traumatic amputation, both legs and arms; multiple lacerations to abdomen; through-and-through fragment wounds, head and chest." '[64]

For Florange, the fact that he received precisely 46 wounds at Novara was far more important than the internal experience of being injured. If the French army of his days had published casualty reports, Florange would have preferred them to enumerate his wounds rather than write an account of his feelings.

We are now in a position to understand the logic behind Shakespeare's Agincourt speech. The scars which the veteran shows his neighbors on St. Crispian days are tangible testament to *mental* qualities. They testify to the honor and power of one's mind, and the authority to speak emanated from that power. The most important qualification for speaking in public was that no lies be told, and honor was the best guarantor of that. A man of honor had the needed commitment and control to always tell the truth. He was not one to tell a lie deliberately, to let slip an error without noticing, or to repeat unfounded gossip as gospel truth. Anything he said was said upon his "word of honor."

If anyone questioned what a man of honor said, it put in doubt his honor, and could be rectified only by a new scar. Accusations of lying were the most common cause of early modern duels. Duels rectified matters by proving one's honor yet again, and *ipso facto* proving the veracity of one's word of honor. When Colonel Augustin von Fritsch wished to assure his readers that he spoke the truth in his memoirs, he stated that the information he gave was 'as true as I am honorable.'[65] Hence the authority to speak granted to soldiers and men of honor was not an undeserved prize. It did not give men who excelled in a field that required only menial dexterity the authority in a field that required intellectual abilities. Rather, it gave men who had proven their mental superiority in battle an authority to speak on all other occasions based on the assumption that their honor is the best guarantor of their truthfulness.

When today a veteran rolls up his sleeve and shows his battle scars to his neighbors, the train of thoughts this is meant to induce in the neighbors' minds is as follows: "This man has been in battle and sustained injuries. He must have gone through very unique experiences, which we never underwent. These experiences must have taught him some deep wisdom, which we are ignorant of. It would be wise to listen to him." (Note that in this case, even if the veteran is known to have run away or to have suffered a mental breakdown, his authority is not necessarily damaged.) Shakespeare's veteran tries to induce a very different train of thoughts: "This man has been in battle and sustained injuries. If he faced such dangers yet continued to fight, it must mean his mind is strong and honorable. If he is such a man of honor, whatever he says must be the truth. It would be wise to listen to him." An additional thought that was usually induced was "Besides, if I question what he says, he may throw me the gauntlet."

Under normal circumstances, soldiers had no need to describe their internal experiences in order to impress society with their superior minds. It was enough to display or enumerate the list of one's battles and injuries. Consequently, when memoirists wrote the story of war as an honorable way of life, they had no place in this story for either revelation or inner experience. The lifestory of a man-of-honor was a collection of honorable deeds rather than a process of inner change. To think of one's lifestory or narrate it to others meant to recollect a certain honorable incident, then another, and then another, without these incidents merging together to form an organic process of change or revelation.[66]

War as a personal instrument

War could also be interpreted as a means by which the individual combatant acquired wealth, status, and power. This was an extremely common interpretation in early modern armies, when combatants and commanders alike were often mercenaries who paid only lip service to the cult of honor, and who had even less interest in their paymaster's war aims. The events of war were narrated and evaluated solely according to their impact on one's personal interests. An event that had a positive impact – for instance, participating in a mutiny against the prince that managed to secure back-pay – was good. An event that had a negative impact – for instance, losing a valuable horse during a victorious battle – was bad. An event that had no impact whatsoever – for instance, seeing a comrade die in combat – was not narrated.

The model combatant of this story was the self-serving military entrepreneur. In his case too, bodily experiences were completely subservient to the aims set by the mind. From the day he enlisted as a penniless youth until the day he retired as a rich grandee, the entrepreneur pursued a single ideal of worldly success. In war he accumulated much practical wisdom that enabled him to achieve his ideal, but war did not change his worldview or the way he understood himself. At the same time, the strength and abilities of the entrepreneur's mind could be judged only by bodily actions and material objects in the outside world. It all boiled down to coins, lands, and lucrative posts – what went on inside him was irrelevant.

For instance, in the memoirs of Sebastian Schertlin von Burtenbach war is most often interpreted as Schertlin's personal instrument, and the main storyline tells how Schertlin rose from the ranks to become a senior commander, accumulating on the way a considerable amount of wealth and power. Schertlin gives little or no importance to experiences, and does not describe any process of inner change.

He mentions that during the siege of Pavia (1524/25) he was a young soldier in the besieged garrison, and that the garrison was reduced to such straits that they had to eat horses, donkeys, and dogs. Yet he does not describe what it felt like to be in such a situation, and he evaluates the campaign as a good one, because he was made a knight and gained 1500 florins.[67] At another campaign he lost all his followers except one servant, 'because they all died.' He does not specify how they died or what he felt about it, and his only comment about this campaign is that he brought home from it 5000 florins.[68] About the war of 1540 he writes that it was 'short and lucky.' For though the big English dog of Duke Henry of Brounschwig bit him, making seven holes in his foot, thanks to God he ended the war with a net profit of 4000 florins.[69] When he became a senior commander Schertlin kept the same viewpoint, evaluating one war as good because he gained in it from salary, presents, and booty 30,000 florins,[70] while evaluating another war as bad because he lost in it 1000 crowns.[71]

Even clearer examples of the story of war as a personal instrument were the "accounts of services rendered." These were standardized martial CVs, which almost every early modern soldier had to write in order to solicit rewards, pardons, transfers, and so forth. For example, at the age of 14 or 15 Alonso de Contreras, who until then served as a part-time helper to an army cook, drew and submitted to the commander of the Spanish army an account of the services he rendered, asking to be enlisted as a regular infantryman.[72]

Early modern memoirs were influenced to a considerable degree by this formal genre, and many memoirs sprang out of accounts of services.[73] These accounts both shaped and reflected the combatants' perception of their martial lifestories. The lifestories shaped by these accounts were collections of services rendered and rewards received. To think of one's lifestory as a combatant, or to narrate that lifestory to others, meant to recollect a certain service one performed and the rewards one gained, then another, and then another, without these services and rewards merging together to form an organic process of inner change or an experiential process of revelation.

War as a collective instrument

When war was viewed as a collective instrument, its aims were defined as the aims of a ruling dynasty, a country, a religious movement, or any other such collective entity. The events of war were narrated and evaluated according to their impact on these collective aims. An event that had a positive impact – for instance, a cavalry charge that secured control of a vital hill – was good. An event that had a negative impact – for instance, a general who exposed himself to danger out of gallantry, got killed, and thereby led to the rout of his army – was bad.[74] An event that had no impact whatsoever – for instance, a young recruit losing his patriotism as he lay dying from dysentery – was not narrated.[75]

The difference between this story and the honorary story is evident, for example, in the advice that Campbell Dalrymple gives in his military manual (1761): In case of a retreat, or if a company is broken, the company's officers should not stay behind for 'it is a ridiculous point of honour, and hurtful to the service, to remain behind and be taken prisoners, or be killed by the enemy advancing.'[76] So much for King François's conduct at Pavia.

The early modern age is often interpreted as the era when the story of war as a collective instrument became the dominant story of Western war and politics. It was an essential part of the Military Revolution and the rise of the state. One of the main questions that preoccupied early modern princes and governments was how to make their subordinates adopt this story. How to make soldiers see war as a collective instrument rather than as a personal instrument or an honorable way of life? How to ensure that soldiers will never mutiny or disobey orders in the name of honor or of their personal interests? The solution that one prince after the other adopted was to take the model of mind-over-body supremacy, translate it into the military sphere, and there carry it to hitherto unimaginable extremes. For this, the dualistic Cartesian model was particularly well-suited.

The Dutch army in which young Descartes served his apprenticeship was commanded by a man who shared Descartes's fantasy to the full, and implemented it in practice. Prince Maurice of Nassau wanted to create an army whose general could control it as firmly as the Cartesian mind was supposed to control the body.

In order to realize his fantasy, Maurice instituted drill as the foundation of military training. Drill identified the commander with mind, and gave him absolute monopoly of thinking and decision making. Drill also identified the common soldiers with body, and treated the soldiers' own mind as a hindrance. Drill was meant to ensure that the commander's decisions were executed by the bodies of the common soldiers with minimum intervention by the common soldiers' own minds. In Maurice's ideal army, common soldiers were not supposed to take any independent initiative. In this ideal army, not only did mind have absolute control over body, but a *single* mind – that of the general – had absolute control over thousands of bodies.[77]

In order to bypass the minds of the common soldiers, Maurice and his aids analyzed the individual skills of the military trade – that is, walking, standing, carrying the weapon, loading, and firing – and broke them down into series of dozens of precise movements, each being allocated a different word of command. Drill consisted of teaching the soldiers these commands and movements separately, then combining them together and repeating them countless times, until the sequence of movements was performed automatically at the word of command.

For instance, an English drill manual of 1637, which copied Maurice's original manual, broke down the sequence involving the firing and reloading of a musket into 32 different movements, each to be performed at the right word of command.[78] To make the life of drill instructors easier, pictures were added to these manuals to illustrate the sequence of movements and the right body postures, much like in a present-day yoga book:

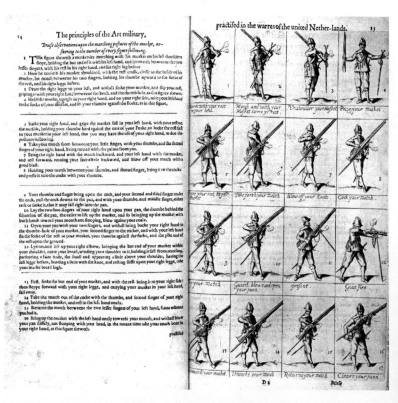

Figure 16 Henry Hexham's *The Principles of the Art Militarie* (1637), showing part of the sequence of movements involving the firing of a musket, together with the words of command[79]

The collective skills of the military trade – that is, standing, moving, and fighting in various formations and velocities – were similarly broken down into geometrically precise series of simple movements, which groups of soldiers repeated again and again, until these movements too could be performed automatically. Mistakes in drill were considered a serious military blunder, and often resulted in severe punishment. A French visitor to eighteenth-century Berlin once saw Prince Ferdinand of Brunswick drilling his regiment:

> Directly in front of me I had a *Junker* of about fifteen, who had seen a soldier of more than fifty years of age commit a slight mistake in the manual drill of arms. He summoned him from the ranks and proceeded to belabour him with repeated blows of his cane on the man's arms and thighs, using all the strength at his disposal. The poor victim burst into tears, but dared not utter a word.[80]

Drill was supposed not only to teach soldiers the right "automatic" way of behavior, but also to iron out all their independent "initiatives." In many cases the soldiers were not expected to show even the minimal initiative involved in aiming their weapons. Thus in order to increase the rate of fire, eighteenth-century Prussian drill positively *forbade* aiming, for it would have slowed the process down. Prussian muskets under Frederick the Great became increasingly simpler to load and *less* accurate.[81]

Ideally, when the time came to fight, the soldiers could maneuver and fire by the beat of the drum and the voice of the commander, going one more time through the series of movements they repeated on the drill-fields, without having any need or opportunity to think and show initiative. Marshal de Saxe expressed a common opinion when he stated that most soldiers should be 'transformed into machines, which can take on life only through the voices of their officers.'[82] The main expectations drill manuals had of the common soldier was that 'In marching or standing, he must have a singular care to keepe his ranke and file, and not to stirre out of it (without command).'[83] The qualities that were sought for in soldiers were 'Silence, Obedience, Secretnes, Sobriety, Hardines, and Truth or Loyalty.' Intelligence was not mentioned, for the soldier's mind was ideally a transparent medium, that transmitted the commands of his superiors without interfering with them.[84] In *The Recruiting Officer*, Captain Plume explains his recruiting policy, saying that "tis a constant maxim among us, that those who know the least, obey the best.'[85] The good common soldier was just a cog in the military machine who sacrificed himself and his personal interests so that the machine could function well and achieve the collective aims.

In addition to drill, draconian discipline was relied upon to check "initiatives" and to habituate soldiers to obey orders automatically. Corporal punishment of great brutality was meted for minor cases of insubordination, whereas major offences such as desertion or mutiny were punished by death.[86] General military wisdom agreed with Rifleman Harris, who wrote in the early nineteenth century that 'I detest the sight of the lash; but I am convinced the British army can never go on without it.'[87]

Maurice's fantasy came closest to realization in Frederick the Great's army of automatons. As Christopher Duffy writes, in the Prussian military machine drill and discipline enabled the commander to compel the machine's parts 'to do what was frequently contrary to their will.' While watching his troops assemble for the invasion of Silesia (1740), Frederick told one of his lieutenants that what struck him most about the scene was that

> we are standing here in perfect safety, looking at sixty thousand men – they are all our enemies, and there is not one of them who is not better armed and stronger than we are, and yet they all tremble in our presence, while we have no reason whatsoever to be afraid of them. This is the miraculous effect of order, subordination and narrow supervision.[88]

Whereas no seventeenth-century soldier preserved an account of these military mechanics, some of the soldiers who served Frederick and who wrote Romantic military memoirs in the late eighteenth century did describe the military machine from the viewpoint of the cog. Ulrich Bräker, who was kidnapped into the Prussian army in 1756, was shocked the first time he went to the parade ground and saw the soldiers drilling. He 'saw the officers so bawling at and striking their men that the sweat dripped from my brow at the thought of what I had coming to me.'[89] Men tried to desert almost daily, and were invariably caught and flogged, sometimes to death. Bräker and his comrades watched the public flogging, whence they 'would look at each other, trembling and deathly pale, and whisper: "The bloody barbarians!"' Events on the drill-field provoked similar reflections on Bräker's part:

Here too there was no end of cursing and whipping by sadistic, jumped-up junkers and the yelling of the flogged in return. We were always amongst the first to move, and really made it snappy. But we were still terribly cut up to see others so mercilessly treated on the slightest provocation and ourselves bullied like this time and time again, standing there stiff as a poker, often whole hours at a stretch, throttled by all our kit, having to march dead-straight here, there and everywhere, uninterruptedly executing lightning manoeuvres – and all on the command of some officer, facing us with a furious expression and raised stick and threatening to lay into us any minute, as if we were so much trash. With such treatment even the toughest couldn't help becoming half-crippled, even the most patient, fuming. And as soon as we'd got back, dead-beat, to our billet, we had to race like mad to get our kit straight, removing every little spot, for, apart from the blue tunic, our whole uniform was white. Musket, cartridge-pouch, belt, every single button on our uniforms – it all had to be got up immaculate. The slightest speck of dirt on any item of equipment or a hair out of place on a soldier when he appeared on the parade-ground, and he'd be welcomed by a rain of lashes.[90]

When officers came to write the story of war, they naturally described common soldiers as mere bodies. Their chief function in the story, as we shall see below, was to display by their movements the superior qualities of their general's mind. As for the soldiers' inner experiences, these were of no importance whatsoever. The lack of interest in the inner experience of individual soldiers was clearly manifested in the way the instrumental story treated their deaths – arguably the most important experience of their life. From the viewpoint of the instrumental paradigm, the death of soldiers was usually important only as a yardstick for victory.[91] Thus in the wake of the battle of Oudenarde (1708) Corporal Matthew Bishop walked over the field and found that 'the number of the enemy's slain exceeded ours; and this pleased me much, as it was an undeniable proof of our having got the victory.'[92] It would have been totally alien to the instrumental interpretation of war to narrate the story of a war as the story of how war experience changed common soldiers, or to condemn war because common soldiers suffered in it.

Sometimes officers were forced to recognize that the soldiers' experience was important, because it influenced their behavior and their obedience. However, officers did so grudgingly, subsuming the soldiers' experiences under the ubiquitous term "morale." The term "morale" was used – and is still used – as a means to avoid any serious discussion of the soldiers' inner experience of war. It lumped together all kinds of feelings – from hunger and fear of punishment to camaraderie and religious enthusiasm – and evaluated them by the single yardstick of whether they increased or decreased obedience. The focus on obedience was so strong, that morale often came to be a synonym for obedience, which in turn was viewed as an almost infallible guarantee of victory. If the army was obedient, and if the army won a victory, it invariably indicated that the soldiers' morale was high. If the army was disobedient, and if the army lost a battle, then unless the army suffered from overwhelming material disadvantages, it always indicated that the soldiers' morale was low.[93] Using circular logic, defeat was proof of low morale, which in turn was used to explain the defeat. I do not recall ever reading about an army with a low morale that won a victory. The possibility that soldiers might have very depressing experiences while winning a great victory was of absolutely no significance to the instrumental story of war.

Common soldiers themselves very rarely wrote memoirs prior to the mid-eighteenth century. Partly because only a minority of them had the economic and cultural resources needed to write and publish such accounts, but also because military culture taught common soldiers to identify with the unthinking body. After years of drilling on the parade ground and the battlefield, it was hard to believe anyone would be interested in their thoughts and opinions about war. Most common soldiers who left accounts of their personal experiences during war did so within the compass of religious narratives, and they were encouraged to write by "civilian" religious doctrines which taught all individuals, no matter how humble, to identify with their soul/mind. It is no wonder, therefore, that common soldiers who wrote religious narratives under the influence of such doctrines tended to sharply contrast their military with their religious personae, and to portray their religious life as having little to do with their military career as "bodies."

Whereas the common soldiers were increasingly seen as automatons, and were taught to identify with the body, officers – who wrote the vast majority of early modern memoirs – were taught to identify with their minds, and to conceive their entire being in the army as that of "minds." They were simultaneously taught to suspect and suppress the thinking of the army's body, and by extension, of their own bodies. This message easily harmonized with the dominant religious teachings of the day.

The good officer was in consequence characterized by three related qualities:

1. His mind was completely devoted to the collective interests.
2. His mind was strong, and was able to compel his body to act in accordance with collective interests even if it meant undergoing suffering or death.
3. His mind was strong, and was able to compel *other people* to act in accordance with collective interests even if it meant undergoing suffering or death.

The only relevant way to evaluate the devotion and strength of the officer's mind was by looking at the actions of his body and the bodies of his subordinates. If these bodies acted in ways that promoted collective interests, then his mind was apparently both devoted and strong. If, say, an officer's company performed badly on the parade ground or on the battlefield, it was decisive evidence that something was amiss with his mental abilities. Whether the failure was one of devotion or of strength mattered little.

Consequently, when early modern officers interpreted war as a collective instrument, they were keen to show their superior mental qualities, but the way to do so was by describing the bodily actions of themselves and their subordinates. When mentioning injuries, hunger, cold, and other miseries, the only important thing was to show that they kept on functioning like loyal cogs. What happened inside them was at best irrelevant.

The duke of Navailles, for example, proudly narrates his exploits at the battle of Civitat (1647): 'I had two horses killed under me; all my men were injured; and I was myself lightly injured in the arm and leg; and at the end I found myself so abandoned and my horse so tired, that I was constrained to take the horse of a cavalryman from the regiment of Piombin.'[94] He nevertheless went on rallying and leading the remnant of his force to battle. Navailles gives a minute description of how he directed various formations to perform this or that maneuver, so that he eventually gained the upper hand despite suffering from numerical inferiority. Yet neither here nor anywhere else in his memoirs does Navailles analyze the inner feelings that caused and enabled him to fight and lead men in such a way. Narrating his brave and successful actions was proof enough that his mind was of superior quality.

The greatest heroes of the instrumental story of war were the Great Captains, men such as Hérnandez Gonzalo de Córdoba (the original *Gran Capitan*), Alexander Farnese, Gustav Adolph, and the duke of Marlborough. Whereas common soldiers were pure body, the ideal Great Captain was pure mind. Unlike the knights of old, and even unlike his subordinate officers, the early modern Great Captain was not supposed to display much fighting prowess. Instead, he was characterized above all by the extraordinary ability of his mind to think rationally, to match means and ends, and to manipulate bodies in space.[95]

Whereas medieval commanders such as Richard the Lion-Heart were envisioned as warrior knights, and often fought in the front ranks, the early modern Great Captain normally ceased to fight himself, and stopped carrying offensive weapons on his person. Indeed, it became reprehensible for generals to risk themselves needlessly.[96] Artists still depicted Captains charging ahead with a drawn sword, but just as often they were now depicted orchestrating the battle from the safety of the rear, carrying nothing but a harmless baton. Such paintings were a mirror of Maurice's Cartesian fantasy. They presented the general as a huge and dominating figure, with thousands of pin-men arranged in nit geometrical formations behind him. This arrangement gave the impression that the general was moving those pin-men around with mathematical precision, as if he were a gigantic chess player or Newtonian physicist.[97]

Figure 17 Jan Saenredam, *Prince Maurice of Nassau* (c. 1600)

The Captain's body, his bodily appetites and humors, and his emotions were suppressed and denied. For the perfect mind of the Great

Captain should have been completely immune to the disruptive influence of sensations and emotions. The Captain was not supposed to be swayed in his thoughts and decisions by hunger and cold; by pity for combatants and civilians; by jealousy of one commander or by fondness for another commander; by sexual and romantic desires; or even by considerations of personal honor.[98]

Robert Parker says of Marlborough that 'He was peculiarly happy in an invincible calmness of temper and serenity of mind; and had a surprising readiness of thought, even in the heat of battle.' Parker rates Prince Eugène as 'equal to the Duke of Marlborough, in every respect but this, that he had not altogether that command of temper, which was his Grace's peculiar excellency: and it was this heat and warmth of his temper, which led him once [...] into a fatal mistake.'[99] Marshal de Saxe agreed, writing in his *Rêveries* that 'A general should be calm and never ill-tempered. He should not know what it is to hate. He should punish without favour, above all those who are his favourites, but he should never get angry.'[100]

The Great Captain could at times make a display of his emotions and sensations, but it was always done in a coldly calculated effort to achieve some rational aim. For instance, Parker describes how in the campaign of 1711 Marlborough first made a show of being sullen and sad, and then drew up a desperate plan of making a frontal assault on the French lines of *Ne Plus Ultra*. He talked about this plan ceaselessly with an 'air of assurance,' so that 'some began to suspect that the ill treatment he had met with at home [...] might have turned his brain, and made him desperate.'[101] The French of course heard of this planned attack, and were ready for it on the appointed night. It then transpired that Marlborough deceived everyone, that his moody displays were a mere trick, and that on that very night he outflanked the entire French position by a bold march. Parker writes that 'never did a player on the stage act a part to greater perfection, than did his Grace through the whole course of this complicated scheme.'[102]

Ideally, even severe illness should not have clouded the thought process of commanders. Marshal de Saxe famously led the French to victory at Fontenoy (1745) from a litter. Francisco de Zurbarán painted the sick Don Fernando Girón directing the defense of Cadiz from a chair (1625). The painting shows Girón sitting in a chair in civilian clothing, far away from the battle, and carrying in his hand nothing but a small baton. Yet, despite the frailty of his body, his mind is in complete control of the situation. The pin-men in the background are apparently moving according to his wishes.[103]

Figure 18   Francisco de Zurbarán, *The Defense of Cadiz* (1634)

The only inner experience that interested the Great Captains' hagiographers was the Captains' thought process. When the career of such a Captain was narrated, either by himself or by others, very lengthy descriptions were given of his thought process: what considerations the Captain made, what factors he weighed, what plans he devised, and how he reached one conclusion rather than the other.[104] The point of such descriptions was again to show the absolute superiority of mind to body. Not only were these thoughts free from the meddling of the Captain's bodily sensations and emotions, but they determined the fate of countless other bodies. The minute descriptions of the Captain's thought process were invariably followed by a description of the maneuvers of thousands of bodies in space, and the message was that these maneuvers were dictated by the Captain's thought process. Not only the maneuvers of his own troops, but even the maneuvers of the enemy were anticipated and controlled by his superior mind. The story of war as a collective instrument thus celebrated war as the victory of human mind over human bodies. The superior reason of the Great Captains moved human bodies around in an immense game of chess,[105] while the patriotic zeal of individual combatants made them sacrifice their bodies for the common good.

It should be stressed that the preceding pages describe images and cultural developments more than military realities. Maurice's Cartesian fantasy was just that – a fantasy. It could not be and was never realized in its totality, not even by Frederick the Great. In particular, not only was it impossible to totally repress the minds of the common soldiers and give Captains monopoly over thinking, but, as we shall see in Chapter 5, it was counterproductive.

Nevertheless, this fantasy had far-reaching consequences. For two centuries armies made repeated practical efforts to realize it, which shaped to a large extent all their activities from recruitment to strategy. At a deeper level, this fantasy had an immense influence on the stories of war and on the image of soldiers, officers, Great Captains, and military maneuvers. Even if in reality war never realized Maurice's Cartesian fantasy, the stories of war presented it as if it did. To this day people still tend to think about armies as gigantic "military machines," about common soldiers as "mindless automatons," and about Great Captains as "pure minds." To this day military histories are often Cartesian fantasies, in which the perfect mind of a Napoleon moves hundreds of thousands of bodies across entire continents, hampered solely by the equally perfect mind of a Wellington. The similarity between the vector diagrams of Newtonian physics and the Cartesian battle diagrams with their square formations and neat arrows has bedazzled and misled generations of military historians, military theorists, and not a few military commanders.

Up till now we spoke about the drilled armies and the automaton soldiers as reflecting a "Cartesian" fantasy. However, we can now take a second look at the relationship between Descartes and his one-time commander. Both chronology and common sense hint that it is perhaps better to speak of Descartes as pursuing a "Maurician" fantasy rather than the other way around. It could well be that Descartes' year of service in Maurice's army influenced his thought far more than historians of philosophy usually concede. It may well be argued that of all the people who populated the planet in the year 1619, officers in Maurice's Dutch army were the most likely to fall under the impression that bodies are mechanical automatons that mind can command at will. Was it pure coincidence that one of these officers was the person who exported this idea to the world of philosophy?

* * *

The conflict between the stories of war as a collective instrument, as a personal instrument, and as an honorable way of life, was the main conflict about the understanding of war in the early modern age. Wars were characterized by an unresolved and ever-present tension between the political interests of the government, the personal interests of the soldiers, and the ideals of chivalric fair play.[106] Combatants and theoreticians debated back and forth whether dishonorable means may be used to gain victory, and whether a combatant's first allegiance should be to his personal honor, to his purse, or to his sovereign.[107]

Repeated efforts were made to end the conflict and reconcile the three stories. With the passing of the centuries and the rise of the state, the story of war as a collective instrument gained the upper hand. It became common to argue that every soldier should adopt the collective interests as his own personal interests. It became equally common to argue that personal honor is gained by serving the collective interests. It was eventually argued that the honor of the collective depends on its being victorious, which made any means that helped secure victory *ipso facto* honorable.[108]

Yet the struggle between the stories was never really settled, and the honorary story in particular was never completely digested by the instrumental story. It has continued to disrupt the instrumental understanding and conduct of war down to the twenty-first century, when the personal honor of commanders still interferes with the smooth pursuit of national interests; when armies and combatants still have qualms about using "dishonorable" means to secure victory;[109] and when defeated armies and combatants still comfort themselves with the thought that they at least fought honorably.[110]

From our perspective, it matters little which of the three stories gained the upper hand in the mind of a particular early modern soldier, because all three agreed that mind must retain absolute mastery over body, and that the quality of a mind is judged by its ability to master bodies and direct them in the right way. Consequently, memoirists who used any of these stories – in whatever combination – to understand war had little interest in inner experiences of war, and could not have had any martial revelations. None of these stories offered a model for how bodily suffering (or joy) may reveal new truths.

Conclusions

War in the early modern period was the supreme model for the victory of mind over body. According to the instrumental and honorary stories alike, war involved a constant inner battle between mind and body. This battle could have only two possible outcomes: In the optimal case of men-of-honor, successful entrepreneurs, good patriots, and Great Captains, mind won, and the lives and deaths of such men advertised the victory of mental ideals over bodily experiences. Alternatively, mind lost, but the victory of the body proved only the cowardice and weakness of that particular man. Between the two options no room was left for questioning old ideals or acquiring new knowledge. Hence war could not be a source for revelation, the experience of war was of no interest, and it was enough to describe the external behavior of combatants in order to gauge the measure of their minds.

Participating in war was accordingly a limited source of authority. If a man passed the tests of war successfully, acting as the dominant ideals of war expected him to act, he was recognized as a man of honor, or a good patriot, which gave him much authority. However, this authority always depended on the ideals of military conduct, and his personal experience did not give him the power to question these ideals.

Let us imagine an encounter between a civilian who never experienced war, and who spoke highly of patriotism and glory, and a veteran soldier who said that only fools believe in patriotism and glory, and that the best thing to do in battle is run away. Today, the weight of authority would lay with the veteran, who could tell the civilian that the latter does not know what he is talking about. In the early modern period, the weight of authority lay with the civilian. Despite his vast military experience, if the soldier had spoken in dishonorable and unpatriotic terms it would merely have branded him a cowardly wretch, one of Erasmus's 'dregs of mankind.'

As we shall see, in the late modern era it was the revolt of the body and the breakdown of mental control that changed the balance of power and gave soldiers a type of experiential authority that was independent of military ideals (though it did depend on new aesthetic and epistemological ideals). The revolt of the body also made it necessary – and interesting – to start describing the experience of war. As the mind lost some control of the thinking process in favor of the body, war no longer resulted in either the complete victory or the complete defeat of the mind. Rather, war became a *Bildungsroman*, in which the body taught the mind through a process of experiential revelation who one really was and what the world was really like. Instead of merely testing the soldiers, war began teaching and changing them.

Part III
The Revolt of the Body: 1740–1865

In the period 1740–1865 a new story of war emerged: the story of war as a revelatory experience. Part III tries to outline the appearance of this story against the background of more general trends in Western culture – namely Sensationism and Romanticism – and related socio-political developments. My main interest is to explain the exact dynamics and internal logic of the emerging story, and to expose its cultural foundations. No attempt is made to give a comprehensive overview of Sensationism and Romanticism, or of contemporary social and political upheavals. Similarly, there is no attempt to give an exhaustive causal explanation for the rise of this story. I am more interested in explaining what happened than why it happened.

Two further apologetic comments are in order.

First, the following chapters discuss several complicated philosophical ideas such as the Kantian sublime. Philosophers and scholars have spilled rivers of ink trying to pin down these ideas and explain their precise meaning. Their efforts often resulted in only greater confusion. When discussing these ideas, I approach them as far as possible from the viewpoint of soldiers. I try to relate them as far as possible to military issues, and to explain ideas such as the Kantian sublime in a way that would have been comprehensible to a typical common soldier or junior officer in the Napoleonic wars. The result may be unpalatable to philosophers, but as explained in the introduction, the privileged audience of this book is military historians.

Secondly, I have adopted a very cavalier attitude toward chronology. The following chapters make no distinction between proto-Romantics, early Romantics, and late Romantics, lumping them all together with the Sensationists of the mid-eighteenth century. Similarly, the following chapters juxtapose military memoirs written in the 1750s with memoirs written in the 1850s, treating them as belonging to the same historical era. This is almost inevitable in a book that tries to encompass more than 500 years of military culture. I believe it is further justified by the fact that soldiers, unlike philosophers and artists, seldom formed part of a self-conscious cultural avant-garde. They were influenced by movements such as Sensationism more slowly and more haphazardly than poets or painters, and therefore cannot be easily compartmentalized into distinct decades or cultural phases.

Instead of a chronological typology, I tried to formulate a thematic typology, and divided memoirs according to the themes that dominate them. The book assumes that the differences between narratives of positive revelation and narratives of disillusionment written in the same year are far more important than between two narratives of disillusionment written 50 years apart.

For convenience sake, and in the absence of a better term, the book refers to military memoirs written in the entire period 1740–1865 as "Romantic" memoirs. Though in many contexts it would be nonsensical to speak of the mid-eighteenth century as a Romantic period, in the context of military memoirs and the rise of the revelatory story of war I believe the epithet is justified. In this I follow those who interpret Romanticism as a continuation of the Enlightenment and the culture of Sensibility, and who speak of the "long" Romantic era stretching from the middle of the eighteenth century to the middle of the nineteenth century (e.g., the recent *Encyclopedia of the Romantic Era, 1760–1850*).

4
Bodies Begin to Think

The War of Austrian Succession and La Mettrie's
L'Homme-machine

In the late twentieth century Joseph Heller could freely write that a
young soldier is indistinguishable from stewed tomatoes. Netiva Ben-
Yehuda did not fear censorship when she compared wounded soldiers to
screaming meat-balls. In the middle of the eighteenth century such ideas
were scandalous, and few dared publish them.[1] One of the first who
dared was a French army doctor, Julian Offray de la Mettrie. A Breton
of middle class origins, La Mettrie was trained in both philosophy and
medicine, thinking at first to pursue an ecclesiastical career, but later
preferring the more lucrative profession of a physician. In 1742 he
was appointed regimental physician of the French Guards. During the
War of the Austrian Succession he accompanied the Guards on several
campaigns, and was present at the battle of Dettingen (1743), the siege
of Freiburg (1744), and the battle of Fontenoy (1745).

As regimental physician during these actions, La Mettrie had to
take care of hundreds of sick and wounded soldiers, dissecting and
amputating bodies by the dozen. After battle, eighteenth-century field
hospitals usually looked like butcher shops flanked by piles of amputated limbs. Effective anesthetics were still a hundred years in the
future; medical facilities were almost non-existent; and many military
"surgeons" were trained in civilian life as barbers, butchers, and
carpenters. The death-rate for thigh-amputation operations during the
period was about 70 percent.[2]

La Mettrie experienced the miseries of war on his own flesh too.
During the siege of Freiburg he had a violent attack of fever. As Frederick

the Great wrote in his eulogy of La Mettrie, 'for a philosopher an illness is a school of physiology.' Utilizing the unique conditions of illness in order to conduct a first-hand investigation of his mind and body, the feverish La Mettrie reached the opposite conclusions of those to which Descartes reached in his warm chamber. He concluded, according to Frederick,

> that thought is but a consequence of the organization of the machine, and the disturbance of the springs has considerable influence on that part of us which the metaphysicians call soul. Filled with these ideas during his convalescence, he boldly bore the torch of experience into the night of metaphysics; he tried to explain by aid of anatomy the thin texture of understanding, and he found only mechanism where others had supposed an essence superior to matter.[3]

La Mettrie was a bold spirit. While his patients were exposing themselves to musketry salvoes and artillery bombardments, he exposed himself to the fury of church and state by publishing the results of his investigation in a treatise titled *Histoire naturelle de l'âme*, which appeared shortly after the battle of Fontenoy (1745). To avoid the full measure of the expected reprisal, La Mettrie published the text anonymously, and pretended that it was but a translation of an English treatise. To safeguard himself further, he published the text in the Netherlands, which was then at war with France. (Dutch forces had just opposed La Mettrie's regiment on the field of Fontenoy.)

These precautions availed him little. The text caused an uproar, the identity of the author was soon discovered, and La Mettrie had to quit his post. It was argued that a heretical doctor could not cure the guards of His Most Catholic Majesty, the king of France. La Mettrie was at first kicked upward, and appointed medical director of the army's rear hospitals, but the persecution continued. In 1746 he had to flee to the Netherlands for fear of his life.

Undaunted, La Mettrie published an even bolder text, which became the manifesto of modern materialism: *L'Homme-machine* (1747). This often misunderstood book presented an extreme anti-Cartesian and anti-Christian view. It abolished the Cartesian dichotomy between mind and body, denied the existence of mind and soul alike, and argued that thinking and feeling were done by matter. These views were so scandalous, that even the tolerant Netherlands could not stomach them. All copies of the text were ordered to be burned. In a rare moment of sectarian unity, Calvinists, Lutherans, and Catholics joined hands to hound La Mettrie, who had to flee again, this time to Prussia. Frederick the Great, the greatest soldier of his age and a self-proclaimed philosopher-king, welcomed the radical doctor to his court, made him a member of the Prussian royal academy of science, supported him until his premature death in 1751, and then wrote a flattering eulogy of him.[4]

L'Homme-machine had two main mottos, which were subsequently adopted by numerous soldier-writers. The first motto was that intellectual speculations produce only baseless theories, whereas truth can be known only through direct physical experience. Philosophers and theologians who enclose themselves in their libraries and monasteries know nothing about the nature of humanity. Only doctors, who cut people open and literally probe their entrails, can form well-founded opinions on the nature of man. La Mettrie wrote that

> Physician-philosophers probe and illuminate the labyrinth that is man. They alone have revealed man's springs hidden under coverings that obscure so many other marvels. [...] these are the only physicians who have the right to speak here. What have others to tell us, above all, theologians? Is it not ridiculous to hear them pronouncing shamelessly on something they are incapable of understanding, from which, on the contrary, they have been completely turned away by obscure studies that have led them to a thousand prejudices, in a word, to fanaticism, which adds further to their ignorance of the mechanisms of bodies?

La Mettrie further explained that

> All the investigations the greatest philosophers have made *a priori*, that is, by wanting to take flight with the winds of the mind, have been in vain. Only *a posteriori*, **by unraveling the soul as one pulls out the guts of the body**, can one, I do not say discover with clarity what the nature of man is, but rather attain the highest degree of probability possible on the subject. Take up, therefore, the staff of experience, and leave behind the history of all the vain opinions of philosophers.

In his next sentence, this regimental doctor, who has pulled out the guts of many a soldier, dismisses as 'useless efforts' all the so-called 'profound meditation' of 'the Descarteses, Malebranches, Leibnizes, Wolffs, etc.'[5] His own treatise, on the other hand, is no such useless meditation. For it is based on first-hand investigations La Mettrie conducted on his own body and on the bodies of the thousands of patients and soldiers he treated. It is no coincidence that the text is full of references to injured soldiers and other cases from La Mettrie's medical career. 'Slit open the guts of man and animals,' says La Mettrie to the philosophers, 'How can you grasp human nature if you never see how the innards of the one exactly parallel the innards of the other?'[6]

As for the relations between bodily experiences and revelation, La Mettrie argued that the truth of revelation must correspond to the truth of bodily experiences, and in effect concluded that bodily experiences are akin to revelation. 'Only by [observing] nature,' he wrote, 'can we discover the meaning of the words of the Gospel, whose true interpreter is experience alone. Indeed, other commentators up to now have only obscured the truth [...] experience alone can make sense of faith.'[7] La Mettrie boasted that his own views are based solely on 'the inner feelings and personal experience of each individual.'[8]

Anticipating the arguments of late modern pacifist materialists, La Mettrie finally contended that the abstract arguments of theologians and philosophers were downright dangerous, for they were the root cause of wars. He defended his atheistic materialism by putting the following words into the mouth of a friend: 'If atheism [...] were generally widespread, all the branches of religion would be cut off at the root and die. No more wars incited by theological arguments, no more soldiers of religion, terrible soldiers!'[9]

The second motto of *L'Homme-machine*, indicated by the title, is that the conclusion of proper experiential investigations is clear-cut and simple: Man is matter, and matter can feel and think. Man is different from clay, or from stewed tomatoes, only in his arrangement. Movement, feeling, and thought can be and are produced by matter, if that matter is arranged in an appropriate way. The secret is in the organization. This is the meaning of the comparison to a machine. If you take a lump of iron and a cartload of wood by themselves, they will neither move nor produce anything. But arrange them into a particular form called "a machine," and they can weave textiles. This does not mean, though, that the iron used for the production of a weaving machine is endowed with some mysterious inner quality of "weaving," which other iron lacks. Similarly, if you take ordinary matter, devoid of any inner quality of "feeling" or "thinking," and arrange it into the appropriate form, it will start feeling and thinking. What has man got that animals do not? Only a few more cogs and springs. Even man's delicate conscience is 'no more foreign to matter than thought is.' 'Is organization therefore sufficient for everything?' asks La Mettrie rhetorically, and immediately answers: 'Yes.'[10]

Since feeling and thinking is done by matter, all human feeling, thought, and ideals are material, and are the result of the material conditions of the body. Whereas previously it was believed that mind can and should resist the enervating influences of the body, La Mettrie emphasized that difficult bodily conditions are *bound* to influence the thinking process, and that nobody can resist material discomfort indefinitely. Illness may well turn the loftiest genius into an idiot, and then 'goodbye to all that precious knowledge acquired at such great cost and with so much trouble!'[11] Apparently speaking of his own experiences in the field hospital, La Mettrie writes about amputated and dying soldiers, saying that 'This one cries like a child at the approach of death, while that one cracks a joke. What would it take to change the intrepidity of Canus Julius, Seneca, and Petronius into pusillanimity or cowardice? An obstruction in the spleen or the liver, a blockage of the portal vein.'[12]

Moving from the effects of illness to those of exhaustion, La Mettrie asks his readers: 'Look at this tired soldier! He snores in the trench to the noise of a hundred cannon! His soul hears nothing, his sleep is perfect apoplexy. A bomb is about to crush him! He will feel this blow less than does an insect underfoot.'[13] Soldiers for La Mettrie, like humans in general, are machines of flesh and blood, even their bravery and cowardice no more than bodily reactions. '[F]eed the body, pour powerful juices and strong liquors into its pipes, and then the soul arms itself with proud courage, and the soldier, whom water would have made run away, becomes ferocious and runs gaily to his death to the beat of the drum [...] the soul dwells in the stomach.'[14]

It should be stressed though that La Mettrie was not upholding what we today call a "mechanistic" worldview. On the contrary, his main idea was that matter can think and feel. This became the basis for all subsequent *organic* worldviews. Due to the ill-chosen title of his book, La Mettrie is usually thought of as some kind of ultra-Cartesian who dispensed with the "ghost in the machine." In fact, La Mettrie animated the world of matter and was a Romantic precursor and groundbreaker.[15]

La Mettrie did not comment on the possibility that his soldiers too might claim for themselves the authority of experience. But it was a very small step from *L'homme-machine*'s arguments to the conclusion that an amputated soldier in a field hospital knows the nature of man better than a learned theologian in his ivory tower.

La Mettrie's ideas were political dynamite for other reasons too. Even Frederick the Great became alarmed when La Mettrie thought of comparing the state to the human body.[16] Such comparisons were traditional. For millennia philosophers and theologians had compared human society and the human body. However, they always concluded that human society must have a sovereign king comparable to the sovereign soul or mind that rules the body. What kind of political philosophy would La Mettrie's materialism produce?

La Mettrie observed in *L'Homme-machine* that in the body, what people called soul or will is far from being sovereign. 'In vain does one protest for the sovereignty of the will. For every order it gives, it submits a hundred times to the yoke.'[17] Though we can perhaps consciously rule over our voluntary muscles, no man can 'take the reins of the whole body to control, suspend, calm, or excite its movements at will!'[18] There is no sovereign soul in the body which does the thinking and gives command to the organs. Rather, it is the organization of the body that animates it and directs it throughout its life. If so, perhaps in human society too one can dispense with the notion of a sovereign head? With the proper organization of society, the body of society might itself do the thinking and regulate its actions. Arrange even the commonest people in the right way, and you can have an excellent government and a well-functioning society.[19]

Frederick would have been even less keen to contemplate the implications of La Mettrie's view for the military field. Superficially, the kingly drill-master with his automaton soldiers should have been pleased by the comparison of humans to machines. But in fact, La Mettrie's *L'homme-machine* undermined the basis of the Frederickian war machine. First, La Mettrie argued that all humans – and not just common soldiers – were mere matter. Secondly, La Mettrie argued that thinking is done by the material body, not by some elevated "mind." Thirdly, La Mettrie argued that the more one distanced oneself from the reality of the body, the less truth there was in one's thoughts. This implied that military thinking could and should be done by common soldiers, and that armies should function as *organisms*. For every decision the Great Captain makes, he must submit a hundred times to the organism's inner dynamics. A hundred years after La Mettrie, Tolstoy's *War and Peace* will describe the 1812 campaign as a blind contest between two immense organisms, with Kutuzov and Napoleon serving as helpless figureheads, unable to really influence the course of events.

In 1773, two French junior officers committed suicide due to their exasperation with their limited opportunities in the royal army. They left a suicide note saying: 'A few grains of gunpowder have just burst the springs of that mass of moving flesh which our haughty brethren like to call king of creatures.'[20] The body of the individual human being, of the state, and of the army was flexing its muscles and preparing to appropriate a share in the thinking process.

Sensationism and sensibility

La Mettrie was not the single-handed creator of late modern war culture. Neither was he the first domino piece in the chain that led to *Catch-22*. Rather, he was a radical vector within a much larger shift in Western civilization that occurred during the eighteenth and early nineteenth century, and that revolutionized war culture along with many other phenomena. This shift has often been tagged "the culture of sensibility."

The culture of sensibility manifested itself in almost all aspects of Western life, from philosophy, religion, psychology, and literature to medicine, education, economics, and government. Scholars are still hotly debating its root causes. Some have highlighted the import-ance of eighteenth-century physiology and its influence on philo-sophy and literature,[21] but alternative narratives could be constructed as well. It is particularly difficult to single out the "first" causes because the borderlines between, say, eighteenth-century physiology, literature, economics, and religion were quite hazy. For instance, La Mettrie was both a physiologist and a philosopher, had a smarting of theology, published numerous works of literature, and was a military man into the bargain.

The following pages describe the culture of sensibility primarily in the context of philosophy and literature because they had the most obvious connections with soldiers' writings. Subsequent chapters examine the manifestations of the culture of sensibility in strictly military contexts. No comment is made on the question of origins; that is, the present book neither makes the grandiose claim that soldiers created the culture of sensibility, nor does it argue that soldiers slavishly copied the ideas of physicians, philosophers, and poets.

In philosophy, the culture of sensibility appeared above all in the guise of Sensationism, 'the most widely accepted way of thinking among eighteenth-century French intellectuals.'[22] Sensationism was domin-ated by French thinkers such as Etienne Bonnot de Condillac, Charles Bonnet, and Claude Adrien Helvétius, but was profoundly influenced by the moral-sense school of the earl of Shaftesbury and Francis Hutcheson, and by eighteenth-century British Empiricists.[23]

Sensationist philosophers refrained from adopting materialist views and from denying the existence of immaterial souls or minds.[24] However, they agreed with La Mettrie that all ideas and all knowledge are the product of bodily sensations. There is nothing in the mind that did not originate in some sensation or the other.[25] They thereby subordinated minds and souls to bodies. Charles Bonnet explained that the divine author of nature has 'subordinated the *Activity* of the Soul to its *Sensibility*, its sensibility to the *Play of Fibers* [in the sense organs]; the Play of Fibers to the *Action* of *Objects.*' Mental ideas, according to Bonnet, are in their origin 'but the movements imprinted by Objects on the Fibers of the *Senses.*'[26] There were no innate ideas. Even 'Our most *abstract* and most *spiritualized* [...] ideas derive thus from *sensory* ideas, as from their natural source. The Idea of GOD, for example, the most *spiritualized* of all our *Ideas*, manifestly comes from the *Senses.*'[27] David Hume went a step further, arguing that thinking itself is an involuntary association of ideas which past experience alone connects with each other.

Sensationists were consequently averse to abstract theories that have no basis in sensory experience. They strongly emphasized that it is meaningless to speak about things which one has not experienced, for any ideas not rooted in the senses are mere delusions. They attacked with equal vigor the scripture-based dogma of theologians and the metaphysical systems of rationalist philosophers. They posited sensation as the only sure source of knowledge, and warned against the use of "big words" and flowery metaphors, which all too easily trick and mystify people.[28] Locke famously wrote that 'many cardinal errors are due to the mistaking of words for things.'[29] From Locke onward, it became *de rigueur* to discredit one's opponents as being entrapped by flights of rhetorical imagination which have no basis in experience. This accusation was commonly leveled by Empiricists thinkers of the Enlightenment against the Rationalists and the Christian theologians. The Romantics subsequently leveled exactly the same accusation against the Enlightenment. Later on it would be the turn of the Romantics to be accused of the same sin by the Realists, which themselves did not escape similar accusations in the twentieth century.

By construing bodily experiences as the ultimate source of all knowledge Sensationists not only undermined the power of all abstract theories, but they simultaneously empowered each individual to challenge established authorities in the name of his or her personal experience. Sensationist thinkers such as Helvétius were adamant that all people had the same bodily sensibility, and had therefore equal aptitude to acquire knowledge. If the upper classes were more knowledgeable than the lower classes, it was due only to differences in education.[30] And if an illiterate soldier directly experienced something that a learned theologian only read about, then the soldier was a better authority on it than the theologian.

Such claims went back, of course, to ancient Greece. The dictum that everything in the mind had originated in the senses was repeated by one school of thought or another in every century from Aristotle to Hobbes. However, whereas previous generations of philosophers voiced it on the basis of logical syllogisms, eighteenth-century Sensationists had at their disposal the novel findings of modern physiological research. These findings enabled those who upheld the claims of sensation to base their arguments on the actual research of sensations rather than on logic. Particularly important were the new physiological studies of the nervous system, and the new language of nerves and fibers, which was developed by the joint efforts of physiologists and poets. This language described human beings as sensitive percussion instruments, made of fibers and nerves, on which external phenomena played. Not only sensations, but also emotions, thoughts, and ideas were nothing more than nervous music.[31] As we shall see in Chapter 6, this new neurological language made a significant contribution to the spread and triumph of Sensationist thought in military circles.

Eighteenth-century Sensationist philosophy differed from earlier sensationist philosophies in one more important respect. Unlike many previous schools, eighteenth-century Sensationism was a wide cultural river rather than a narrow intellectual stream. In the second half of the eighteenth century the "cult of sensibility" swept Europe and America, popularizing Sensationist ideas, and shaping Western "sensibilities" to this day.[32]

The cult of sensibility – as against the more intellectual variants of Sensationism – was characterized by its interest in everyday emotional life. It emphasized the sensory nature of human emotions. Condillac, for example, said that 'desires, passions, etc., are only sensation itself which is transformed differently.'[33] The more radical branches of Sensationist psychology ultimately reduced all human emotions, vices, and virtues to the pursuit of sensory pleasure or avoidance of sensory pain.[34] 'Physical pain and pleasure,' said Helvétius, 'are the unknown principles of all human actions.'[35] Emotions were normally described by physiological language of vibrating fibers and tensing nerves, and the discourse of sensibility was used by physicians and poets alike. Talk of "aching hearts" and "gut sensations" which is today taken figuratively was still understood literally. The twentieth-century distinction between feeling emotions (connected with the mind) and feeling sensations (connected with the body) was only beginning to take shape, and the two were habitually conflated.[36]

For instance, Joseph Reed remembered that when the American army fled before the British at Harlem Heights (1776), 'the enemy appeared in open view and in a most insulting manner sounded their bugle horns as is usual after a fox chase. I never felt such a sensation before; it seemed to crown our disgrace.'[37] Reed is obviously referring here to what today we would call an "emotion." George Gleig wrote that the prospect of fighting, 'instead of creating gloomy sensations, was viewed with sincere delight.'[38] We would speak of "gloomy emotions." Conversely, John Shipp recounted that when he underwent his basic training under a cruel drill-sergeant, the latter 'did not fail to enforce his authority and dignity in a manner by no means agreeable to my feelings, especially to those of my back.'[39] Even today the word "sensation" means both a feeling on the body and an event of great emotional impact.

There was nothing new in seeing emotions as bodily phenomena closely related to sensations. For centuries the Galenic, Christian, and Cartesian schemes considered emotions to be either pure bodily functions or the result of bodily movements. For instance, carnal love, jealousy, anger, and hot temper in general were considered "hot" emotions, connected with particular types of hot bodily fluids, hot sensations, hot foods, and hot climates.[40]

However, while the cult of sensibility agreed with traditional opinions that the emotions were closely related to bodily sensations, it interpreted this fact in a radically new way. Traditionally, the close identification with the body resulted in the denigration of emotions compared to pure mental ideas. They were considered a fickle and untrustworthy source for making judgments and gaining knowledge. The eighteenth-century culture of sensibility argued along opposite lines. If emotions were really sensations, and sensations were the root of all knowledge, it followed that emotions were central for the acquisition of knowledge, and had a more exalted status than intellectual speculations. Feeling began to denote not only having sensations and having emotions, but also having knowledge. Feeling became synonymous with knowing, and to this day Westerners often say "I feel" when they actually mean "I think." As Charles Taylor explains, though reason could still guide and correct feelings when they deviated from the right path, feelings yielded crucial insights that reason could never produce by itself.[41] In particular, ethical and aesthetical judgments, hitherto the indisputable domain of reason, from now onward were increasingly appropriated by feeling.

Goethe's Faust exclaims that 'Feeling is all.' Marianne, the heroine of Marivaux's *La Vie de Marianne* (1736–41), explains that 'I believe that only feeling can give us reliable information about ourselves and that we must not put too much trust in what our minds twist to their own convenience, for they seem to me great dreamers.' Diderot argued that 'The passions always inspire us rightly, for they inspire us only with the desire for happiness. It is the mind that misleads us and makes us take false roads.' Hamann wrote that 'Thinking, feeling and understanding all depend on the heart.'[42] In his *Sentimental Journey* (1768) Laurence Sterne compared sensibility to God:

> Dear sensibility! source inexhausted of all that's precious in our joys, or costly in our sorrows! thou chainest thy martyr down upon his bed of straw, and 'tis thou who lift'st him up to HEAVEN. Eternal fountain of our feelings! 'tis here I trace thee, and this is thy *'divinity which stirs within me'* [...] all comes from thee, great, great SENSORIUM of the world! which vibrates, if a hair of our heads but falls upon the ground, in the remotest desert of thy creation.[43]

Rousseau summed it all up in his *Émile*, the new sentimental Bible: 'Too often does reason deceive us, we have only too good a right to doubt her.' When looking for our rules of conduct, we should therefore abandon rational calculations. Instead, explained the great sentimental guru, 'I find [my rules of conduct] in the depths of my heart, traced by nature in characters which nothing can efface. I need only consult myself with regard to what I wish to do; what I feel to be good is good, what I feel to be bad is bad [tout ce que je sens être bien est bien, tout ce que je sens être mal est mal].'[44] Later on he explains that it is vital

> to distinguish between our acquired ideas and our natural feelings; for feeling precedes knowledge [...] The decrees of conscience are not judgments but feelings. Although all our ideas come from without, the feelings by which they are weighed are within us, and it is by these feelings alone that we perceive fitness or unfitness of things in relation to ourselves, which leads us to seek or shun these things. To exist is to feel [Exister pour nous, c'est sentir], our feeling is undoubtedly earlier than our intelligence, and we had feelings before we had ideas. Whatever may be the cause of our being, it has provided for our preservation by giving us feelings suited to our nature.[45]

Nineteenth-century Romanticists whole-heartedly adopted this eighteenth-century legacy. Whether they upheld religion, nature mysticism, nationalism, or any other ideal, they based it primarily on feeling.[46] In Friedrich Schiller's *Wallenstein*, Max Piccolomini has to decide whether to rebel against his father Octavio, and against the Emperor Ferdinand, or whether to abandon his sweetheart Thekla, and her father Wallenstein. When Octavio counsels him to remain loyal to the Emperor, Max refuses to be persuaded, saying that 'Your judgment may speak false, but not my heart.'[47] He then goes to confront Thekla and her domineering aunt, the Countess Terzky. Max asks Thekla to decide his fate. The Countess tries to influence Thekla, urging her 'Think well. . . .' But before she could complete the sentence, Max interrupts and exclaims, 'No, do not think. Say what you feel.' He then adds that 'Lay all this in the balance [. . .] then speak, / And let your heart decide it.'[48] Later on Gordon, the commander of Eger fortress, exclaims: 'The heart is God's own voice, the work of man / Is all the calculation of our cunning.'[49]

Many revolutionaries in the late eighteenth and nineteenth century similarly built their political philosophies upon the inner voice of feeling, arguing that if that voice was freed from the tyranny of kings and religions, it would always favor what was good and right. 'Feeling,' explains Steven Bruhm in *Gothic Bodies*, 'was the origin of all reformist and enlightened thought.' The Utilitarians in particular saw human feelings of suffering and happiness as the ultimate object of ethics, and the same human feelings were also the ultimate judges of right and wrong. Cesare Beccaria argued that 'no lasting advantage is to be hoped for from political morality if it is not founded on the ineradicable feelings of mankind.'[50]

Of course, as Rousseau hinted, it was not easy to discern the truthful voice of inner feeling from the sly tricks of abstract reason. The cult of sensibility consequently gave birth to a new type of sage: a person who is fully "connected" and attuned to his or her sensations and emotions, and able to easily discern the wheat of feeling from the chaff of logical acrobatics.

Since the cult of sensibility was not an abstract philosophy, its theoretical maxims are of lesser importance than the practical lessons it taught people. Two such practical lessons, which could be followed in day-to-day life, were particularly important.

First, one should pay as close an attention as possible to one's minutest sensations and emotions, and open oneself up to their influences. By the late eighteenth century, "sensibility" – defined as 'habitude of mind, which disposes a man to be *easily moved*, and *powerfully affected*, by surrounding objects and passing events'[51] – came to be one of the most prized characteristic of elite men and women. Whereas classical, medieval, and early modern elites valued constancy and immutability in the face of external events and objects, eighteenth-century elites began to value the opposite. According to a 1796 issue of *The Monthly Magazine*, at least in the late eighteenth century 'height of breeding was measured by delicacy of feeling, and no fine lady, or gentleman, was ashamed to be seen sighing over a pathetic story, or weeping at a deep-wrought tragedy.'[52]

For instance, in her article on sensibility and the American War of Independence, Sarah Knott has shown how both British *and* American officers (as against American common soldiers) publicly wept at the execution of Major André (Benedict Arnold's British accomplice). One American officer stated that he left the field 'in a flood of tears,' another wrote that the scene excited the 'compassion of every man of feeling and sentiment.'[53] Indeed, Knott argues that sensibility became a required characteristic of aspiring American officers, and a distinguishing mark from the coarse common soldiers. General Anthony Wayne wrote to the president of the Pennsylvania House of Assembly that gentlemen 'of Spirit and Sensibility [...] are the very men we want to render our arms formidable to our Enemy & Respectable to our friends.'[54]

It should be stressed though that the cult of sensibility praised sensitivity, not weakness. Sensitivity required strength, which was increasingly seen as bodily strength. The ideal sensitive person possessed a nervous system which was both sensitive *and* strong. This enabled the person to experience the world fully, but without being overpowered. People possessed of a sensitive but weak nervous system were in almost as great a predicament as insensitive brutes.

The second practical lesson taught by the cult of sensibility was that people should not only open themselves up to any experiences that came their way, but *actively* expand their range of sensations and emotions as far as possible. 'The more one feels,' argued Sensationist philosophers, 'the more fully one exists.'[55] The basic formula of the cult of sensibility thus reads as follows:

$$\text{sensibility} \times \text{experience} = \text{knowledge}$$

A person needed both sensibility and a variety of experiences in order to gain knowledge and increase his or her wisdom. Sharpening one's sensibility and seeking novel experiences therefore became the two most important exercises in the Sensationist quest for knowledge.

Experiencing new tastes, new sights, new smells, new emotions became a key to expanding one's horizons and wisdom. People began pursuing new, exciting, and "exotic" sensations for their own sake, and gave themselves liberty and encouragement to experience and express wider spectrums of emotions.

The painter J. M. W. Turner lashed himself to the mast of a ship in order to experience the ferocity of a snowstorm at sea. His experience resulted in the painting *Snowstorm with a Steamship*.[56] James Boswell often went to Tyburn to see criminals executed in order to investigate the experience both of the condemned persons and of himself. Henry Mackenzie in his *Man of Feeling* (1769) highlighted the wisdom that could be garnered from experiences of suffering: 'Is it that we delight in observing the effects of the stronger passions? for we are all *philosophers* in this respect; and it is perhaps among the spectators of Tyburn that the most genuine are to be found.'[57] Watching executions was, of course, a favorite European pastime since Roman times. Watching them in order to conduct first-hand philosophical investigations, however, was a novel phenomenon.

Travel too was hailed as a means for acquiring new experiences and therefore as a privileged means of education. It became so fashionable to travel in order to seek truth by experience that the model was even used by the author of a pornographic tale titled *An Account of Several Experiments Made by a Lady Who Had Adopted the System of Sympathy*. In this tale, a certain Florentine Lady

> reflected, that all sound Philosophy is founded upon Experiment; and that she might be at Liberty to try such Experiments as she thought requisite, she had Recourse to a Stratagem. She drest herself in Man's Clothes; and, attended only by her Woman in the same Disguise, made a Tour to *France*.

At Lyons the lady, disguised as an Italian Marquis, met a French officer. The officer invited "the Marquis" to share his bed. The lady was at first taken aback by the offer, but 'by the Dint of Philosophy [she] had surmounted the Timidity of her Sex.'[58] In Voltaire's *Candide*, the first sexual escapade of Candide and Cunégonde is similarly described as a philosophical experiment.[59]

The modern tourist, who sets out to experience new lands, new sights, and new cuisines, and who often breaks on tourist resorts the taboos he is forced to keep at home, is an heir to the cult of sensibility. Bungee-jumping and roller-coasters promise instant (and safe) experiences of fear. Backpackers often travel half way around the world in order to enjoy on their vacations from unfamiliar degrees of danger, destitution, and discomfort as much as from good food or beautiful sights. The memory of a 24-hour train trip in a second-class Indian train compartment, suffering from diarrhea and heat, is not infrequently the most exciting and exquisite tale such tourists take with them back home.[60]

The cult of sensibility had a darker side. Modern tourists are as much heirs to the libertine heroes of the marquis de Sade as to the sensitive souls of sentimental novels. Sade – a radical Sensationist and materialist who also served for several years as a junior officer in the French army – pursued Sensationist ideas to their logical conclusion. Sade wrote of men (and some women) who gave completely free rein to their pursuit of new sensations, emotions, and experiences. In his utopian castles of sensory extremes, upper class men raped, tortured, and killed their victims (of all ages and sexes), and were themselves subjected from time to time to rape and torture (mostly by extra-virile men), stopping short only of suicide. Any customary boundary set on sensory experiences – whether a moral, legal, or biological boundary – was for them an invitation for exploration. These libertines were Sensationist truth seekers on a quest, and their holy grail resided at the extremes of pain and pleasure. If scientists tortured animals for the sake of medical truth, why not torture people for the sake of philosophical truth?[61]

Sade would probably have recognized Ernst Jünger's veterans, made wise by killing and getting killed in the trenches of World War I, as direct descendants of his libertines. To this day, a distinct strand of militaristic culture presents war as a Sade-ist utopia, in which men get the opportunity to indulge in otherwise forbidden pleasures and pains, and thereby acquire forbidden knowledge.[62]

This section has stressed the rising importance of feeling and sensibility in eighteenth-century culture. It would be wrong, however, to conclude that reason and constancy were completely devalued. The eighteenth century was still the Age of Reason, as well as of sensibility. Even the most ardent adherents of the cult of sensibility regarded reason as vital. Whereas they made the inner voice of feeling ("the heart") the supreme judge of goals and values, translating those goals and values into effective action in the external world still relied heavily on reason. British and American officers may have openly wept for Major André, but in the war councils of General Clinton and General Washington they were still expected to speak their minds more than their hearts.[63]

Sensibility also has many sworn enemies, who sharply criticized it for its alleged irrationality.[64] Sensibility was often equated with 'emotional excess, moral degeneracy, and physical debilitation.'[65] In the religious arena Quakers, Shakers, and Methodists were all derided as irrational "enthusiasts."[66] In the political arena it was attacked from right and left alike. Some British conservatives in the 1790s equated sensibility with Jacobinism.[67] Proto-Marxist thinkers interested in social reform argued that only a rational analysis of social systems could bring about real change. The moral voices of sentiment merely placed presentable plasters on the wounds of society, without heeling them.[68]

Hence, we should beware of describing the late eighteenth century and early nineteenth century as an era ruled by feeling and sensibility. What we can safely say is that the era was ruled by *discussions* of sensibility, and that though sensibility did not dethrone reason, it did upset the overall cultural and political balance, raising the value of sensations and feelings. The cultural symphony of the Western world continued to be dominated by the voice of reason, but a new leitmotif of feeling was added. Often, the combination of the old voice of reason with this new leitmotif of feeling resulted in a new harmony, called "common sense." Common sense – as Thomas Paine christened his best-selling pamphlet (1776) – was the united voice of reason and feeling. Those who spoke for common *sense* condemned with equal vigor the sentimental excesses of "hysterical" women and religious enthusiasts, and the over-intellectualizations of ivory tower philosophers and dogmatic theologians. Samuel Johnson's gesture of kicking a stone in order to disprove Bishop Berkeley's Idealist philosophy is the equivalent of slapping the proverbial hysterical woman – it signals that we should not let our imagination *or* our reason carry us too far from our senses.

The new importance of feelings enabled even the humblest person to at least gain a hearing in the public arena on the basis of his or her personal feelings, even though many remained unconvinced by such passionate appeals. Armies continued to understand wars primarily in the rational language of military manuals, but for the first time common soldiers could compose alternative war narratives of personal experiences – and expect these narratives to be published and read. Again and again they would describe the numbing cold in the trenches and the stench of military hospitals, seeking to disprove by this appeal to common sensations the strategic and historical chimeras born from the minds of generals, politicians, and metaphysicians.

The novel of sensibility, the *Bildungsroman*, and the ideals of *Erlebnis* and *Bildung*[69]

In order to translate the abstract ideas of Sensationist philosophy into tangible terms, the cult of sensibility relied perhaps above all on the novel of sensibility and the *Bildungsroman*. The rise of the novel was one of the greatest cultural movements of the eighteenth century. By the late eighteenth century, over 70 percent of the books borrowed in German, British, and North American libraries were novels, and the novel became a major vehicle for educating literate people and acquainting them with new ideas and attitudes.[69] The novel of sensibility, which by the late eighteenth century spawned the *Bildungsroman*, was probably the most influential literary genre of the period. (It is worth noting that in 1785 Second Lieutenant Napoleon Bonaparte sketched out a sentimental novel in his free time.[70]) The crucial task of the novel was to show people what a sensible life actually looked like, day after day, year after year.[71]

The hero or heroine of these novels was almost always a naïve youth, who acquired knowledge by encountering a succession of different experiences. Wilhelm Dilthey, who is largely responsible for disseminating the term *Bildungsroman*, defined *Bildungsromane* in the following words:

> they all portray a young man [...] how he enters life in a happy state of naiveté seeking kindred souls, finds friendship and love, how he comes into conflict with the hard realities of the world, how he grows to maturity through diverse life-experiences, finds himself, and attains certainty about his purpose in the world.[72]

Sensibility on the part of the hero, and a rich spectrum of experiences – often provided by travel and calamity – were the key to the learning process and to the youth's eventual transformation into a wise and socially adept man or woman.

Travel narratives in which the hero encountered a succession of experiences and persons were nothing new. They were a staple of both medieval and early modern literature. However, in previous such narratives the hero set out to *test* his mettle and perform worthy deeds, and the focus was on external events (alternatively, as in the case of *Don Quixote*, the hero's travels were just an excuse for telling a string of secondary stories). The hero seldom underwent any significant process of inner change. Particularly in adventure narratives and chivalric romances the hero's chief characteristic was steadfastness and resistance to change. No matter what novel sensations he encountered – be they the most painful or joyful – the hero's mental control remained firm and his ideals and mentality relatively unchanged.

The unique feature of the novel of sensibility and the *Bildungsroman* was that the hero or heroine underwent profound changes, and that the narrative focused overwhelmingly on this inner process of change. External events were important mainly as catalysts for inner change. Following Sensationist ideas, in the *Bildungsroman* encounters with new sensations and emotions usually produced new ideas and changed the hero's mental configurations. Conversely, no serious mental change could occur without the prior input of external experiences.

In his *Versuch Über den Roman* (1774) Friedrich von Blanckenburg emphasized that the novel was superior to the epic because the latter described only external events whereas the former focused on the protagonist inner development (*Bildung*). Blanckenburg explained that 'every event in nature contributes something to the formation and development of our character' because it 'influences our thinking, and our thinking in turn has an effect in the next instance according to the idea received from it and merged into all its other ideas.' This complex process amounted to 'the shaping (*Bildung*) of our way of thought, to the formation of our entire being.' A good novel should describe 'how our manner of thinking and acting has been shaped into what it is through the influence of the events we have encountered.'[73] Blanckenburg further explained that

> The universe is arranged in such a way that a person cannot receive his education (*Bildung*) without passing through a variety of events. The poet must [...] capture this when he shapes his figure into a real person or wants to give us the inner history of a person.'[74]

Five years earlier Henry Mackenzie was busy writing *The Man of Feeling* (1769). He explained that his literary project consisted of 'introducing a man of sensibility into different scenes where his feelings might be seen in their effects.'[75] Ann Jessie Van Sant writes that for Yorick, the hero of Laurence Sterne's *A Sentimental Journey* (1768),

> The world [...] is an instrument for stirring his sensations. He goes on the road not to rescue widows and virgins but to watch them – and record his experiences. In his journey to see Maria, Yorick involves himself in the distress of the 'disordered maid,' in order to create

a psychological event in himself. After experiencing 'undescribable emotions' during the encounter with her, he can exclaim: 'I am positive I have a soul; nor can all the books with which the materialists have pester'd the world ever convince me of the contrary'.[76]

Elsewhere an exchange of snuff boxes between Yorick and Father Lorenzo becomes a complete drama, comparable to the epic encounters of Homeric and chivalric heroes, except that the adventure takes place 'in nerves, fibers, and blood vessels.'[77] In another scene, Yorick meets a woman and shakes her hand, describing the handshake in several paragraphs. Yorick explains that 'The pulsations of the arteries along my fingers pressing across hers, told her what was passing within me [...] in this interval, I must have made some slight efforts towards a closer compression of her hand, from a subtle sensation I felt in the palm of my own – not as if she was going to withdraw hers but as if she thought about it.'[78] Van Sant concludes that in the novels of sensibility 'not only is sensation the basic unit of experience; it replaces adventure as the basic unit of narrative.'[79]

The novels of sensibility and the *Bildungsromane* thus implanted two ideals of the greatest importance into late modern consciousness:

(1) *Erlebnis*: The English word "experience" has two distinct meanings. One meaning is practical, empirical knowledge gained by direct experiments, as, for example, when a scientist says that she knows by experience that a water molecule is composed of an atom of oxygen and two atoms of hydrogen. "Experience" in this sense is often contrasted with logical rationalizations, scriptural authority, religious dogma, and hearsay. The other meaning of experience is the lived moment of sensing and feeling something. In German, the word *Erlebnis* is reserved for this latter meaning.

Baconian scientists made experience in the sense of "experiment" a leading ideal of Western culture at least since the sixteenth century, depicting it as the most reliable source of scientific knowledge. Baconian narratives transformed the experiment into the basic building block of science. The progress of science, and the personal history of individual scientists, was conceived as a string of experiments, each resulting in some new piece of knowledge and each leading to further experiments. In order to make sense of the world, a scientist had to understand and narrate his experiments with the utmost clarity, establishing all the different factors and forces operating within the experiment, delineating its components and its boundaries in space and time.[80]

Thus in *Observations on the Sensibility and Irritability of the Parts of Men and Other Animals* (1768), Robert Whytt – a leading physiologist – described an experiment he conducted on a frog:

> I laid open the whole *abdomen* and *thorax* of a frog; and at 28 minutes past seven in the morning, immersed it in a turbid solution of *opium* [...] At forty minutes after seven, I turned the frog on its back, and observed its heart beating between ten and eleven times a minute. [Eight minutes later], Observing the heart without motion, I opened the *pericardium*; which producing no effect, I cut the heart out of the body, and laid it upon a plate, when it beat twice or thrice, and never after moved, although it was pricked once and again with a pin.[81]

Novels of sensibility and *Bildungsromane* have done a comparable service for *Erlebnis*, elevating it too to the status of a Western ideal, and presenting it too as a privileged source for knowledge. They identified units of experience rather than units of external action as the basic and most important building blocks of human lifestories, and they made the ability to clearly narrate and make sense of experiences the most important skill of authors, psychologists, and truth-seekers. It was no longer enough to merely tell what happened in the outside world and what different people did. It became necessary to untangle the experience thread by thread, paying particular attention to the moment-by-moment flow of sensations, emotions, and thoughts within the hero.[82] Sterne describes the exchange of snuff boxes between Yorick and Father Lorenzo with even more care and exactness than Whytt describes the dissection of the frog.

It is telling that nineteenth-century historians, in their search for a way to scientifically understand past humanity, have adopted the ideal of *Erlebnis* as a means. Wilhelm Dilthey in particular made *Erlebnis* the foundation of historical reason and of all attempts to understand human reality. *Erlebnis* was for him 'the "primordial cell" of the human-historical world and the basic empirical datum of the human sciences.'[83] He argued against the abstract philosophical systems of Kant and the British Empiricists alike. 'There is no real blood,' he wrote,

> flowing in the veins of the knowing subject fabricated by Locke, Hume, and Kant, but only the diluted juice of reason as mere mental activity. But dealing with the whole man in history and psychology led me to take the whole man – in the multiplicity of his powers: this willing-feeling-perceiving being – as the basis for explaining knowledge and its concepts.[84]

Elsewhere Dilthey emphasized that neither thought nor reason is the core of life, but rather 'the core of what we call life is instinct, feeling, passions, and volitions.'[85]

(2) *Bildung*: In an attuned person, the accumulation of lived experiences resulted in *Bildung*. *Bildung* meant an evolutionary process of inner change, leading from ignorance to enlightenment by means of undergoing experiences and learning from them. The full development of one's potential for self-knowledge and knowledge of the world through a large variety of intellectual, emotional, and bodily experiences became the highest aim of life, and narrating that development – one experience after another – became the master narrative of late modern lifestories.[86]

For instance, Wilehlm von Humboldt, one of the formulators of the *Bildung* ideal, thought that the aim of human life was 'a distillation of the widest possible experience of life into wisdom.'[87] Elsewhere he wrote that 'there is only one summit in life, to have taken the measure *in feeling* of everything human,'[88] and that 'He who can say to himself when he dies: "I have grasped and made into a part of my humanity as much of the world as I could", that man has reached fulfillment [...] In the higher sense of the word, he has really lived.'[89]

Humboldt's ambitions could be realized only if people pursued them as a life-long project. Note that such projects and such *Bildung* narratives are markedly different from many traditional narratives of enlightenment, in which people retire from the world and try to *minimize* their experiences in order to look inside themselves more attentively. Strict codes control the lives of Christian and Buddhist monks, purposely limiting the types and numbers of "experiences" they could have. Modern scholars and scientists fortify themselves inside their sterilized libraries and laboratories, seeking wisdom through learning and experiments, but not through experience. Like monastic codes, the ethical and professional codes of libraries, laboratories, and universities often forbid scholars to have any Romantic "experiences" within their walls. (In *Bildungsromane*, sexual affairs are amongst the most important and most enlightening experiences. Such affairs are forbidden to monks, and often seem "unprofessional" in strictly academic contexts.)

The most unfortunate and derided people in the era of *Bildung* have been people who due to one reason or the other encountered a very limited spectrum of experiences (e.g., monks),[90] or coarse people who are insensitive to the experiences that come their way and therefore cannot learn anything from them. Early modern military memoirs usually bore and alienate late modern readers because their authors seem to be extremely coarse and boorish men. Their lives have brought them into contact with awesome experiences, yet they seem to be completely insensitive to them. They are obsessive about narrating external facts, while paying almost no attention to *Erlebnis*. Their lifestories are consequently a dry catalog of events, without a trace of *Bildung*.

Boswell went to Tyburn to "experience" executions. In *Sentimental Journey*, Sterne transforms the varying pressure of a woman's handshake into a fully developed literary episode. What would they have thought of the marquis de Chouppes who had absolutely nothing to report about his first campaigns, battles, and injuries; or about Andrew Melville, who remained untouched by his near-execution in 1648, and who had nothing to record about his inner experience when he saw his would-be executioner loading the musket, taking aim, and pressing the trigger?

Romanticism, nature, and the sublime[92]

Romanticism is often considered a reaction against the over-rationalization of eighteenth-century Enlightenment. Traditional accounts of the Enlightenment discount the culture of sensibility, and depict the Enlightenment as a cult of pure reason, which believed that human reason can understand everything and accomplish anything. According to this account, Romanticism was a rebellion against this notion, which stressed and celebrated the limitations of reason.

Things are not so clear-cut. The Enlightenment itself contained a sharp critique of reason, in the shape of the culture of sensibility. To a considerable extent, Romanticism merely developed the ideas of sensibility further, and can thus be seen as an offshoot of the Enlightenment rather than a rebellion against it.

The culture of sensibility argued, as we saw, that

$$\text{knowledge} = \text{sensibility} \times \text{experience}$$

There was a hitch in this formula, however. If one failed to experience things "authentically," and if the experience was "contaminated" by cultural preconceptions, the result would be contaminated and inferior knowledge. Many Sensationist philosophers illustrated the process of sensory enlightenment by the fable of the awakening statue. In this fable, a marble statue comes to life and begins to experience sensations. Since the statue has no memory and no cultural baggage, its sensations are pure experience, and whatever knowledge it gains is similarly pure. Unfortunately, such a *tabula rasa* could not be found in real life. As postmodernist studies emphasize, every moment of lived experiences is culturally constructed, and reflects cultural preconceptions as much as physical reality. This was obvious already in the eighteenth century. Sensationists were consequently confronted by a severe problem: When sensitive persons tried to get attuned to their sensations and emotions, how could they be sure that they were not actually getting attuned to their own cultural constructions? How could they be sure that instead of receiving pure wisdom, they were not strengthening old cultural prejudices? When Max Piccolomini asked Thekla von Wallenstein to allow her heart to decide his fate, how could he be sure that her "heart" was not in fact her father's reason?

The Romantics identified nature as the remedy. As O'Neal explains, already in the high days of the Enlightenment, 'writers invariably identified nature with an original experience whose truth was authentic and not based on anything that might be considered artificial or abstract.'[93] Nature had no ideas. It was pure experience. It was 'the source of intelligence, the guarantee of reason, the home of wisdom and goodness.'[94] People who lived in the state of nature – such as the famous noble savages – were completely free from culture's hindrances, and were completely attuned to their inner natural selves.

Romanticism accordingly created a powerful variation on the basic theme of *Bildung*, in which nature played a prominent role. The crucial experiences of Romantic *Bildung* often involved travels to "nature" and encounters with "nature." As long as one lived in the midst of the city, in palaces, salons, and coffeehouses, the chatter and clatter of culture prevented one from connecting to one's inner natural wisdom, in the shape of sensations and emotions. The solution was to go out to the woods and the mountains. There one had to remain connected to one's sensations in order to survive; and one was drawn by natural phenomena away from the harmful influences of culture.[95] By connecting to "nature" without, one was able to get in tune with "nature" within, and hear what Charles Taylor called 'the inner voice of nature' over and above the cacophony of decadent culture. This 'inner voice of nature' in its turn became the source for ethics, aesthetics, politics, and art.[96]

Not any natural phenomenon would do, though. A unique class of phenomena, labeled "sublime," was identified as holding the all-important key that unlocked the mysteries of outer and inner nature. The idea of the sublime was developed in eighteenth-century aesthetics, most notably by Edmund Burke,[97] Immanuel Kant,[98] and Friedrich Schiller – who like La Mettrie was a regimental doctor for a while.[99]

The sublime was most often contrasted with the beautiful. A beautiful phenomenon was, for example, the geometrically arranged gardens of Versailles, or the geometrically arranged battlefields of eighteenth-century paintings. The symmetrical arrangement of the objects made it easy for viewers to grasp them, and fitted exactly to one's ingrained preconceptions. It thereby gave viewers a pleasant feeling of mastery and security.

A sublime phenomenon, in contrast, overwhelmed the viewers' perception and broke their preconceptions. It had no clearly defined boundaries, it seemed to obey no known rules, and its power seemed without measure. It often threatened one's sense of self-preservation, inspiring awe, terror, and a feeling of helplessness.[100]

Philosophers had different hair-splitting theories about what actually happened during a sublime experience. Burke, following the traditional stance of Longinus, believed that when a person encounters a sublime phenomenon, the resulting sensations completely overpower the mind, and the normal thinking process grounds to a halt. All the mind's preconceptions and normal cognitive schemata are incapable of handling and interpreting the overwhelming experience. All the motions of the mind 'are suspended [...] the mind is so entirely filled with its object, that it cannot entertain any other, nor by consequence reason on that object which employs it. Hence arises the great power of the sublime, that far from being produced by them, it anticipates our reasonings.'[101] Everything one ever knew is, at least for that precious moment, suspended.

Kant and Schiller argued that the sublime is a two-stage experience. In the first stage, one is indeed overwhelmed and astounded by the experience. But only our imagination and our sensuous nature, which cannot grasp and master the experience, are overwhelmed. Our reason can still function. And when our reason realizes that it is still functioning and still able to make free choices without the help of the imagination and in the face of overwhelming physical forces, it is a moment of spiritual triumph and of intense delight. Humans discover that despite the fragility of their body and the narrowness of their imagination, their reason and their ethical judgment are divine sparks that are superior even to the breathtaking vistas of the Alps, to the raging ocean, or to the terrors of the battlefield. In sublime moments humans realize their true nature: physical dependence coupled with complete rational and moral independence.[102]

Despite the differences between them, Burke, Kant, and Schiller all agreed that whereas the beautiful encourages complacent illusions by strengthening our preconceptions, truth resides in sublime encounters. Wordsworth would later christen these encounters "spots of time," and James Joyce would call them "epiphanies." For Burke and for the Romantics who distrusted reason's ability to grasp the totality of truth, these epiphanies were rare windows of opportunity in which the barriers of both culture *and* reason were let down, and a person was fully open to higher states of awareness and to new inspiration and knowledge.

For Kant and Schiller, who still believed in the supremacy of reason, sublime epiphanies were also rare windows of opportunity in which the barriers of the imagination were destroyed, and naked reason faced the world and could finally grasp its own overwhelming power and the world's true nature, free from the limits imposed by our weak imagination. In *On the Sublime* Schiller argues that the beautiful imprisons people within the sensuous world, softening them, and causing their innermost moral commitments to decay. But a single sublime experience may break open this soothing spiderweb, and give people back their moral freedom. He compares the beautiful to the goddess Calypso who enchanted Odysseus, and would have imprisoned him forever on her island, if a sublime impression sent from the gods did not awaken him to his true duty and destiny.

The differences between the Burkean and Kantian sublime had all kinds of philosophical, artistic, and political implications, but they were lost on most ordinary people, including most soldiers. What people did grasp was that during extreme experiences cultural preconceptions stop functioning, "contaminated" knowledge disappears, and one discovers pure and superior truths which remain otherwise inaccessible.[103]

European savants and ordinary people alike began to actively pursue such sublime experiences, and to publish accounts of the resulting epiphanies and of the truths they uncovered. For example, in 1798 Helen Maria Williams traveled to the Alps, where she saw a mountain cataract 'rushing with wild impetuosity over those broken unequal rocks.' She described the resulting experience in the following terms:

> never, never can I forget the sensations of that moment! when with a sort of annihilation of self, with every part impression erased from my memory, I felt as if my heart were bursting with emotions too strong to be sustained. – Oh, majestic torrent! which hath conveyed a new image of nature to my soul, the moments I have passed in contemplating thy sublimity will form an epoch in my short span![104]

In *Les Rêveries du promeneur solitaire* (1782), Jean-Jacque Rousseau wrote in similarly ecstatic terms about a brush he had with death. As he was walking in the countryside around Paris, a large dog came running by, and knocked the old philosopher to the ground. Rousseau hit his head on the hard surface, and for a moment lost consciousness. As he came back to his senses,

> I glimpsed the sky, a few stars, and a patch of greenery. This first sensation was enchanting. I was aware of that and no more. I drifted into consciousness at that moment and felt as if I, with my unsubstantial existence, were breathing life into all the objects I could see. Wholly in the present, I remembered nothing; I had no clear notion of my individuality, not the slightest idea what had happened to me; I could not tell who I was or where I was; I felt neither pain, nor fear, nor anxiety. I watched the blood flow out of me as if it were a running brook, without once thinking that the blood belonged to me. I felt blissful rapture pervade every vein in me, which, each time I recall it, compares to nothing else in the scale of familiar pleasures.[105]

Rousseau found his accident so enrapturing because it enabled him to be completely absorbed in nature, without any cultural inhibitions. For a split second, he was a pure child of nature, like the fabled marble statue waking into consciousness.

The truths revealed by such epiphanies came in all shapes and colors. Some authors described epiphanies as moments of religious ecstasy, others as moments of poetic inspiration, and still others as moments of metaphysical or ideological revelation. An Alpine cliff could 'awe an atheist into belief' according to Thomas Gray (1739).[106] The sublime view from the Monte Sacro in Rome inspired Simon Bolivar to envisage the liberation of South America. Burke believed that the humbling experience of the sublime, which confronted people with their finitude and their limitations, would give rise to 'a strong sense of humility and sympathy' which would encourage us 'to relieve our pain by relieving that of others.'[107] The late modern tradition of Pacifist Materialism, represented, for example, by Heller's *Catch-22* and Scarry's *The Body in Pain*, is heir to this Burkean idea.

Though the truths revealed by sublime epiphanies were diverse, the common assumption was that a truth revealed in such a manner was superior to truths which were reached by any other means. The sublime was the Romantic counterpart of religious revelation. It was, however, secular in essence, for it depended on encounters with immanent reality in the shape of mountains or storms, rather than on encounters with a transcendental reality. The sublime may be seen as the vacuum left in the field of human knowledge once the Enlightenment removed God from the scene.

The rise of the Romantic sublime had a revolutionary impact on the image and culture of war. In discussing the sublime, scholars tend to give prime of place to natural phenomena such as mountains. Yet war fitted the definition of the sublime far better than mountains.[108] It is particularly noteworthy that Burke, Kant, and Schiller grounded the sublime in the sense of self-preservation, arguing that terror and fear of death are at the bottom of the sublime experience.[109] Obviously, a fierce cannonade is far more terrible and threatening than an Alpine view. John Shipp writes about the storming of Bhurtpoor (1805):

[The fort's] ramparts seemed like some great volcano vomiting tremendous volumes of fiery matter; the roaring of the great guns shook the earth beneath our feet; their small arms seemed like the rolling of ten thousand drums; and their war trumpets rent the air asunder [...] The scene was awfully grand, and must have been sublimely beautiful to the distant spectator.[110]

(Shipp was only a rough uneducated soldier, not a philosopher of aesthetics. Hence his oxymoronic reference to the "sublimely beautiful" must be excused).

In his *Critique of Judgment*, Kant himself chose to illustrate the appeal of the sublime by noting that in all human societies, from the most savage to the most civilized, the sublime figure of the brave soldier is 'the object of the greatest admiration.' Kant further affirmed that aesthetically the general is a more attractive figure than the statesman, and that

War itself [...] has something sublime about it, and gives nations that carry it on [...] a stamp of mind only the more sublime the more numerous the dangers to which they are exposed, and which they are able to meet with fortitude. On the other hand, a prolonged peace favours the predominance of a mere commercial spirit, and with it a debasing self-interest, cowardice, and effeminacy, and tends to degrade the character of the nation.[111]

In the following two centuries, war has increasingly been described as a sublime experience. Countless war narratives, knowingly or unknowingly, modeled themselves on Rousseau's encounter with the Parisian dog. Note, for instance, the similarities between that encounter and Shawn Nelson's description of the battle of Mogadishu (1993):

he had never felt so completely alive. [...] In those hours on the street he had not been Shawn Nelson, he had no connection to the larger world, no bills to pay, no emotional ties, nothing. He had just been a human being staying alive from one nano-second to the next, drawing one breath after another.[112]

The resemblance to Prince Andrei's epiphany on the battlefield of Austerlitz is even more striking. Did Tolstoy plagiarize Rousseau? It would be extremely ironic if the most famous combat epiphany of the late modern era is in fact modeled on an unfortunate clash between a large dog and an old Parisian gentleman out for a walk.

Andrew Melville did not describe his near-execution in 1648 as a moment of epiphanic revelation because he was unfamiliar with either Burkean or Kantian conceptions of the sublime. From around 1740 onward soldiers such as Shawn Nelson and Leo Tolstoy increasingly recognized the sublime nature of war. They accordingly described war as something that released them from their cultural preconceptions and offered them a glimpse of pure truth – whatever it may be.

Obviously, most late modern memoirists did not read Burke or Kant. Yet they imbibed Burkean and Kantian conceptions of the sublime through myriad intermediaries. To give one example, millions of European boys who joined the Boy Scouts or the *Wandervogel* were taken to the mountains to have sublime experiences, and were usually told in no uncertain terms what kinds of revelation to expect.

* * *

We began this discussion with La Mettrie's stark materialism and, after covering a very wide spectrum of opinions and works, have ended it with the early nineteenth-century Romantics, some of whom were extreme idealists who denied the very existence of matter (e.g., Fichte), or at least argued for the superiority of soul and mind over body and matter. The bond that nevertheless unites this entire spectrum from La Mettrie to Fichte is the importance given to sensations, emotions, and external natural influences as sources for knowledge.

We should not be led astray by the Romantic enthusiasm for "soul" and "spirit." This enthusiasm was in fact a close relative of La Mettrie's materialism. For the soul admired by the Romantics was the sensitive soul of the poet, and the mind they worshipped was the passionate and intuitive mind of the genius, not the calculating rational mind of Cartesian philosophy or the transcendent spark of Christian theology.[113] Nowhere is this clearer than in the growing cult of the military genius.

When describing Napoleon's genius, Clausewitz wrote that at the battle of Lodi (1796)

> he was drunk with victory, by which I mean he was in that elevated state of hope, courage, and confidence by which the soul raises itself above the mundane calculations of reason – he sees his opponent running away in a state of confused terror – and in that moment there is almost nothing he cannot do! [...] This enthusiasm represents an elevation of spirit and feeling above calculation. War is not waged by reason alone and action in war is not just a matter of arithmetic. It is the whole man who wages war.[114]

Feeling above calculation. How different is this from Parker's description of Marlborough as a perfect calculating machine? Granted, Clausewitz still places the soul at the pinnacle, but his soul is something that feels and that is connected to "the whole man." It is clearly different from the Cartesian computer.

The supremacy of feeling over reason is also evident in the writing of the Russian officer Denis Davidov. Davidov explained the failure of General Bennigsen to win the battle of Eylau (1807) in the following terms:

> Calculation and prudence were the hallmarks of our general's thinking and planning, the logical outcome of a sound, precise mind. But although equal to the task of grappling with minds of a similar type, he was not up to dealing with flashes of genius, sudden events which defy foresight, and touches of inspiration.[115]

Davidov further explained that

> In order to take advantage of such opportunities [...] it is not enough to have a thorough knowledge of one's craft, to show a determined spirit or possess a sharp mind. None of this is of any avail without inspiration – that inexplicable impulse which is as instantaneous as an electric spark, and which is as essential to the poet as it is to the military commander. To Napoleon and Suvorov, inspiration was innate, just as it was to poets such as Pindar and Mirabeau, with their command over words.[116]

Gone is the commander as chess-player – enter the military artist.

It is hard to exaggerate the importance of this change. For Descartes and Maurice of Nassau feeling was a base bodily function, whereas the primary occupation of mind was thinking. For the Romantics –

including Romantic officers – the primary function of the mind/soul became feeling. The new military genius created by Clausewitz, Davidov, and others was a genius of sensibility rather than of calculation. The supreme quality of this genius was not an ability to plan and foresee everything, but rather to remain attuned to the minutest changes in the battlefield, to "sense" or "smell" the battle, and feel what is the exact moment in which, say, to order an attack.

In consequence, the wide gulf that previously separated "I feel" from "I think," and "heart" from "soul," all but disappeared. In many cases – especially amongst the unsophisticated rank and file of Napoleonic armies – body had simply taken over soul, appropriating even its name. People such as Clausewitz kept talking about the superiority of soul or mind over body, without realizing that what they call "soul" is what their grandparents had called "body!"

Even the rationalist tendencies evident in Kant's and Schiller's analysis of the sublime still gave a vital role to the body and its sensations. Though Kantian sublime experiences were supposed to result in the eventual triumph of reason, this could be accomplished only by passing through the crucible of sensory experiences. Whereas Descartes was able to "discover" the supremacy of reason enclosed within a well-heated room, Schiller's Prometheus – the sublime Romantic hero *par excellence* – could reach the same conclusion only when he was tied up to a remote mountain peak in the Caucasus and assaulted by a terrifying vulture. Reason's triumph for Descartes was the conclusion of a rational debate. For Schiller, it was the conclusion of a sublime *sensory* experience.

We can conclude our own investigation by highlighting the crucial difference between methods of inquiry and the inquiry's results. Thinkers in the eighteenth and early nineteenth century reached all kinds of conclusions about the relationship between mind, soul, body, and matter. Many still argued for the supremacy of soul or mind. However, in their *method* of investigation even the adherents of mind gave unprecedented importance to sensory experiences. We can imagine, say, La Mettrie and Fichte arguing whether reason is superior to the sensations, and whether reason is capable of functioning under extreme conditions such as those of battle. Such arguments had been going on for millennia. The novelty of the age of sensibility was that a common soldier who overheard the two philosophers could feel he had the full support of his culture to dismiss their reasoning as idle chatter, and to recount his own battlefield experiences as a superior source for truth. Indeed, there was a good chance that the philosophers themselves were bound by their own logic to respect his views. Compared to that momentous change, whether the soldier's views upheld the supremacy of reason or the supremacy of the sensations was of incidental importance.

5
The Rise of the Common Soldier

Common soldiers begin to think

The culture of sensibility made a deep impact on the military sphere. One of its most important and enduring contributions involved the common soldiers. Just as sensibility gave a tremendous boost to the status of sensations and emotions and handed them a significant part to play in the thinking process, so in the military sphere sensibility gave a boost to the status of common soldiers and helped give them a role in the military thinking process. In order to appreciate this, we should take another look at the situation of common soldiers in old regime armies.

In no era of Western history was the status and image of the common soldier lower than in the seventeenth century and early eighteenth century. This resulted from a vicious triple-bind.

First, the leading military fantasy of that era was the Cartesian army: a machine made of mindless automatons, whose every movement is controlled by the single rational mind of a Great Captain. The perfect soldier of this fantasy was completely devoid of thought and initiative. This fantasy was fueled to a large extent by fear of its nightmarish shadow. Monarchs, commanders, and the civilian population still remembered the mutinous and rapacious hordes of the Thirty Years War and the sixteenth century, which usually made war serve their own ends and interests at the expense of their paymasters and their taxpayers.

Secondly, the vast majority of seventeenth- and eighteenth-century common soldiers came from amongst the poorest and most despised members of society. Many were forced into the army against their will, others were tricked by means of alcohol and false promises, and not a few were literally kidnapped by press gangs. Most (though not all) of those who still joined willingly did so because they had few alternative means to feed and cloth themselves. Military commanders – who came from the upper strata of society – tended to look down on their soldiers, and expected the very worst from them. They saw them as coarse creatures, devoid of the finer qualities of mind and intellect, and full of brutal urges and peasants' cunning. The only initiatives they were thought capable of were to distort and disobey orders, desert, mutiny, skulk, loot, rape, and get drunk.[1] It did not improve matters that many soldiers were foreigners who owed no national loyalty to their army and commanders, and who could hardly care less about the political outcome of the war.[2]

Saint-Germain, the French minister of war, said in 1779 that 'armies must inevitably be composed of the filth of the nation, and everything which is useless and harmful to society.'[3] Another well-placed commentator wrote about recruitment to Maria Theresa's army that

> We should not allow ourselves to be blinded by delusions about "love of country" or "inclination toward military service". If we take the trouble to investigate the most important impulses which bring the lads to the free recruiting table, we shall find that they are things like drunkenness, a frenzy of passions, love of idleness, a horror of any useful trade, a wish to escape from parental discipline, inclination toward debauchery, an imaginary hope of untrammeled freedom, sheer desperation, the fear of punishment after some sordid crime, or however else you care to define the motives of worthless people like these.[4]

This widespread opinion, and the military policies it bred, was a self-fulfilling prophecy. Recruits behaved as was expected from them, and self-respecting "honest" men almost never enlisted in the first place. Even if a military thinker wanted to give more room in his schemes to the free initiative of the soldiers, prevailing views on the abilities of these men would have rendered such a scheme unpalatable.

Military culture thus produced two dominant images: The ideal soldier was an unthinking automaton. The real soldier was a rather creative criminal. The problem facing commanders and military educators was how to transform criminals into automatons. Here we come across the decisive third factor in the vicious circle of old regime military culture: contemporary ideas of education.

In the early modern era, it was commonly believed that education had its limits. A person was born with innate ideas, tendencies, and intellectual abilities, and no amount of education could overcome that.

Moreover, it was believed that mind was superior to body, and that it was consequently far more difficult to shape minds than to shape bodies. Military education was based on these assumptions, and tried to transform criminals into automatons by means of drill and discipline.

Drill was a profoundly pessimistic form of education. No matter how brutal the drill-masters of Maurice, Marlborough, and Frederick were, they had no illusions that they could completely erase the recruit's past identity and then build him anew from scratch. It was assumed that despite all the drill and disciplinary measures, the soldiers' old identity will always lurk just beneath the surface waiting for its opportunity. Drill and discipline were meant only to keep this innate monster chained, and impose a superficial military identity on top of it.[5] When it came to intellectual abilities, the drill-masters had an even grimmer outlook. The vices of the soldiers could perhaps be kept in check, but what could be done about their innate stupidity? Not much, except make them blindly obey the orders of their more intelligent superiors.

Old regime armies had to pay a very high price for their Cartesian ideals. In major field battles they functioned relatively well. They functioned even better during regular sieges, which were often conducted with Newtonian precision.[6] During these major actions, old regime armies came closer than any armies in history to the "chess game" model, enabling their commanders to move regiments and companies about like so many chess pieces. Yet once they stepped off the chess board, things became awry. It was almost impossible to execute their complicated drills in rough terrain such as woods, marshes, and hills, or during night-time and under adverse weather conditions. Like physicists who try to ignore friction by solving a theoretical problem in "frictionless conditions," eighteenth-century drill-masters did their best to ignore the friction of war. They built "frictionless" parade grounds on which to train their soldiers, and almost never exercised them under realistic conditions, for instance in woody hills.[7] When the time came for combat, commanders tried to adopt a similar approach. Since their troops could not execute their parade-ground maneuvers in rough terrain, commanders did their best to avoid fighting in rough terrain, which obviously had far-reaching operational and strategic implications. Heinrich von Bülow sarcastically remarked about this parade-ground mentality that drill ceased to be a preparation for combat, and became 'something complete within itself, in the sense of Goethe's and Schiller's aesthetic principles. It has its own purpose. Its purpose is to shine on the parade-ground ... "Will you dogs keep in step!" would have been the command even during surprise attacks at night.'[8]

The operational abilities of old regime armies were further crippled by their fear of desertion and insubordination.[9] Commanders worried that without the close supervision of officers, many soldiers would skulk or desert, and the rest would be unable to function effectively.[10] They were consequently very reluctant to allow their troops to march or fight in open order and in rough terrain, and restricted the use of scouting and foraging parties. In 1707 Prince Eugene ordered that any soldier found more than a hundred paces away from the army on the march, or more than a thousand away from camp, should be hanged.[11]

Frederick the Great believed that it was 'one of the most essential duties of Generals who command armies or detachments, to prevent desertions.' In order to prevent desertion, he gave commanders the following instructions: Avoid night marches. When the infantry crosses woods, send patrols of hussars to the right and left of the column. Do not encamp too close to woods or forests, unless sufficient reasons necessitate it. When camping in any place, send hussars to patrol the country round about. At night, a strong guard of elite loyal soldiers should be placed around the camp. In any case, never let soldiers wander by themselves. Strictly forbid the soldiers to quit the ranks during march, and severely punish marauders.[12] Elsewhere Frederick wrote that 'For my own part, I am determined never to attack by night, on account of the confusion which darkness necessarily occasions, and because the major part of the soldiery require the eye of their officers, and the fear of punishments, to induce them to do their duty.'[13] Frederick's instructions greatly hampered military operations, particularly at night and in rough terrain. It is telling that Prussian light cavalrymen had to be diverted from reconnaissance missions to watching over their own comrades.[14]

Paret explains that

[the] fear of laxness and desertion, of seeing the tight formations unravel into clusters of possibly willing but necessarily ineffective individuals...made it difficult to exploit a victory once it had been won....Disciplinary and tactical demands not only stood in the way of achieving decisive results in battle, but acted as a retarding element throughout the campaign. They handicapped reconnaissance, precluded improvisation, favored systematic rather than rapid movement, and placed the heaviest of burdens on the supply and transportation system.[15]

Consequently, in any operation that involved moving and fighting in open order, with small groups of soldiers and individual men acting independently, old regime armies were at a decided disadvantage. All their operations – from foraging and scouting, through counterinsurgency warfare, to exploiting victories in set-piece battles – were severely handicapped.

In actuality, old regime armies were often forced to rely to some extent on the initiative of their common soldiers. A researcher who would put aside the rare spectacle of Blenheim and focus instead on the guerrilla and counterinsurgency warfare of the Camisard rebellion would encounter many thinking common soldiers.[16] However, these facts were ignored in old regime military culture, and had little influence on military theory or on the cultural image and political power of the soldier. To the age-old question at the heart of military theory – how to maneuver soldiers in a disciplined way? – old regime military culture had a firm answer: Drill would ensure maneuverability, and harsh external supervision would ensure discipline.

Before leaving the armies of the old regime, it is pertinent to address one common misunderstanding. The difficulties that old regime armies suffered from were largely due to lack of initiative, not lack of motivation. Old regime soldiers – after being properly trained – were often highly motivated, not only by fear and greed, but also by professional pride, *esprit de corps*, small unit cohesion, personal honor, masculinist ideals, and occasionally by patriotism and even religious fervor. As T. Blanning noted, old regime armies 'were capable of feats of heroism, both individual and collective, which cannot be explained in terms of iron discipline making the soldiers fear their officers more than the enemy.'[17]

Yet old regime commanders and old regime military theory made a very clear distinction between motivation and initiative, which influenced old regime military practices. Even when commanders recognized that soldiers could be highly motivated and could act courageously, they were reluctant to trust in their initiative. First, it was believed that even highly motivated soldiers did not possess the intelligence needed to make independent decisions. Secondly, it was feared that once soldiers were given an opportunity to think, their innate wickedness would rise to the surface and cause them to act in non-virtuous ways. The same soldier who would bravely storm an enemy position when blindly obeying orders, may well desert if he was asked to make up his own mind (as we shall see in the following chapter, Ulrich Bräker charged bravely with his comrades at the battle of Lobositz, but deserted as soon as he was left to his own devices).

This is something we find hard to grasp today, because in our minds, motivation and initiative are two sides of the same coin. Once the former is secured, the latter is taken for granted. In this, as in so much else, we are heirs to the revolutionary military ideas of the late eighteenth century, and at odds with early modern military ways of thinking.

The revolution in military education

The era of the common soldier dawned toward the end of the eighteenth century, and went hand-in-hand with one of the greatest military revolutions of the modern age. During the Napoleonic era, coercion was replaced by cooptation as the main method of training and employing soldiers, which released immense new sources of energy for the use of armies.

Old regime armies assumed that most of the personal energy of each soldier – his intelligence, resourcefulness, cunning – was a dangerous source of trouble that would forever endanger the army and would always have to be kept in check. Consequently, old regime armies not only wasted a large part of their energy on controlling and supervising their soldiers, but could tap only a very limited part of the soldiers' initiative and energy. In contrast, Napoleonic armies assumed that this very same energy – the intelligence and resourcefulness of the soldiers – could be coopted and made to serve the army's aims. Accordingly, Napoleonic armies needed to waste a far smaller amount of energy on controlling and supervising their soldiers, while tapping far more of the soldiers' initiative and energy.

What made it possible to replace coercion by cooptation? The following pages cannot provide an in-depth answer to this question, which is one of the most important and most difficult questions of modern military history. There was nothing obvious or inevitable about this change. In the early modern era, Western armies followed an opposite trajectory, and there were good historical reasons to fear that any relaxation in hierarchical military control might result in a return to the anarchical days of the sixteenth century. What the following pages do highlight are the cultural factors that induced contemporaries to replace coercion by cooptation, and that *contributed* to the outstanding success of this experiment. Whether these factors tell the entire story is, however, doubtful, and a full explanation of this momentous change must await a future research.

On a cultural level, it is clear that the replacement of coercion by cooptation in armies was connected to a general revolution in education that was itself part and parcel of the culture of sensibility. By emphasizing that all knowledge came from sensory experiences, the culture of sensibility opened amazing new vistas of education. There were no innate ideas, tendencies, and intellectual abilities. Everything in the mind had got there from the senses, and was nothing but the product of past experiences. Ergo, humans *of all classes* were in essence blank slates (*tabula rasa*), and 'L'éducation peut tout' – education can do anything, in Helvétius's famous words.[18] The potential of every human being – a king or a pauper – was not determined at his or her birth, and was essentially unlimited. Napoleon expressed this idea in military garb when he said that "every soldier carries the marshal's baton in his knapsack."[19]

This Sensationist *credo* became the cornerstone of numerous educational campaigns. In almost every field attempts were made to "educate," "reform," and "perfect" children, peasants, workers, criminals, vagabonds, lunatics, and prostitutes. The advent of the Romantic movement did not turn back this rising tide of educational utopianism. In theory, education was the one field in which the Romantics should have made a clean break with the Sensationists. No idea was more alien to the Romantics than that of the *tabula rasa*. They emphasized the unfathomable natural depths of the human psyche, and portrayed Man as a sack full of seeds rather than a blank slate. In practical terms, however, Romantic educational ideas were very similar to Sensationist ideas. Both stood in opposition to the old authoritarian views according to which humans were born with innate tendencies and abilities, from which they could not diverge. Though the Romantics agreed that humans were born with a particular potential, they believed that the potential of all humans was immense and unfathomable, and that the seeds of this potential could not germinate and grow without the help of external experiences.

J. Z. Hahn, the great Saxon educational thinker, wrote in 1800 as follows:

Who can determine with certainty what fate has firmly decided? Just because someone is born into a lower class can I say that fate has placed him into that low estate and thus limited his measure of enlightenment?... Nature knows no social classes according to which she distributed her gifts and abilities among mankind. [Consequently] wisdom and higher education must not be made into a privilege of certain levels of society... every breast harbors feelings which, if they are nurtured, developed, made conscious, are vitalized and ennobled by advanced education, can ripen into the most glorious deeds...The powers and abilities of intelligent creatures should be developed as fully as possible.[20]

Lieutenant Christian Nagel wrote about the way he trained and educated the men of his Jäger company that 'even in the coarsest man there always glows a spark by means of which, through breath or storm, the spirit is kindled.'[21]

Thus the Romantic "sack full of seeds" was surprisingly similar to the Sensationist *tabula rasa*. Both gave unlimited opportunities for experience to educate and reform humans. They differed only in the way they explained the power of experience. For Sensationists, educational experiences "created" new qualities ex nihilio. For Romantics, educational experiences merely cultivated pre-existing seeds. (It is much like arguing whether a marble slab is a *tabula rasa* out of which an artist can sculpt anything he likes, or whether it already contains numerous possible sculptures, out of which the artist can choose to uncover one).

Both Sensationists and Romantics also shared similar views about the nature of educational methods. Because they believed that every person could be cultivated to achieve impressive results, they rejected "pessimistic" methods which involved brutal discipline and learning by rote, and instead emphasized the importance of comprehension, independent judgment, and more humane treatment of the pupils (here the contribution of Locke, Basedow, Herder, Pestalozzi, and Rousseau is particularly conspicuous).[22]

The new belief in the unlimited power of education began to spill into the military sphere from the middle of the eighteenth century.[23] The second half of the century witnessed the blooming of the Military Enlightenment, the publication of quite a few military periodicals, and the appearance of numerous military academies for senior officers and of regimental schools for junior officers, NCOs, and common soldiers.[24] Several armies even established schools for the children of common soldiers.[25]

More importantly, the new ideas of education began to be applied to the military training of soldiers. In the 1760s the Welsh military thinker Henry Humphrey Evans Lloyd was one of the first to undertake a systematic study of military psychology. He started from the Sensationist maxim that 'Fear of, and an aversion to pain, and the desire for pleasure, are the spring and cause of all actions, both in man and other species of animals.'[26] He then explained how a general could manipulate the motivation of his soldiers, so that 'he becomes entirely master of their inclinations and disposes of their forces with unlimited authority.'[27] That is, mastery of bodily movements through drill was replaced in Lloyd's Sensationist scheme by mastery of mental inclinations through education and manipulation.

In 1798 Georg Heinrich von Berenhorst published his influential *Reflections on the Art of War*.[28] Berenhorst argued that in war the motivation of the common soldiers counted for far more than their drill or even the intellectual abilities of their officers, and that precise drill and brutal discipline should therefore be replaced by a humane system of training aimed to inflame the soldiers with an unbeatable fighting-spirit.[29]

Colonel von Tschammer, Clausewitz's regimental commander, founded in the 1790s schools for both the soldiers' children and for the junior officers and NCOs of his regiment. He believed that 'the soldier should not stand apart from the general progress of civilization' and that 'the primary function of education was not the acquisition of knowledge but the development of judgment, without which the soldier was only an animal. Courage and coolness...result from a healthy self-confidence, which in turn is the product of education and experience.'[30]

Clausewitz himself expounded similar views. In *On War* (1832) he continually emphasized that war is governed by psychological factors and cannot be reduced to the mathematical precision of the parade ground, and that consequently the spirit of the army counts for more than its proficiency in drill.[31] Already in 1809 Clausewitz wrote in a letter to Johann Gottlieb Fichte that the 'true spirit of war seems to me to lie in mobilizing the energies of every individual in the army to the greatest possible extent, and in infusing him with bellicose feelings, so that the fire of war spreads to all elements of the army.'[32]

Clausewitz, a deeply Romantic thinker, speaks about mobilizing pre-existing energies, whereas the Sensationist Lloyd spoke of external manipulation. However, both agree on a new ideal of military education. Though most recruits were still "the dregs of society," the mind of these dregs was malleable. If you exposed even a coarse and ignorant peasant boy to the right experiences, there was no limit to what you could produce from him. By a proper course of physical, mental, and ideological education, virtuous qualities could be either implanted or cultivated even in the "dregs of society." The brute common soldier could be transformed into a virtuous and even intelligent being. And once an army was composed of virtuous and intelligent beings the basic problem of how to maneuver soldiers in a disciplined way could be solved in a radically new fashion. Maneuverability could be based less on drill and more on intelligent personal initiative. Discipline could be based less on harsh external supervision and more on internal commitment and understanding. In short, cooptation could replace coercion, and soldiers could then be given greater room for independent action, without fear that they would desert or act as vicious and stupid oafs.[33]

Accordingly, in the late eighteenth century military training began to change. Boot camp was born. By the careful application of particular experiences armies sought to completely wipe out the civilian identity of their recruits and transform them into a *tabula rasa*. The army could then inscribe on this newly formed *tabula rasa* whatever it wished and needed. A soldier could be created, whose interests, values, and intellectual abilities fitted the requirements of the army, and who could therefore be trusted to think and initiate action without endangering the army. (The Romantics would put it differently. In the course of training, armies first cut down the wild weeds of the soldiers' past experiences, and then carefully cultivated the hitherto dormant good seeds.)

If all went well, a *tabula rasa* such as private Jean-Baptiste Bernadotte could yet become Marshal of France and King Charles XIV of Sweden. On a more moderate scale, nineteenth-century Britain was flooded with soldiers' memoirs that narrated how the dregs of society became model soldiers and citizens. For instance, John Shipp was a destitute orphan, who spent the first years of his life in the village poorhouse, and then became a troublesome brat and a source of nuisance for the entire neighborhood. The village elders were only too glad to enlist him in the army at the age of 13. In the army he became a responsible and diligent soldier, was commissioned as an officer, and ended his life as the Superintendent of Liverpool's Night Watch and Master of the Liverpool Workhouse.[34]

It is debatable to what extent military training in the late eighteenth and early nineteenth century really managed to transform recruits into a *tabula rasa* and then create virtuous soldiers out of them. Many remained suspicious of the new ideas, and adhered to the old drillfield way of thinking. In 1779 Alexander Hamilton wrote about the Continental Army: 'Let the officers be men of sense and sentiment, and the nearer the soldiers approach to machines perhaps the better.'[35] Yet more and more commanders adopted the new educational ethos, and showed far greater willingness to trust in the initiative of their soldiers.

The first products of the military educational revolution were the light infantry.[36] The term "light infantry" connoted highly maneuverable infantry, and particularly infantry that could maneuver and fight in open order and over rough terrain. Light infantry contrasted with "line infantry," which was expected to execute only the linear maneuvers of the parade ground. From the middle of the eighteenth century, old regime armies utilized light infantrymen for all the tasks that were beyond the abilities of the line infantry. They were often used in small independent groups, moving and fighting in irregular and dispersed formations. They were ideal for scouting, foraging, skirmishing, and fighting in rough terrain, where line troops could not execute their drill-field dances, and where the danger of desertion was greatest.

Though some light infantrymen were armed with rifles rather than muskets, their higher maneuverability was not due to a change in armament.[37] Rather, it was due to the increased initiative and self-assurance of junior officers, NCOs, and individual troopers, which were in turn the result of novel systems of military education. Light infantrymen were not drilled like automatons, but were educated to think and show responsible initiative. In addition, whereas the line troops were usually drilled in frictionless "laboratory" conditions, the light troops were increasingly given far more realistic training that imitated combat conditions.[38] In particular, they were given training in marksmanship that encouraged them to select their own targets, and to load and fire at their own discretion.[39]

In Britain's rifle regiments, each rifleman was trained 'to act for himself, and on his own judgment, in taking advantage of the ground on which it may be his lot to engage the enemy... [since] it is impossible that an officer or sergeant can always be at his elbow to set him right.'[40] David Dundas, the spokesman of British military conservatism in the Napoleonic era, complained bitterly about the light infantry that 'By their present open order and independent ideas, they are under very little control of their officers; and their practice seems founded on a supposition of the spirit and exertion of each individual.'[41] For Dundas, it must be explained, "independent ideas" and "individual exertion" were not compliments.

The Austrian military manual of 1807 instructed that soldiers chosen to serve as light infantrymen should be '[the] brightest, most cunning, and most reliable... [soldiers] whose concepts are not limited to maintaining physical contact with the men in front of them.'[42] In Prussia, Jäger forces enjoyed a comparatively relaxed system of discipline, and devoted far less time than line regiments to formal drill.[43] Instead of drill, they were exercised under realistic conditions, and learned to load and aim their rifles independently. The Prussian General Yorck explained: 'The rifle was not made for drill, and drilling is not the *Jäger's* purpose.'[44]

The Prussian infantry regulation of 1788 stipulated that a soldier chosen to serve as a sharpshooter 'must be intelligent, and have all those qualities which enable him to become an NCO.'[45] In April 1793 a Prussian line general witnessed for the first time a successful attack by an allied Hessian Jäger company. He was amazed by it, saying that 'Each [soldier] had without orders taken the utmost advantage of even the smallest terrain feature, something he had never seen before, indeed never had believed possible.'[46]

In the French revolutionary army it was believed that drilling was simply irrelevant for light infantry action. Jean Colin commented on the 1791 official French drill book that 'It was found... that it was absurd and a nuisance to draft regulations to fix the number and the mode of action of [light infantry].' General Le Couturier, a light infantry expert, commented on light infantry action that 'It is in effect so simple that *intelligence can take the place of rules*, and that some wise advice, given in writing or verbally, is worth more than artistically composed and described maneuvers.'[47] By calling for the replacement of rules by intelligence, La Couturier put in a nutshell the entire educational revolution.

It is crucial to realize that the armies of the old regime began to experiment with light troops already before 1776, and that they subsequently became a pivotal part of "reactionary" armies as well as revolutionary ones. The Croat, Pandour, and Grenzer light infantry of the Habsburg army was reputedly the best in Europe, and played a particularly important role during the War of the Austrian Succession. In 1756 they comprised almost a quarter of the Austrian army. By 1808 it contained 62 light infantry battalions.[48] The Prussian army began to train and raise Jägers in the 1740s, seeking to enlist to them recruits characterized by intelligence, nimbleness, and reliability.[49] In Russia, Count Rumyantsev raised the first Jäger units in 1761,[50] and by 1796 the Russian army had 40 Jäger battalions.[51] Britain raised light infantry from the 1750s. From 1771 a light company was formed in every battalion of British infantry, and men were selected for this elite service for 'intelligence, energy and marksmanship.'[52] During the American War of Independence British light infantry played a key role, and was generally superior in skirmishing and marksmanship not only to regular but also to irregular American forces. In 1788 the conservative military thinker Dundas complained that light infantry had become so trendy, that it had eclipsed the importance and pride of the line troops.[53] France raised *chasseurs à pied* from the middle of the century, and already in the early 1770s Guibert estimated that light troops amounted to a fifth of total French forces.[54] In 1789 there were 12 *chasseurs à pied* battalions, in

addition to light companies in line battalions.[55] Even the tiny ecclesiastical principality of Mayence raised a unit of Jägers in the 1770s,
which henceforth constituted the "elite" force of the Prince-Bishop's
ramshackle army,[56] whereas in later years Portugal's main contribution
to Wellington's forces were its *Caçadores*.[57]

The light infantry forces exemplified how one could take "the scum
of society," cultivate their virtues, self-confidence, and intelligence, and
transform them into elite *thinking* soldiers. The next step in the military
educational revolution was taken when armies tried to do the same with
masses of line troops. It was obvious that if all troops in an army could
maneuver and act with the same flexibility as light infantry, the tactical,
logistical, and strategic benefits would be immense.

To be sure, drill continued to be of great significance in the training
of line troops.[58] Yet it was given considerably less importance than in
the previous era, and its complexities were reduced as far as possible.[59]
Commanders no longer looked on it – in Bülow's words – as 'something complete within itself,' and many thought that evolutions that
could be executed only on the parade ground should be dispensed with.
Wellington commented of his Peninsula soldiers in 1813 that

> if his regiment here was in its present state to pass in review in
> Wimbledon Common, the whole would be sent to drill immedi-
> ately, and declared quite unfit for service. Indeed, he added, that
> the men had now got into such a way of doing everything in the
> easiest manner...He did not mention this by way of complaint, but
> as showing how ideas here and at home differed.[60]

In the 1820s veteran French officers called to abolish the drill regulations
of 1791, arguing from their experience that 'few of the complex drills
of the Ordonnance were ever executed in war.'[61]

Instead of drill, commanders began to cultivate the initiative of their
line soldiers by a campaign of psychological grooming and by more
realistic and open-minded training. The brutal disciplinary measures
of old regime armies – and in particular corporal punishment – were
criticized for destroying the soldiers' self-esteem. Instead, armies adopted
more "humane" systems of discipline, which were based on shaming and
on promises of reward, and which were supposed to make the soldiers
feel proud of themselves (see below for changes in military punishments
and in the service conditions of soldiers).[62] Instead of teaching soldiers
to follow commands blindly, new training methods sought to explain

to the soldiers the aim and rationale of their maneuvers, and left room for independent action.

Yet the key problem of loyalty remained. Could regular line soldiers be left to their own devices and trusted (a) not to desert, and (b) to try and accomplish something useful? How could armies make sure that soldiers used their newly cultivated initiative to further *collective* aims? Showing trust and respect for the soldiers helped to cultivate their loyalty as well as their self-esteem, but it was not enough in the case of masses of line troops. To further safeguard this loyalty, contemporaries relied on campaigns of ideological education. The late eighteenth century witnessed the rise of two major ideological movements: nationalism and republicanism. Both reenvisioned the state as a cooperative enterprise, and emphasized that each citizen shared the collective interests of the nation, and was bound to do his utmost to further them. This outlook was translated in war into the concept of 'the nation in arms.' It was repeatedly argued that if a state imbued the mass of its citizens with nationalist or republican sentiments, it could rely on them to serve as loyal soldiers in times of war. Patriotic or republican soldiers could be trusted to use their independent initiative to further the collective aims of the nation, with little fear that they would desert or utilize the war only for their own selfish purposes.[63] This line of argument was hardly new, going back to Renaissance military treatises such as Machiavelli's and of course to Greek and Roman writings. It was developed already under the old regime, for instance in Guibert's *Essai general de tactique* (1772) and in Servan's *Le soldat-citoyen* (1781). However, whereas events in the sixteenth century gave the lie to Machiavelli's dreams of a national militia, events in the late eighteenth century seemed to prove their veracity. The two most potent contemporary examples were the revolutionary armies of the American Colonies and France.

Friedrich Wilhelm Von Steuben, the drill-master of the nascent American army, famously wrote about his soldiers that

> The genius of this nation is not in the least to be compared with that of the Prussians, Austrians or French. You say to your [European] soldier: 'Do this!' and then he does it. But I am obliged to say, 'This is the reason you ought to do it', and then he does it.[64]

Johann Ewald, who fought against the Americans, also paid tribute to their unique qualities: 'With what soldiers in the world,' he asked rhetorically, could one do what was done by these men, who go about nearly naked and in the greatest privation. Deny the best disciplined soldiers of Europe what is due to them and they will run away in droves, and the general will soon be alone. But from this one can perceive what enthusiasm – what these poor fellows call Liberty – can do![65]

In France, the revolutionary leadership was fully aware of this rationale, and launched a massive propaganda campaign whose hero was the patriotic common soldier. French propaganda portrayed the French soldiers as intelligent free men fighting enthusiastically for their liberty against the oppressed automatons of the old order, and raised morale by arguing that free men enjoy inherent tactical superiority over servile automatons. This tactical superiority was supposed to manifest itself in two ways. First, free soldiers defending their liberty charged with far greater enthusiasm than the oppressed hirelings of despots. On the battlefield, this rhetoric was translated into the cult of the bayonet and of the mass attack column. Secondly, free soldiers using their intelligence could fight far better in open order than their unthinking opponents, and could be trusted more by their commanders.[66] Accordingly, in the French revolutionary armies it was an ideological expectation that all units would be capable of fighting in open order *en tirailleur*. As Duhesmes, a contemporary light infantry specialist, put it: 'The French armies had only light infantry.'[67] At least in several engagements and battles, such as Hondschoote (1793), the entire French army indeed fought *en tirailleur*.[68]

Translating abstract political ideology into down-to-earth tactical disposition always involves a lot of wishful thinking, but at least in the case of the *tirailleurs*, it seems to have worked. Even if most French troops were armed with normal muskets and had little training in specialized light infantry tactics, they could be counted upon to fight in open order without deserting *en masse*. They thereby overcame what Lynn defined as 'the greatest single barrier to a wider use of light infantry earlier in the century.'[69]

Not only French propagandists, but foreign observers too believed that the new educational ethos of the French army – which combined ideological indoctrination with cultivation of personal initiative – was the key to their military successes. The future Prussian reformer Gerhard von Scharnhorst wrote about the success of the revolutionary armies that

The physical agility and high intelligence of the common man enables the French *tirailleurs* to profit from all advantages offered by the terrain and the general situation, while the phlegmatic Germans, Bohemians, and Dutch form on open ground and do nothing but what their officer orders them to do...[the French] took account of these circumstances and based on them the system of always waging war in broken and covered terrain...and [aimed to] wear out the Allies by skirmishes, outpost affairs, and isolated attacks in woods and ravines.[70]

Another Prussian observer, the future Field Marshal von dem Knese-beck (a die-hard conservative), commented in 1794 about the French superiority in light infantry tactics: 'It is here that the education [Aufklärung] of the individual is of such great benefit to the Repub-licans, because situations too often occur during the combat of light forces in which the officer's control ceases completely...in which each man acts on his own.'[71] The influential Hessian military educator Hein-rich von Porbeck concluded that against French *tirailleurs* the Allied line infantrymen – 'soldiers, whom the art of our lungs and sticks had partly transformed into stiff machines' – were useless. For, 'the more enlightened the common people are, the more they reason, and the more they are suited and ready for skirmishing.'[72]

If France led the way here, Germany brought up the rearguard, and was dominated even in the early 1800s by the Frederickian heritage of automaton soldiers. When Lord Cornwallis witnessed the Prussian field exercises after the American War of Independence, he criticized them harshly, saying that that they were ridiculous and bore no rela-tion to the realities of war.[73] From the 1790s military reformers such as Scharnhorst tried to push through sweeping reform in the Prussian and other German armies, which included better education for officers and NCOs, promotion by talent, more humane methods of military justice, greater reliance on light infantry and skirmishing, operational independence for subordinated commanders, realistic training instead of drill, and greater reliance on popular conscription.[74] Yet such views were strongly resisted by the Prussian establishment.

A good example of the gap between the new educational methods characteristic of the French armies and the old methods characteristic of German armies was given in late 1805, when the Prince of Isenburg – Birstein raised a regiment to serve in Napoleon's army. The regiment was recruited mainly from Austrian and Russians prisoners of war, but included also a number of German volunteers. One of these volunteers was the 15-years-old Johann Konrad Friederich, a Frankfurter of good bourgeois stock. Friederich decided to join the French army because he dreamt of military glory and hoped that he would be able to advance more easily in the egalitarian French army than in the various German armies, which still put a premium on nobility.

The regiment's commanders were also mostly German, and they decided to train and discipline their regiment 'the German way.' Friederich was exasperated by the experience.

> I soon began to be deeply disgusted with the everlasting nerve-racking monotony: musket up, musket down, right and left in the flanks, turn to the right, loading in twelve tempoes and eighteen movements, positioning, walk in single file etc. were the spirited occupations I enjoyed with all the others three to four hours in the morning, and the same length of time in the afternoon. The prince had intro-duced German command, because he claimed it was a German regi-ment, although it had almost more Russians, Poles, Hungarians, and Bohemians than Germans...

> Even worse than the German command was, that German beating too was introduced to the regiment, on the advice of several officers who had in the past been in Austrian, Prussian or other German services, and claimed that discipline could be sustained only by the use of German beating. Very soon this was regularly awarded with great bounty in portions of twenty-five, fifty and hundred by former Austrian corporals, who best understood how to ply it. This method had two major disadvantages for the regiment. For one thing, all sense of honor was choked in the soldiers, and for another thing, the regiment was looked upon with great contempt by the French troops that it met in the field or in the garrisons. The officers of French and even Italian regiments criticized its officers for the beating. Certainly *salle de police* and *salle de discipline*, as prescribed by the French regu-lations, would have had the same, or even much better effect. But all the ideas of some reasonable officers did not help and could not convince the Prince. The beatings continued.[75]

Friederich also complained about the suppression of initiative under the regime of 'German training.' Officers reacted to any objection to their commands, or even to mere suggestions made by the men, with severe beating until the soldier's 'lights are punched out' [dass die Schwarte kracht].

> How totally different was it in the French army, where even the common soldier was allowed to make without concerns all kinds of

suggestions to his colonel or general, being sure, that they were not only heard with amicability and benevolence, but incorporated, when they proved to be justified. Our German cane heroes [Stock-helden], in contrast, stared with numb eyes at everything that solely tasted like reason and were only masters of the meanest blustering and cursing.[76]

Another contemporary testament to the same effect comes from the memoirs of Johan Christian Mämpel. He was another German who found himself serving in the French army, being conscripted in 1806.

> In the beginning of my career, I imbibed a powerful aversion to the duties I was subjected to; nor was this without reason; since, during my former residence in Germany, I had frequent opportunities of witnessing military exercises, and recollected perfectly well the brutal treatment experienced by the unfortunate novices at the hand of their task-masters.... my compassion was constantly awakened by the sufferings of these poor people... But I soon found, to me delight, that this system was not followed up by my [French] instructors, who exercised towards their pupils great kindness and forbearance.[77]

During that very same year, 1806, the Prussian army was crushed by the *Grande Armée* at Jena and Auerstadt. This debacle proved – at least in the eyes of contemporaries – the superiority of the new flexible armies over the old 'automatic' armies, and paved the way for the triumph of the reform movement in Prussia. Soul-searching Prussian commanders and politicians concluded that the reformers were right all along, and that it was the French superiority in light infantry tactics and in soldiers' initiative that brought about the humiliating defeat. For the purposes of this study, it matters little whether their conclusion was accurate, and whether fighting in open order was really as effective as contemporary ideologues, propagandists, and commanders believed it to be. The crucial thing is that both military men and civilians believed it was so, which helped transform not only the military practices of Prussia, but also the cultural standing of the common soldier.

In the period 1807–13 the Prussian state and army underwent radical reforms under the supervision of Stein, Scharnhorst, and Gneisenau.[78] The Frederickian heritage of automaton soldiers was discarded, and the Prussian army was rebuilt as an army of thinking and highly motivated soldiers, which could fully tap the psychological and intellectual energies of its recruits. Drill was replaced to some extent by realistic training which 'placed new emphasis on the initiative of the trained, committed, thinking soldier.'[79] The first realistic field exercises were undertaken by the Prussian army in 1810. Leaving the parade ground, troops practiced patrolling, ambushing, and night attacks.[80] A concentrated effort was made to train a third of each line regiment as skirmishers, and to train all infantrymen in marksmanship.[81] A British officer remarked about the new Prussian army that 'It forms part of the discipline in the Prussian army to manage soldiers by exciting their feelings and national spirit in substitution of the old system of making them up into highly drilled machines.'[82] From 1807 up to World War II, the independent initiative of their junior officers, NCOs, and common soldiers became the hallmark of the Prussian and German armies.[83]

The Prussian establishment finally agreed to these sweeping reforms due not only to the shock of defeat. By 1807 these reforms seemed far less frightening than in 1793, because in the meantime it became apparent that soldiers' initiative did not entail republicanism. Though it was – and still is – tempting to connect initiative in combat with initiative in politics, there was overwhelming evidence that the former could be groomed without encouraging the latter.

In France itself the change from republic to military despotism was not accompanied by any decrease in the willingness of French soldiers to harness their personal initiative in the service of the army. In fact, the professional army of the Empire was greatly superior to the republican armies of the early 1790s.[84] Reactionary powers such as Austria and Russia similarly found that they could tap the initiative of their common soldiers without undergoing any political reforms and without risking a revolution. During the 1799 Alps campaign Field-Marshal Alexander Suvorov – the champion of the reactionary powers – explained to his subordinates that

> It is not enough that only the senior commanders should be notified about the plan of operations. It is necessary that the junior officers would keep it in their minds as well, so they could lead their troops accordingly. Furthermore: even battalion, squadron and company commanders should know it for the same reason, and so are the NCOs and private soldiers. Each combatant should understand his maneuver.[85]

The Russian common soldiers justified Suvorov's trust, and Russian armies were able to function well while fighting in open order. For instance, on the second day of the battle of Mutalal (1799) the Russian army fought almost entirely in open order, defeating a superior French force.[86]

In Britain, Samuel Johnson observed already in 1760 that the initiative of the common soldiers had little to do with liberal ideology. In *The Bravery of the English Common Soldier* Johnson argued that English common soldiers were the bravest in the world. He began by saying that an army is usually made formidable by confidence in the commander, discipline, and drill (which Johnson called 'regularity'). He explained that 'Regularity may, in time, produce a kind of mechanical obedience to signals and commands, like that which the perverse Cartesians impute to animals; discipline may impress such awe upon the mind, that any danger shall be less dreaded than the danger of punishment.'[87] However, whereas he cited 'the troops of the Russian Empress, and Prussian Monarch' as examples of drilled and disciplined troops, he said that English forces lack such drill and discipline.

What then was the secret of their bravery? Johnson refuted the claim that the common soldier fought so bravely because in liberal Britain he had a greater stake in his country's defense than in more authoritarian regimes. 'What has the English,' asked Johnson,

> more than the French soldier? Property they are both commonly without. Liberty is, to the lowest rank of every nation, little more than the choice of working or starving; and this choice is, I suppose, equally allowed in every country. The English soldier seldom has his head very full of the constitution.[88]

Instead, Johnson attributed the bravery of the English common soldier to 'that dissolution of dependence' which obliged every man to depend on his own best efforts, which raised his self-esteem, and which made him think of himself as equal to his leaders. He concluded by saying that 'they who complain, in peace, of the insolence of the populace, must remember, that their insolence in peace is bravery in war.'[89]

The Prussian gamble that military cooptation could be decoupled from republican politics proved correct. From 1807 to 1945, Prussian and German armies were arguably the most liberal in the world in terms of their encouragement of soldiers' initiative, yet they served a succession of authoritarian regimes. It has often been commented that during World War II, the German military education system was far superior to that of the Western democracies, and that the Wehrmacht relied on the initiative of its junior officers, NCOs, and common soldiers far more than the French, British, or American armies. In many situations when leaderless British and American troops ceased to function, German troops continued to fight efficiently under the guidance of a sergeant, a corporal, or even a private.[90]

We can therefore conclude that the cultivation of soldiers' initiative was a vital ingredient of the Napoleonic military revolution, and that it gave a tremendous boost to the cultural standing of the common soldier. We can also conclude that it had little to do with republicanism. As long as the cultivation of soldiers' initiative was confined to small professional bodies such as the light infantry, it could be achieved without the support of any accompanying political ideology. Elitist *esprit de corp* was sufficient. In order to cultivate the initiative of masses of recruits, some additional ideological motivation was needed, but it could be provided by authoritarian nationalism and even old-fashioned religious devotion as much as by liberal republicanism.

The revolution in military recruitment

As the horizons of military education broadened, they broadened with them the horizons of military recruitment. Old regime armies were small compared to the armies of the Napoleonic period. This resulted to a large extent from two interconnected difficulties.

First, it was thought that relentless drill and strict discipline were indispensable for creating efficient and reliable soldiers, and that drilling and disciplining were impossible in a mass army. In old regime armies, it took recruits at least a year to master the intricacies of individual and collective drill,[91] and perfection was often attained only after three years.[92] Even with well-drilled soldiers, constant supervision by NCOs and officers was needed to insure discipline. There was simply not enough time, money, and officers to educate and supervise a mass army in the old fashion way.[93]

Secondly, even if an army of hundreds of thousands of men could be raised and trained, the command-and-control difficulties involved in controlling such an army were thought to be insurmountable. The Cartesian military ideal envisioned a single Great Captain controlling the movements of the entire army, as a puppeteer controls a puppet. Though this could be done effectively in armies of 50,000 men, it could not be done in armies of 150,000 men. Such huge armies could not function unless the Great Captain delegated as much responsibility as possible down to his lieutenants, and they delegated responsibility further along the ladder all the way down to the junior officer, NCO, and common soldier. As long as armies thought along Cartesian lines, and as long as military education cultivated blind obedience, such delegation of responsibility was anathema. Marshal de Saxe thought that the ideal size of an operational army was 46,000, and harshly criticized suggestions for raising larger armies.[94]

Once armies absorbed the new ideals of the culture of sensibility, both of the above problems were solved. First, sensible cooptation was far cheaper and faster than brutal coercion. The handful of officers and NCOs in charge of green companies could not hope to teach military drill to dozens of civilian bodies in a matter of a few months. However, by creating the right experiences they were able to change their civilian minds into military minds. In Napoleonic armies, far larger numbers of recruits were trained far faster by giving them less training in drill coupled with greater emphasis on cooptation, initiative, and self-discipline. The Prussian conscripts of 1813 were sent to battle after a training period of only nine weeks.[95]

Secondly, once the military machine was reenvisioned as a sensitive organic machine rather than a lifeless puppet, it greatly eased the command-and-control difficulties. Sensationist thinkers such as La Mettrie pointed out that the human body is an incredibly large and complicated mechanism, which can function only because its various limbs are authorized to make many decisions by themselves (even decisions affecting the entire organism). On most occasions, the liver dictates the mood, thoughts, and actions of the conscious mind, rather than the other way around. If this principle was applied to armies, it could ease their command-and-control difficulties and enable them to expand greatly. Of course, already in the high-days of Cartesian armies subordinates had to make many independent decisions. But in those days it was an embarrassing deviation from the ideal, which military thinkers swept under the carpet, and which commanders sought to restrict as much as possible by keeping armies small. From the late eighteenth century it became *the ideal*.

A revolutionary new type of military machine was envisioned. From Napoleon's *Grande Armée* to Hitler's *Wehrmacht*, the military machine was recreated as a gigantic sensitive organism, conforming to La Mettrie's vision rather than to Descartes's. Discipline was still of paramount importance, and if the mind issued a command, the hand was still bound to obey it. Yet every cell in the new organism was meant to think and react with maximum autonomy and initiative, and for most of the time the mind interfered as little as possible with the action of these cells.

The way to mass recruitment was thereby opened. In 1793 the French Republic proclaimed the *levée en masse*, leading to a quick expansion in the size of its military forces. In the following century, one country after the other – irrespective of their political ideology – followed suit.[96] Once mass armies began to be recruited, an escalating magic circle was created. Sensationist education meant that far bigger armies could be recruited more quickly and more cheaply; bigger armies meant far more command-and-control problems; command-and-control problems meant that more responsibility had to be delegated; Sensationist ideas of education meant that junior officers, NCOs, and common soldiers could be educated to bear responsibility better. The circle was closed, and the small mechanistic armies of old regime Europe were gradually over-whelmed and replaced by the mass organic armies of the late modern era. (I have no intention of arguing that the French revolutionary armies defeated the old regime armies. That is far from being true. What I mean is that both revolutionary *and* reactionary powers gradually replaced their small automatic armies with mass organic armies.)

It is a mistake to think that the new mass armies overcame and replaced the old professional armies thanks to sheer numbers. That never worked in history. Instead of mere mass, the new armies were a maneuverable and disciplined mass. The secret of their success was that Sensationist ideals of education and function enabled them to replace coercion and supervision with cooptation and independent initiative, which enabled them in their turn to recruit and maneuver their superior numbers cheaply yet with a tolerable measure of discipline.[97]

The larger size and higher initiative of the new armies more than compensated for their lack of drill and expertise. Commanders who previously husbanded their well-drilled automatons could now expand far more freely the lives of their cheap and relatively enthusiastic recruits. Marshal de Saxe observed about old regime soldiers that 'It is better to put off the attack for several days than to expose oneself to losing rashly a single grenadier: he has been twenty years in the making.'[98] In the Napoleonic era, manpower became so cheap that Napoleon could have famously observed to Metternich: 'Un home comme moi ne regarde pas à un million de morts.'[99]

On the battlefield, thick clouds of light skirmishers constantly harassed the enemy, and when a concentration of maneuverable force was needed, undrilled troops were bunched together in heavy attack columns. (Such columns were rarely used by old regime armies because they were wasteful in firepower and costly in lives. The new mass armies could afford them far more easily.[100]) The new mass armies proved their success far more persuasively off the major battlefields. When it came to operational maneuvers, Elzéar Blaze explained that Napoleon could often execute very hard marches because he did not have to wait for the slowest soldier in his army, and did not fear desertion so much.[101] 'Sometimes half the soldiers were left behind, but – since they did not lack good will – they arrived later, but they did arrive.'[102] Furthermore, explained Blaze, the French armies could travel light because they relied for their supply on the efforts of free marauders

> who traveled along the side roads, from one to three leagues [5 to 15 kilometers] distant from their column. Sometimes they were attacked by the enemy, but one can say that the French soldier's intelligence equals his bravery. These gentlemen chose a leader among themselves who commanded like a dictator, and often these improvised generals fought serious engagements and reported victories.

> When General Moore's English army made its retreat to Corunna, our advance guard which pursued it was very surprised to encounter a palisaded village. The French tricolor floated from the clock tower, the sentinels wore French uniforms. The officers who investigated it soon learned that 200 marauders held the village. Cut off from our army they had established themselves in the village and forti-fied it. Often attacked, they had always repulsed the enemy. Their commanding general was a corporal…The corporal, with his old-soldier experience, had fortified the village as well as an engineer officer could have done.[103]

Such a corporal was hardly imaginable in the armies of Prince Eugene or Frederick the Great – though he had all too many forerunners in the armies of the Thirty Years War.

The new armies (of Napoleon *and* of his enemies) had an equally impressive edge in holding down countries and civilian populations, and in guerilla and counterinsurgency warfare. In such situations their numbers and initiative gave them overwhelming superiority over the old small armies of professional automatons. Already in the 'Forage War' in New Jersey (1776–77), the raw American militia proved that in *petite guerre* a large popular force could overcome a smaller profes-sional army, provided the popular force had enough initiative to compensate for its lack of training.[104] The British Colonel William Harcourt observed about the New Jersey militia that they 'seem to be ignorant of the precision and order, and even of the principles, by which large bodies are moved ... [but] they possess ... extreme cunning, great industry in moving ground and felling of wood, activity and a spirit of enterprise upon any advantage.'[105] It is again important to note that there was little connection between *petite guerre* and ideology. In the 1790s republican French armies encountered great difficulties when faced by popular insurgencies and guerilla warfare which supported the reactionary powers.[106] The most vicious and successful guerilla campaign of the era, in Spain, was ultra-conservative in its ideology.

It is also vital to note that soldiers' initiative played a key role in the *suppression* of popular insurrection and guerillas. Johann Konrad Friederich spent much of his military career fighting against insurgents in Italy and Spain. He comments about this *petite guerre* that

> no other way of waging war is so informing and so rich in experiences as this one. One learns from it especially to use every terrain properly, to gain a very sharp eye and a right overview of all dangers, and to take advantage of every little favourable situation. The constant alertness that one necessarily needs on all forays on such a broken terrain extraordinarily sharpens view and mind. *Every single man often gets there in a situation, where he has to mobilize all his intelligence and abilities* not to become the victim of any default or carelessness, which often has to be paid for with life. The experiences and dangers of such a war prepare one for all higher command posts and for leading the most important expeditions.[107]

Thanks to the initiative of their soldiers, who mobilized 'all their intelligence and abilities,' Napoleonic armies were generally successful in suppressing insurrections and guerrillas, except when the latter were supported by regular armies (as happened in Spain).[108]

The common soldier as cultural icon

The changing attitude toward the recruitment, education, and employment of common soldiers was accompanied by a radical change in their public image. Throughout the early modern period common soldiers were seen primarily as the criminal dregs of society. Even though the soldiery collective was often lauded, individual common soldiers were usually depicted as either criminal or comical figures.[109] Positive images of common soldiers could be found mainly in picaresque narratives, which celebrated in a similar fashion other rogues and outcasts.[110] Respectable military heroes were almost always officers.

In the middle of the eighteenth century, the picaresque criminals and simpletons of earlier days were well on their way to becoming the brave sons of the motherland.[111] A good example of the changing cultural trends is the semi-fictional *Life and Adventures of Mrs. Christian Davies, commonly called Mother Ross* (1740), which was published on the outbreak of the War of Austrian Succession, and which narrated the adventures of a woman camp-follower and occasional combatant. The book was heavily influenced by previous picaresque narratives of female heroines (such as Grimmelshausen's *Mother Courage*), and contains many farcical episodes, but it gives the soldiers and Mother Ross in particular a less criminal and more patriotic twist. It represented a general trend in eighteenth-century military picaresque narratives, which began to present common soldiers as wholly positive figures who fought for the social order rather than against (or alongside) it.

On one of her campaigns Mother Ross went foraging outside the British camp, and discovered that the French army was preparing to attack, unbeknown to the British commanders. Ross hurried back to the camp to sound the alert, and found the British commander, the Duke of Argyle, busy playing chess with the Lord Mark Kerr. 'I asked them with some warmth, in a Language which only became a Soldier, and a Freedom allowed my Sex, what they meant by having no better Intelligence and idling their Time at Chess, while the French were on the point of cannonading us.' The Lord Mark Kerr told Argyle that Ross was 'a foolish drunken woman, and not worth Notice; To which the Duke replied, he would as soon take my Advice as that of any Brigadier in the Army.'[112] This passage not only praises 'the insolence of the populace.' It also contrasts the highly rational but unrealistic chess game played by the senior commanders in their headquarters with the healthy initiative of a female camp-follower who actually goes over the contested ground and who saves the army from disaster.[113]

When the War of Austrian Succession ended in a defeat for Britain, the Whig opposition adopted the spirit of *Mother Ross*. The Whigs sharply criticized the incompetence of the senior military and political echelons, who were blamed for the defeat, while simultaneously heaping praise on the common soldiers for their gallantry and faithful service.[114] This potent image of 'lions led by donkeys' would later be used again and again in the modern public sphere, most notably in the aftermath of the Crimean War and World War I. It became well-nigh sacrilegious to criticize the common soldiers, and failures were always blamed on the commanders. Even if the troops behaved badly, this too was laid at the door of the commanders. Since education was thought omnipotent, if soldiers misbehaved, it was because commanders failed to educate them properly.[115]

By the end of the eighteenth century, individual common soldiers were celebrated as national heroes. In France 13-years-old Joseph Bara, who died fighting against the Vendean insurgents, became a hero of the Republic. He was the subject of a virtual cult, medallions and paintings recorded his heroic death, and Robespierre intended to hold a national festival in his honor and transfer his remains to the Pantheon. After Robespierre's fall, the Convention commissioned Jacque-Louis David to paint Bara's death with the intention of distributing copies to primary schools 'to provide a constant reminder to the young people of France of the most perfect instance of patriotism and filial devotion.' In the late nineteenth century, under the Third Republic, the story of Bara became a mandatory part of the education of French schoolchildren.[116]

Commanders of course still retained their special aura, but even in the field of command, a considerable part of public attention and admiration shifted from the senior to the junior ranks. Whereas senior commanders came under increasing criticism, lieutenants, captains, and majors basked in the sunshine of popular acclaim as never before.

In France, examples include Ensign Joseph Coulon de Jumonville, who became a national hero in France during the Seven Years War,[117] and Captain Théophile Malo Corret de la Tour d'Auvergne, 'The First Grenadier of the Republic,' whose tomb became a national monument under Napoleon.[118] Another example was the unfortunate Major André, whom the British press often referred to, mistakenly, as Major *Saint*-André.[119] Quite a few wars in history were named after kings and conquerors: The Napoleonic Wars, The War of the Three Henries, King Philip's War, and so forth. The only war in history named after a junior officer erupted in 1739 between Britain and Spain. The captain of the brig *Rebecca*, master mariner Robert Jenkins, was arrested by a Spanish ship and having been accused of smuggling, had one of his ears cut off. The ear was displayed in the British Parliament with an accompanying sentimental description of his miseries and his patriotic devotion, which helped spark the War of Jenkins' Ear (1739–48).

The more positive appreciation of the role and abilities of common soldiers was reflected in a myriad ways. Military honors and medals, which previously were reserved for officers and noblemen, began to be distributed to common soldiers too.[120] New avenues of promotion were opened to the soldiers, and increasing numbers of senior officers rose from the ranks. Though in practice it was still very hard to advance up the ladder, and few made it from the bottom all the way to the top, those who succeeded were viewed as ideal models, and the cultural status of all common soldiers received a great boost once they began to be looked at as candidate-marshals.[121]

It might be argued that the new military awards and the new dreams of promotion were nothing but 'opium for the masses.' Yet from the perspective of cultural history, what type of opium the masses consume is an extremely important sign of the times. Napoleon may have laughed at his soldiers, saying that he could make them die for a colored ribbon. Yet the way they looked at themselves, and the way they were looked at by family members, friends, and neighbors really changed thanks to those flashy pieces of cloth and metal.

Another sign of the times was the changing cultural attitude toward guerilla warfare. Guerilla warfare existed throughout the early modern era, but like the common soldiers, it was either invisible or disreputable. This was to a large extent because guerilla and counterinsurgency warfare relied on the initiative of junior officers and common soldiers rather than on the Newtonian maneuvers of a few Great Captains. The Napoleonic era witnessed a drastic shift in the image of guerilla warfare. In the Vendée, Russia, the Austrian Tyrol, and above all in Spain, guerilla warfare was given central stage in war culture, and was encouraged and celebrated even by autocratic governments.[122] After the 1812 campaign Russia established the Silver Medal 'For Love of the Fatherland,' which was awarded to partisans and other non-regular soldiers.[123]

In the fledgling United States the shift was even more pronounced. In 1776 Washington and the Continental Congress still adhered to the old military ideals and sought to create a European-style drilled professional army. Military historians today have repeatedly argued that British regular light troops were superior to the American militia in their maneuverability and tactical initiative, and that drilled American line troops played a key role in the American victory. Nevertheless, already in the late eighteenth century American public opinion downplayed the role of the regular Continental Army in the War of Independence. Instead, it seized upon the image of the undrilled militiaman stalking the unthinking British regular from behind the cover of trees and hedges as a symbol for the superiority of American free initiative over old regime obedience.[124] The free-thinking common soldier and the patriotic *guerillero* were launched on a collision course with the Great Captain as the model military hero.

Equally momentous changes took place in public attitude toward the soldiers' living and dying conditions. Up to the late eighteenth century the main concern of the civilian public was to ensure that soldiers were kept under maximum discipline, and that the civilian population was protected from their depredations. From the mid-eighteenth century the public became increasingly interested in the lot of the soldiers themselves, and in the negative results of harsh military discipline.

Corporal punishment was greatly restricted and in many cases abolished.[125] For instance, in July 1834 a private soldier in Charing Cross Barracks received 300 lashes for being drunk on sentry duty and trying to strike his sergeant. The case became a *cause celebre*, the popular press raised an outcry, and petitions were submitted to Parliament. In Oxford, 1648 inhabitants signed a petition that denounced the flogging as 'a disreputable, cowardly, unmanly, unfeeling, brutal, inhuman and bloody mode of punishment.'[126] A century earlier 300 lashes would have been considered a mild punishment, and if the general public ever heard of such a case, it was more likely to show concern about the insubordination of drunken soldiers than pity for their cruel treatment.[127]

The public similarly began to criticize the faulty arrangements of military logistical and medical systems. For centuries, armies had suffered far more casualties from hunger and disease than from enemy action, and even where military hospitals were available, admittance to them was usually considered a death sentence.[128] To take one example out of a myriad, of the 60,000 Imperialist troops that invaded Provence on July 24, 1536, less than 30,000 emaciated survivors struggled back to Italy on September 11, 1536. They have not fought a single major action in between, and succumbed only to hunger and an outbreak of dysentery, which were the result of French scorched-earth strategy and bad management of the Imperialist supply system. (It is notable that the Imperialists were campaigning in Provence at the height of today's *vacance* season – not in some frozen Russian winter[129]). No scandal erupted in Spain, Germany, or Italy following this disaster. Taxpayers might have grumbled about the cost, but public opinion in Emperor Charles V's domains did not care an iota about the fate of the emperor's sick and dying mercenaries.

Around 1800, things began to change. One scandal after the other erupted in situations which would not have raised an eyebrow previously. In France, one of the blackest spots on Napoleon's reputation was his callous treatment of sick French soldiers at Jaffa (1799). In Britain, heart-rending accounts were published of the misery of the common soldiers on the retreat to Corunna (1809) and on the failed expedition to Walcheren (1809).[130] These various scandals were completely overshadowed by two events that became ever after potent icons for the misery of the common soldier in war: the retreat from Moscow (1812) and the siege of Sebastopol (1854–55).

The retreat from Moscow was indeed a catastrophe of unprecedented proportions, but there was nothing in the magnitude of the disaster that made it inevitable to focus on the misery of the French common soldiers (rather than, say, on the misery of the Russian civilians).[131] In the case of the Crimean War, there was nothing unique either about the overall number of British dead (about 20,000), or about the breakdown of this figure: 2255 soldiers were killed in action, 1847 died of wounds, and 17,225 died from disease.[132] Yet the cultural standing of the common soldier in Britain of the 1850s was completely different from the cultural standing of the common soldier in the Habsburg Empire of the 1530s, which made the misery of the soldiers seem intolerable to British public opinion. Even before the Crimean War ended, an unprecedented campaign was launched to better the living conditions of the common soldiers, and to completely reform the military medical system.[133]

Throughout history, the image of common soldier was built around a basic tension between heroism and criminality. The soldier was half-hero, half-criminal, who stood apart and above from normal civilian society. All societies made huge efforts to reward and strengthen the heroic half and to discourage the criminal part. The campaigns of 1812 and of Sebastopol marked a turning point in military history, when this simple tension became a complex three-way struggle. To the heroic and the criminal soldier was now added the victimized soldier. By the late twentieth century, this image became dominant in the minds of civilians, so that, for example, Vietnam War veterans came to be seen in the United States as the chief *victims* of the war. Even when Vietnam veterans were accused of heinous crimes, the dominant tendency was to absolve them from responsibility to these crimes. The soldier's crimes were really the fault of the generals and politicians who victimized him and placed him in an impossible situation.

The common soldiers of the Old Regime were subject to a vicious magic circle: The prevailing negative cultural image of soldiers caused only the dregs of society to enlist, caused soldiers to have a low self-esteem, and caused commanders to distrust their soldiers and treat them as criminals or robots. The fact that only the dregs of society enlisted, that soldiers suffered from low self-esteem, and that commanders treated them as criminals and robots, naturally fueled the negative cultural image of the soldiery.

From about 1750 a new magic circle began raising the common soldier to giddy heights. A more positive cultural image of soldiers caused more "respectable" men to enlist, caused soldiers to view themselves far more favorably, and caused commanders to treat their soldiers with far greater respect. These tendencies were mutually reinforcing, and they all fueled an ever greater improvement in the cultural image of the soldiery, which was an essential characteristic of the new mass recruitment armies.[134]

Common soldiers begin to write

As the common soldiers became the beloved sons of the Motherland, they received a much more prominent place within the culture of war. From mere extras they became the chief heroes of numerous paintings, plays, and poems, as well as of fictional memoirs. As Peter Paret writes,

> The end of the eighteenth century marks a deep incision in the fluctuating course of the common soldier's appearance and disappearance in images of war. After the French Revolution he no longer fades from view. For some generations he shares the focus with those who lead him, but he gradually displaces them... In the serious work of art senior officers almost disappear, except in such attacks on their class as the works of George Grosz. By the time of the First World War... the common soldier has not only become the central figure in images of war, increasingly the images are drawn or painted from perspectives that seek to be his.[135]

More importantly for the present research, in the late eighteenth century Western culture began for the first time to solicit and listen attentively to the authentic voices of the common soldiers themselves. In the early modern age the vast majority of autobiographical war narratives were composed by noblemen or by officers of medium and senior ranks. In the rare cases when a common soldier or junior officer published a narrative of war, he usually presented it as a general history rather than a personal narrative.[136] From the middle of the eighteenth century more and more junior officers and common soldiers composed and published self-proclaimed *personal* narratives of war. By the early nineteenth century, these subaltern military narratives for the first time in history matched and even outstripped the narratives of senior officers in their numbers and public visibility.[137] It is crucial to note that this was true not only in post-revolutionary France and the United States, but also in conservative powers such as Britain and Prussia.

This shift in the culture of war resulted from two sets of changes. First, Western culture in general became far more open to the narratives of subaltern groups. The culture of sensibility contended that knowledge and authority were based on experience, and that extreme experiences in particular were a privileged source for knowing and telling the truth. Simultaneously, the culture of sensibility encouraged 'sensitive' men and women of the higher classes to sharpen and display their sensibility by listening with sympathy to the woeful narratives of their social inferiors.[138]

This opened the way for a flood of autobiographical and semi-autobiographical narratives of previously silenced groups: criminals, slaves, prisoners, paupers, prostitutes, and peasants.[139] In 1771, Reverend Johann Kaspar Lavater summed up this trend, saying that a 'faithful and circumstantial moral [i.e. psychological] history of the most common and unromantic character is infinitely more important and fitter for improving the human heart than the most extraordinary and interesting novel.'[140] For a few months in 1775 the favorite book of the Parisian salons was *Le Paysan perverti*, a semi-fictional autobiography of a workingman, written by a self-educated peasant with literary aspirations.[141] The subaltern soldiers that began to publish their narratives of war were part of a much larger bonanza of subaltern publication.

Yet the mass publication of subaltern soldiers' war narratives also resulted from a set of other factors, which were unique to the military sphere:

1. As noted earlier, general culture became far more sympathetic toward the common soldiers. From criminals they came to be seen as patriotic heroes. Though in the culture of sensibility a criminal too had some authority to speak, it was obviously preferable to speak as a patriotic hero.
2. As armies came to rely more on the initiative of their soldiers, Western culture came to see soldiers as *thinking* beings. Their intellectual qualities were more appreciated, and their opinions and stories consequently carried more weight.
3. As armies came to rely more on the initiative of their soldiers and treated their soldiers better, the soldiers themselves became more self-confident and more willing to express their opinions. It is indicative that the percentage of soldiers' war narratives published by veterans of light forces was far bigger than the percentage of light forces in contemporary armies, reflecting the higher self-confidence and cultural status of light troops.[142]

4. Due to changes in recruitment policies, military education, and civilian education, common soldiers c.1800 were far more literate than their predecessors c.1700.[143] In 1775/76 the volunteer army of New England was the first army in history in which most privates could read and write.[144] Around the same time it was apparently expected of every sergeant in the Russian, Austrian and British armies, and even of most corporals, to be able to read and write.[145] In 1768 Bennett Cuthbertson recommended that in every British regiment a school should be set up in which illiterate soldiers, as well as the children of the regiment, would learn to read and write.[146]

5. Last but not least, the experiences that authorized soldiers to speak in public were sublime experiences, whereas many of the experiences that authorized slaves, prostitutes, and peasants to speak in public were more pathetic than sublime. Around 1800, the Western public was certainly willing to listen to the voice of the pathetic, but it was even more willing to listen to the voice of the sublime. In addition, whereas the voice of the pathetic was usually listened to with sympathy and condensation, the voice of the sublime was listened to with awe and humility. Whereas most subaltern narratives in the era of sensibility could therefore command only sympathy, common soldiers' narratives possessed far more formidable authority.

Consequently, while common soldiers and junior officers in the early modern age had to disguise their autobiographical writings as 'history,' and often apologized for their temerity in writing anything at all, the soldiers of the Romantic era felt very confident about their ability and right to tell their stories to the public and to command the public's attention. The publisher of *Vicissitudes in the Life of a Scottish Soldier* (1827) wrote confidently that

> We possess already many works which present all the grand and general features of our Continental campaigns; but we know very little about the minuter details that gave the Peninsular war its peculiar character and colouring. The courage of our soldiers, their constancy under daily sufferings and privations, their kindness to the foreigners they were protecting, and their generosity to the foe they opposed, have been lauded, in aggregate, both in prose and in rhyme; but there are few traits preserved of individual prowess and of individual adventure, – of the light-heartedness, the misery, the ludicrous or lamentable incidents, the vices and the virtues that diversify the life and character of a private soldier. The single subject here selected

for a picture will, in the main points, illustrate the personal condition of the whole of our army; and, from such a story, many particulars may be learned regarding the conduct of the officers engaged in the Peninsular War, which could in no other way be obtained.[147]

The rising tide of military subaltern narratives was far more than a literary trend. As the following pages argue, subaltern narratives were amongst the chief vehicles that transformed Western war culture. They reinterpreted war as a sublime revelation and created archetypical war stories that have dominated Western war culture ever since.

Conclusions: War and *Bildung*

The rise of the common soldier and his transformation from cog to thinking cell may seem to us natural, but it stands in sharp contrast to the general trends of late modern professional life. The industrial-capitalist revolution of the late modern era involved an unprecedented process of alienation amongst the mass of workers. Whereas the early modern shoemaker had to employ his personal initiative, ingenuity, and craftsmanship to produce a shoe, the worker in the twentieth-century mass-production shoe factory was required only to operate a machine with a minimal investment of initiative (much the same could be said of the white-collar bureaucrat). It is striking to realize that just when the mass of civilian workers became cogs in a vast industrial machine, the military machine was rolling in the opposite direction. Just when the worker became a cog, the soldier was recognized as an independent thinking cell.

The result of these contrasting movements was that war became a Romantic preserve within an alienated industrial economy. For the majority of late modern workers, 'work' was an alienated and narrow-minded activity, which did not cultivate any process of *Bildung*. Work did not require the full investment of one's potential, it did not involve any novel experiences, it did not sharpen one's sensibilities, and it did not result in acquiring new knowledge about oneself and the world. War, on the other hand, was reconceived as a Romantic preserve of initiative, novelty, and exploration. Even if one belonged to a giant 'military machine,' and even if this giant machine was extremely narrow-minded during peacetime, in times of war this machine expected one to show independent initiative, and allowed one far more scope for exercising this initiative than any civilian job. As we shall see in the following pages, the great attraction of late modern war was the chance to escape from the deadening world of work, and to explore and develop one's full human potential.

Nothing captures this spirit better than the U.S. Army recruitment slogan in the period 1981–2001: 'Be All You Can Be.' Nobody has ever summarized the ideal of *Bildung* better. The slogan's message is that by exposing soldiers to the widest possible range of experiences, the army enables them to develop the full range of their human potential, which would otherwise remain dormant. When they die – in or out of combat – the veterans can consequently say with von Humboldt that they have indeed 'taken the measure in feeling of everything human,' and that they had 'really lived.' Civilians, in contrast, working in the factory or the office, never realize all that they can be, and consequently never know who they really are. *Nike* may try to sell its shoes to consumers with the catchy slogan 'Just do It!,' which seems to promise adventure and exploration. It could not possibly lure potential factory workers or accountants by promising to them 'Work for *Nike* – be all you can be.' That would simply sound ridiculous, if not downgrading. Nobody would like to think that all he or she could be is a *Nike* employee.

When in 2001 the U.S. Army switched to a new recruiting slogan – 'An Army of One' – the chief promise to volunteers, in addition to pay, remained the promise of *Bildung*. One 2003 recruitment poster shows a soldier in full gear with the caption saying 'Most job training teaches you how to make something. Mine taught me what I'm made of.' The contrast here is between the alienated peacetime "job" that teaches only mechanical skills (like making shoes) and the *Bildung* promised by the army.

It is easy to be cynical about these recruitment promises, but in a way, armies are serious about them, because they have a genuine stake in them. We noted Field Marshal von dem Knesebeck's comment that the *Aufklärung* of the individual soldier is of great benefit to the army. Today, it has become common to speak of "the strategic corporal": the corporal whose decision in some remote outpost may make it within hours to news headlines all around the world. From the late eighteenth century, armies have gambled that they *can* produce enlightened strategic corporals, and more importantly, that these enlightened corporals – for all their independent thoughts – *can* be co-opted to the army's purposes. So far this gamble seems amply justified. There is still room for cynicism, because as institutions, armies are interested only in co-opted enlightenment rather than in enlightenment per se. Yet in this respect, armies are not far worse than schools, universities, and churches.

Figure 19 US Army Recruitment Poster (2003)

The preceding pages explained why armies acquired a genuine stake in the new Romantic vision of war, and why it became believable to depict armies as ideal hotbeds for *Bildung*. The following chapter explores the various variants of the new Romantic view of war, as expressed by the soldiers themselves.

6
The Rise of the Revelatory Interpretation of War

In the early modern era the combatants' view of war was dominated by the tension between the interpretation of war as a collective instrument, as a personal instrument, and as an honorable way of life. All three interpretations assumed the supremacy of mind over body, and all three gave very little importance to the experience of war. Once the culture of sensibility was absorbed into the military sphere, a new interpretation of war began to take shape. The new interpretation moved the experience of war from the sidelines to the limelight of military culture. It no longer saw war as an instrument to achieve some outer goal, or as an honorable way of life. Rather, it saw war first and foremost as a sublime experience that was capable of revealing deep truths and changing people in fundamental ways.

As the experience of war moved into the limelight, the relationship between body and mind in war also acquired unprecedented complexity and importance. Hitherto, this relationship was a straightforward affair of the mind's absolute supremacy over the body, which most authors dealt with – if at all – by a few platitudes. The culture of sensibility turned the tables and placed the body in a position to control, teach, and change the mind. The extreme bodily experiences of war suddenly became a far more interesting and important subject than they had ever been before. From tests for a warrior's prowess and steadfastness, they became a sublime gateway to otherwise inaccessible truths and realities, which *change* the warrior instead of merely testing him.

In consequence, military culture and military authors came to show increasing interest in the relationship between body and mind in war, and recognized it as a subject of enormous complexity and importance, capable of destabilizing and even overturning age-old narratives and conventions. Not only great names such as Stendhal and Tolstoy but also ordinary soldiers reconceived war stories to be a above all a philosophical study of the relationship between body and mind, compared to which the study of narrow political and military questions pale into insignificance.

Carl Daniel Küster, a chaplain in Frederick the Great's army, wrote in 1790 about his experiences in the Seven Years War that

> The events of war which are important for reason, heart, humanity, fatherland and for one's own life, write themselves with deeply engraved flame-script in the table of the human soul. After having overcome the shiver of combat in the bloody hours of battle, *all nerves of the senses and of the spirit stand excellently, in almost unbelievably powerful tension and restless activity, to accept and create a host of ideas and to give material to benumbing, but happy thoughts.* For the reader will see in the following, that either in or after the turmoil of combat, high and precious beams of happiness rush through the soul and can give momentary amusement [...] The battle [of Hochkirch, 1758] is important and rich for the hero of war. – To the moralist, explorer of human beings and worshiper of God, the battle opens space for many true, significant commentaries.[1]

Wilhelm von Humboldt put things more succinctly when he said that war is 'one of the most beneficial phenomena for the *Bildung* of mankind.'[2]

It should be noted though that the rise of the revelatory interpretation of war was a slow affair, and even today this interpretation often plays second or third fiddle to the instrumental interpretation. The present chapter makes no attempt to evaluate accurately the relative importance of these various interpretations between 1740 and 1865. Still less does the chapter attempt to offer a picture of "the experience of war" in the Napoleonic era. The number and variety of military memoirs alone – not to mention other types of sources – is so huge that any number of passages can be quoted to prove or disprove any theory.

Instead, the chapter attempts only to highlight and map the novel features of Romantic military memoirs, which clearly distinguish them from early modern memoirs. During the Romantic era, a new culture of war was created, with a new language and a new set of images and values. Potentially, all memoirists could have made use of these new cultural resources. In actuality, many of them made only very limited use of the new resources, and some memoirists made no use of them whatsoever.

The chapter's chief aim is to create an inventory of these new cultural resources. To what extent they were actually used by authors in different countries and different decades is a question that only future research could answer.

Sentimentalizing and Romanticizing war

On the shallowest level, Sensationism and Romanticism transformed military memoirs by changing their language, their scenery, and their imagery. This is a fit subject for an entire book. I wish only to exemplify the transformation by focusing on four issues: sensations, nerves, sympathy, and nature.

Sensations – The first thing that strikes one when comparing Romantic with early modern memoirs is the richness of sensory descriptions, and the attention given to sensations. Early modern memoirists usually tell only what they did and what they saw. In the rare cases when they also tell what they felt, and try to translate the described events into sensory terms, their vocabulary is very limited and dull. In contrast, Romantic memoirists often take great care to explain how events *felt*, and they employ a very rich and diverse language for that purpose. No examples need be given here, as the following pages contain an abundance of them.

Nerves – Sensationist philosophers, poets, and scientists developed in the eighteenth century a new sensory and emotional language which centered on the concept of nerves and fibers. In the twentieth century this language eventually came to dominate military psychology and military experience, as in the contemporary discourse of trauma. Yet it began to infiltrate and influence military discourse already in the Romantic era. Alexander Graydon wrote about leaving Philadelphia in 1776 at the head of his company that 'To say it was a disruption of my heart strings, would be a language neither too forcible nor figurative for the occasion.'[3] John Blakiston said that when he left his family to go serve in India, 'it seemed to me as if my heart-strings were torn asunder.'[4]

Nowhere was this new language of sensitive fibers more apparent than in the changing concepts of fear and courage. We saw that in the early modern era courage involved a simple dynamic between mind and body. Back then, courage was a purely mental quality, a strength of the mind. It was the ability of the mind to overcome the body's fearful messages and make the body act in complete subordination to the mind's will. Even if combatants felt fear, if their mind was strong they could overcome this base sensation. Paragons of courage such as Bayard and Scaevola were so steadfast that they never felt fear at all.

In the eighteenth century a new interpretation of courage appeared. This Sensationist interpretation understood courage to be a bodily strength, belonging to the nervous system rather than to the mind.[5] A strong nervous system, like a strong percussion instrument, could pass on extreme sensations without breaking down. A weak nervous system collapsed under the strain, and could not function. The mind had, at best, only a limited control over the person's capacity. Thus one British officer who was wounded in the Peninsular War had to retire from service due his "nervousness." 'I am grown so nervous,' he wrote, 'that when there is any service to be done it works upon my mind so that it is impossible for me to sleep at night. I cannot possibly stand it, and I shall be forced to retire.'[6]

"Nervous" – originally a neutral term – became synonymous for "fearful." Colonel Landmann remarked about the cannon shots at the battle of Vimeiro (1808) that '[t]he noise made by such a missile, when passing within a yard or so of a person's head, is, to say the least of it, exceedingly disagreeable, and the stoutest nerves would not always save the individual from this highly reprehensible bobbing' ('bobbing' means lowering the head on hearing the approach of a missile, which some thought to be a display of nervousness/cowardice).[7] That "nerves" were a bodily rather than spiritual quality is obvious from the fact that Landmann attributes it to animals as well as men. He wrote that he was 'much pleased and surprised at the readiness with which my horse's nerves had been reconciled to the violent explosions of Artillery.'[8]

In *On War* Clausewitz defines 'presence of mind' as an essential quality of the good commander. 'Whether this splendid quality is due to a special cast of mind or to steady nerves depends on the nature of the incident, but neither can ever be entirely lacking. A quick retort shows wit; resourcefulness in sudden danger calls, above all, for steady nerves.' Though at first Clausewitz refuses to judge the relative importance of mind and body, the examples he gives clearly reveal his hand. If one wants a witty commander, a good cast of mind is enough. But if the commander needs to be resourceful in dangerous situations, a strong nervous system is more important.[9]

Later on Clausewitz discusses four types of commanders, differentiated by how sensitive they are to outside influences. The first type consists of phlegmatic men, who have a 'small capacity for being roused.' The second are men who are extremely active, but whose feelings never rise above a certain level, men whom we know to be sensitive but calm. Third, there are men whose passions are easily inflamed, in whom excitement flares up suddenly but soon burns out [...] And finally we come to those who do not react to minor matters, who will be moved only very gradually, not suddenly, but whose emotions attain great strength and durability. These are the men whose passions are strong, deep, and concealed. These variants are probably related to the *physical forces* operating in the human being – they are part of that dual organism we call the nervous system, one side of which is physical, the other psychological.[10]

Despite Clausewitz's vacillating language, it is again quite clear that the different characteristics of commanders result primarily from their nervous systems. Throughout most of *On War* Clausewitz gives great importance to psychological factors, but in this passage he makes it evident that these psychological factors are ultimately based upon the physical forces of the nervous system. He has little else to say about neurology simply because, in his opinion, contemporary science still lacked the physiological knowledge needed to speak intelligently about the matter.

This new neurological image of courage was not powerful enough to completely dislodge the traditional "spiritual" view of courage. The traditional view probably remained the dominant one throughout the Romantic era and, indeed, down to our own day. However, the neurological view did succeed in transforming the hitherto straightforward discourse of courage into a far more complex and interesting one. Around 1700, it was quite obvious what courage was. Memoirists in particular felt very little need to discuss and explain this issue. Describing the outer activity of people was usually comment enough on their courage, and any reflexion on courage usually consisted of a few platitudes.

Around 1800, it was already far less obvious what courage was. Not only were there now two contending views, but neurological theories also succeeded in subtly influencing those who still adhered to the traditional view. As long as courage was thought to be a purely mental quality, it was associated with other qualities of the mind: It was potentially constant and inexhaustible. Now, thanks to the influences of neurological theories, even those who believed that courage was a spiritual quality began to suspect that it was neither constant nor inexhaustible. It became accepted to argue that a man could be courageous in one action, and cowardly in another, and that every man had some limit to his courage.

For instance, Elzéar Blaze emphasized that fear and courage are not constant qualities, but an ever-changing phenomenon. He writes that

> Frederick the Great often repeated to those who would listen, 'Do not say that a man is brave, but that he was brave on such and such a day.' Indeed, our actions are so intermixed, our feelings sometimes produce such unexpected results that it is impossible for us to say whether we shall be able to do tomorrow that which we have done today.
>
> [...] I shall not boast here like a matamore captain, claiming that I never have been afraid – something I have often heard others say repeatedly. I declare, to the contrary, that when the first bullet whistles overhead, I salute it by an involuntary movement [...] Yes, certainly one must have a breast lined with triple steel to remain perfectly cool amid shot and shell. *I have often analyzed the sensations I have felt during that ceremony*, and I admit that I have been afraid.[11]

Many other memoirists felt obliged to offer complex explanations and critiques of courage, which usually focused on the delicate relations between mind and body. In order to understand courage, it became necessary to describe not only one's external actions, but also the inner feelings involved. This was one of the main reasons why Napoleonic memoirs became far more experiential than early modern memoirs.

After describing how he volunteered to lead the forlorn hope at the storming of Bhurtpoor (1805), John Shipp poses to meditate upon the nature of courage.

> I have heard some men say that they would as soon fight as eat their breakfast; and others, that they "dearly loved fighting". If this were true, what blood-thirsty dogs they must be! But I should be almost illiberal enough to suspect these boasters of not possessing even ordinary courage. [...] [I will ask] these terrific soldiers to account to me why, some hours previously to storming a fort, or fighting a battle, are men pensive, thoughtful, heavy, restless, weighed down with apparent solicitude and care? [...] *A man, situated as I have supposed, who did not, even amid the cannon's roar and the din of war, experience anxieties approaching to what I have described,*

may, by possibility, have the courage of a lion, but he cannot possess the feelings of a man.[12]

We saw that in the early modern period, the ideal was to be like Bayard and Scaevola: completely without fear. Any inner trembling was a sign of weakness, and few admitted the presence of such sensations. Shipp, and the entire sentimental tradition, argued along opposite lines. Courage and honor now depended on inner sensations and emotions of fear. A man was honorable *because* he felt fearful sensations and emotions, yet acted bravely. Someone who did not *feel* fear was for Shipp a mere animal.[13]

John Malcolm repeated the same idea:

I have occasionally met with men who professed to have no such feelings [of fear], and who boasted that, when in similar circumstances, they never once had a thought or a fear of death. Let us hope, for the honour of humanity and of themselves, that this was not true, and that they had been induced to say so from an idea, that a contrary confession might be construed into a want of courage. But surely a mere brute insensibility to danger, goaded on by animal impulse, is not entitled to the name [courage]; and, however paradoxical the assertion may seem, where there is no sense of fear, there can be no courage.[14]

Similarly in Tolstoy's *Sebastopol in August 1855*, the only character who does not experience fear is a common soldier called Melnikoff. When Melnikoff refuses to take shelter during a heavy bombardment, the story's hero – the officer Volodia – who struggles with his own fears, asks the other soldiers about Melnikoff. They tell him that 'He is, your Excellency, an animal who is afraid of nothing.'[15] Not knowing fear is the characteristic of an insensitive animal.[16]

In 1868/69 Ardant du Picq brought the new discourse of fear and courage into the field of professional military theory. After centuries in which the vast majority of military theoreticians focused almost exclusively on tactical disposition and strategic movements, and devoted only a few banalities to the soldiers' psychology, in *Battle Studies* Du Picq revolutionized military theory by placing the psychology of the common soldier at the very center of military thought.

Du Picq assumed that the question of fear and courage is indeed a very complex one, and that the old views of it are nothing more than flowery rhetoric. His main maxim (which is similar to Henry Lloyd's) was that 'Man does not enter battle to fight but for victory. He does everything that he can to avoid the first and obtain the second.'[17] Like the Sensationists, Du Picq assumed that man is dominated by the instinct of self-preservation, and that fighting is therefore unnatural for him and can result only from some complicated mechanisms. To decipher the secrets of military psychology, Du Picq laid aside millennia of martial rhetoric and historiography, and began the study of war afresh with positivist sociological and psychological research. He distributed questionnaires to thousands of combatants, asking them about their *experience* of war. Both in his methods and in his conclusions Du Picq blazed the trail along which S. L. A. Marshall, John Keegan, and the whole modern school of military psychology and "Face of Battle" studies would follow in the twentieth century.[18]

The new neurological language also began to forge the connection between war and madness, with weak nerves and extreme experiences serving as a link. Ulrich Bräker tells of recruits who became mentally unstable due to the shock of recruitment and basic training. One Mecklenburg recruit would stand at night outside the barracks, and shout obscenities at his officers and King Frederick. Bräker and the other recruits tried to calm him: ' "Listen, mate! [...] if you're not careful, the way you're going, one day you'll find yourself in the mad-house." ' Bräker then saw another recruit who hang by himself and was very quiet. When he was told that the man is mad, Bräker's enlightened curiosity arose. 'This account made me keen to getting to know the man more closely. [...] The physiognomy alone of a poor body in such straits was sacred to me.'[19]

Thomas Morris was once ordered for a general parade to witness the execution of a soldier. 'The guard, with their loaded muskets, were waiting only for the fatal word, when the officer commanding, intimated to the prisoner, that the Duke [of Wellington] had been graciously pleased to pardon him. This sudden and unexpected announcement, had the effect of depriving the poor wretch of his reason, and he left the ground a *maniac.*'[20] James Campbell mentions a young dragoon in his regiment who was severely wounded in battle. 'His wound had produced mental imbecility, which was strikingly depicted on his countenance, and was, besides, perceptible by his manner of playing with a clod of the ploughed field.'[21]

Heinrich Vossler wrote about the retreat from Moscow that

> not only men's bodies suffered unspeakably, their minds, too, became deeply affected by the combined assault of extreme cold and hunger. [...] Dull despair or raving madness had taken possession of many

and they died muttering, with their last breath, the most horrible imprecations against God and man. Others became childish and perished as a result, though their physical strength might otherwise have carried them through. Yet others again fell into a torpor which prevented them from grasping the means of salvation when they presented themselves and thus they, too, stumbled to their deaths. All, without exception, had suffered some impairment, at least temporary, of their mental powers, which often manifested itself in a sort of dumb lethargy. The troops called it "the Moscow dumps."[22]

Sympathy – Wars in the early modern era engendered a tremendous amount of human suffering, and memoirists often made little effort to hide this fact. However, though they often mentioned suffering in a matter-of-fact way, they seldom described it in sympathetic detail. In contrast, Romantic memoirists customarily incorporated into their narratives detailed descriptions of pathetic scenes, rendered in the most emotional terms. The purpose of these scenes was to display the author's sensibility, and to enable the readers to display and develop their own sensibilities.

For instance, in his introduction to a story of British captives in India, William Thomson wrote that 'The Narrative of what happened to our men under confinement with the Barbarians is not only affecting, but in some measure instructing. As natural convulsions discover the hidden strata of the earth and ocean, so violent moral situations tear up and display the passions and powers of the human soul. The sensibility of our captive countrymen and friends was powerfully excited.'[23] The duke of Montesquiou-Fezensac says at the end of his narrative of the 1812 campaign that '[o]f those who read what I have written I ask only that they share the emotions which I feel as I conclude this account: I ask them to join me in admiration for so much courage and sorrow for so much misfortune.'[24] Memoirists such as Montesquiou-Fezensac no longer seek just to inform the readers – they seek to develop their sensibility.

It was also of great importance to memoirists to illustrate that they and their fellow soldiers were men-of-feeling rather than brutes. Lieutenant John Shipp insists throughout his narrative that it is not true that 'soldiers, inured to the scenes of war, do not possess the nicer feelings of the heart.'[25] When the British commander-in-chief in India reviewed the survivors of the 22nd regiment, which was decimated in a failed attack, 'he was seen to turn from them, and the tear fell down his cheek; but, fearful it might be observed, he took off his hat and cheered them.

This was not the tear of Judas, for his lordship often shed tears of sorrow for our great loss at this place.'[26]

On another occasion, after the bombardment and surrender of the fort of Dhamoony (1817), a British gunner entered the fort to see what damage his battery inflicted. Shipp pointed out to the gunner an Indian woman whose legs were shot off, and who was still carrying a baby in her arms. Shipp, who objected to the bombardment, addressed the gunner:

> "Well, sergeant, I hope you are now compensated for your trouble in the erection of your battery." He turned his head to where I pointed, and said (I shall never forget his pathetic manner), "By my conscience, your honour, if I had thought I should ever have seen such a murderous sight, I would not have come near the place." I saw him wipe the tear of sympathy from his eye with the back of his hand, and he continued, "Shall I take the poor creature to the hospital?"[27]

Shipp continually describes the British soldiers as men of feeling, whereas he criticized their Indian enemies for their lack of feeling. On one occasion the British offer, out of sympathy, good surrender terms to a fort under bombardment.

> We could distinctly hear the moaning of the wounded; and sad must have been the fate of those poor fellows whose gaping wounds were left bleeding, the shattered bones protruding through the lacerated flesh. The very idea makes the sympathetic mind shudder; but the hearts of these unfortunate creatures were as impenetrable as the stubborn rock on which their fort was erected. Yet, this very fact serves but to increase our sorrow for their benighted souls, influenced and guided by some hypocritical priest or mendicant impostor, who leads them blindfold to destruction.[28]

Shipp disdains to describe the scenes he saw inside the fort after it eventually fell, so as not to hurt his readers' feelings, 'and, should these Memoirs ever meet the eye of any of my fair countrywomen, I am confident they will thank me for the omission.'[29]

Similar "sympathetic" scenes became common in visual art as well. For instance, one of Joseph Wright's most successful paintings, *The Dead Soldier* (1789), depicted a dead soldier with his widow and orphaned baby in a way that may seem to present-day viewers a bit too sentimental, but which appealed to Wright's contemporaries.

Figure 20 Joseph Wright, *The Dead Soldier* (1789)

Nature – When reading military memoirs from the early modern age, it is easy to imagine that the described events took place in a blank environment. With few exceptions,[30] the authors show only the most meager interest in the natural setting of war. Woods, mountains, oceans, sunsets, ancient towns, ruined castles, and thunderstorms occasionally appear in the texts, but only when they have some obvious military significance, and even then they are noted rather than described. If something had no obvious bearing on the public or private aims of war, or on matters of honor, it was deemed unworthy of being recorded.

In the Romantic scheme, however, nature could not be ignored. The sensations and experiences resulting from the natural setting shaped not only the mood of individual people, but the character of entire nations and the outcome of great enterprises. "Going into nature" was an extremely important way of acquiring wisdom and insight, and connecting to one's inner nature and to one's collective identity. Nature occasionally defined the very aims of war. The war aims of revolutionary France were famously defined by Danton as the achievement of "natural" frontiers. 'The frontiers of France,' he said in the National

Convention, 'have been mapped by nature, and we shall reach them at the four corners of the horizons, on the banks of the Rhine, by the side of the ocean and at the Alps.'[31] Consequently, it became impossible to describe a military campaign without giving a "romantic" description of its natural settings and the experiential impact this setting had on the combatants.[32]

Moreover, the fact that combatants spent much of their days in the open, camping, marching, and fighting "in nature," greatly enhanced their cultural standing and the authority they could command. War itself was a sublime event, but the fact that it took place in "nature," with the combatants often encountering wild terrain and camping in the open, made war all the more sublime, and gained added authority for veterans.[33]

Military memoirists were clearly aware of these cultural developments, and reflected them in their writings. For example, in 1807 Clausewitz recollected his first campaign in the following terms:

> With much pleasure I still recall [...] an experience when the Prussian army in 1793 left the Vosges. We had spent half a year in these thickly wooded, raw, poor, and melancholy mountains, and with a kind of resignation our eyes had grown accustomed never to see more than a few steps of the path that we followed. Our psychological existence was similar: the physical surroundings perfectly reflected our mood. The soldier's extremely restricted horizon barely permits him to survey the next few hours. Often he hears the voice of battle, which is near and yet remains invisible, and he approaches his fate like a danger in the night. – At last, after an arduous march, we suddenly reached the magnificent valley of the Rhine, from Landau to Worms. At that moment life seemed to me to change from ominous gravity to friendliness, from tears to smiles.[34]

Lieutenant Ernst-Friedrich von Barsewisch, an officer in Frederick the Great's army, was deeply influenced by the mountains through which his unit marched:

> The greatness and wonderful creation of God, and the grand and omniscient creator himself cannot be admired enough given the various shape of the earth. The omnipotence and greatness of God has always seemed to me far more majestic and glorious on the cliffy backs of the mountains, which lose themselves in the clouds, than in the lowlands, especially when I, during a strong storm, under flashes

and cracking, thought of the mountain Sinai and of God's command-
ments, which were on this mountain under lightning and thunder
given and revealed to the human race through Moses.[35]

Peter Leslie describes the march from Calcutta to the Punjab with similar
enthusiasm, insisting that 'no good-thinking being can view the beauties
of nature unmoved,' that India's nature is 'awfully sublime,' and that 'He
must, indeed, feel little of devotion within his breast who can witness an
Indian thunderstorm without being convinced of a "great First Cause,"
and that an Almighty God "reigneth in heaven and amongst the inhabitants of the earth." ' [36]

John Shipp was similarly enthralled by the wonders of India's nature.
Whenever he describes a battle or a siege, he devotes a paragraph or two
to describe the natural settings in exceedingly 'romantic' language. For
example, on campaign against the Nepalese, one morning

> The sun rose in majestic splendour, and the scene before us was
> a little world of woody hills and valleys. The brilliant rays of the
> luminary day exhibited to the eye nature's masterpiece in scenery.
> Golden woods, that would have defied the pencil of an artist, and
> which surpassed the sublimest creation of the imagination; glittering
> hills, that vied in brilliancy with the rising sun; rippling rills, that
> whispered, "Come, yet thirsty souls, and drink of the crystal brooks;
> and, ye passing seraphs, stay and dip your wings in the pure stream,
> ere ye ascend to the realm of love;" [...] and cataracts, that rushed
> headlong down the rocky cliff, and imparted a wild beauty to the
> whole, beyond the power of words to describe. [...] Oh, that ever
> human blood should defile these beautiful scenes! or that the horrors
> of war should disturb the sweet harmony established by nature in
> the fertile valleys of this sweet and picturesque country![37]

Only after two pages of such descriptions does Shipp go on to describe
the disposition of the Nepalese forces and the maneuvers of the British
army.[38]

The new "natural" language of war is perhaps most evident in three of
the iconic images of revolutionary warfare: Napoleon crossing the Alps,
Washington crossing the Delaware, and Russia's "General Winter."

The Alps were a busy military highway throughout the early modern
age. During the Italian Wars, for example, French armies crossed and
recrossed the mountain ranges almost every year. Yet no contemporary
memoirist thought of describing the grandeur of the Alps. They were just

a physical obstacle to the troops and the supply columns. For instance, the lord of Florange described the 1515 crossing of the Alps by François I in the following terms:

> The heavy artillery of the king and some infantrymen took the road through the mountains of Geneva to descend to Susa [through the Mount Cenis pass], because there was no mountain passage through which the artillery could cross except there. And the king and the light artillery took the road to Guylestre, which was three mountain ranges away, and made their descent to a castle on a mountain, with a small town adjacent, called Rocquespervet, adjoining the Marquisate of Saluce.[39]

In 1524 François again led his army across the Alps in a forced march, aimed to catch his enemies unaware.

> He divided his army into three to make the crossing through three passages: the Swiss through Guillestre and the landsknechts with them, and my lord de la Pallice with the vanguard and the king through another passage near Notre Dame d'Aulbyn to Susa. The artillery and the rest of the infantrymen went through the mountains of Geneva, which was their crossing.

Florange explains that it was impossible to supply the army well due to the suddenness of the movement and the difficulty of the terrain. The Swiss in particular could not find bread or wine for eight or ten days, yet they traveled with astonishing rapidity. Though he aims to impress the readers with the boldness of François's sudden stroke, Florange never describes the Alps themselves, and cares nothing for the grandeur and sublimity of the natural setting.[40] None of François's court painters thought of producing a picture of "François I crossing the Alps," and though both in 1515 and in 1524 François's move resulted in a (temporary) French victory, the crossing itself was overlooked in the celebration of success.

In contrast, Napoleon's crossing of the Alps in 1800 became one of the most famous scenes of the Napoleonic era, immortalized in numerous poems and paintings as well as military memoirs, and symbolizing the victory of the new forces released by the revolution over the old order that hitherto seemed as immutable and insurmountable as the Alps.

Figure 21   Jacques-Louis David, *Napoleon Crossing the St. Bernard* (1800)

Why did Napoleon's Alpine crossing attain such cultural prominence whereas François I's crossing did not? The essential reason is that in 1800 European elites had for decades been fed on a diet of sublime Alpine crossings. In such atmosphere, Napoleon's crossing was not just a fit object of study for logistic experts, but a sublime event of inescapable import. It was easy to imagine that in confronting and overcoming the Alps, Napoleon saw a sublime vision of a new world order. (It is curious to note that in 1791 Second Lieutenant Bonaparte submitted an essay to a prize competition of the Academy of Lion on the question "What truths and feelings are most important to instill happiness in men?"

In his essay, the young officer advised readers to climb the peak of Mont-Blanc and watch the sunrise.[41])

Across the Atlantic, Washington's crossing of the Delaware River before the battle of Trenton (December 25, 1776), undertaken during a severe winter storm, became the most famous visual icon of American military history.[42] Again, the forces of nature – the icy river and the roaring storm – symbolized the immense obstacles against which the revolutionaries struggled, and the confrontation with these forces could not but be interpreted as a confrontation with the sublime. Washington's gaze must be seeing, through the storm, a sublime vision of the new order.

Figure 22   Emanuel Gottlieb Leutze, *Washington Crossing the Delaware* (1851)

Needless to say, rivers had been crossed in numerous early modern wars, occasionally under conditions quiet similar to those prevailing at the Delaware in 1776. For example, in December 1503 the Spanish army under Hérnandez Gonzalo de Córdoba confronted a superior French army across the Garigliano River. Utilizing a dark and stormy night, on December 29, 1503 Córdoba bridged the river by a fit of engineering that stupefied contemporaries. He took the French by surprise, and routed them. To the best of my knowledge, no early modern artist thought to immortalize the crossing of the Garigliano.

A final example is the campaign of 1812. Contemporaries were quick to ascribe Napoleon's defeat to the working of "General Winter," and numerous written and visual accounts from all sides described in great detail the awesome power of the Russian winter.[43] Winter had defeated countless armies on previous occasions, yet rarely was it personified and described in such a way. When in 1588 a severe storm wrecked the Spanish Armada and saved England from invasion, contemporaries attributed the defeat to Divine Providence rather than to Admiral Storm.

The key experiences of war

In addition to using new language, scenery, and imagery, Romantic military memoirs began to evaluate the events of war from a new perspective. Events were no longer judged by their military impact or by their honor. Instead, events became "experiences," and began to be judged by their impact on the *Bildung* process of the individual. Key experiences such as one's enlistment or baptism of fire were moved into the limelight even if they had no impact on the collective war aims, on one's personal aims, and on matters of honor.[44]

Sir James Campbell of Ardkinglass, in his memoirs of the Seven Years War, explains how he chose which incidents to narrate:

> It appears to me that circumstances, which, if now occurring, I should regard as unworthy of observation or remark, but which, at the moment when they did occur, took such a hold of my imagination as to imprint themselves on my memory, and leave there a distinct impression at the distance of many years, have some claim to be recorded from that very circumstance, **without any reference to their intrinsic merits.** Of this nature is the fact I am about to set down. [...] At the siege of Marburg, I observed a shell in its descent pass through the dead body of a man lying by me on the ground, and immediately afterwards explode. When the explosion had taken place, I naturally looked all round me in expectation of seeing some of the mangled remains of the poor soldier, but strange to say, not a vestige of them was to be discovered in any direction.[45]

In Sir James's logic one can detect the first notes of the Freudian leit-motif. Sergeant Bourgogne anticipated Freud even more closely when explaining how he chose what to narrate about the retreat from Moscow (1812): 'For the honour of humanity, perhaps, I ought not to describe all these scenes of horror, but I have determined to write down all I saw. I cannot do otherwise, and, besides, all these things have taken such possession of my mind that I think if I write them down they will cease to trouble me.'[46] Further on Bourgogne explains that whenever he meets with other veterans, and they begin to speak of their past campaigns, it is always to the retreat from Moscow 'that our memories take us; and I have noticed that with them, as with me, indelible impressions are left.'[47]

The following section surveys the key military experiences identified by the new stories of military *Bildung*. We shall see in a subsequent section how these individual experiences were combined to create a number of meta-narratives that have characterized Western war culture ever since.

Note that when memoirists describe these key experiences, they often add to them general insights about war and other issues. By incorporating these insights into descriptions of key experiences, which often have a sublime nature, the memoirists give them the authority of revelation.

Basic training

The events of basic training usually had no impact on military actions and objectives, and it was similarly impossible to acquire honor in them. Basic training was consequently left out of almost all early modern memoirs. However, in the era of *Bildung* basic training acquired immense importance. It was recognized not only by the army but also by the recruits as a crucial identity crisis. With hindsight, veterans remembered basic training as one of the most significant periods of their military career and of their entire life. They encountered for the first time in their life a whole plethora of extreme experiences, sensations and emotions, which within a few weeks brought about radical changes in their personality and worldview.

For instance, whereas Chouppes and Navailles summed up their first years of campaigning in a few sentences, John Shipp devoted 50 pages to describe his enlistment, basic training, and his experiences in the army up to his first combat (1797). His memoirs include one of the first specimens of the "military haircut scene":

> I was taken to a barber's, and deprived of my curly brown locks. My hair curled beautifully, but in a minute my poor little head was nearly bald, except a small patch behind, which was reserved for a future operation. I was then paraded to the tailor's shop, and deprived of my new clothes – coat, leathers, and hat – for which I received, in exchange, a red jacket, red waistcoat, red pantaloons, and red foraging-cap. The change, or metamorphosis, was so complete, that I could hardly imagine it to be the same dapper little fellow. [...]

My pride was humbled, my spirits drooped, and I followed the drum-major, hanging my head like a felon going to the place of execution. I cut such a queer figure, that all who met me turned round and stared at me. [...] Passing some drummers on their way to practice, I got finely roasted. "Twig the raw-skin!" – "Smoke his pantaloons!" – "Them there trousers is what I calls a knowing cut!" – "Look at the sign of the Red Man!" &c., &c. [...] I sat myself down on a stool, which might not inaptly have been styled the stool of repentance; for here I began first to think that soldiering did not possess quite so much delight as I had pictured to myself.[48]

Ulrich Bräker describes in detail how he was tricked by a Prussian recruiting officer and pressed into Prussian service against his will. He then gives a minute description of the life and thoughts of a Prussian recruit in the barracks and on the drilling field, complete with sadistic drill-sergeants, merciless kit inspections, and recruits who go nuts.[49]

An Irish youth joined the British Army in 1806, attracted by 'the roll of the spirit-stirring drum, the glittering file of bayonets, with the pomp and circumstance of military parade, not unmingled perhaps with undefined thoughts of ultimate promotion.' In his memoirs he gave a minute description of his first night in the barracks. He was tormented by thoughts of his poor mother, and was further appalled by the material conditions. He was lodged in a large room, full of young soldiers, drinking, cursing, and fighting, and 'altogether the coalition of discordant verbiage was such as to beggar all description [...] Never will the occurrence of that night be effaced from my mind. Surely, thought I, hell from beneath is moved to engulf us all.'[50]

In 1838 an anonymous British soldier even published an *Autobiography of a Private Soldier*, which focused exclusively on the author's experiences during his period of basic training. The aim of this short narrative was to warn youths of the difficulties and dangers of enlisting, and the author hoped that the profits of this publication would enable him to buy his own discharge from the service![51]

Baptism of fire

Early modern memoirists dwelt on their first combat experience only if they covered themselves with glory, or if it was an important histor-ical event in its own right. In contrast, Romantic memoirists began describing their first combat experience in detail even if it was a petty skirmish and even if they themselves performed no memorable deed. Their focus was neither on the military impact of the action nor on honor, but rather on the novel sensations and emotions they encountered, and the effect these novelties had on them.[52]

For example, Peter Leslie described his first combat experience in a chapter of his autobiography which he titled 'Baptism of Fire.' On October 26, 1863 he took part in a minor skirmish in the north-west of India, 'on which occasion one private was killed and five were wounded.'[53] Most early modern memoirists would not have bothered to even mention such a trivial incident. Yet for Leslie it was one of the decisive moments of his life. 'Such, then, was my first – and as yet only – taste of the "Baptism of fire," and never till my dying day can I efface its scenes from my mind.' After experiencing combat he takes stock of his earlier fantasies of war:

> Often, as I have already said, had I read and pondered over the glorious deeds performed by my countrymen upon the field of battle, and longed to share in their well-merited honours, now that I had become a soldier; but when the stern reality was placed before me, and I had to meet such a foe face to face, I must confess I felt an indescribable thrill pass through me, and again when my front rank man rolled over a corpse and I had to step up into his place to keep the "thin red line" unbroken, all finer feelings gave way as I saw at once at what cost "Duty must be done," and how true was the exclamation of the Psalmist when he said – "Come see what desolations war has brought."[54]

Leslie's baptism of fire is a typical example of how the narration of a key experience is utilized to give the authority of revelation to a general insight about war.

Major-General Sir George Bell wrote that as he and his comrades went 'to be baptised in blood' at their first battle (Arroyo Dos Molinos, 1811), 'I began to have a queer feeling of mortal danger stirring my nerves.' He heard the noise of an approaching cannonball 'such as I had never heard before,' and shortly after 'I saw two men cut across by that last shot, the first I had ever seen killed. I was horrified, but said nothing.'[55]

John Blakiston comments about his baptism of fire at the siege of Ahmednaghur (1803):

> This was the first time I had ever heard the whistling of balls. The reader will perhaps expect that I should exultingly exclaim with Charles the Twelfth, 'Henceforth this shall be my music!' But candour obliges me to confess that such a noble idea did not enter my

thoughts, for, however harmonious the balls may have sounded in the ears of the Swedish hero, to me they certainly did not convey the same degree of pleasure that I have since experienced from the voice of a Catalani, or from the bow of a Linley. On the contrary, the noise which they made, as they glanced past my head, raised about the precincts of my heart a kind of awkward sensation, not at all allied to pleasure, and partaking more of what is vulgarly called fear, but which, as a military man, I dare not designate by that name.[56]

Nadezhda Andreevna Durova had opposite impressions of her first battle:

May 22, 1807. Guttstadt. For the first time I have seen a battle and been in it. What a lot of absurd things they told me about the first battle, about the fear, timidity, and the last, desperate courage! What rubbish! [...] The novelty of the scene absorbed all my attention: the menacing and majestic boom of cannon fire, the roar or kind of rumble of the flying balls, the mounted troops galloping by, the glittering bayonets of the infantry, the roll of drums, and the firm pace and calm look with which our infantry regiments advanced on the enemy – all this filled my soul with sensations that I have no words to express.[57]

The Baptism of Fire became such a clichéd experience that in the *Charterhouse of Parma* (1839) Stendhal, a veteran of the Napoleonic Wars, already felt obliged to satirize it.[58] Fabrizio, the novel's hero, is a young Italian who traveled to the Low Countries in 1815 to join Napoleon and "experience" combat. His experience of Waterloo was dominated by a peculiar obsession: He was keen to have his Baptism of Fire, but everything he experienced did not seem to him exalted enough to be considered such a sublime event.

When he first came under fire, and enemy cannonballs killed some nearby soldiers, Fabrizio was ecstatic: " 'Ah! So I am under fire at last!" he said to himself. "I have seen shots fired!" he repeated with a sense of satisfaction. "Now I am a real soldier." ' [59] However, upon reflection, he became dissatisfied with the experience, because he had merely been under fire, without doing anything himself. He now came to believe that "experiencing" battle required firing at the enemy and killing a man. Fabrizio wandered over the field of battle, but never got a chance to fire his weapon. At last, after the French were defeated and the route began, Fabrizio got a chance to shoot some pursuing allied cavalrymen. 'Fabrizio was supremely happy. "Now I am going to do some real fighting," he said to himself, "and kill one of the enemy. This morning they were sending cannonballs over, and I did nothing but expose myself and risk getting killed; that's a fool's game." '[60]

He killed a man, but still remained in doubt whether he really "experienced" battle. When he separated from two soldiers who accompanied him during the retreat, he became distressed. 'What distressed him most was that he had not asked Corporal Aubry the question: "Have I really taken part in a battle?" It seemed to him that he had, and his happiness would have known no bounds could he have been certain of this.'[61]

After Waterloo

> Fabrizio became another man, so many and profound were his reflexions on the things that had happened to him. He had remained a child upon one point only: what he had seen, was it a battle; and, if so, was that battle Waterloo? For the first time in his life he found pleasure in reading; he was always hoping to find in the newspapers, or in the published accounts of the battle, some description which would enable him to identify the ground he had covered with Marshal Ney's escort, and afterwards with the other general.[62]

The irony of Fabrizio's story is of course that he not only "experienced" a battle, but he had experienced the most famous battle of modern times.

The eve of combat

In early modern memoirs the only thing that was usually told about the preliminaries of battle was the disposition and strength of the opposing armies. In Romantic memoirs the eve of combat was elevated to the status of an epiphanic experience, during which the expectant troops became acquainted with extreme psychological and physical states.

In Schiller's *Wallenstein's Death* (1799) Wallenstein tells Fieldmarshal Illo about his experiences before the battle of Lützen:

> Know there are moments in the life of man / When he stands closer than at other times / To the directing spirit of the world, / And may put question to his destiny. / It was at such an instant, when, the night / Before the action that we fought at Lützen, / I leant against a tree, alone, in thought, / And gazed out on the plain. The camp-fires burned / With dismal glow to pierce the swirling mists, / The muffled clang of weapons and the cry / Of sentinels alone disturbed the silence. / Then in that moment all my life, both past / And future,

sped before my inward eye, / And on the coming morning's fate my spirit / In ranging dreams hung all that was to come.[63]

George Gleig writes about his own experiences (1813):

> It would be difficult to convey to the mind of an ordinary reader anything like a correct notion of the state of feeling which takes possession of a man waiting for the commencement of battle. In the first place, time appears to move upon leaden wings; every minute seems an hour, and every hour a day. Then there is a strange commingling of levity and seriousness within him – a levity which prompts him to laugh, he scarce knows why; and a seriousness which urges him ever and anon to lift up a mental prayer to the Throne of Grace. [...] On these occasions, too, the faces of the bravest often change colour, and the limbs of the most resolute tremble, not with fear, but with anxiety; whilst watches are consulted, till the individuals who consult them grow absolutely weary of the employment. On the whole, it is a situation of higher excitement, and darker and deeper agitation, than any other in human life; *nor can he be said to have felt all which man is capable of feeling, who has not filled [sic] it.*[64]

Which means that to fulfill von Humboldt's ideal of "taking the measure in feeling of everything human,"[65] combat experience was indispensable.

Combat

Naturally, combat too was described as an epiphany. For instance, John Shipp wrote that

> In action man is quite another being: the softer feelings of the roused heart are absorbed in the vortex of danger, and the necessity for self-preservation, and give place to others more adapted to the occasion. In these moments there is an indescribable elation of spirits; the soul rises above its wonted serenity into a kind of frenzied apathy to the scene before you – a heroism bordering on ferocity; the nerves become tight and contracted; the eye full and open, moving quickly in its socket, with almost maniac wildness; the head is in constant motion; the nostril extended wide, and the mouth apparently gasping. If an artist could truly delineate the features of a soldier in the battle's heat, and compare them with the lineaments of the same man in

the peaceful calm of domestic life, they would be found to be two different portraits.[66]

Elzéar Blaze agreed, writing that 'When you maneuver, when you fire, when you are fully engaged, your feelings disappear – the smoke, the uproar of the cannon, the shouts of the combatants intoxicate everyone. You don't have time to think of yourself.'[67] Commanders too described combat as an emotional epiphany rather than a game of chess. Jean-Jacques Pelet writes regarding his emotions when his troops were almost caught by the British after Bussaco (1810): 'Never will I suffer as much as I did during that cruel night, when exhaustion and rain were nothing compared with my mental anguish and many fears.' When he saw that his troops were safe, 'I was in ecstasy. I can say that my soul was over-flowing with happiness.'[68]

Injury and brushes with death

Death was at the basis of all sublime experiences. Not surprisingly then, when combat involved a close brush with death, it could give rise to even more novel sensations and experiences, which could result in important revelations. For instance, Lieutenant Jakob Friedrich von Lemcke of the Prussian army describes his injury in a battle against the Russians (1759) as an extreme experience that culminated in an early example of the Kantian sublime (written well before Kant's *Critique of Judgment*). As Lemcke was trying to push his soldiers to attack, a cannonball smashed his left foot. His men fled, and the pursuing Russians passed him by. A Russian marauder then came along, and prepared to shoot Lemcke at point-blank range:

> As I could see now right into the muzzle of the musket, it was awful to me, to have my murderer so close in front of me, so I plunked myself lengthwise on the earth and lay on my belly. It was, as if all my senses had left me and I may have lay a long time in my numbness, when I recovered again through a heavy stroke, which the Cossack had given me with the butt [of the musket].

The Cossack merely robbed him, and left him to his fate. Some Prussian soldiers tried to carry him away, but the pain was too terrible, and he could not be moved.

> Here I wished all the time, that one of the cannon balls, that so often rolled past my place, would hit me, so that I would soon be redeemed from the agony, because I most certainly believed, that I would have

to die, and considered it impossible to live on any longer. And I cannot describe how relaxed I was and how much I wanted to die.

He somehow survived, and continued to just lay there in the midst of the battle,

> stripped to my sheer shirt, heavily bleeding, exhausted, and so thirsty, that the tongue stuck to the roof of the mouth, – but still the cruel death did not want to come, how much soever I asked God to dissolve me, ***but I recognized, that my mind and heart were quite powerful.***[69]

In Tolstoy's *War and Peace* young Nikolai Rostov had a brush with death in a minor cavalry skirmish during the 1805 campaign. His cavalry squadron was given an order to charge. Rostov was excited. '"If only they would be quick," thought Rostov, feeling that at last the time had come to experience the intoxication of a charge, of which he had heard so much from his fellow hussars.' To Rostov's dismay, the French drove the Russians before them, and Rostov himself was knocked down. After some time, he saw French soldiers approaching, and found it hard to credit what is happening.

> "Who are these men?" thought Rostov, unable to believe his own eyes. "Can they be the French?" He looked at the approaching Frenchmen, and in spite of the fact that only a moment before he had been dashing forward solely for the purpose of getting at these same Frenchmen to hack them to pieces their proximity now seemed so awful that he could not believe his eyes. "Who are they? Are they coming at me? Can they be running at me? And why? To kill me? *Me* whom everyone is so fond of?" He thought of his mother's love for him, of his family's and his friends', and the enemy's intention of killing him seemed impossible. "But perhaps they will!" For over ten seconds he stood rooted to the spot, not realizing the situation.

Eventually, 'A single unmixed instinct of fear for his young and happy life possessed his whole being,' and he managed to escape. Looking back at the French he thought, '"No, there's some mistake [...] They can't have meant to kill me."'[70]

Inflicting death

Inflicting death on others was another "key experience" which could make a deep impact on memoirists. During the War of American Independence, the severest trial James Collins had to undergo was when he was given a spear and asked by one of his comrades to kill in cold blood a Tory captive. He was even offered money to do the deed. Collins describes the experience in detail, explaining that this was 'a trial that I have not forgotten, nor will ever forget.' Eventually he resisted the temptation. '[H]ad I committed the deed,' he writes, 'the ghost of that old man would have haunted me to this day.'[71]

General Marbot recounted how he was once attacked by two Cossack officers, youths of about 18 or 20, who were accompanied by their old governor. The elder one charged Marbot. Marbot easily vanquished him, but spared his life. The Cossack then brought out two pistols, and treacherously shot dead Marbot's aide. 'Besides myself with rage, I dashed on the madman, who was taking aim at me with his second pistol. But as he met my eye he seemed fascinated, and cried out in good French, "Oh God! I see death in your eyes! I see death in your eyes!" "Ay, scoundrel, and you see right!" And he dropped.'

Marbot, in a towering rage, then charged the other Cossack and the governor. He caught the youth in the throat, and raised his sword to strike him, when the old man cried, 'For your mother's sake pardon this one, who has done nothing!'

> On hearing him invoke that revered name, my mind, overwrought by the surroundings, was struck with hallucination: I thought I saw a well-known white hand laid upon the young man's breast, which I was on the point of piercing, and I seemed to hear my mother's voice saying "Pardon! Pardon!". My sword point dropped, and I had the youth and his governor taken to the rear. So great was my emotion after this incident that I could not have given any word of command if the fight had lasted much longer.[72]

Durova's memories of her first kill in war were more painful. The victim was a goose that she robbed from a deserted village during the 1812 campaign.

> Poor geese! The sight of them reminded me of Podjampolsky's appeal, reminded me that one of them must surely die. Oh, how ashamed I am to write this! How ashamed to confess such inhumanity! With my noble saber I cut off the head of an innocent bird!! It was the first blood I had ever shed in my life. And, although it was the blood of a bird, please believe me, you who will someday read my *Notes*, that the memory of it weighs heavily on my mind.[73]

Was she being ironic? I really do not know. Anything is possible with these Romantic authors.

Witnessing death

Even when death was not the memoirist's fault, witnessing it was a key experience. During combat in the Pyrenees (1814), John Malcolm witnessed the death of a fellow officer, and his reaction anticipated that of Yossarian in *Catch-22*. The officer was firing upon the enemy with much courage and coolness.

> I happened to turn about my head for a moment, and when I looked back again, he was lying stretched on his back, the blood welling from his breast, and his feet quivering in the last convulsions of expiring nature. [...] He had joined us only two or three days previous to the battle, and was standing close beside me in the flush of youth, and health, and hope – in the very moment of victory – the proudest one of life: His eye but twinkled once, and he lay a corpse at my feet!
>
> > "What art thou Spirit undefin'd,
> > That passest with man's breath away,
> > That giv'st him feeling, sense, and mind,
> > And leav'st him cold unconscious clay?".[74]

George Blennie saw several men killed in action during one of his first battles (1799). One death scene in particular shocked him. 'I was so struck with this man's ghastly appearance, that I thought with myself, "Were I a poet, I would choose, as my subject, the horrors of war, that I might persuade mankind not to engage in it." '[75]

Robert Blakeney remembered with awe not only the first time he saw a soldier killed, but even the first time he saw a soldier injured. It happened during exercises in England.

> Never shall I forget the thrilling emotion which agitated my whole frame at seeing the blood fall from the hand of one of the soldiers, wounded through the clumsy manner in which he fixed his flint. I eyed each precious drop that fell with glowing sensations such as would blaze in the breast of a Napoleon on beholding an old dynasty diadem, or inflame the heart of a Scot in contemplating a new place in the Treasury.[76]

Around the same time, civilian artists too began to create sentimental "death in battle" scenes which focused on the knowing stare of the depicted soldiers. Relying on the model of religious Pietas, they painted the death of soldiers in combat as a revelation for their surrounding comrades. Benjamin West's *The Death of General Wolfe* (1770) is probably the most famous specimen of this emerging genre (note that West painted the surgeon inserting his hand into the open wound on the general's side – an obvious allusion to Doubting Thomas and Christ).

Figure 23   Benjamin West, *The Death of General Wolfe* (1770)

Particularly interesting is the "noble savage" in the foreground. Painted in the classical pose of Western meditation, he seems to be studying the dying general with philosophical interest, much like Boswell studying executed criminals at Tyburn or Robert Whytt studying a dying frog. It is doubly interesting that the noble savage has the most imposing *bodily* presence of any of the men in the picture. Whereas all the others are fully clothed, he is almost naked. Whereas the dying general seems to be as weak as a fleeting spirit, the savage – apparently a Native American common warrior rather than a chief – is depicted with bulging muscles. Though West himself probably thought along opposite lines, *The Death of General Wolfe* can well be seen as symbolic for the victory of body over mind, and for the way body has appropriated the traditional prerogative of mind: thinking. Whereas the emblematic picture of the early modern era showed a general standing on a high hill, his mind controlling the fate of thousands of pin-men, the emblematic picture of the Romantic era shows a weak and dying general whose death is an object of meditation for a very corporeal common soldier.

While West still distanced the dying general from the battlefield, in the following decades artists placed such scenes in the midst of combat, as in the case of John Singleton Copley's *The Death of Major Peirson* (1783). Note the similarity between the group of soldiers holding Major Peirson, and earlier Pieta and entombment images (such as Raphael's *Deposition*) which focused on a group of saints holding Christ's body.

Figure 24 John Singleton Copley, *The Death of Major Peirson, 6 January 1781* (1783)

In contrast to Urs Graf's *Battlefield*, in these sentimental battle paintings the painted soldiers forget for a moment about the surrounding dangers, and focus their stare on their dying comrade. Their stares register the experience of combat; and the message to the viewers is that the soldiers are undergoing a deep experience, that the soldiers know they are undergoing a deep experience, and that we viewers are in an inferior position to understand and know what they experience. Death in battle is no longer just heroism. It has also become "an experience." By noticing it and taking in the experience, the soldiers themselves have emerged from ignorance to knowledge.

The rising importance of the soldiers' knowing stare was reflected in contemporary literature as well. In *War and Peace* Tolstoy describes a scene of young soldiers marching into their first battle: 'Without turning their heads the soldiers glanced at one another out of the corners of their eyes, curious to see the effect on their comrades. Every face, from Denisov's to the bugler's, showed around lips and chin one common expression of conflict, excitement and agitation.'[77] The soldier's stare, of no importance in Urs Graf's *Battlefield*, has come to dominate the cultural landscape of combat.

The wake of battle

Just as the eve of battle was an epiphanic experience replete with extreme sensations and emotions, so also visiting a battlefield in the wake of battle became a key experience, during which combatants encountered unparalleled scenes of misery and were given a chance to reflect on them. These wake-of-battle scenes were the context in which the new military macabre flourished. Whereas early modern memoirists ignored the macabre potential of war, Romantic memoirists finally discovered it.[78]

We have noted how Andrew Melville summed up his meeting with a corpse after the battle of Worcester (1651) by dryly writing that 'they threw a dead body into the same place, with its legs right over me, which absolutely prevented my moving.'[79] Nothing more. Two centuries later, when Sergeant Bourgogne was placed in a similar situation, he remembered it with much more emotion. During the retreat from Moscow (1812), Bourgogne fell on top of three dead bodies:

> My head was down lower than my legs, and my face resting on one of the dead hands. I had been accustomed for long enough to this sort of company, but now [...] an awful feeling of terror came over me. It was like a nightmare. I could not move, and I began screaming like a madman, as if something were holding me. But, in spite of all my efforts, I could not move. I tried to help myself up by my arm, but I found my hand on a face, and my thumb went into its mouth!
>
> At that moment the moon came out and showed me all my dreadful surroundings. [...] a wild sort of frenzy, instead of terror, took possession of me. I got up, raving and swearing, and trod on anything that came near me – faces, arms, and legs, not caring which; and I cursed the sky above me, defying it.[80]

Particularly relevant for wake-of-battle scenes was Schiller's concept of the "pathetically sublime." In pathetically sublime experiences people encountered sublime phenomena from a safe distance, and were given an opportunity to exercise their sympathy and moral freedom.[81] Battlefields in the wake of battle were ideal locations to experience the pathetically sublime. Soldiers witnessed death and extreme suffering while being themselves safe, and could develop their sympathy and moral feelings by musing on the nature of war, and by helping casualties and enemy prisoners.

The "preachings of the dead" in the wake of battle, ignored by the vast majority of early modern memoirists and dismissed even by Colonel Blackader in a sentence, consequently became an elaborate pageant of pathetically sublime scenes, geared to shock and educate both the protagonist and the audience. One memoirist after the other began describing his wandering through the debris of the military charnel house as a Virgilian or Dantesque descent into Hades. Anything one learned during this descent had the authority of sublime revelation behind it, which made these scenes a favorite occasion for the memoirists to present their general outlook on war.

Sergeant Thomas describes how after a battle against the Danes near Copenhagen (1807), he felt 'subdued beyond all I ever felt before.' As he traversed the battlefield, and saw the corpses of Danish soldiers, his wrath of the day before disappeared. 'They were said to be enemy, but I felt that they and myself were partakers of one common nature.' He wondered how this scene of desolation had the power to transform 'views and sensations.'[82]

Heinrich Vossler described the field of Borodino (1812) in the wake of the battle thus:

Without pausing I continued to thread my way through the corpses, the horror of the scene mounting as I progressed. [...] the corpses lay piled higher and ever higher around a position that had changed hands again and again. The ditches were filled to the brim with bodies. [...] Men and horses had been gashed and maimed in every conceivable way, and on the faces of the fallen Frenchmen you could still discern the various emotions in which death had overtaken them: courage, desperation, defiance, cold, unbearable pain; and among the Russians passionate fury, apathy and stupor. [...] For a long time my gaze stayed riveted to the fearful sight which seared my soul so that I shall not forget it until my dying day.[83]

John Malcolm similarly wrote that the scene in the wake of the storming of St. Sebastian (1813) 'will haunt me as long as I live'[84] Vivian Dering Majendie said about the wake of battle that 'it is difficult to describe the sensations with which one first beholds such a spot as this,'[85] whereas General George Bell wrote that after the battle of Balaclava (1854), he went over the battlefield and inspected a burial pit where 'a hundred of the human race were lying on top of each other, in all the distorted, frightful positions in which they fell. I gazed down upon this hideous spectacle of mangled humanity, and shocked my own nerves with the sight.'[86]

William Martin wrote about the wake of the Alma (1854) that 'it was a sight once seen one could never wholly efface from his memory.'[87] William Mason also described the scene in the wake of the Alma, and commented: 'Who wants war let him go and look over the battle field, and if his heart does not sicken at the sight, he will have a hard one. I am not one of those who say peace at any price; but I do say that before war is resorted to, every other means for an amicable settlement should have failed, for war is horrible.'[88]

Wake-of battle scenes became a favorite topic for poets,[89] and painters too. In 1807 French public opinion was appalled by the number of casualities sustained at the battle of Eylau (15,000 dead and 20,000 wounded).[90] Criticism of Napoleon's military ambitions mounted, and Le was accused of being an insensitive ego-maniac who sacrificed tens of thousands to his ambitions. Napoleon countered by announcing a prize-winning contest for a painting of the battle. According to the terms of the contest, contestants had to paint not some glorious scene of victory, but rather a scene in which Napoleon visited the battlefield in the wake of battle, and showed sympathy to captive and wounded enemy soldiers. The winning painting, Gros's *Napoleon on the Battlefield of Eylau* (1808), does not depict Napolean as a military chess-master directing thousands of pin-men from on high. Rather, Napolean appears as a sympathetic man-of-feeling who is fully aware of war's horrors and who comes to witness and alleviate the suffering of the common soldiers.[91]

It is interesting to compare Gros's *Eylau* with Urs Graf's *Battlefield*. In both cases the painting's foreground is filled with mutilated corpses. Yet whereas in Graf's painting none of the painted figures notices the horrendous scene, in Gros's painting Napoleon himself – not to mention numerous men of lesser status – comes to bear witness to the carnage.

Many who are familiar with Fussell's *The Great War and Modern Memory*, and the studies that followed its lead, would perhaps be

Figure 25 Antoine-Jean Gros, *Napoleon on the Battlefield of Eylau* (1808)

surprised by the fact that already around 1800 it was common in Western war culture to focus on the pathetic side of "famous victories" and to show sympathy for the sufferings of the common soldiers. My own impression is that there is a persistent and mistaken belief that the mere exposure of war's miseries is enough to end them, and that if wars continue, it must mean that their miseries are concealed. Jean Norton Cru expressed this belief when he wrote that 'man comes to the point of making war only by a miracle of persuasion and deception practiced on the future combatants, in peace time, by false literature, false history, and false war psychology [...] if people knew what the soldier learns at his baptism of fire, nobody would consent to a solution by force of arms.'[92]

It is a main argument of the present book that this is simply not true. Throughout the last 200 years, the miseries of war have been exposed by war culture in very stark terms, and it did comparatively little to lessen either these miseries or the recurrence of war. Those who believe that mere exposure can solve the problem tend to ignore the numerous counter-precedents. Every war generation in the last 200 years had somehow managed to convince itself that it is the first to fully appreciate and expose war's true face. The sinister message of the *Eylau* painting is that Napoleon's was fully acquainted with the miseries of war, and sympathetic to the soldiers' fate, and yet five years after Eylau launched his catastrophic invasion of Russia.[93]

The joys of comradeship

A wholly positive source of sublime revelations in war was comradeship. In Romantic culture love and friendship were presented as sublime emotions, and falling in love as an epiphany whose force equals that of the wild elements of nature.[94] Just as military authors presented war as a sublime event incorporating and surpassing anything "civilian" nature had to offer, so they also presented the comradeship that springs up between soldiers as something that incorporated and surpassed the civilian love between men and women. Just as civilians could not experience horrors as intense as those of battle, so they could not experience love and joy as intense as those between comrades-in-arms.[95]

For instance, an officer of the 95th Rifles Regiment said about the troops with whom he served: 'I love them as I hope to do my better half (when I come to be divided).'[96] In Schiller's *Wallenstein*, Wallenstein gives a classical description of his comradeship with Octavio Piccolomini, explaining that 'For thirty years / We lived and bore the toils of war together. / We two have slept together in one bed, / Drunk from one glass, and shared one bite of bread.'[97] Probably the most famous contemporary example was the comradeship of Alexander Dumas's Musketeers, immortalized in their motto: "One for all and all for one."

The trope of comradeship became so well established that in the *Charterhouse of Parma* Stendhal satirized it along with the baptism of fire. During the battle of Waterloo Fabrizio bought a bottle of brandy and distributed it among some cavalrymen, who looked upon him kindly. Fabrizio becomes convinced that a sublime bond of comradeship has sprung up between them. However, the cavalrymen end up stealing Fabrizio's horse. Fabrizio's heart was broken.

> He could find no consolation for so great an infamy, and, leaning his back against a willow, began to shed hot tears. He abandoned one by one all those beautiful dreams of a chivalrous and sublime friendship, like that of the heroes of the *Gerusaleme Liberata*. To see death come to one was nothing, surrounded by heroic and tender hearts, by noble friends who clasp one by the hand as one yields one's dying breath! But to retain one's enthusiasm surrounded by a pack of vile scoundrels![98]

Returning home

One last stock experience that sealed the soldier's *Bildung* process was the homecoming. Most often, soldiers narrated how upon coming back home their parents, siblings, spouses, or friends failed to recognize them – which proved how much war had matured and changed them.[99]

When Ulrich Bräker returned home after deserting the Prussian army (1756),

> I hurried to our house. It was a beautiful autumn evening. As I entered the parlour (Father and Mother were not at home) I soon noticed that not a single one of my own brothers and sisters recognized me, and that they were pretty scared at the unusual spectacle of a Prussian soldier addressing them there in full kit, with large pack on back, hat pulled down low, and a luxoriant moustache. The little ones trembled; the eldest boy reached for a hayfork, and – made off. Nevertheless I was determined not to reveal myself until my parents were there. At last my mother came. I asked her for lodgings for the night. She had her doubts; her husband was not at home, etc. I couldn't restrain myself any longer, seized her hand, saying: 'Mother! Mother! Don't you know me any more?' Oh, first there were tumultuous cries of joy from large and small, from time to time mingled with tears...[100]

When Alfred Laverack arrived back home after ten years of absence, his father came to meet him at the Leeds train station.

> As I stepped out of the carriage he looked at me and saw the 98th number in my cap, but said to a granddaughter who accompanied him, "That's not my Alfred." He then turned away to go down the platform to see if any more soldiers were there [...] When my eye rested on him, I knew him at a glance [...] With a full heart I could only articulate the one word, "Father," when falling upon his neck we wept together. Stepping into a cab, we drove off home; but neither my mother, brothers, nor sisters knew me. In order to make sure of my identity, my mother looked for a scar upon my jaw, cheek, and the back of my head; when finding them, she was satisfied that it was her long absent boy.[101]

Flesh-witnessing: Those who weren't there cannot understand

Side-by-side with the development of these key military experiences, Romantic memoirs also developed the ideal of flesh-witnessing as a potent new source of authority. This usually involved little more than translating general Romantic thinking on the sublime into the unique language of war. Henceforth, a central tenet of the new stories of war was that those who did not undergo the key experiences of war cannot understand these experiences and cannot understand war in general.

Two stock expressions repeat themselves in Romantic memoirs: "It is impossible to describe it" and "You had to undergo the experience yourself in order to understand it."[102] Fifer John Greenwood said about the crossing of the Delaware (1776) that 'What I suffered on the march cannot be described [...] They who were with us know best about these things, others cannot believe the tenth part, so I shall say nothing further.'[103]

Robert Butler wrote about the miseries of campaigning in India:

> I need not labour to make you enter into my feelings, for that would be impossible, unless you had experienced what I have done. However, I would not advise you to try the experiment to gratify your curiosity, or you may think it dear bought; and, in all probability, never come home to tell the tidings. I must say, indeed, that I was quite overjoyed when we received the route to go to India; but if I had known beforehand what I was to be subjected to in that country, I think, and not without cause, that I never would have been able to support the afflictions and hardships which fell to my lot.[104]

About another incident he wrote that

> Now, my dear reader, if you have been placing yourself all along in my circumstances, you will certainly partake, in part, of my feelings; but, after all, it will only be in part; for although the power of imagination is great, yet I am persuaded you will come far short of the reality.[105]

Joachim Nettelbeck wrote that the relief of Kolberg (1813) brought about indescribable joy to the garrison and the citizens:

> Whose pen is capable of describing the drunken elation, that took hold of all minds! One really has to have been in this situation in person, to have completely given up oneself and his beloved, together with life and prosperity, in order to sympathise with this new, almost unbelievable feeling of quietness and security, in which one gets over and forgets, at least for moments, the distress one has suffered. It is like a bad dream which one has finally shaken off and from which one now returns to full joyful consciousness.[106]

By the late nineteenth century a nurse in a Confederate military hospital could already anticipate World War I poets by exclaiming, 'Nothing that I had ever heard or read had given me the faintest idea of the horrors witnessed here. I do not think that words are in our vocabulary expressive enough to present to the mind the realities of that sad scene.'[107]

The authority of flesh-witnessing created by these expressions was often utilized to attack the views of civilians and stay-at-homes. John Deane, a common soldier who fought in the War of Spanish Succession, wrote about the siege of Lille (1708) that people back in England criticized the army for taking so much time to capture the city. 'However,' said Deane (anticipating Guy Sajer even in the reference to coffee!),

> it cannot be expected by any man of reason that a place of such vast bigness and strength can be so soon taken; but by those over their glases of wine or strong beer, haveing their heads full of ffoolish [sic] notions, thinking themselves a Second St Mickell, and wiser than the best of Generals of the mightest of Potents on earth [...] for such Coffee house Warriors that think a souldier earns not his pay, I doe hartely wish they were to take the place of many a brave officer and souldier that hath been and may be lost upon this occasion.[108]

Matthew Bishop voiced similar feelings regarding the siege of Aire (1710). Bishop wrote that

> Our gentlemen soldiers in England little think of the hardships we endure abroad; therefore I thought proper to make them sensible of them at this juncture. They think it a great hardship to stand in a sentry box [...] A man in England is not apprised of those things, therefore I thought it high time to acquaint him, lest he should think things hard which are not, in regard to true military employment. But as I have given you a kind of an abstract of the manner in which we performed our duty, I think proper to explain how we lived in the trenches. We got two or three bushels of beans, and a bushel of wheat at a time [...] In the beginning of the siege we had very fine weather, but the latter end was excessively wet and uncomfortable; so that we were obliged to lay fascines upon the bottom of the trenches, and flakes upon that [...] I generally drank coffee in the morning, which I found very refreshing, after a night's duty upon the cold ground, where we were obliged to relieve one another upon our hands and knees.[109]

It is crucial to note that when Bishop takes on the "gentlemen soldiers" in England, he focuses his attention on the sensory day-to-day realities of life in the trenches: On the meager diet, the bad weather, the mud, the cold ground, the hot coffee (this time it is the soldiers who drink it ...). What stay-at-homes are oblivious of are the sensory experiences of war – not the strategic abstractions of the high command.

Veterans criticized with particular vehemence the newspapers and the official proclamations for their glossy coverage of war. Whereas early modern memoirists usually complained about factual mistakes and the unfair distribution of honor, Romantic memoirists were angry that the experience of war was distorted. Sergeant Thomas wrote about the Napoleonic Wars:

> let it not be supposed that I consider war as an immaterial occurrence, and a light evil: on the contrary, experience has shown me that it is one of the worst, and most destructive calamities by which humanity can be visited.

He then complained that people in England heard of war only through the newspapers, and did not experience its full force, and hence

> we are apt to overlook the mischief inflicted on those, upon whose peaceful residences the unwelcome avalanche has broken. The dispatches of naval and military Commanders being written in an official and rather glossy style, tend naturally to maintain the deception, and inflame vanity, that longs to catch the igniting spark. [...] nothing was more common during the late bitter and protracted war, than accounts in the daily journals, of actions fought on the high seas [...] in which might be perceived the same ingenious rejection of unpleasant allusions, while victory and conquest, as though they cost nothing, rejoiced in every sentence. Some variation was, of course, observable in these spirit-stirring epistles; but the main point of communication were generally similar: "Discovered a suspicious sail on the weather beam; gave chase immediately, and cleared for action. She proved to be a fine vessel, almost new, of superior force, and full of men. Got within range at two P.M., and gave her a broadside, which did prodigious execution. Having disabled her rigging, we ran her on board; and though the resistance was desperate, in ten minutes the capture was complete. We had only ten killed and thirteen wounded; while the enemy, in consequence of his peculiar obstinacy, lost more than three times that number."

Certain officers are then recommended for promotion; the gallant crew are presented to the notice of the Lords of the Admirality; and the affair, emblazoned by thousands of impressions, is conveyed by the obsequious press, from Berwick-upon-Tweed to the Scilly Isles. It is true, souls have been hurried, by mortal strife, into the eternal world; the widow's tear will flow; orphans will be left to sigh in sadness and destitution: but their grief will expend itself in silence and secrecy; for in the exultation of victory and triumph, who can find time to turn aside and weep?[110]

Sergeant Thomas would have been delighted to read John Keegan's *Face of Battle* or Paul Fussell's *Great War and Modern Memory*.

Captain Elzéar Blaze was equally critical of people who learn of war only from hearsay and books. He particularly ridiculed the accounts published in newspapers.[111] As for history books, he wrote that 'After having read some history, civilians generally think that a battle resembles a review on the *Champ de Mars* and that 100,000 men placed facing another 100,000 amuse themselves by firing as they please with the accompaniment of cannon to produce the effect of contra-basses in an orchestra.' To counter this false view, Blaze announces to his readers that 'I shall enlighten them as to how a battle is fought.'[112]

However, before enlightening the readers and describing a typical battle, Blaze warns them that even his description is far from realistic. To illustrate this, he tells a story about a jealous apothecary from Avignon who kept his pretty wife at home at all times. When she complained and wanted to go to theater, the husband reassured her that he would read to her whatever play they staged that day.

The lady pouted, but had to give in. The husband took his book and the play began. At the end of each act, after having drunk his customary glass of sugar and water, he never failed to comment on what he had just read. "You see, my dear, when the actors say that they are going to fight, or promenade, or leave for America, you must not think that they're really going to do so – they remain offstage in the wings".

When you have finished reading my chapter on the battles, you will know as much as the apothecary's wife.[113]

In Blaze's view, one had to experience war first hand in order to understand it, and in particular one had to experience its sensory miseries.

Blaze's comrade, Labourie, went as far as arguing that people who have not experienced battle are ignorant not only about war, but about everything else as well. Labourie thought that the battle of Eylau (1807) was the yardstick of all human knowledge.

> That battle of Eylau always came up in his talk. It served as a standard of comparison and was for him the superlative of misery. No one had any merit in Labourie's estimation if he had not fought on the field of Eylau. We received the *Journal of the Empire*. One day, after having read it, I told Labourie, "They advertise a book which I want to order from Paris."
>
> "What is it?"/
> "The *Précis of World Geography*"
> "Who wrote that?"
> "Malte-Brun."
> "Who is your Malte-Brun?"
> "He is one of our best geographers"
> "What's his regiment?"
> "He's not a soldier, he's a savant, a man of very high reputation. He lives in Paris."
> "He's a precious rabbit, your Malte-Brun. I would have liked to see him at Eylau, with his geography and the snow up to his knees – with his science and no bread – with his reputation and nothing to drink. Had it happened that he had been there, we would have seen if he could write those books!"' [114]

Heinrich von Brandt was equally critical of the philosopher Michel de Montaigne. In his memoirs Brandt notes that he once read the works of 'the famous skeptic,' in which Montaigne wrote that 'There is nothing more pleasant than military life.' 'This remark,' says Brandt, 'only goes to show that Montaigne had never served in the army.'[115]

Such views were occasionally adopted by civilians too. Coleridge, who had no combat experience of his own, wrote in "Fears in Solitude" (1798):

> Boys and girls,
> And women, that would groan to see a child
> Pull off an insect's leg, all read of war,
> The best amusement for our morning meal!
> The poor wretch, who has learnt his only prayers

From curses, who knows scarcely words enough
To ask a blessing from his Heavenly Father,
Becomes a fluent phraseman, absolute
And technical in victories and defeats,
And all our dainty terms for fratricide;
Terms which we trundle smoothly o'er our tongues
Like mere abstractions, empty sounds to which
We join no feeling and attach no form!
As if the soldier died without a wound;
As if the fibres of this godlike frame
Were gored without a pang; as if the wretch,
Who fell in battle, doing bloody deeds,
Passed off to Heaven, translated and not killed.[116]

It is particularly interesting to note that Clausewitz's masterpiece, *On War*, not only recognized this line of thinking, but was founded on it. In a chapter titled 'On Danger in War' Clausewitz wrote about the ignorance of those who lack personal experience of war:

To someone who has never experienced danger, the idea is attractive rather than alarming. You charge the enemy, ignoring bullets and casualties, in a surge of excitement. Blindly you hurl yourself toward icy death, not knowing whether you or anyone else will escape him. Before you lies that golden prize, victory, the fruit that quenches the thirst of ambition. Can that be so difficult?

To dispel such fanciful delusions, Clausewitz takes us on an imaginary guided tour of battle. 'Let us accompany a novice to the battlefield,' he writes. He describes in the first-person plural how 'as we approach the rumble of guns grows louder' and 'Shots begin to strike close around us.' Clausewitz then goes through a list of stock key experiences:

someone you know is wounded [...] you yourself are not as steady and collected as you were: even the bravest can become slightly distracted. Now we enter the battle raging before us [...] Shot is falling like hail, and the thunder of our own guns adds to the din. [...] Cannonballs tear past, whizzing in all directions, and musketballs begin to whistle around us. A little further we reach the firing line, where the infantry endures the hammering for hours with incredible steadfastness. The air is filled with hissing bullets that sound like a sharp crack if they pass close to one's head. For a final shock, the sight of men being killed and mutilated moves our pounding hearts to awe and pity.

The novice cannot pass through these layers of increasing intensity of danger without sensing that here ideas are governed by other factors, that the light of reason is refracted in a manner quite different from that which is normal in academic speculation. [...] Danger is part of the friction of war. Without an accurate conception of danger we cannot understand war.[117]

Clausewitz draws far-reaching conclusions from this thought experiment:

If no one had the right to give his views on military operations except when he is frozen, or faint from heat and thirst, or depressed from privation and fatigue, objective and accurate views would be even rarer than they are. But they would at least be subjectively valid, for the speaker's experience would precisely determine his judgment.[118]

Based on this observation, Clausewitz developed one of his most original and important theoretical concepts: friction. Clausewitz argued, with some measure of truth, that all previous military thinkers (e.g., the Marquis de Puységur, Adam von Bülow, and above all Antoine Henry Jomini) were engaged in theoretical abstractions that bear very little resemblance to the reality of war. They built "mathematical" systems of war, which were inspired by Newtonian physics and Vauban's precise rules for siege warfare, and which sought to reduce the conduct of war in general to a similarly precise system of rules.[119]

Like all Romantic thinkers, Clausewitz was averse to such over-rationalization.[120] Just as La Mettrie attacked the abstract logical systems of the metaphysicians, so Clausewitz attacked the mathematically precise systems of military rationalists. Just as Samuel Johnson sought to disprove Berkeley by kicking a stone, Clausewitz sought to disprove Jomini by sticking his foot into a mud-pool. All mathematical and "Newtonian" systems of war are a useless chimera, he argued, because a myriad uncontrollable factors hamper the execution of all military plans: supply wagons sticking fast in a sudden rainsquall, an aide-de-camp losing his way while carrying a vital message, a general's horse stumbling at the wrong moment, a scout arriving with false reports of the enemy's movements; in short, the chaotic element of war that can bring down a kingdom for want of a nail. Clausewitz named these factors collectively "friction."[121]

Clausewitz's friction was a fundamentally Romantic concept, because it set limits on the flights of human reason. Clausewitz argued that nobody could ever monitor and take into account all the factors that constitute friction, and that consequently a commander's ability to make and execute reasonable plans is always limited. Any commander who would trust in his reason to formulate perfect plans and would further trust that these perfect plans could actually be carried out is doomed to be defeated by the intervention of friction. The aim of military theory, argued Clausewitz, was not to find a set of precise rules for war, but rather to help commanders deal with – and utilize to their own benefit – this universal friction. Whereas the greatest achievement of the Maurician Great Captain was to exclude chance from war, the greatest achievement of the Clausewitzian commander was to take advantages of the opportunities chance presented him.[122]

Clausewitz repeatedly emphasized both that friction was the most important feature of military operations and that nobody can understand friction unless he experienced it at first hand. In the chapter 'Friction in War,' Clausewitz wrote as follows:

> If one has never personally experienced war, one cannot understand in what the difficulties constantly mentioned really consist, nor why a commander should need any brilliance and exceptional ability. Everything looks simple; the knowledge required does not look remarkable, the strategic options are so obvious that by comparison the simplest problem of higher mathematics has an impressive scientific dignity. Once war has actually been seen the difficulties become clear; but it is still extremely hard to describe the unseen, all-pervading element that brings about this change of perspective. Everything in war is very simple, but the simplest thing is difficult. The difficulties accumulate and end by producing a kind of friction that is inconceivable unless one has experienced war.[123]

Clausewitz repeats – with some elaboration – the arguments made earlier by Deane, Bishop, and Blaze, arguments that would be repeated countless times in the subsequent two centuries. It is extremely ironic that in the twentieth century "mud" would become the main symbol of military disasters resulting from the discrepancy between grand theories and mundane realities of war. The concept of "mud," which goes back to the iconic mud of Passchendaele (1917), was attached in the twentieth and twenty-first centuries to numerous military embroilments irrespective of whether they took place in jungle or desert (e.g., the Vietnam mud, the Afghanistan mud, the Lebanon mud, the Iraq mud).

The image it conjures up is of a president or a general sitting in his cushy air-conditioned headquarters, drawing neat colorful arrows on a map, which bear absolutely no relation to reality because on the ground infantrymen, guns, and lorries are stuck fast in mud.

The irony is that back in 1832 Clausewitz's *On War* made this exact same image the bedrock of late modern military theory, and that the generals of World War I and of the Vietnam War read Clausewitz as their Bible. Military friction, the real hero of *The Good Soldier Svejk*, of *Catch-22*, and of numerous other late modern satires of war, is also the hero of late modern military theory. We thus find that the late modern satirical critique of war is barging into a wide open door (or is it perhaps co-opted by mainstream military thinking?). Contrary to what journalists, common soldiers, and war satirists seem to believe, generals are fully aware of the chasm between military theory and the muddy reality. It is written in golden letters in the contemporary military Bible. Instead of undermining the authority of generals, the concepts of "mud" and "friction" strengthen it. Since war is governed by friction, only those who have experienced this friction should talk about it and direct it. Academic historians, journalists, politicians, and civilian voters who are ignorant of military friction should remain silent and allow generals to do their job.

The master narratives of late modern military experience

By the first half of the nineteenth century, all the ingredients of the master narratives of late modern war experience were in place: The basic ideals of *Bildung* and of the sublime; the new language of nerves, sensations, and emotions; a set of key military experiences; and the maxim that "those who weren't there can't understand anything." When these ingredients were combined they resulted in a number of different and even contradictory master narratives, which nevertheless shared common assumptions and a common view of war as a process of experiential revelation. They were all based on the basic Sensationist formula: sensibility × experience = knowledge.

War as a positive revelation

One master narrative viewed war as a process of positive *Bildung*, which revealed positive realities and truths about oneself and the world. This master narrative emphasized the numbing characteristics, mercantile mentality, and limited horizons of peacetime existence, and set up war as a time of excitement, intense vitality, extraordinary growth, and spiritual flowering.[124] It re-enacted the basic Romantic fantasy of "going into nature," with war functioning as a stand-in for nature. The rough conditions of war scratched off one's decadent outer shells and uncovered the inner "natural man" or the inner "noble savage."[125]

The contrast between the limited horizons of peacetime and the excitement and open vistas of wartime is evident, for example, in the memoirs of Peter Leslie. Born to a family of miners in Fife, he went down to the mine at the age of 10, and never left Fife until he was 20. He eventually enlisted in the British army primarily because he wanted to "see the world," and being uneducated, had no other means of escaping the mines. He was very disappointed to spend his first 15 months of service in training and garrison duty. When they were at last ordered to go to war, he was enthusiastic: 'We are at last to get *a taste of life.*'[126]

Durova similarly writes about her reaction on hearing that Napoleon has declared war on Russia (1812):

> Oh, how this situation has revived all my sensations! My heart teems with emotions, and my head with ideas, plans, dreams, conjectures; my imagination paints pictures for me glittering with all the rays and colors that exist in the kingdom of nature and of possibilities. What a life! What a full, joyous, active life! How can it be compared to that which I lived [on garrison] in Dubrowica? Every day and every hour now I live and feel alive. Oh, this way of life is a thousand times superior! Balls, dances, flirtation, music ... Oh, God, what trivial and boring pastimes![127]

Note that in 1812 Durova was not a recruit, and had ample previous experience of the realities of war.

The lifestory of Dr. Christian Nagel (1787–1827) harps upon the same theme. It is worthwhile to examine it in detail, since it is an excellent prototype of the military *Bildungsroman*. The book, published in Cleve in 1829, was composed by two of Nagel's friends and admirers – Friedrich von Ammon and Theodor Herold – on the basis of Nagel's own journal. It contains copious quotations and renditions from Nagel's journal, with linking passages written by Ammon and Herold themselves. The resultant volume is a typical example of early-nineteenth-century patriotic edifying texts. To finance it, the book was subscribed by Nagel's friends, so that its very composition was a tribute to the ideal of comradeship.

Nagel studied theology and humanities in the universities of Rostock and Heidelberg. After completing his studies in 1809 he yearned to volunteer for the Austrian army, and avenge Germany's humiliation at the hands of Napoleon. However, the dire economic situation of his family forced him to travel back home, where he began working as a private tutor for rich families. Nagel hated the petty life of a civilian tutor, and suffered grave inner torments. 'At that time, he began to recognize with increasing clarity that only by giving himself up to the stress of violent effort, toil, and danger in which he would be striving daily for the highest interests of his country and of mankind, would he lose himself; in other words, only in war would he be able to find himself and fulfill his destiny.'[128]

For more than three years he endured his numbing civilian existence.

> Did the life of a tutor ordinarily appear too narrow an existence for one who desired a life of deeds, in times such as these it must have appeared to him a tomb which he longed to rend asunder, to burst forth and passionately follow the will of the Fatherland to strength and freedom.
>
> And the tomb was shattered, and a light shone through the darkness, and a voice from heaven rang out and awakened the people to arise from the long night of shame; and everyone took courage and followed the sacred call and pledged his earthly life and goods for freedom and honor.
>
> At Prussia's call, her sons and the sons of other German states thirsting for freedom and revenge gathered with lightning speed to place themselves under arms; and Nagel was among the first of those who, with oppressed hearts beating anew, hastened to the assembly cantonment for freedom's soldiers at Breslau.[129]

Nagel joined the Lützow *Freycorps*, a volunteer formation, 'in which the flower of German youth was at that time gathered and in which he met many like-minded friends. With this step a new and momentous epoch begins in the life of our friend – the youth has become a man.'[130] How far are we from Saint-Germain's army, 'composed of the filth of the nation, and everything which is useless and harmful to society'?

Now began a period of transformation for the ex-student from Heidelberg, thanks to the alchemical power of comradeship and of military experiences.

The fellowship with so many admirable and spirited young men, all animated like himself and striving for the highest ideals, had a fundamental influence on the development of Nagel's mind and character without restricting his own individuality. Through the constant use of his faculties in iron-hard strife, he gained in insight and experience and developed more and more independence, worldly knowledge, and understanding of human nature.[131]

Nagel himself wrote,

With my whole soul I have given myself to the matter in hand, for which I gave up so much that was dear, and daily I grow stronger and my spirit is lifted by thousandfold stimuli and contact with like-minded comrades-in-arms. The temper of my mind becomes more and more serious, elevated, and intense, the closer I approach the great moment where life stands out in its highest and most important meaning [i.e., battle].

[...] *Seldom have I experienced the goodness of living more keenly, felt more sweetly chained by the bonds of the present;* but at the same time how easy, how pleasant a death that would unite one with those noble souls. The splendid Amor von Mengs [an eighteenth-century Saxon painter who specialized in religious subjects] has penetrated my mind like a vision from heaven; the lofty circle of Olympians stand exalted before me over lowly mankind. I saw the sun go down in the ground of Plauen, brought in tune with the purest awareness of the present by the ennobling beauties of the day and the enchanting surroundings.[132]

Soon after, Nagel was elected corporal by his comrades – an unheard-of method of promotion in the old Prussian army – and later he was elected sergeant-major of the elite Jäger company. On May 16, 1813 he was elected lieutenant of the Jäger company. His only disappointment was that so far they were merely exercising and marching, and have not taken part in any battle. 'With intense longing he looked forward to battle, even though it might bring about his own downfall.'[133]

Finally they were called for, and 'they marched to battle to the thunder of cannon, and Nagel's heart beat stronger with joy and satisfaction.'[134] Nagel recorded in his journal the exact moment when he first heard a shot fired in anger, and the narrative describes his first skirmish in glowing terms.[135] Comrades began to fall as 'martyrs for the Fatherland's cause.' The narrative commemorates their sacrifice in the most flowery terms.[136]

The main thing that troubled Nagel was that peace might be concluded too soon. For he gradually recognized that the war was an extremely positive force that not only liberated and uplifted himself, but liberated and uplifted the entire German nation. 'No peace with Napoleon!' he exclaimed in his journal, 'Prevent it, our Guardian Spirit; let no hand grasp at the life of Napoleon, for he has become the sharpener and whetstone for German heart and hand, a torch on which German life joyfully and strongly ignites.'[137]

German nature itself participated in the joys and revelations of war. At the climax of the war, when he marched through Münster and basked in the adoration of the liberated population, nature too embraced him:

> How different man and nature appear since the foreign yoke is broken, and the black veil that covered our great heaven has been rent asunder. A proud feeling over our possessions lifted our hearts. In harmony we shared in that richest reward of the soldier, the joy of the inhabitants over the arrival of their liberators. Shortly before Elberfeld, our road turned to the left and there we camped. With some friends I climbed to a high point on the rim of a quarry, which gave a panoramic view. The enchanted valley lay there like the prize creation of an efflorescent fantasy, which my eyes greedily drank in and my heart and all my senses feasted on.[138]

When the army finally reached the majestic Rhine and the city of Cologne, Nagel was transported in ecstasy.

> How I wish I might plunge down and submerge in your stream, hallowed Rhine [...] Lead me as God wills it to an honorable death – or as an upright victor into the arms of my dear ones. How gloriously the inner strength and excellence of the Germans has been revealed [...] but better that the pen should pause before I try to put the indescribable within the bounds of words. [...] O! my German people, what can compare with you in greatness, power, and grandeur![139]

Our ears, after two centuries of ultra-nationalist histrionics and two world wars, cannot listen to such passages without cynicism and even disgust. In the Romantic 1810s and 1820s, this was novel and inspiring rhetoric.

Next came the siege of Julich, in which the *Freycorps* suffered from difficult living conditions. Nagel describes the difficulties, but believes they too had a positive effect. '[T]he mettle of the Corps,' he writes, 'was established by the manifold testing it received there.'[140] In May peace was concluded, far too soon for Nagel's taste. 'He believed that a longer period of sharing of both common dangers and honors was needed to draw tight the bond of brotherly unity about the sons of the Fatherland who had been separated for so long in unnatural enmity.'[141] Nagel was deeply saddened by his personal prospects too. Going back from the excitement and grandeur of war to the petty life of a private tutor was unthinkable. Staying in the army in peacetime was equally distasteful, 'for his mind, which strove for a freer and larger field of usefulness in intellectual work, was not inclined towards the narrow forms, the little concerns and labors of garrison life.'[142]

He might well have echoed the trooper in Schiller's *Wallenstein* that complained, 'Did I run away from my desk in the school / Only to find the same labour and rule, / The narrow study, the toil and the cramp / Awaiting me here in the soldier's camp? / I want to live well, not to have too much to do, / Every day of my life see something new, / Cheerfully seize the moment, in sum, / Not brood on the past, nor on things to come.'[143]

Then, a miracle. Napoleon fled Elba to France, and war was upon them again. The 'tremendous crash shattered the tiresome sameness of Nagel's existence, and soon the storm was again raging in every part of his being.'[144] In the description of the following campaign, Ammon and Herold make fewer alterations and interjections.

[L]et our Nagel himself tell about these momentous days of his life. Even though the story of these notable happenings is in general well enough known, yet it should not in itself be without interest to learn about the subjective interpretations of these events from a participant. It is especially important, however, for the portrayal of the character of our friend for us to accompany him during these days and to observe his thoughts and actions.[145]

The description of the Waterloo campaign need not concern us too much, as it is largely more of the same. It is interesting to note, however, that after describing the great battle, Nagel gives a lengthy and pathetic description of the wake-of-battle scenes.

As the sun rose, what a battlefield it brought to light! Already in the woods that yesterday hid us, the wounded were moaning and their number, as also the number of the dead, grew constantly. The approaches to Planchenoit were almost blocked with corpses; part of the village was still burning. [...] the horrible sight of the mangled bodies shocked my whole being. Six French Light Line Infantrymen whose feet had been shot off, all together in a row, still lived; what a pitiable picture! The bodies of many men of refinement and high rank lay about, as one could recognize partly by their noble form and partly by the fine linen that was still left them, for the carrion crew had otherwise already plundered everything. Whole swarms of peasants and other rustics went about in search of booty. [...] The most sorrowful were the bodies crushed on the road by horse and wagon, and of which there seemed to be no end [...]

We [...] came upon the great highway from Brussels to Charleroi [...] Here first, the real horror began, where the dead of previous days lay heaped with the others, so crushed into the earth and mangled by cannon and wagon that they were no longer distinguishable as bodies from the other carcasses and mire.[146]

The sights did little to disillusion Nagel. The following pages are crammed with the same patriotic paeans to war as before. The one thing that really disturbed Nagel was that his regiment was disgraced due to the conduct of many soldiers who fled from the battle of Ligny, and he conducted a vigorous and rather angry campaign to reclaim the regiment's honor. Ammon and Herold felt uneasy about this chapter in Nagel's life. Fearing that 'rational temperate critics' might censure this attachment to worldly honor as a weakness, they suggest that it might have resulted from some peculiarity in his 'nervous system [Nervensystem].' To further exonerate Nagel, they quote a passage from his journal where he explains that 'not for me do I rage, for no one can besmirch my honor but I, myself, through ignoble deed [...] what above all incites me – the fallen comrades whose honorable tomb they dare to profane.'[147] True honor for Nagel, Ammon, and Herold has thus become above all an inner quality, something between a man and his conscience.

After the war was over, Nagel found the life of an officer in peace-time increasingly boring. In particular, he was appalled by the return of old-fashion drill and discipline. When he witnessed 'the monotonous cycle of military exercises' meant to teach the soldiers 'the mechanics, tricks, and skills of the drill ground,' sad thoughts oppressed him. In his journal, Nagel sketched plans for a new army and a new training system. At present, he lamented, 'Months are wasted so that the soldier learns to walk and place each finger correctly on his musket,' and in the end what it produces is 'dull masses who of themselves are unable to act beyond the instructions that are hammered into their heads.' Instead, the army should develop the physical and mental strength of the soldiers, and particularly their freedom of thought. 'Only one thing would I impress upon those who stand at the top; if you wish to be the leaders of a free and honorable people, then begin with youth. Everything must spring from education.'[148]

'For such ideals,' explain Ammon and Herold, 'the realities of that time might not have been suitable [...] This might be expected when one considers the contrasts between war and peace and in the case of the latter the necessarily greater quiet and monotony, when consideration and concentration upon unimportant external thing become all the more apparent than in the previous magnificent stormy time when fixed habit had receded and only the spirit ruled.'[149] Peace is equated here with triviality and numbness, whereas war is a magnificent spiritual storm.

This time no Napoleon came to Nagel's help, and eventually the 'deadly boredom' of military reviews caused him to quit the army.[150] He went to study at the University of Halle in 1816, and in 1817 was appointed headmaster of the Gymnasium in Cleve. He devoted the rest of his life to the education of German youth. His chief motto in education was "Religion, Learning, Fatherland," and he was also deeply influenced by the gymnastic school of Friedrich Jahn, which emphasized the importance of physical sports in patriotic education. Nagel emphasized to his students that 'Without Fatherland, no knowledge; without body, no soul.'[151]

Nagel's story received an important twist in 1821 with the eruption of the Greek War of Independence. This war was the nineteenth-century equivalent of the Spanish Civil War. It inspired the Romantic "International" just as the Spanish struggle inspired the Socialist International in the following century. And just as hundreds of European youth who missed World War I flocked to Spain to join the International Brigade, so hundreds of Romantic youths who missed the Napoleonic Wars flocked to Greece in the 1820s to join the Philhellenic Army of General Normann (which was really no bigger than a battalion).[152] One of them was Nagel's youngest brother, Gustav.

Gustav was inspired by the example and stories of his brother, whom he sought to emulate. Nagel at first tried to stop Gustav, largely because their ailing father refused to part with his Benjamin. Eventually the father gave Gustav his blessing in a letter. When the letter arrived, allowing Gustav to go to Greece, Nagel writes that his whole heart was moved with joy. In a letter of his own Nagel wrote that he fully supported Gustav's venture, and that 'his undertaking arose from the purest indomitable urge of his heart. God be with you, dear brother! If you return, you will bring with you *a consciousness and experience that gold can not buy.'* If he was destined to fall, however, 'for a holier cause, man can not sacrifice himself.'[153]

In the battle of Péta (1822) the Philhellenic Army was destroyed,[154] and Gustav too was killed. For Nagel it was a cruel blow. 'My whole being was as though shattered. Gustav had so completely engrossed me; nothing else could I experience or think of than his loss.'[155] Six months later he wrote, 'every day my heart breaks again in fresh sorrow. When I lie down to sleep, his picture in bloody death-struggle stands before me and when I awake, it is again there and accompanies me through every minute of the day. Wherever I look, hear, what I think and perceive is connected with my dear brother; I myself know not how. O my Gustav, the strength and joy of life is shattered with you.'[156]

Though Nagel felt the loss keenly for the rest of his life, he never reproached himself and his overblown idealism for his brother's death (at least no such reproach is recorded in the book). He continued to believe in his old ideals, and continued to educate his students in light of them. If he had any reproach, it was solely toward General Normann, who brought about the disaster of Péta by his incompetence. A donkey leading lions.

Nagel interpreted Gustav's death as a heroic sacrifice, called upon by God and humanity. 'Truly! The more I review and consider everything, the more I recognize that it was an inviolable call from above, which with an irresistible urge of his heart drew him there, where his earthly life would dissolve and clarify and be transfigured into an eternal life filled with light and freedom. Yes! Light and Freedom!'[157] And again 'it is no small comfort about Schmidt and Gustav that they found the noblest and most stately death, death for a noble and holy cause; that they fell in company of so many fine and brave who, as they, flowed and strove and sealed the purity of their spirit with their blood.'[158]

Though narratives such as Nagel's deeply offend twenty-first-century sensibilities we should not make life easy for ourselves by setting him up as a scarecrow. It is often said that positive war stories paint war as an ecstatic experience while hiding its uglier side, and that they thereby brainwash future generations and contribute to the rise of militarism and the eruption of more wars. In particular, such narratives are blamed for leading future youths to their deaths by planting delusions of military grandeur in their minds. Twenty-first-century readers might only too easily identify Christian Nagel with Erich Maria Remarque's Kantorek, the high school teacher whose nationalistic and militaristic rhetoric seduced Paul Baumer and his friends to enlist and find their death in the trenches of World War I.

Nagel's narrative is certainly militaristic. It depicts peacetime as a numbing prison and wartime as an ecstatic adventure, in which alone men can fully experience life and develop their abilities and virtues. However, it is a complex and self-conscious narrative. Unlike Remarque's Kantorek, Christian Nagel had ample war experience. He occasionally depicts the horrors and miseries of war in gruesome detail, and criticizes the political leadership on quite a few instances. More importantly, built into the narrative is the story of Gustav's enchantment with war and eventual death. Gustav's fate gives Nagel, Ammon, and Herold – and the readers – a chance to witness at first hand the effects of Nagel's war stories and patriotic rhetoric. The reader, who drinks in Nagel's story, finds himself in Gustav's shoes, and cannot help but contemplate Gustav's fate.

Hence the book cannot be construed as a starry-eyed romance of war, unconscious of its potential harmful impact. It is fully aware that the romance of war can lead youths to their death, and moreover, can cause great miseries to their bereaved families. And yet, taking all this into consideration, the book's final verdict on war remains highly positive. Knowing perfectly well what the results might be, the book recommends to future readers that they too should fight "for the Fatherland," for if they live, they will bring back "a consciousness and experience that gold cannot buy," and if they die, they will "seal the purity of their spirit with their blood" and be rewarded with "eternal life filled with light and freedom."

The story of war as a positive process of *Bildung* quickly became the dominant story of military experience in the nineteenth century and the first half of the twentieth century. In the second half of the twentieth century, the impact of two world wars and a threatening nuclear war dimmed the luster of this story. Yet even then it did not disappear. Many contemporary war stories still depict war as an experience of positive revelation. Even clearly disillusioned and pacifist war stories cannot help but incorporate at least some of its ingredients: the adoration of comradeship, getting close to nature, escaping the petty worries of peacetime, drinking the cup of life to the full.[159]

These beneficial experiences of war have caused numerous memoirists from the late eighteenth century onward, including many of the authors of the so-called "anti-war" memoirs, to conclude that whether good or bad, war was the most important experience of their life, and that they would not have missed it for the world. For instance, Jean Jacques

Pelet wrote about the Portugal campaign of 1810–11 that despite the privations and the eventual defeat

> this adventurous situation, not only full of boldness and hazard but also brilliant with glory, pleased and thrilled me so much that there are few memories in my life with as much charm for me. Perhaps it was the pure air, the beautiful climate, which made us appreciate life more – this could have contributed much to my attitude. Nevertheless, more than anything else, I liked all the old scenes, the strong emotions of war, and the great movement of the soul in the midst of success or reverse. Some memories ennobled us, others touched us.[160]

Rifleman Harris wrote that 'For my own part I can only say that I enjoyed life more whilst on active service than I have ever done since; and as I sit at work in my shop in Richmond Street, Soho, I look back upon that portion of my spent in the fields of the Peninsula as the only part worthy of remembrance.'[161] After Matthew Bishop was discharged from the army he became so miserable that 'I wished there might have been a perpetual war.'[162] A young Philadelphia officer wrote about the battle of Princeton (1776) that 'I would not have been absent from it for all the money I ever expect to be worth.'[163]

William Martin, after giving a very graphic and detailed description of the miserable conditions in the siege trench around Sebastopol (1854–55), assures the readers that despite these miseries, and though half his tent-mates were either killed or wounded during the siege,

> I do not think there was any time of my life that I enjoyed more than that at the Siege of Sebastopol. It was good weather, and though those who went into the trenches never all came back, this did not cast any shade of gloom on our lives; but, on the contrary, the danger we daily and hourly encountered gave a zest to life that nothing else can give.[164]

Religious narratives of military conversion

In the twentieth century the idea that war may cause a religious revival or a religious conversion has become widespread. It has become common to argue that "there are no atheists in the trenches," and that under the stresses and miseries of war, men naturally turn to religion for consolation.[165] Jay Winter has argued that this represents a "traditional" response to war. In particular, it has been argued that the spiritual responses to World War I illustrate the fact that this war was not a clean break with the past, and that many people coped with it by falling back on time-honored attitudes rather than by adopting novel modern attitudes.[166]

Though interpreting war in religious terms is certainly a "traditional" attitude going back to biblical times, the expectation that war would play a *positive* religious role in converting people from ignorance and sin to knowledge and piety seems to be a decidedly late modern phenomenon. Moreover, it is quite clear that the narratives of religious conversion in war that began to appear in the nineteenth century imitated secular Romantic narratives of military revelation rather than the other way around.

Due to limitations of space and time, I cannot survey the entire spectrum of eighteenth- and nineteenth-century religious-military narratives, and instead focus on one stream of military conversion narratives that was particularly prominent, namely the narratives of soldiers who converted to Methodism and similar evangelical movements in Britain and the United States.[167]

Methodism warrants particular attention due to several reasons: First, in Methodist conversion narratives, a single eye-opening experience often played a dominant part, and personal experience was considered an important religious authority.[168] Secondly, Methodism was an "enthusiastic" religion. Methodist sermons and mass "revival" meetings were often characterized by the arousal and display of excited emotions, and were clearly influenced by Sensationist ideas.[169] Thirdly, Methodism was a "working class" religion, and from its very inception it singled out soldiers as an important target for missionary activity. Not only many of the first converts but also many of the first Methodist preachers were soldiers. More than a quarter of the preachers whose lives were included in *The Lives of Early Methodist Preachers* were ex-soldiers.[170] For instance, around 1740 the dragoon John Haime was converted to Methodism by Charles Wesley, and became a very active preacher. By the time of the battle of Fontenoy (1745), Haime had converted 300 men, appointed 6 more preachers, and built a chapel in the British camp.[171] Another famous soldier-preacher was Captain Thomas Webb, who served under Wolfe in Canada, and helped form the first Methodist circles in America.[172]

Like the Puritans before them, Methodist and Evangelical teachers actively encouraged converts to write down and publish their narratives of conversion. Taking a ride on the bonanza of soldiers' memoirs following the Napoleonic Wars, soldier-converts were particularly encouraged to write dual narratives of military adventure and religious conversion, which often hid their missionary zeal under an innocuous martial title. Dr. John Brown encouraged Sergeant Robert Butler to publish his memoirs under the title *Narrative of the Life and Travels of Serjeant Butler* (1823), arguing that the book would be

> useful to a very numerous class of readers, who, though disinclined to look into a book that bore a religious title, might be disposed to peruse the Narrative of a Soldier's Life and Travels, written by himself, expecting to find in it something novel and entertaining, and, in his opinion, this expectation would not be disappointed; and while only seeking amusement, they might find what, by the blessing of God, might awaken serious thought, and lead to a saving conversion.[173]

As a result, a significant number of military conversion narratives were written and published by Methodist and other evangelical soldiers. Due to the unique characteristics of these narratives and of the Methodist movement in general, there seems to be no better place than these narratives to look for descriptions of war as a positive experience of religious revelation.

Yet surprisingly, most of these military conversion narratives up to the mid-nineteenth century followed medieval and early modern conventions, and largely ignored war's revelatory potential. John Haime's conversion narrative is a case in point. Haime himself was converted during peacetime in England, before experiencing combat. For a long time he struggled against the evil ways of his comrades in the barracks by reading religious tracts and going to church every day. He then found in his quarters Bunyan's *Grace Abounding*, and read it 'with utmost attention.' He wavered between faith and despair for some time, until he had several deep religious experiences, while walking along the River Tweed and again when watering his horse.[174] He then met Charles Wesley, was deeply influenced by him, and by the time he went on active duty in Germany he was already a confirmed Methodist.[175]

The battles of Dettingen (1743) and Fontenoy (1745) were a deep religious experience for him, but they made no difference to his convictions. More importantly, Haime does not claim that they converted any of his fellow soldiers. He narrates the stories of numerous men whom he converted in the army, yet they were all converted by preaching and reading. He does not attribute the conversion of a single one of them to combat. He describes the death and injury of many of these converts at Fontenoy as martyrdoms, yet Fontenoy too did not convert a single soldier to Methodism. Indeed, Haime laments that not only were many Methodist soldiers and several preachers killed there, but two of the preachers 'fell into Antinomianism' in the wake of the battle.[176] Haime himself grew complacent after the battle and began to eat more and covet, and God became so angry with him that he took away his eyesight. For eight months Haime was almost blind. As in the case of St. Francis of Assisi, modern readers may be quick to connect Haime's fall and blindness with "battle trauma" (there are known cases of Post-Traumatic Stress Disorder manifesting itself in blindness).[177] Yet Haime makes no such connection, and ascribes his fall to negligence in praying and reading Scripture.[178]

James Downing was a private in the British army, who lost his eyesight during the 1801 campaign in Egypt and was subsequently converted. He wrote his autobiography in verse, and published it in 1811. This autobiography portrays soldiers as terrible sinners, and stresses that war by itself is totally incapable of reforming them:

> What instances do soldiers see,
> Of sudden deaths around,
> Some of the land are snatch'd away,
> Some in the seas are drown'd.
>
> Oh! if like David they would cry,
> "Lord, number out my days,"
> That we may set out hearts on thee,
> And so shew forth thy praise.
>
> [...] But things with us were quite reverse,
> And shameful thus to tell,
> I still went headlong down the road
> That leads to death and hell.
>
> Though many awful instances
> Had been before my eyes;
> Though God hath call'd to me by death,
> His calls I did despise.
>
> Though I to danger was expos'd
> Upon the land and seas,
> My language was, I do not want
> The knowledge of thy ways.[179]

Downing explains why war is such an ineffective means for converting soldiers. He describes the mental stages soldiers pass through in combat:

> I know at first through fear of death,
> You eagerly will say,
> O Lord have mercy on my soul,
> And rescue me this day.
>
> But when you have engag'd awhile,
> You loose all shame and fear,
> Your thoughts of death, and judgment too,
> They quickly disappear.
>
> My brother soldiers, pray reflect
> Upon your awful state,
> > Pray to the Lord for pard'ning grace,
> > Before it be too late.[180]

Eventually Downing was stricken with a severe eye infection, lost his eyesight, and was discharged from the army. Even blindness did not open his spiritual eyes. His situation continued to deteriorate, and for four years he lived in sin, full of resentment and bitterness about his fate, and drowning his misery in liquor. He was eventually converted in London, at peacetime, by the grace of God and through listening to sermons.[181]

In 1835 an ex-sergeant of the 43rd light infantry regiment, known only as Thomas, published a narrative of his conversion, which similarly stressed the inability of war to convert sinners. Within hours of a hard battle, 'our recent perils and exposure to sudden mortality were soon forgotten, or remembered only for amusement.'[182] All the deaths and miseries he encountered in the army made no impact on him, and he was eventually converted after his discharge, by reading Methodist tracts and hearing Methodist sermons.[183]

Following his conversion, Thomas often thought about his former days in the army:

> I am amazed that at the season of life now described although just escaped almost miraculously from the jaws of death, not the smallest sense of gratitude to the Almighty seemed to enter the minds either of my comrades or myself. That this acknowledgment is discreditable to myself, I am sensible; but since such was the fact, – and I am determined to represent things as they really were, – it

must not be suppressed merely for the purpose of putting a gloss upon conduct essentially wrong. [...] Subsequent reflection upon the debased condition of my mind at that time has shown me, and my experience has borne out the fact, that man by nature is spiritually insensible, and in a condition that exactly verifies the declaration of holy writ. His soul is touched with an iceberg. The faculties are chained down by invincible ignorance.

The only thing that can break this deadlock and melt the frozen heart is divine power, and not human reason or combat experience.[184]

Probably the most moving and most profound of these narratives was composed by George Blennie, a private soldier in the Gordon Highlanders regiment. (If you are going to a read but a single volume of Romantic memoirs in your life, I would heartily recommend Blennie's.) Blennie's narrative is outstanding both for his realistic descriptions of camps, battles, and hospital wards, and for the minute descriptions he gives of his state of mind. In his introduction he explains that 'my chief object is, to give a history of the workings of my mind, during the past part of my life, rather than the particulars of my life itself; but I shall narrate as much of these particulars as is necessary to account for, and illustrate, the history of my mind.'[185]

The history of Blennie's mind follows a cyclical pattern: the dangers and horrors of combat and the miseries he witnessed and suffered in military hospitals led him to momentary bouts of repentance and supposed revelations and conversions, but his deep-seated sinfulness, his pride, and the evil influence of his comrades always returned him to the path of sin. For instance, after a severe battle in the Netherlands (1799) 'I reflected on the dangers we had escaped, [and] I was filled with wonder; but I soon forgot them all; and during the few days that we lay in the town of Helder, my conduct, in place of being better, was worse than ordinary.'[186]

Blennie repeatedly emphasizes the inability of war to really influence and change the ways of soldiers. After being wounded at Alexandria (1801), Blennie was taken onboard a hospital ship, where dozens of injured men lay, many in the last agonies of death:

If any one wishes to know what were the topics of conversation among so many men in such circumstances, it pains me to state, that our conversation was about any thing but that one thing which most concerned us, and which ought to have engrossed our whole attention. About that world to which so many of us were daily departing, and about that God before whom so many were so soon to make their appearance, there was not a word to be heard, except it was in taking his name in vain. The groans of the dying were to be heard in various quarters of the ship, but no one, either asking or telling how a sinner could be saved. Nor was I better than others. I did not improve my mercies. I had been wounded in a comparatively merciful manner, but I forgot the God to whom I had made my supplication, and neglected my Bible. [...] death was becoming familiar to me, and I looked at it with a careless indifference.[187]

Further on Blennie explains that in the entire hospital in which he was, not a single person seemed to have possessed true saving knowledge, and no person was attempting to find such knowledge. 'And this was the case, not in this hospital only, but in all the hospitals I was in, both before and afterwards.'[188]

Blennie insists throughout the narrative that mere experience – no matter how extreme – is never enough to uncover the truth and to redeem soldiers. He attacks head-on the idea of sublime "revelations" in combat, and exposes the sublime as an ephemeral sensation whose influence passes quickly without leaving any real trace. All the "revelations" and "conversions" that people claim to experience in combat, or when lying in hospitals on their deathbed, are mere delusions.

> The approach of death, and the fear of hell, and remorse of conscience, arising out of convictions of sin, may greatly alarm you; but this will not change your heart, nor save your soul. Such a state of mind is neither repentance nor conversion. How often was I in danger, and imagined I repented; and, when I was at the point of death, I thought I had repented in truth. But my conduct after I had recovered showed that I had deceived myself; and had I died in the state I then was in, I must have perished.[189]

Instead of experience, Blennie holds up Scripture as the only means to true knowledge. '[R]evelation alone,' he writes, 'either does or can make any provision for a certain ground of hope for futurity. God alone can tell how he will forgive sin; he has done this in the Scriptures, and there alone. O be sure you examine what is revealed in them upon this subject, and build your hope for eternity only upon what God has revealed to a sinner to trust in.'[190] Addressing fellow soldiers he writes, 'Unless your repentance be that of the Bible, and your faith in Jesus genuine, arising from a scriptural understanding of your own character as guilty and helpless sinner in the sight of God, and a scriptural discernment of the rich grace and almighty power of Christ, you will not be able to stand.'[191]

Such statements in favor of Scripture and against experience seem paradoxical in a personal account written by a private soldier. Blennie is aware of the paradox. He explains that though personal experience is useless as a guide to the saving truth, it nevertheless has one value: it can show people the depth of human sinfulness and weakness. And even here he quickly adds that knowledge of sinfulness and weakness too is derived primarily from Scriptures, with personal experience serving as no more than an optional illustration: 'I do not refer to *my* experience, as an exclusive proof of [the weakness of sinners]; but I refer to it as an instance of the truth of God's word, which declares that sinners are "*without strength*." Rom. v. 6.'[192]

Hence even in the early nineteenth century, soldiers were still widely seen as confirmed sinners and war was seen as a ticket to perdition. If soldiers were sometimes converted, it usually occurred in peacetime, and thanks to reading Scriptures or listening to sermons rather than to their war experience.[193] Why was war such a bad path to religious revelation? Most probably due to the same reason that made early modern culture separate the macabre from war: War could expose the truth of mortality perfectly well, but it had absolutely no means of revealing the far more important truths of resurrection and salvation.

Religious conversion narratives resisted the influences of the Romantic war story for almost a century, but eventually they too succumbed to its sublime temptations.[194] Around 1850, the experience of war began to be sacralized. Though it was still a widespread opinion that soldiers were the worst of sinners, and that joining the army and going to war was a sure recipe for damnation,[195] alternative views became more common. Narratives of religious conversion began to describe war as a positive agent of revelation. As noted in the introduction, the most famous example is the conversion of Prince Andrei in Tolstoy's *War and Peace*. It began on the battlefield of Austerlitz with Andrei's vision of the eternal sky, and ended on the battlefield of Borodino (1812), where Andrei was mortally wounded and had a second mystical revelation.[196]

The American Civil War was the first war in which combat was widely expected to bring about religious conversion. The Southern armies fully answered these expectations. Numerous mass "revivals" took place during the war, in some of which up to 5000 soldiers participated, and it was observed that 'the most dramatic outbursts [...] followed fierce and bloody battles.'[197] It was observed that 'the army showed more devotional fervor than civilians did. Chaplains reported that revival crowds were larger than before the war, that the soldiers' morals were superior to noncombatants, that the revival spirit was deeper than it had been for decades.'[198] William Jones argued that 150,000 Confederate soldiers were "born again" during the war.[199] Lieutenant Randolph McKim, a chaplain serving in Lee's army, wrote that in 'forty-five years of ministerial life [...] I have never found men so open to the frank discussion of the subject of personal religion as the officers and men of Lee's army.'

A letter to the *Charleston Courier* explained that

> There is something irresistible in the appeal which the Almighty makes when he strikes from your side, in the twinkling of an eye, your friends and comrades [...] Every man unconsciously asks himself, "whose turn will come next?" [...] In this aspect, the recent battles have done more to make converts than all the homilies and exhortations ever uttered from the pulpit. A man who has stood upon the threshold of eternity while in the din and carnage of the fight, has listened to eloquence more fiery and impressive than ever came from mortal lips.[200]

Modern researchers have been quick to adopt such claims. Drew Faust tries to explain the revivals in the Confederate armies by arguing that for the soldiers 'perhaps the ever-present threat of death gave battle a transcendent, rather than primarily worldly, significance.'[201] Richard Schweitzer comments that the belief that war causes religious revival is widespread even amongst scholars, on the assumption that 'wars produce great emotional strains [which] are mediated through religion as individuals take solace in God.'[202]

The North had its own share of revivals and conversions. In 1872 Chaplain A. S. Billingsley of the Union army published *From the Flag to the Cross; or, Scenes and Incidents of Christianity in the War*, which contained numerous military conversion narratives, in which war played a crucial part.[203] Whereas early modern writers viewed soldiers as the worst of sinners and as being particularly blind to the truth, Billingsley insisted on the unique susceptibility of combatants to the truths of Christianity:

> There is something connected with army life and with battle scenes well calculated to impress and awaken the sinner. The solemn pause,

the awful suspense just before a battle, together with the dread of death and the awful foreboding of the eternal world, are well calculated to arouse the most *careless*. Hence, conversions among the most wayward are not unfrequent [sic] in the army. [...] He who shoots his arrows when, where, and how he pleases, can make the whizzing of a bullet, the groans of the dying, or the lightning's vivid flash, the means of the soul's salvation.[204]

Billingsley concludes that 'doubtless many have been converted in the army who never would have been reached at home.'[205]

Billingsley included in his book many accounts of conversion. It is noteworthy that the majority of these conversions were caused by preaching and reading.[206] However, Billingsley narrates a few cases of soldiers who were directly converted by the experience of combat. One Union soldier told him how 'I have been a very great sinner; but I believe, now, God has converted my soul and forgiven my sins.' When the chaplain asked how and where God accomplished that, the soldier explained as follows:

In the battle of Hatcher's Run. There, amidst the shock of battle, I saw so many falling around me, and thinking how soon it might be my turn, and what an awful thing it would be to die for my country, and lose my own soul; there, with balls and bullets whistling close by me, and shells bursting around me, together with the groans of the wounded and dying, I cried to God for mercy; and there, I believe, he changed my heart.[207]

In Britain too things changed around that time, and the Methodist Reverend Arthur Male wrote in the late nineteenth century that 'The time for regarding the ranks of the British Army as filled with the scum and off-scouring of society has gone by.' He insisted that through their military experience 'many a man has become a better man.'[208] By the time World War I erupted, it was widely expected that war would bring about a religious revival, and many claimed after the war that this is exactly what happened.[209]

Soldiers were thus transformed from confirmed sinners into potential converts, and war was transformed from a ticket to perdition into a path of revelation. This transformation had much to do with changes in recruitment policy. Whereas it was easy to view the sixteenth-century mercenary or the eighteenth-century professional soldier as a wicked sinner, it was far harder to view in like manner "our boys," who enlisted *en masse* to the armies of the American Civil War or World War I. Yet recruitment and social prestige were only half the story. Early modern *officers* had an excellent social standing, yet their war experience was not seen as a path to revelation. What early modern officers lacked was Romanticism and its sublime ideals. It was the Romantic models of secular military revelation that finally helped sacralize war experience in the late nineteenth century. The story of religious revelation in combat owes far more to Burke and Schiller than to St. Paul and St. Augustine.

The decisive contribution of Sensationism and Romanticism to the military conversion narrative is made clear in the writing of Pierre Teilhard de Chardin, a Jesuit who served as a stretcher bearer in World War I. Chardin wrote about his war experience that

> The unforgettable experience of the front, to my mind, is an immense freedom [...] There is a world of feelings I would never have known or suspected, were it not for the war. Only those who were there can ever experience the memory charged with wonder of the Ypres plain in April 1915, when the Flanders air smelled of chlorine, and shells were cutting down the poplars [...] Those more than earthly hours instill into life a tenacious, unsurpassable essence of exaltation and initiation, as if they were part of the absolute. All the enchantments of the Orient, all the spiritual warmth of Paris, are not worth the experience of the mud of Douaumont [...] Through the war, a rent had been made in the crust of banality and convention. A window was opened on the secret mechanisms and deepest layers of human development. A region was formed where it was possible for men to breathe an air drenched with heaven [...] Those men are fortunate, perhaps, who were taken by death in the very act and atmosphere of war, when they were robed and animated by a responsibility, an awareness, a freedom greater than their own, when they were exalted to the very edge of the world, and close to God![210]

What would St. Ignatius Loyola have made of this latter-day Jesuit? Would he have recognized his own experiences at Pampeluna in this military mysticism?

Disillusionment

Sensationism and Romanticism lent themselves not only for the creation of new positive stories of war, but also for a powerful wave of disillusionment. *Bildung* very often involved disillusionment with old ideals as much as the acquirement of new ones. From the second half of the eighteenth century, disillusionment with the ideals of the Enlightenment and with ideals in general became a cultural trope of unprecedented importance in which war played a central part.

Voltaire's *Candide* (1759) is the ironic archetype of all subsequent military disillusionment narratives. As a youth, Candide dwells in the peaceful and idealic castle of Baron Thunder-Ten-Tronckh, where the philosopher Pangloss teaches him an extremely positive and naïve view of the world. Candide begins an affair with the baron's daughter, the lovely Cunégonde. When it is discovered, he is forced to flee the castle, enlisting into the Bulgar army (a stand-in for the Prussian army). The Bulgars subsequently wage war on the Abares. In his first battle, while the 'heroic butchery' proceeds, Candide hides himself 'trembling like a philosopher.'[211] He then deserts the Bulgar army and flees.

When he next meets Pangloss, Candide is shocked to learn that the Bulgars have pillaged Thunder-Ten-Tronckh castle, and murdered the baron's family. Pangloss tells him that Cunégonde

> was disemboweled by the Bulgar soldiers, after having been raped to the absolute limit of human endurance; they smashed the Baron's head when he tried to defend her, cut the Baroness to bits, and treated my poor pupil exactly like his sister. As for the castle, not one stone was left on another, not a shed, not a sheep, not a duck, not a tree; but we had the satisfaction of revenge, for the Abares did exactly the same thing to a nearby barony belonging to a Bulgar nobleman.[212]

Now follows a long string of calamities and horrors, most of them due to a series of wars. Throughout all these calamities Candide and Pangloss refuse to be disillusioned, and continue to adhere to their naïve peacetime philosophy. Yet their refusal is clearly ironic, and it is obvious to the readers that anyone who is not disillusioned by war's horrors must be a complete fool.

Goethe's *Wilhelm Meister* is another archetypical disillusionment story. As a boy, Wilhelm Meister is given a puppet theater, on which he stages a number of warlike puppet shows (mainly the biblical combat between David and Goliath, and scenes from Tasso's *Gerusalemme Liberata*). He develops childish fantasies, not about becoming a warrior but rather about becoming an actor and artist. The rest of the book describes how Wilhelm goes out into the world in pursuit of his fantasies, but his encounters with reality gradually disillusion him.[213] Most *Bildungsromane* describe similar processes, and it has often been argued that the typical hero of the *Bildungs-sroman* 'sets out on his life's journey as an adolescent with many youthful dreams, aspirations, and illusions, and his experiences lead him to a healthy realism, to the abandonment of such dreams as illusions.'[214]

In Schiller's *Robbers*, when the youth Kosinsky wishes to join Karl Moor's robber band, Moor tries to dissuade him from taking such a step:

> Has your tutor been telling you tales of Robin Hood? – They should clap such careless creatures in irons, and send them to the galleys – exciting your childish imagination, and infecting you with delusions of greatness? Do you itch for fame and honour? Would you buy immortality with murder and arson? Be warned, ambitious youth! Murderers earn no laurels!

Kosinsky answers that he does not fear death in the least, an answer that wins only ridicule from Moor:

> Splendid! incomparable! You learnt your lessons like a good boy, I see you know your Seneca by heart. – But my friend, fine phrases like that will not talk away the sufferings of your flesh, will never blunt the darts of your pain. Consider well, my son! Let me advise you as a father – see how deep is the abyss, before you jump into it![215]

In Hölderlin's *Hyperion* (1797–99) war's role is even more central. The book describes how Hyperion led the Greeks in rebellion against the Turks, his head full of Romantic fantasies about love, patriotism, comradeship, and justice. Yet reality proves a bitter disappointment. The Turks eventually gain the upper hand, and Hyperion becomes disgusted with his own troops who plunder and murder their compatriots while fleeing at the first sign of danger. Though Hölderlin was describing the Greek revolt of 1770, he unwittingly anticipated the events of the Greek War of Independence. Many of the Romantic Philhellens who flocked to Greece hoping to encounter the heroes of the *Iliad* and of the age of Pericles and Demosthenes were utterly disgusted by the rapacious klephts and corrupted politicians whom they actually encountered. Instead of a heroic struggle, they found themselves caught up in a cruel civil war, suffering from every possible moral and material deprivation.[216]

The most famous incident of the Greek War was Lord Byron's death, which was again a bitter disillusionment. Byron failed to participate in any military action, and instead of falling on the glorious field of battle, he slowly succumbed to the ravages of illness, eventually dying from a severe attack of cold (1824). Byron actually had little illusions about the glories of war. The seventh and eighth Cantos of Byron's *Don Juan*, composed six years before his death, describe the siege of Ismaïl (1790) in cynical terms, constantly snapping at 'glory, and all that immortal stuff.'[217] Thus Byron asks rhetorically, 'I wonder (although Mars no doubt's a god I / Praise) if a man's name in a *bulletin* / May make up for a *bullet* in his body?'[218]

The French Revolution in particular played a decisive role in this "culture of disillusionment," anticipating in many ways the role played by World War I in twentieth-century cynicism. The cynical use made by the French revolutionaries and by Napoleon of the ideals of the Enlightenment, and the crimes and wars committed in the names of these ideals, disillusioned many former adherents of Liberty, Equality, and Fraternity.[219] In the *Memoirs of Thomas Holcroft* (1816), William Hazlitt wrote that

> Kind feelings and generous actions there always have been, and there always will be, while the intercourse of mankind shall endure; but the hope, that such feelings and such actions might become universal, rose and set with the French Revolution [...] The French Revolution was the only match that ever took place between philosophy and experience: and waking from the trance of theory to the sense of reality, we hear the words *truth, reason, virtue, liberty,* with the same indifference or contempt, that the cynic who has married a jilt or a termagant, listens to the rhapsodies of lovers.[220]

In *The Plain Speaker* (1826) Hazlitt further wrote

> As for my old opinions, I am heartily sick of them. I have reason, for they have deceived me badly. I was taught to think, and I was willing to believe, that genius was not a bawd – that virtue was not a mask – that liberty was not a name – that love had its seat in the human heart. Now I would care little if these words were struck out of my dictionary, or if I had never heard them. They are become to my ears mockery and a dream.[221]

By the mid-nineteenth century, disillusionment was established as a trademark of modernity, and the disillusioned young man, completely disgusted with the ideals of his society and his elders, became a stock figure of European culture.[222] For example, Mikhail Lermontov's Pechorin, the hero of *A Hero of Our Time* (1840), is a young officer serving on the Caucasus front who is completely disillusioned about any and every ideal, be it love, comradeship, patriotism, or glory. When he arrives on the frontline, he is at first excited. 'This was the happiest time of my life. I hoped that boredom could not survive under Chechen bullets – but in vain. A month later I was so accustomed to their buzzing and to the proximity of death that, indeed, I paid more attention to the mosquitoes.'[223] The narrator comments about Pechorin that 'disenchantment, like all fashions, having begun with the highest tiers of society, had descended to the lowest.'[224]

Accordingly, the Romantic period witnessed not only the flowering of the war story of positive revelation, but also the birth of the disillusioned war story. This story usually begins with youthful Candide-like innocence and Wilhelm-Meister-like fantasies, passes through various sobering experiences, and ends with Hyperion-like bitter disillusionment or even Pechorin-like nihilistic cynicism. It was a story of negative enlightenment, of waking up from a rosy dream to a brutal reality.[225]

The milder versions of the disillusionment narrative were made up of four interconnected threads: describing the miseries of war in detailed Sensationist terms; exposing the positive ideals of war as false or at least as incapable of redeeming war's miseries; questioning the integrity of the leadership and the rightfulness of the war; and exposing atrocities committed by one's own side.

The first and most essential thread of disillusionment narratives was to describe the miseries of war in the greatest possible detail and precision. The new language of sensations was particularly important in this respect. By appealing to sensations, memoirists brought their readers down from the high-flying metaphors of war rhetoric to the reality of war. They took to heart Locke's maxim that 'many cardinal errors are due to the mistaking of words for things,'[226] and strove to expose the "things" of war in terms of sensations. In this they foreshadowed Emile Zola's technique of heightened realism, which would subsequently be used by the disillusioned veterans of twentieth-century wars.[227]

For instance, the battle of Borodino (1812), celebrated by generations of Russian authors as the epitome of Russian heroism, was described by Durova from the viewpoint of her freezing fingers. She wrote almost nothing about strategy, tactics, and heroism, and instead gave a minute description of her cold sensations, asking the reader at the end, 'What can valor do against the cold?'[228]

Sensationist descriptions of war's miseries were essential for disillusionment narratives, but in themselves they were not enough. As we saw in cases such as the *Araucana* and Nagel's narrative, detailed descriptions of miseries could quite easily be combined with appeals to positive ideals that redeemed these miseries. In such cases, the focus on the miseries of war actually served to exalt its spiritual ideals. Describing the difficulties experienced by a hero was essential to make readers appreciate his heroism (just as in martyrdom stories, the most gruesome descriptions of material miseries served to exalt the spiritual ideals that redeemed these miseries).

Hence, the second essential thread of disillusionment narratives was to disconnect the miseries of war from any redeeming spiritual ideals such as patriotism or heroism. Some memoirists chose to attack these spiritual ideals head on. Doing so was not easy. If a memoirist wished to mount such an attack, he needed all the authority he could get. Most memoirists who chose this difficult path found the necessary authority in the shape of experiences of sublime suffering. Turning the heroic formula on its head, instead of utilizing material suffering to proclaim the victory of spirit over matter, they proclaimed the victory of matter over spirit. They argued that in sublime moments of suffering, what is revealed is the illusionary nature of spiritual ideals and their utter inability to compensate for the suffering. Such a topsy-turvy argument was made possible thanks only to the revolutionary ideas of the secular culture of sensibility.

One narrative that followed this path was composed by Johan Christian Mämpel, and edited by none other than Goethe. Mämpel began the book with an account of his eldest brother's heroic exploits. That brother was unwillingly conscripted into the French army, but soon acquired a taste for war and glory. He fought at Marengo, 'where General Desaix closed a life of heroism by a death of glory' and then at Austeriltz. 'For his good conduct and bravery in this action, my brother was invested with the cross of honor; but he had, to counterbalance this fortune, the ill fate to lose his left leg, which was dashed to pieces by a spent ball.'[229] Despite the injury, Mämpel's brother spoke enthusiastically about war.

> "Every young man," said he, "who is healthy, and possessed of sufficient strength to bear the inconveniences of the service, ought to repair with ardor to the standard of his country, whenever that country is threatened with danger. I know of no calling so honorable as that of a soldier, who endures, for a slight remuneration,

all the privations and horrors of war; – who, reckless of danger, every day exposes his own life for the preservation of his kindred and fellow citizens from the invading enemy. If he falls, he dies the death of glory. Does he become mutilated? – He leaves the scene of his honorable exploits, and carries home with him the esteem of his comrades, receiving there the welcome of affection and respect".[230]

Unlike Gustav Nagel, Mämpel was hardly convinced by his brother's example, and says that 'I had always cherished the hope of drawing a free lot, which would have exempted me from service.' However, in 1806 he drew a bad number and was compelled to enlist.

My mother was inconsolable; but my father's sensibility had been blunted by renewed accessions of evil, and he now shielded himself with the feeling of indifference. My brother encouraged me; and when I cast my eye on the red riband of the cross of honor which decorated his button-hole, a spark of emulation darted athwart my mind, and I felt excited to acquire a similar mark of distinction; an ardor however which was speedily abated on glancing a little lower down upon his wooden leg.[231]

Mämpel did not mistake words for things. In the contest between the cross of honor and the wooden leg, the latter carried the day.

After his enlistment Mämpel's fears abated for a time. He and the other common soldiers were pleasantly surprised by the good treatment they received in the French army. Moreover,

veterans related to us their former expeditions and achievements – not in the spirit of boasting, or to impress upon our minds the hardships of a military life; but in order to lay before their youthful auditors an example of the manner in which they ought to behave themselves when called on for active service. Thus the days passed cheerfully on; and a positive desire was awakened in our hearts to join the ranks of our regiment, in order that we might display to our aged friends how much we had profited by their lessons.[232]

They just missed participating in the 1806 Prussian campaign, and 'our disappointment was great in being doomed to remain inactive in quarters while these glorious events were going forward.' In 1807 their chance for glory finally arrived. They received the orders to proceed to

Spain with great joy, and the march through Germany and France 'was the pleasantest I ever experienced in the course of my military life.'[233] His first year in the army thus brought Mämpel round to his brother's viewpoint, awakening in him an appreciation of the joys and glories of war.

However, when Mämpel finally experienced war in Spain, his illusions were shattered. The narrative becomes a litany of terrible privations and equally terrible atrocities (committed by French and Spaniards alike), which are not redeemed by any spiritual ideals. Mämpel fell into Spanish captivity at the defeat of Baylen (1808), and spent three extremely wretched years in a POW camp. He carefully chronicled the miseries of the camp, paying close attention to the bodily deprivations and the miserable sensory experiences.

After three years of woe, Mämpel extricated himself by enlisting into the British army. For the first time in three years he was thoroughly cleaned and was given new cloths to wear. 'Never did I experience sensations so perfectly delightful as those which followed this replenishment of the outer man. A voluptuous irritation, if I may so express myself, spread over my whole frame, and did not subside for several days.'[234] In the narrative, these sensations counterbalance the ignominy of desertion.[235]

Despite the improvement in the material conditions, his life as a common soldier remained very hard, and 'neither the esteem of my officers, nor the friendship of my comrades, both of which, I rejoice to say, I enjoyed, could repress my longing to change the military for the domestic life.' He writes that there were many other soldiers in his regiment 'who cursed the day on which they left [home] to follow a life of toil and bloodshed.' Almost every week soldiers tried to desert or mutilated themselves in order to acquire a discharge. Particularly telling is the story of one soldier who shot himself through the hand, which had to be amputated. This amputated limb seems to recall the wooden leg of Mämpel's brother, indicating that its warnings were far truer to the reality of war than the colorful lies of the Cross of Honor.[236]

Mämpel eventually returned home after more than ten years abroad. 'With a host of mingled emotions, well nigh overpowering utterance, did I enter beneath the shelter of my parental roof.' He found that his parents are both dead, and his brother received him coldly at first, not recognizing the stranger. 'I must have presented a curious contrast to the youthful, rosy-cheeked lad they had bid adieu to some ten years before. My face was embrowned by the heat of a tropical sun; while long subjection to the storms of fate had disposed me a good deal to serious reflection, and conveyed over the lines of my countenance an expression of considerably more advanced age than I actually had attained to.'[237]

When Mämpel comes to evaluate war, he puts on one side of the scales the flashy riband of glory. On the other side he piles up high the missing limbs, the years of toil and misery, the dead comrades, his own lost youth, and his premature old age. These miseries cannot possibly be redeemed by the riband. Instead, they prove that just as he suspected in his childhood days, the riband was a hollow illusion.

Elzéar Blaze was far more sarcastic and direct. He summarized war as follows:

> Behold 100,000 men; they are going to fight under the command of a single individual for reasons they do not understand and for which not one of them gives a damn. Some were brought there by force, others because they like it, but all of them will risk all possible dangers out of self respect. They will be killed, possibly crippled, or mutilated – which often is worse than death. They will endure every hardship, fatigue, and kind of bad weather. If one of these men disobeys his commander, he will be killed [...] While these 100,000 men leave their country to pick a fight with their neighbors, those who remain behind in their native land must labor to feed and clothe them and especially to make up for the vast waste which war is always a pretext. The 100,000 men return, wounded, crippled by rheumatism, and in rags – and for a reward they can admire the statue of their general in a public square.[238]

Blaze throws on one side of the scales the hardship of campaign, the dead, crippled, and mutilated soldiers, and the rag-tag veterans. The only thing he throws on the other side is the glorious statue of the general. The fact that people try to balance these miseries with the help of a statue makes the statue a symbol for cynicism and cruelty rather than for glory.

Other disillusioned memoirists condemned war's ideals in more reserved terms. These memoirists paid lip service to the ideals of war and agreed that they had some truth in them, but they were still not powerful enough to redeem the miseries of war. After the costly storming of Lucknow (1857), Vivian Majendie mused about the price of war:

> It is a sad moment that, when the excitement which hurried you on, and bore you unshrinkingly through the heat of battle, has died

away, and you have nothing left but to count over the friends who are gone, and to familiarize yourself with the cruel thought that never again will that hand grasp yours, and that the dear eyes are closed for ever. A wretched waking it is on the morn which succeeds an action – a blank and joyless day that follows. It is hard to seek in the glory you have won for the companions you have lost, and poorly does the success of yesterday fill up the gaps which shot and steel have made – the 'old familiar faces' that you miss – the well-known footsteps that you hear no more – the kind voice, with its cheering accents of friendship and brotherhood – where are they now? Oh! Who among us soldiers has not in the course of his career had to ask this pitiful question? How few among us are there who, in the course of this wretched rebellion and its attendant war, have not felt that dreary blank and vacuum in their hearts as they mourned over some dear and well-loved comrade? It is not when the blow first strikes upon the heart that it is felt most keenly, but it is the bruise which it leaves behind, and which refuses to be healed, that is the hardest to be borne. How cruelly in those days of sorrowing do we apply nature's probes – truth and affection – to the gaping wound, and search into it, and feel its depth, and measure its extent, and realize for ourselves the greatness and the fullness of our grief! Then it is, as day follows day, and the void remains still unfilled, and the slow cure seems still to stand aloof, that we suffer most; then, while the world rolls on as it did before, and folks around us pass to and fro upon their several paths, careless and gay as ever, and heedless of our loss, that the anguish gnaws fiercest at our souls. War is but poor work after all – a little glory, a little glitter, to season much sorrow, grief, and woe![239]

In Majendie's scales, the glory and glitter of war do carry a little weight, but not hardly enough to compensate for war's sorrow, grief, and woe.

Jean-Baptiste Barrès, writing about the brilliant campaign of 1805 after the victory of Ulm and the occupation of Vienna, narrates little else except a litany of physical miseries. He reflects that

We left Paris quite content to go campaigning rather than march to Boulogne. I was especially so, for war was the one thing in wanted. I was young, full of health and courage, and I thought one could wish for nothing better than to fight against all possible odds; moreover, I was broken to marching; everything conspired to make me regard a campaign as a pleasant excursion, on which, even if one lost one's head, arms, or legs, one should at least find some diversion. I wanted, too, to see the country, the siege of a fortress, a battlefield. I reasoned, in those days, like a child, and at the moment of writing this, the boredom which is consuming me in cantonments (at Schönbrunn) and four months of marching about, months of fatigue and wretchedness, have proved to me that nothing is more hideous, more miserable, than war. And yet our suffering in the Guard are not to be compared with those of the line.[240]

Most memoirists did not feel powerful enough to mount such direct attacks on the positive ideals of war. They therefore separated the miseries of war from any redeeming spiritual ideals simply by not mentioning the latter. In particular, they downplayed combat and emphasized instead unheroic aspects of war such as hunger and disease, which were intrinsically far more resistant to redemption.

For example, Friedrich Christian Laukhard's memoirs of the 1792 invasion of France gave very detailed descriptions of the condition of sick and wounded soldiers, which were not balanced by any appeal to spiritual ideals. Shortly after the allied army crossed into France, the soldiers began to suffer from dysentery.

If I told, on that subject, everything that I witnessed, those of my readers who are a bit delicate would be nauseated. But after all I do not write to [over] sensitive and refined men. My book is addressed to men of good will, who want to know the truth, and resolved to hear, even when it is inconvenient, everything that our troops suffered in their campaigns against the Revolution, in order to learn lessons and profit from it. So I will take a chance and write a few facts.

Though the toilets were cleaned every day, they presented such a terrible aspect, in the morning, that it was enough to see them in order to fall ill! On all side one could see pools of pus and blood, within which sometimes bodies were laying. The camp itself was soiled with bloody excrement, deposed by the men who were attacked by so violent a dysentery, that they could not arrive to the toilets, no matter at what distance they were! I am persuaded that more than 5/8 of the army had the dysentery when we departed that place.[241]

Laukhard is one of the first in the long line of late modern military memoirists who give a detailed description of a military latrine. (In the 1920s and 1930s right-wing critics of disillusioned World War I memoirs christened these books the 'lavatory school' of war novels.[242])

Yet Laukhard's most shocking descriptions are reserved for the fate of the wounded and sick soldiers in military hospitals. Laukhard recounts how he went to visit a sick friend in the military hospital at Longwy, and was appalled by the prevailing conditions. He explains that 'I honestly want to acquaint the reader with what I have seen there, yet with the condition, that the too delicate reader may skip this chapter.'[243] As he entered the hospital,

> how horrified I was, when I saw everything gleaming from excrements right in the entrance. I could not find even a single spot to step on unsullied. The general toilet did not at all suffice for so many persons sick with dysentery, most of whom were also missing the strength to reach it, and chamber pots I hardly ever saw. So the unfortunate only skulked outside the parlor, and then deposited everything there, wherever and however they could. It is abhorrent [...] that I even saw dead bodies lying in this filth. I slipped fast through it into a room, but then an abhorrent smell immediately obtruded on me, so that I would have liked to faint. The smell was much worse than if one [...] stood in summer where animals are skinned.

Laukhard goes on to narrate the miserable conditions inside the rooms, the lack of food and medicine, and the feelings of anger and sympathy the experience caused him. He later went to visit other field hospitals, and found 'even more horrors.' At the hospital in Bingen he was shocked in particular by the attitude of the medical staff.

> People were laying there, who had been brought there already four or more days previously, and were not bandaged yet. One had an arm shot broken, another one a leg, and the people moaned, so that one's breast would become uneasy from sympathy. But the revered army doctors and the mischievous caregivers comforted the poor people only with curses and maledictions. "Is it my fault", I heard an army doctor say, "that you are injured? I would have preferred that the bullet had gone into the a– of the devil, so I would not have to bother about you now! I will bandage you, but you have to wait! Dammit, I have more things to do."
> And therewith the thug went out of the door.

Laukhard concludes this tale of misery by addressing the readers with cautionary words: 'See, humans, that is what people like you count for in war!'[244]

A third thread of disillusionment narratives involved questioning the integrity of the leadership and the rightfulness of the war. This strengthened the impression that war's miseries were unredeemed, because they were not suffered for any worthy cause. Of course, criticism of generals and politicians was nothing new in military memoirs. But whereas previously they were criticized for incompetence, for taking all the honor and riches to themselves, and for distributing rewards unfairly, now commanders were increasingly criticized for playing with their troops' lives and for sacrificing them for unworthy causes.

Alexander Graydon criticized General Mifflin of the Continental Army, saying that 'he was considerably happy in the display of that apathy to human carnage, which is affected by great commanders, in the spirit of which the great Frederick tells us, that "When sovereigns play for provinces, the lives of men are but as counters." So much 'tis better to direct the game, than be a component part of its machinery!'[245] French graffiti in Spain said that 'This war in Spain means death for the men; ruin for the officers; a fortune for the generals!'[246]

General Marbot wrote about an unnecessary attack ordered by General Heudelet in 1807 that 'He was again repulsed with some thirty men killed and wounded, among them a captain of engineers, a most promising officer. I have always felt disgusted by this contempt of human life, which at times leads generals to sacrifice their men to their desire of seeing themselves mentioned in dispatches.'[247] Marbot was far more sweeping in his criticism of the Spanish war.

> As a soldier I was bound to fight any who attacked the French army, but I could not help recognizing in my inmost conscience that our cause was a bad one, and that the Spaniards were quite right in trying to drive out strangers, who, after coming among them in the guise of friends, were wishing to dethrone their sovereign and take forcible possession of the kingdom. This, therefore, seemed to me wicked, but I was a soldier, and I must march or be charged with cowardice. The greater part of the army thought as I did, and like me, obeyed orders all the same.[248]

Occasionally, memoirists even blamed commanders that they deliberately planted illusionary ideals of war in the minds of the soldiers in order to manipulate them for their own selfish ends. In the *Charterhouse of Parma* Fabrizio concludes from his experiences at Waterloo that 'war was no longer that noble and universal uplifting of souls athirst for glory which he had imagined it to be from Napoleon's proclamations!'[249]

Napoleon is tacitly criticized here for spreading ideas of glory which he must have known from his experience to be false. Characteristically, Stendhal balances the high rhetoric of Napoleon's proclamation against a sensory experience. On the morning after the battle, writes Stendhal, 'Our hero was [...] the coolest man in the world; the amount of blood he had shed had liberated him from all the romantic element in his character.'[250]

Johann Konrad Friederich repeatedly criticized the false ideals planted in his head by cynical generals. When the young Friederich marched through Italy, he was inspired by Napoleon's words to his soldiers: 'You have nothing, and there is everything you desire!' To these words, the mature Friederich cynically comments, Napoleon should have added 'and that you won't gain.' For 'What did these conquests give to the simple man or the subordinate officer? Only some leaders robbed themselves rich.'[251] As for himself, Friederich writes that for years he served Napoleon loyally, because 'I was at that time a blinded fool like the others.'[252]

It is interesting to note that Friederich's narrative of disillusionment was inspired directly by Goethe's *Wilhelm Meister*. In his youth, Friederich – like Wilhelm Meister – wanted to be an actor, and he claims to have discussed this idea with Goethe himself at Weimar.[253] He then changed his fantasy, and enlisted into the French army dreaming of imitating Napoleon and rising through the ranks. '[I] hoped, that I too would one day command an army, [a task] from which merciful heaven saved me, for which I sincerely thank heaven, now that the absurd nothingness of all these human, if also often very bloody, puppet shows has become terribly clear to me.'[254] The hint at Wilhelm Meister's puppet theater may well have been intended.

The fourth thread that made up the typical disillusionment narrative consisted of exposing war crimes committed by one's own side. That was not a Romantic novelty. Early modern memoirists often mentioned such crimes, and early modern soldiers were often described as criminals. However, within the context of Romantic memoirs this thread acquired a new importance, because it counterbalanced the rising positive image of the common soldiers, and made it more difficult for readers to believe that their own moral purity somehow uplifted and redeemed the soldiers' miseries.

For instance, Jean-Baptiste Barrès wrote about the first time he saw his comrades sack a village, during the victorious campaign of 1805:

Then, for the first time, I witnessed an example of the horrors of war. As the cold was very bitter some men were detached to fetch wood, in order to bivouac. The village whither they went for it was devastated in a moment; not content with taking the wood, they carried off the furniture, the farm implements, the linen and other movables [...] This spectacle, new to me, wounded me to the heart. I shed tears over the fate of these poor villagers, who had in a moment lost all their possessions. But what I saw later caused me to regard them as still happy in their misfortune. As I was a novice in the military art, all that was contrary to the principles in which I had been trained surprised me.[255]

Ulrich Bräker took things to their logical conclusion. If war was such a misery, which was unredeemed by any spiritual ideal or moral purity, and which resulted from the cynical manipulation of heartless generals and politicians, a really wise and enlightened man should do his best to absent himself from war. Bräker was a Swiss peasant who was deeply influenced by the Enlightenment. Though of very limited means, he was nevertheless a leading member in a local literary club, and besides writing an autobiography, also wrote over 3,000 pages of journals, a criticism of Shakespeare, a volume of poetry, and a novel. His autobiography was published in 1789, and won him a modest literary fame. His description of his military career was clearly influenced by *Candide*.

As we saw in previous chapters, in his youth Bräker was forced into the Prussian army (1756). Though he had an extremely pitiful time during his basic training, once war broke out he was caught up in the general war enthusiasm. He was very keen to experience battle and show his mettle, and did his best to shine on parade in order to ensure that he will be sent to the front rather than left at depot.[256] (It is interesting to note that like Mämpel, Bräker too says that as a green recruit he had no military inclinations whatsoever, and that it was boot camp that implanted in him aspirations for military glory.)

The few marches the army made from Berlin to Pirna (1756) were enough to disillusion Bräker, and he writes, ' "Up to now the Lord has helped!" These words were our padre's first text at Pirna. You're telling me He has! I thought: Well, let's hope He keeps it up – and sees me safely back home – 'cos I couldn't care less about your wars!'[257] From Pirna onward, he thought only of desertion. His description of the battle of Lobositz (1756) reads like an expanded version of Candide's first battle.

As soon as battle was joined, 'all my courage sank into my breeches; my only wish was to creep into the bowels of the earth, and a similar fear, indeed deathly pallor, could be seen on all faces, even of those who'd always made out how tough they were.' His regiment was sent to fight some Austrian light infantrymen on a steep hill overlooking the main battlefield. As they engaged the Austrians his fear abated, and at the height of the action 'I slewed about all over the place like a mad thing, and immune to the slightest fear, in *one* burst I shot off well nigh all 60 of my rounds till my musket was pretty well red-hot [...] I don't believe I hit a living soul though – it all went into the air.' On the plain below him, he saw the battle 'But who shall attempt to describe it? – the smoke and fumes [...] the crashing and thundering [...] the moans and groans from so many thousands of wretched, mangled, half-dead victims of this day: it dazed all the senses!'

Then he had a moment of revelation. 'As I stood there a little way up the slope, staring at the plain as into a murky thunder – and hailstorm – that very moment it occurred to me, or rather it was my guardian angle prompting me, that it was high time I fled for safety. [...] to the left I saw vineyards, bushes, copses, just the odd Prussian, pandour or hussar dotted about, and of these more dead and wounded than living. There! there! that direction, I thought; otherwise you haven't a hope in hell!' He began to hedge slowly toward the safety of the rough ground. 'I was scared stiff, I must admit. But as soon as I'd got so far no one could see me any more, I doubled, trebled, quadrupled, quintupled, sextupled my speed, looked to left and right like a huntsman, still saw away in the distance – for the last time in my life – wholesale murder; then in full gallop I skirted a small wood that lay full of dead hussars, pandours and horses, ran full tilt down towards the river and now found myself in a dell.' He surrendered himself to some Austrian soldiers, who took away his musket – 'good riddance!' comments Bräker. He still had one fight ahead of him, having to struggle with a crowd of fugitive women for a place on a ferryboat.

In the Austrian camp, he saw some Prussian prisoners-of-war, 'a pitiful sight! Scarcely one who'd got off without wounds or bruises, some slashed all over the face, others in the neck, others across the ears, across the shoulders, the thighs, etc. Nothing but moaning and groaning from all sides. Didn't these poor wretches call us fortunate to have so luckily escaped a like fate, and didn't we ourselves thank the Lord we had!'[258]

Bräker's description of Lobositz is similar in many respects to Estebanillo Gonzalez's description of Nördlingen, but with three important differences: First, Bräker does not describe himself as a buffoon, but as an intelligent man of the Enlightenment. His conclusions about war should be taken seriously. Secondly, whereas Estebanillo is a through-and-through coward, Bräker has moments of courage and of war-enthusiasm, which makes it easier for the average reader to identify with him and to respect his views. He was not an innate coward. Rather, it was his war experiences that taught him not to throw away his life for nothing. Thirdly and most importantly, Estebanillo is a fictional person, and even if his story was based on authentic experiences, no real person was willing to be identified with him. Bräker, on the other hand, was *proud* to be recognized as the deserter from Lobositz.

There was, however, one ideal which was never attacked in the milder versions of the disillusionment narratives: comradeship. Indeed, in disillusioned narratives such as Bräker's, comradeship was described in positive terms, and the positive force of comradeship was occasionally relied upon to expose the fraud of other war ideals. Patriotism and heroism were blamed for the death of comrades, and soldiers found in comradeship the spiritual and practical basis needed to withstand the brainwashing of the establishment. Thus Bräker's comrades assure one another that it is not base cowardice to desert the army, and they help one another to actually desert.

Some disillusioned narratives, however, began to expose comradeship too as an illusionary ideal. One such example is contained in the memoirs of Karl August Varnhagen von Ense. A student at Halle, in 1809 Varnhagen enthusiastically rushed to join the Austrian army, volunteering to serve as an ensign in the infantry. Wondering through the Austrian camp at Wagram, 'I almost fancied myself in the midst of the soldiers described by Schiller in Wallenstein's camp.'[259] He soon became disillusioned about his fellow officers, who

> were but sorry companions. The views taken by northern Germans were incomprehensible to the Austrians, who saw in war merely a trade from which to gain all the advantage they could, and who looked forward with pleasure to garrison life in Prague. The colonel was the only one who knew Gentz, and had heard of Friedrich Schlegel [...] There was no enthusiasm, no poetry.[260]

During the battle of Wagram Varnhagen received a shot in the leg, and was evacuated in a cart along with other wounded men. 'The jolting of the cart gave me excruciating pain, and when the flow of blood, which had continued until now, ceased, my whole leg grew cold and stiff. Like the others, I suffered from extreme thirst, and the chill of the night air was hard to bear.'[261] As day rose, he was tormented by the blistering sun. Mercifully, the cart was covered by the boughs of a tree.

I found such a relief from the shade and the sight of the green boughs, that I no longer felt the torture of my wounds, and occasionally fell into a sort of pleasant dreamy state, in which I even made verses in honour of the tree which had done me such signal service. I cannot now remember the actual words, but the sensations which gave rise to them are still present to my mind. Unluckily these feelings were frequently broken by the cry of pain wrung from me by the stumble of the horse, or the jolting of the rough wagon.[262]

When this Romantic poet reached the hospital, he was increasingly dismayed by the difficult conditions and the prevailing moral atmosphere. 'My interest in public events was at first so intense, as to make me forget my own personal griefs; but this decreased every day, as the accounts got worse and worse.' He was disappointed by the defeatism and provincialism of the Austrians, and longed to be back in Berlin. 'My patience was heavily taxed. The two officers who shared my room were but sorry companions, and too dull to understand my feelings.' He asked for books to pass the time with, and received a load of trashy novels, 'into the midst of which I plunged, seizing with all avidity upon the stray quotations from Goethe and Schiller which they contained.'[263]

Varnhagen thus stands in sharp contrast to Nagel, and anticipates the disillusioned bourgeois volunteers of 1914. Varnhagen, like the 1914 volunteers described by Eric Leed, joined war with Romantic expectations of universal comradeship, only to discover that these very expectations were a middle-class fantasy, which marked him off and set him apart from his social inferiors.[264]

Varnhagen's narrative is quite unique inasmuch as it expressed disillusionment with the ideal of comradeship while retaining its belief in patriotism and glory. The most extreme disillusionment narratives of the Romantic era described the miseries of war in the most detailed Sensationist terms, while simultaneously expressing disillusionment with all military ideals *including* comradeship.

The largest crop of such extreme disillusionment narratives emanated from Napoleon's ill-fated invasion of Russia (1812). As noted earlier, the retreat from Moscow became a universal symbol for military disillusionment and for the misery of the common soldiers in war. Numerous memoirists of all the nations that took part in the invasion described the miseries of the retreat in the most harrowing terms. These narratives were particularly shocking because their almost unreadable descriptions of physical sufferings were not compensated for by *any* spiritual ideals, not even comradeship. Indeed, the narratives usually described the moral collapse of the army in even greater detail than its physical collapse. According to many memoirs, the *Grande Armée* became a decidedly un-heroic mob of frightened, half-crazed, and egotistical fugitives.

The most poignant of these memoirs is perhaps that of Sergeant Bourgogne. From all the military memoirs I have read during this research, including those of the two World Wars, I have found Bourgogne's account of the retreat from Moscow the hardest to stomach. The only equivalents that came to my mind were memoirs of Holocaust survivors. Napoleon's soldiers in Bourgogne's account not only endure extremes of suffering, but many of them lose all trace of humane feelings. To note just a few scenes: Five French soldiers 'fighting like dogs' over a frozen horse leg.[265] Bourgogne himself hiding a few potatoes he had found from his mess-mates and closest comrades.[266] Hundreds of French soldiers locked themselves up in a barn, which then accidentally caught fire. Soldiers flocked to the burning barn to warm themselves by its fire, oblivious to the terrible shrieks coming from within.[267] A member of the Imperial Guard stripping the clothes of a dying comrade, while the victim in vain tries to resist and strikes the ground helplessly with his fists.[268] Bourgogne and some comrades expel by the point of the bayonet a weaker group of soldiers who sheltered themselves in a church. The next morning 'we found many of the poor wretches dead by the side of

Figure 26 Christian Wilhelm Faber du Faur, *Near Oschimany, 4 December* (1812–1830)

the road. Others had dropped down further on, while trying to find a place of shelter. We passed by these dead bodies in silence. We ought, no doubt, to have felt guilty and miserable at this sad spectacle, of which we were partly the cause; but we had arrived at the point of complete indifference to everything, even the most tragic events.'[269]

Almost as shocking is Major Christian Wilhelm Faber du Faur's pictorial memoirs of the 1812 campaign (sketched *in situ* in 1812, and later drawn up and colored in 1827–1830). The scene below, for example, shows how the able-bodied survivors stripped their weaker comrades while the latter were still alive. The person at the bottom right shows clear signs of madness. The accompanying text reads 'The strongest pillaged the weakest, the sick were stripped of their clothing and the dying were robbed of their clothes and left to die in the deep snow. An instinct of self-preservation had snuffed out all traces of humanity in the human heart.'[270]

The duke of Montesquiou-Fezensac describes the universal image left by the retreat from Moscow:

> Imagine vast snow-covered plains stretching as far as the eye can see, deep pine forests, half-burned and deserted villages, and marching through this mournful countryside an immense column of miserable wretches, almost all without weapons, moving along rag-tag and bobtail, slipping on the ice at each step and falling down beside the carcasses of horses and the corpses of their comrades. Their faces bore the impress of resignation or despair, their eyes were dead, their features without expression and blackened with dirt and smoke. Sheepskins and strips of cloth served them as shoes; their heads were wrapped in rags, their shoulders covered with horse blankets, women's skirts, or half-cured hides. As soon as one of them fell from exhaustion, his comrades stripped him before he was dead and dressed in his rags.[271]

'All human compassion vanished,' wrote Heinrich Vossler, 'each thought and cared only for himself and be damned to his comrade. With complete indifference he watched him lie down and die, without emotion he seated himself on his corpse by the fireside.'[272] Vossler concludes his memoirs by noting that during 1812 he suffered from every conceivable misery.

> My health, once robust, was ruined. My feet were a mass of open sores, my stomach greatly weakened, unable to absorb any but the slightest of diets. My chest ached with every sudden movement. Nor had the two campaigns proved any less ruinous for my finances. [...]

Centuries will pass and breed many more wars. Yet the horrors of the war of 1812 and the misfortunes that befell the French army and its allies will not soon be forgotten. [273]

No ideal – either heroism, patriotism, or camaraderie – appears in these concluding lines to balance the wounded feet, the weakened stomach, the aching chest, and the empty purse.

To summarize, the disillusionment narratives of the Romantic era mostly adopted a worldview that can be labeled "Materialist Pacifism." They emphasized the reality of war's material miseries, while exposing the emptiness of its spiritual ideals. Imitating the attacks of the Radical Enlightenment on Christianity, Materialist Pacifism argued that war is a horrible material experience that people engage in only because they are deceived by the empty spiritual promises of cynical generals and politicians. If people would stop believing in these spiritual charades, peace would reign on earth.

Thus, paradoxically, there was at least one good thing all disillusioned memoirs could say about war: War experience revealed the truth about war, thereby disillusioning people and promoting peace. From the Napoleonic era onward, the more terrible a war was, the easier it was for people to imagine that it must be the last war.

Despite the above examples, the disillusionment narratives of the Napoleonic era remained a subdued and secondary current within military culture. For every Mämpel, there were a dozen Nagels. With the passing of the years, the Sun of Austerlitz eclipsed the frozen fields of 1812.[274] Even those memoirists that attacked war seldom did so with the same force and bitterness that would characterize their twentieth-century counterparts. Their criticism of war was usually confined to isolated statements and passages, and the force of these passages was often lost within the larger narrative. (This is in contrast to twentieth-century texts such as *All Quiet on the Western Front*, which from beginning to end were an all-out and unremitting assault on war and on military ideals.[275])

Twentieth-century military disillusionment nevertheless owed a great debt to the Romantic tradition. Romantic memoirists such as Mämpel *and* Nagel established the image of war as an experiential revelation of truth, and established the flesh-witnessing authority of subaltern soldiers. It was thanks to this authority that Erich Maria Remarque and Wilfred Owen could storm and shake the bastions of twentieth-century militarism. In a way that Voltaire, Goethe, Hölderlin, Byron, and Lermontov would have found perfectly predictable, the greatest revelation of twentieth-century war was that militaristic ideals are dangerous frauds, and that people had better distrust 'glory, and all that immortal stuff.' For all the radicalism of twentieth-century military disillusionment narratives, they too were part and parcel of the legacy of Romanticism.[276]

Combinations

Positive revelations and disillusionment did not always contradict each other. Since both relied on the authority of flesh-witnessing and both accepted the aesthetics and epistemology of the sublime, they could be combined with surprising ease. In particular, they could be grafted unto the two-stage structure of the Kantian sublime. In the first stage, encounters with the sublime experiences of war overwhelm the combatant and disillusion him about many of his peacetime ideas and ideals. Yet by releasing the combatant from his peacetime illusions these experiences make room for a better and more authentic perception of reality. The combatant then enjoys various positive revelations, which more than compensate for his initial disappointment, particularly because these new revelations bear the authenticating mark of reality.

In its simplest form the process ends with the firm adoption of a new ideal. For instance, in *Mein Kampf* Hitler's World War I experience begins with shallow patriotism – the product of the imagination. Then come horror and fear, which wipe away shallow patriotism. Yet fear in its turn is overcome by the inner voice of duty, and Hitler discovers his absolute moral independence: 'At last my will was undisputed master. If in the first days I went over the top with rejoicing and laughter, I was now calm and determined. And this was enduring. Now Fate could bring on the ultimate tests without my nerves shattering or my reason failing.'[277]

In its more complex variants, this process becomes a type of never-ending revelation, akin to many Puritan and Methodist conversion narratives. The initial conversion experience is followed by further struggles and further conversions. A prototypical example is Leo Tolstoy's Sebastopol sketches of 1854–55. Tolstoy was a 25-year-old junior artillery officer when he joined the garrison of besieged Sebastopol during the Crimean War. At first he was full of patriotic enthusiasm, and shortly after his arrival he published a short story titled *Sebastopol in December 1854*, which described the Russian army in glowing terms, although it included many realistic and shocking scenes of war. The story was written in the second person, and presented as a guided tour of the battlefield. Tolstoy invites the reader to accompany him through the city, and experience different aspects of war.

Thus he comments about an artillery duel that 'The enemy replies, and you experience interesting sensations.'[278] On the whole these experiences have a beneficial impact. Tolstoy tells the reader that if one looked at the brave soldiers in the frontline trenches, 'You will also see that danger, misery, and suffering in the war will have imprinted on these faces the consciousness of their dignity, of high thoughts, of a sentiment.'[279]

In conclusion, Tolstoy says to the reader that

> You have just seen the defenders of Sebastopol on the very place of the defence, and, strange to say, you will retrace your steps without paying the least attention to the bullets and balls which continue to whistle the whole length of the road as far as the ruins of the theatre. You walk with calmness, your soul elevated and strengthened, for you bring away the consoling conviction that never, and in no place, can the strength of the Russian people be broken; and you have gained this conviction not from the solidity of the parapets [...] but from the eyes, the words, the bearing, from what may be called the spirit of the defenders of Sebastopol.[280]

As the siege progressed, Tolstoy became disillusioned, and published another story, titled *Sebastopol in May 1855*. That story contained far more somber and even cynical descriptions of various characters and scenes inside the besieged city. Particularly noteworthy is a minute description he gives of the train of thoughts that passes through the mind of an officer called Praskoukine in the last few seconds of his life. A shell landed near Praskoukine.

> A second, which appeared to him an hour, passed, and the shell did not burst. Praskoukine was frightened; then he asked himself what cause he had for fear. Perhaps it had fallen farther away, and he wrongly imagined that he heard the fuse hissing near him. Opening his eyes [...] he perceived, a yard off, the lighted fuse of the shell spinning around like a top. A glacial terror, which stifled every thought, every sentiment, took possession of his soul. He hid his face in his hands.
>
> Another second passed, during which a whole world of thoughts, of hopes, of sensations, and of souvenirs passed through his mind.
>
> "Whom will it kill? Me or Mikhaïloff, or indeed both of us together? If it is I, where will it hit me? If in the head, it will be all over; if on the foot, they will cut it off, then I shall insist that they give

me chloroform, and I may get well. Perhaps Mikhaïloff alone will be killed, and later I will tell how we were close together, and how I was covered with his blood. No, no! it is nearer me – it will be I!"

Then he remembered the twelve rubles he owed Mikhaïloff, and another debt left at Petersburg, which ought to have been paid long ago. A Bohemian air that he sang the evening before came to his mind. He also saw in his imagination the lady he was in love with in her lilac trimmed bonnet; the man who had insulted him five years before, and whom he had never taken vengeance on. But in the midst of these and many other souvenirs the present feeling – the expectation of death – did not leave him. "Perhaps it isn't going to explode!" he thought, and was on the point of opening his eyes with desperate boldness. But at this instant a red fire struck his eyeballs through the closed lids, something hit him in the middle of the chest with a terrible crash. He ran forward at random, entangled his feet in his sword, stumbled, and fell on his side.

"God be praised, I am only bruised."

This was his first thought, and he wanted to feel his breast, but his hands seemed as if they were tied. A vice griped his head, soldiers ran before his eyes, and he mechanically counted them:

"One, two, three soldiers, and, besides, an officer who is losing his cloak!"

A new light flashed; he wondered what had fired. Was it a mortar or a cannon? Doubtless a cannon. Another shot, more soldiers – five, six, seven. They passed in front of him, and suddenly he became terribly afraid of being crushed by them. He wanted to cry out, to say that he was bruised, but his lips were dry, his tongue was glued to the roof of his mouth. He had a burning thirst. He felt that his breast was damp, and the sensation of this moisture made him think of water [...] He would have liked to drink that which drenched him.

"I must have knocked the skin off in falling," he said to himself, more and more frightened at the idea of being crushed by the soldiers who were running in crowds before him. He tried again to cry out,

"Take me!"

But instead of that he uttered a groan so terrible that he was frightened at it himself. Then red sparks danced before his eyes; it seemed as if the soldiers were piling stones on him. The sparks danced more rapidly, the stones piled on him stifled him more and more. He stretched himself out, he ceased to see, to hear, to think, to feel. He had been killed instantly by a piece of shell striking him full in the breast.[281]

It is probable that never before, and seldom since, has the death of an officer on the field of battle been described with such brutal candor.

After presenting his readers with a kaleidoscope of realistic scenes and protagonists, Tolstoy rhetorically asks who is the hero of his tale. He answers that it is neither this soldier, nor that, nor the other. 'No; the hero of my tale, the one I love with all the power of my soul, the one I have tried to reproduce in all his beauty, just as he has been [...] is Truth.'[282]

Shortly after, Tolstoy published a third story, *Sebastopol in August 1855*, which closed the circle. It tells the fictional story of a young artillery officer named Volodia, who had just left the military school at St. Petersburg and reached Sebastopol with high expectations of glory. A short distance from Sebastopol he meets his elder brother, Michael, who had been serving in the besieged garrison for several months already, and together they cover the last few kilometers in a carriage. Tolstoy describes with marked irony Volodia's glorious day-dreaming as he rides in the carriage:

We will surely get there [Sebastopol] today [...] We go straight to the bastion – I with the artillery, my brother with his company. Suddenly the French throw themselves upon us. I fire on the spot, I kill a crowd of them, but they run just the same straight upon me. Impossible to fire – I am lost! but my brother dashes forward, sword in hand. I seize my musket and we run together; the soldiers follow us. The French throw themselves on my brother. I run up; I kill first one, then another, and I save Micha. I am wounded in the arm; I take my musket in the other hand and run on. My brother is killed at my side by a bullet; I stop a moment, I look at him sadly, I rise and cry, "Forward with me! let us avenge him!" I add, "I loved my brother above everything; I have lost him. Let us avenge ourselves, kill our enemies, or all die together!" All follow me, shouting. But there is the whole French army, Pélissier at their head. We kill all of them, but I am wounded once, twice, and the third time mortally. They gather around me. Gortschakoff comes and asks what I wish for. I reply that I wish for nothing – I wish for only one thing, to be placed beside my brother and to die with him. They carry me and lay me down besides his bloody corpse. I raise myself up and say, "Yes, you could not appreciate two men who sincerely loved their country. They are killed – may God pardon you!" and thereupon I die.[283]

Having finished day-dreaming, Volodia asks his brother, 'Have you ever been in a hand-to-hand fight?,' and Michael answers, 'No, never.

We have lost two thousand men in our regiment, but always in the works. I was wounded there. War is not carried out on as you imagine, Volodia.'[284]

The experiences Volodia himself undergoes in the next few hours quickly damp his spirits. By the end of his first day in Sebastopol, he is crestfallen.

> When they arrive, at nightfall, at the great bridge over the bay, Volodia was not exactly in bad humor, but a terrible weight lay on his heart. Everything he saw, everything he heard, harmonized so little with the last impressions that had been left in his mind by the great, light examination-hall with polished floor, the voices of his comrades and the gayety of their sympathetic bursts of laughter, his new uniform, the well-beloved Czar [...] yes, everything he saw little harmonized with his rich dreams sparkling from a thousand facets.[285]

His fantasies are replaced by fears and anxieties. As shells begin to fall near him, he is seized by a terrible fear, being convinced that any minute a shell will hit him. " 'My God! shall I really be killed – I? Oh, my God, have mercy on me.' "[286] A subsequent visit to a field hospital leaves him completely horrified. He begins to fear that he is in fact a coward:

> Volodia went forward alone. No longer hearing behind him Nikolaïeff's sighs, he felt himself abandoned for good and all. The feeling of this desertion in the presence of danger, of death, as he believed, oppressed his heart with the glacial weight of a stone. Halting in the middle of the place, he looked all about him to see if he was observed, and taking his head in both hands, he murmured, with a voice broken by terror, "My God! am I really a despicable poltroon, a coward? I who have lately dreamed of dying for my country, for my Czar, and that with joy! Yes, I am an unfortunate and despicable being!" he cried, in profound despair, and quite undeceived about himself.[287]

Yet now begins a new process of revelation. Volodia abandons for good his childish fantasies, which is made evident when he meets the other subaltern officers in his battery. The only one of them whom he dislikes is Tchernovitzky. Tchernovitzky is in fact very polite, but he continually 'related with factitious enthusiasm the heroic exploits accomplished at Sebastopol, expressed his regrets at the small number of true patriots, [and] made a show of a great deal of knowledge, of wit, of exceedingly noble sentiments.' Volodia finds that 'without being able to tell why, all these discourses sounded false in his ears, and he even noticed that the officers in general avoided speaking to Tchernovitzky.'[288]

Once the childish fantasies are abandoned to humbugs like Tchernovitzky, Volodia begins to discover the real truth about himself and about war, and is surprised to find that this truth is not altogether negative. When he receives his first combat mission – to command two mortars in a forward position – he is 'happy and surprised to feel that the dread of danger, especially the fear of passing for a coward, was less strong than on the evening before. His impressions of the day and his occupation had partly contributed to diminish the violence of this; and then it is well known that an acute sensation cannot last long without weakening. In a word, his fear was being cured.'[289] During the subsequent experiences Volodia's feelings ebb and flow: at times he experiences courage, at other times fear. Yet on the whole, he grows accustomed to combat, and becomes an efficient and kind officer, beloved by his men. 'The joy he felt at doing his duty well, at being no longer a coward, at feeling himself, on the contrary, full of courage, the feeling of commanding and the presence of twenty men, who he knew were watching him with curiosity, had made a real hero of him.'[290]

After a few days Volodia is killed in combat, commanding his battery bravely. Tolstoy portrays his death scene realistically. Volodia behaves honorably, but not as heroically as in his day-dreams in the carriage, and his action has no bearing on the battle, which ends in a Russian defeat. The last sight we have of him is 'A shapeless thing, clothed in a gray overcoat, lay, face to earth, on the spot where Volodia stood, and the whole place was filled by the French, who were firing at our men.'[291] Tolstoy then describes the Russian route, as men, horses, and wagons flee Sebastopol. 'Although the attention was distracted by a thousand details, the feeling of self-preservation, and the desire to fly as soon as possible from that fatal spot, filled each one's soul.'[292]

Tolstoy's three Sebastopol sketches as a whole, and the *August 1855* sketch in itself, draw a complex picture of war. The process of positive revelation and the process of disillusionment both hold part of the truth, but taken in isolation they are a lie. War is a process of revelation, but it reveals a multifaceted and ever-changing reality. Tolstoy does not end *August 1855* with a clear-cut reaffirmation of some martial ideal. Rather, the hero of *August 1855* is identical to the hero of *May 1855* – it is Truth.

What *August 1855* reaffirms above all is the positive value of truth and of flesh-witnessing. It is a mistake to believe that soldiers in general and oneself in particular are "heroic" or "cowardly," "patriotic" or "disillusioned." Rather, courage and cowardice, patriotism and disillusionment, follow one another and change the one into the other repeatedly. The most positive revelation of all is that one is able to know this changing reality and embrace it without having to cling to any immutable and secure ideal. This of course resonates with – and fulfills – the ideal of the "man of feeling": a seismographer who remains open and sensitive to the tiniest changes, not blocking and numbing himself by blind adhesion to any theoretical view of reality. Even the conclusions drawn from yesterday's battle – for example, that one is courageous – have today become a theoretical view. The man of feeling keeps open the possibility that today fear may assert itself yet again.

Desensitizing [293]

Both the interpretation of war as a positive revelation and the interpretation of war as an experience of disillusionment assume that if all knowledge ultimately depends on sensations, then more intense sensory experiences necessarily produce deeper knowledge. Since war is an extreme sensory experience, it must produce deep knowledge. This was and still is a very common way of thinking, but it involves a problematic logical jump, whose dangers were apparent already to eighteenth-century Sensationists and nineteenth-century Romantics.[294]

Even if knowledge is rooted in sensory experience, it does not follow that there is a direct correspondence between the intensity of the experience and the depth of the acquired knowledge. Opposite arguments could be and were made in the name of Sensationism. Many argued that the more sensitive a person is, the less need there is of external stimulation in order to acquire knowledge. Highly sensitive persons – such as the heroes of eighteenth-century sentimental novels – acquire profound knowledge of themselves and of the world by attending to the most ordinary everyday experiences. Extreme experiences are useful only for people who have no inclination to attend to their sensations – and need a rude reminder – or for people with very dull sensibility, who cannot attend to subtle stimulations.

Moreover, all people, even those possessing the strongest nervous systems, have a limit to what they can take. Whereas the soul and the mind were traditionally imagined as infinite in their capacities, the body was always viewed as finite. Since sensibility depends to a large extent on one's nervous system, it too is necessarily finite, for even the strongest nerves are material fibers, which would break if put under too great a strain. Consequently, if a person is bombarded by over-powerful sensory stimulations, the result is likely to be desensitizing rather than revelation. For in order to cope with this over-stimulation, people develop defense mechanisms that lessen their sensibility.

The model of desensitizing was only a variation on the basic formula of Sensationism. As we saw in Chapter 4 this basic formula reads as follows:

$$\text{sensibility} \times \text{experience} = \text{knowledge}$$

Narratives of positive revelation and of disillusionment understood this formula in a naïve way. They took sensibility as more or less a constant, experience as a variable, and knowledge as the inevitable result. They were thereby led to the conclusion that any increase in "experience" – that is, encountering more extreme and stimulating experiences – necessarily results in more knowledge.

Narratives of desensitizing took a more nuanced approach toward this formula. They pointed out that sensibility and knowledge too are variables. If people do not have the means – the "knowledge" – to face an extreme experience, they may react to an increase in the volume of experience by *lowering their sensibility*. The formula from the desensitizing viewpoint reads as follows:

$$\text{sensibility} = \text{knowledge} / \text{experience}$$

In this case, any increase in "experience" – that is, encountering more extreme and stimulating experiences – may result only in the decrease of sensibility.

The dangers of over-stimulations were a known threat to the devotees of the cult of sensibility, and authors who believed in the Sensationist formula (sensibility × experience = knowledge) not infrequently switched to its desensitizing variant (sensibility = knowledge / experience). Sade's libertine heroes, for example, constantly worried about the danger of desensitizing, and required stronger and stronger doses of stimulation to overcome their growing numbness. In his theory of the sublime, Burke argued that the most beneficial sublime experiences involve only a limited amount of danger. Burke believed that sublime experiences depended upon sensations and upon the strength of one's nervous system, and that consequently there should be a margin of safety for the observers, otherwise they are likely to experience only unmitigated terror, and emerge from their experience weaker rather than wiser. 'When danger or pain press too nearly, they are incapable of giving any delight, and are simply terrible; but at certain distances, and with certain modifications, they may be, and they are delightful.'[295] Kant similarly remarked about fearful things in nature that *'provided our own position is secure*, their aspect is all the more attractive for its fearfulness.'[296]

Schiller explained things with the greatest clarity and candor.

> In order to experience something frightening as sublime and take pleasure in it, inner freedom on the part of the mind is an absolute requisite. [...] Actual and serious fear, however, overcomes all freedom of mind. Therefore, the sublime object must, of course, be frightening, but it may not incite actual fear. Fear is a condition of *suffering* and *violence*; only in a detached consideration of something and through the feeling of the activity inside ourselves can we take pleasure in something sublime. Thus either the fearful object may not direct its power at us at all, or, if this happens, then our spirit must remain free, while our sensuous nature is being overwhelmed. This latter case is, however, extremely rare, and demands an *elevation* of human nature that can scarcely be considered possible in an individual. For where we actually find ourselves in danger, where we ourselves are the object of an inimical natural power, aesthetic judgment is finished.

For example, writes Schiller, a storm at sea is sublime to those observing it from the safety of the shore, but seldom to those caught up in a drowning ship.[297] According to this line of thinking, being in great danger is potentially a sublime experience that may reveal the deepest truths, but only if one has already got such an "elevated nature" that enables one to experience the danger with wisdom and detachment. For the vast majority of humans, it will result only in unmitigated terror.

Accordingly, a strong undercurrent of Romantic thought viewed war as an experience of over-stimulation that may terrorize and desensitize rather than enlighten combatants. What combatants take with them from war is stronger defense mechanisms and weaker sensibility rather than knowledge. Coarse persons are likely to emerge from war coarser than ever, while sensitive persons are likely to be "burnt out" by war ("traumatized," in today's language).

This somber vision emptied the sublime of most of its appeal, and most Romantic writers – including Schiller – preferred to sweep it under the carpet. Yet it occasionally emerged in the writing of almost all Romantic writers, even those who normally focused on the brighter side of the equation. Christian Nagel describes how in the wake of Waterloo 'the horrible sight of the mangled bodies shocked my whole being,' until eventually 'I went, like my horse, indifferent and unfeeling, onwards over the dead.'[298] (Nagel's ability to ignore the corpses is reminiscent of the bravery of people who know no fear – it is the quality of an animal.)

Elzéar Blaze wrote that 'You should see the faces of the conscripts when they [...] see the first dead men. They will detour twenty feet around them, for fear of touching them. Soon they can come nearer to them; later they walk over them without a thought.'[299] In his first battle Rifleman Harris saw Sergeant Frazer die a horrible death:

> It was, indeed, dreadful to look upon him; the froth came from his mouth, and the perspiration poured from his face. Thank Heaven! he was soon out of pain; and, laying him down, I returned to my place. Poor fellow! he suffered more for the short time that he was dying than any man I think I ever saw in the same circumstances. I had the curiosity to return and look at him after the battle. A musket-ball, I found, had taken him sideways, and gone through both groins.
>
> Within about half an hour after this I left Sergeant Frazer, and, indeed, for the time, had as completely forgotten him as if he had died a hundred years back. The sight of so much bloodshed around will not suffer the mind to dwell long on any particular casualty, even though it happen to one's dearest friend.[300]

It is notable that in this and similar cases, the described scene still has a sublime touch, which gives Harris's musing on the nature of the human mind the authority of revelation.

After the battle of Vimeiro (1808), Harris came across three French bodies. They had already been plundered, and a quantity of biscuits were scattered around. Harris comments about his subsequent action:

> War is a sad blunter of the feelings I have often thought since those days. The contemplation of three ghastly bodies in this lonely spot failed then in making the slightest impression upon me. The sight had become, even in the short time I had been engaged in the trade, but too familiar. The biscuits, however, which lay in my path, I thought a blessed windfall, and, stooping, I gathered them up, scraped the blood with which they were sprinkled with my bayonet, and ate them ravenously.[301]

General Marbot wrote that when he saw the Russian soldiers drowning in icy water during their retreat from Austerlitz (1805), he felt no inclination to help them:

> I do not wish to make myself out better than I am, so I will admit that just having taken part in a battle where I had seen thousands of dead and dying, the edge had been taken off my sensibility, and I did not feel philanthropic enough to run the risk of a bad cold by contesting with the ice floes the life of an enemy. I felt quite content with deploring his sad fate.[302]

Alexander Graydon wrote that

> War, indeed, in its essence is cruelty, especially civil war: Its tendency is to make men ferocious and merciless. In conflicts, in which our lives are continually at stake, we at length become callous even to the loss of our own party, and have, of course, still less concern for the destruction of our adversaries, notwithstanding, that particular situations may sometimes call forth striking examples of sympathy and generosity. [...] Such seems to be the nature of man.[303]

Gleig gives a minute description – four pages long – of the horrors he saw when visiting St. Sebastian shortly after its capture (1813). After visiting the place, he says that he and his comrades 'turned our backs upon St Sebastian's, not without a chilling sense of the horrible points in our profession. But this gradually wore off as we approached the quarters of our host, and soon gave place to the more cheering influence of a substantial dinner, and a few cups of indifferently good wine.'[304] Gleig writes that the common soldiers in particular were prone to become desensitized. On one occasion Gleig resolved, 'after a short struggle with my weaker feelings,' to go see the execution of some British deserters. The common soldiers of the corps were forced to do the same, willing or not. Gleig devotes three pages to the description of this solemn event, yet regarding its influence on the soldiers, he remarks ironically that 'long before dark the scene of the morning was forgotten. [...] pity soon died away, and every feeling of disgust, if, indeed, any such feeling had at all arisen, was obliterated.'[305] Tolstoy concurs, writing about the common soldiers in the Sebastopol garrison that 'The only consolation of a life the conditions of which freeze with horror the coldest imagination [...] is forgetfulness, annihilation of the consciousness of the reality.'[306]

These descriptions of desensitizing experiences recall the attitude of early modern and Napoleonic religious conversion narratives. They affirm the observations of Blackader, Downing, and Sergeant Thomas that the horrors of battle fail to enlighten soldiers, and are more likely to make them run after sensual pleasures than to open their eyes to the eternal truth. The logic of desensitizing may also explain why Louis de Pontis was converted by the peaceful death of his civilian friend whereas numerous violent deaths he previously witnessed had no impact on him. At least for a sensitive person, limited stimulation coupled with ample leisure for meditation was a far better path to wisdom then a barrage of overwhelming stimulation.

The model of desensitizing corroded the authority of flesh-witnessing, and was politically useful to curtail the power of the soldiers. It was especially handy for political and ideological groups who needed to explain why many soldiers did not gain the "right" knowledge from war.

For example, desensitizing served – and still serves – as a convenient explanation for the empirical failure of Materialist Pacifism. In the wake of World War I many veterans composed narratives of disillusionment that argued that war is waged due only to ignorance of its conditions, and that if civilians and politicians knew how soldiers lived and died – or if soldiers themselves became politicians – there will no longer be wars. Yet a few years later, an ex-corporal, veteran of the Western Front's trenches, leading a movement which included numerous other such veterans, launched an even more devastating world war. From a Sensationist viewpoint, desensitizing was the best answer for this puzzling development. According to the logic of desensitizing, a beaten child has all the more chances of becoming a beating parent. A veteran soldier, no matter how much suffering he experienced on his flesh, is all the more likely to inflict suffering upon others. For his suffering hardens his heart and makes him insensitive to the suffering he inflicts.

The expectations that war would result in revelation and the expectations that war would result in desensitizing still shared the same basic assumptions and the same basic formula: sensibility × experience = knowledge. We can best appreciate their similarities, and we can also discover the outer limit of the military culture of sensibility, by looking at an example which completely undermines the Sensationist formula. The one thing this formula cannot stomach is a situation when a man of acute sensibility undergoes extreme experiences and keeps his sensibility intact while failing to acquire knowledge. A good example of such a situation is provided by the memoirs of Rudolph Höss, the commandant of Auschwitz.

Höss was heir to the rich German culture of *Bildung*. In his memoirs he interprets war primarily as an experience of *Bildung*, and portrays himself throughout the narrative as a "man of feeling." In the introduction Höss writes that

> In the following narrative I will try to write about my deepest personal thoughts and feelings. I will attempt to recall, to the best of my memory, all the important events, all the highs and lows of my psychological life, and the experiences which affected me.[307]

In 1914 Höss was too young to enlist, and therefore volunteered to the Red Cross. 'I can still see the blood-soaked head and arm bandages,' he writes, 'the uniforms smeared with blood and dirt, our grey prewar uniforms, and the blue French uniforms with the red trousers. I can still hear the suppressed moaning during the loading of the wounded into the hastily requisitioned streetcars, as I ran among them passing out refreshments.'[308]

These experiences hardly lessened his desire to enlist, and when he turned 16 he lied about his age and got himself recruited. He was sent to help the Turks in the Middle East:

> I had many new experiences during our layover in Istanbul, which was still rich in Oriental tradition, and on the horseback ride to the distant Iraqi front line. I've forgotten most of these impressions because they weren't important. But I do remember my first firefight with the enemy.
>
> [...] The English attacked [...] Comrade after comrade fell wounded, and the one lying next to me didn't answer my calls. When I turned to look at him, I saw he was bleeding from a large head wound and was already dead. Never again in my entire life did I experience the horror that seized me then, and the tremendous fear that the same would happen to me. If I had been alone, I would have run as the Turks did. Something kept forcing me to look at my dead comrade.

He looked at his captain, who was firing coolly, and took courage from him.

> Then, suddenly, a strange, rigid, calm came over me that I had never known before. It became clear that I was also supposed to fire. Until then, I had not fired a single shot as I fearfully watched the

slowly advancing Indians [in the English army]. I can still picture to this day a tall, broad Indian with a distinct black beard [...] For a moment I hesitated, the body next to me filling my whole mind, then I pulled myself together even though I was very much shaken. I fired and watched the Indian slump forward during his jump. He didn't move. I really can't say if I aimed correctly. He was my first kill! The spell was broken. Still unsure of myself, I began firing and firing, just as they had taught me in training. I didn't think about the danger anymore because my captain who was nearby kept shouting encouragement.

[...] During the advance I hesitated and reluctantly looked at my kill. It made me feel a little squeamish. It was so exciting for me that I can't say whether I wounded or killed any more Indians during this first firefight. After the first shot I aimed and shot carefully at those who emerged from cover. My captain mentioned his amazement at how cool I was during this, my first firefight, my baptism of fire. If he had only known what was really going on inside me![309]

Höss summarizes his war experiences thus:

World War I ended. I had matured far beyond my age, both inside and out. The experience of war had put an indelible mark on me. I had torn myself from the security of my parents' home and my horizons had widened. In two and a half years I had seen and experienced a great deal. I met people from all walks of life and had seen their needs and weaknesses. The schoolboy who had run away from home and trembled with fear during his first battle had become a rough, tough soldier.[310]

Up till now Höss's memoirs are a typical example of a "Kantian" narrative, in which initial disillusionment and stupefaction is followed by positive revelation. However, for anyone who does not embrace Nazism, the following chapters are much harder to stomach. The toughened youth subsequently joined the SS. In describing his experiences in the concentration camps, Höss is acutely aware of the danger of desensitizing, and stresses repeatedly that he had always remained a very sensitive person. When he supervised the flogging of prisoners,

I stood in the first rank and I was, therefore, forced to watch the entire procedure in detail. I say forced because if I would have stood further back, I would not have looked. Hot and cold chills ran through me when the screaming started. In fact the whole procedure, even the first beating, made me shiver.[311]

Höss analyzes his behavior and his reaction to these punishments, and subsequently analyzes in a similar manner his behavior at executions, just as Boswell and other eighteenth-century "men of feeling" analyzed their reactions to the executions at Tyburn.[312]

As commandant of Auschwitz

I had to make a tremendous effort to pull myself together in order not to show, not even once, in all the excitement after an incident, or to allow my inner doubts and depressions to come out in the open. I had to appear cold and heartless during these events which tear the heart apart in anyone who had any kind of human feelings. I couldn't even turn away when deep human emotion rose within me. Coldly I had to stand and watch as the mothers went into the gas chambers with their laughing or crying children.

On one occasion two little children were involved in a game they were playing and their mother just couldn't tear them away from it. Even the Jews of the Sonderkommando didn't want to pick up the children. I will never forget the pleading look on the face of the mother, who certainly knew what was happening. The people in the gas chamber were becoming restless. Everyone was looking at me. I had to act. I gave the sergeant in charge a wave, and he picked up the screaming, kicking children in his arms and brought them into the gas chamber along with the mother, who was weeping in the most heart-breaking fashion. Believe me, I felt like shrinking into the ground out of pity, but I was not allowed to show the slightest emotion.

Hour upon hour I had to witness all that happened. I had to watch day and night, whether it was the dragging and burning of the bodies, the teeth being ripped out, the cutting of the hair; I had to watch all this horror. For hours I had to stand in the horrible, haunting stench while the mass graves were dug open, and the bodies were dragged out and burned. I also had to watch the process of death itself through the peephole of the gas chamber because the doctors called my attention to it. I had to do all of this because I was the one to whom everyone looked, and because I had to show everybody that I was not only the one who gave the orders and issues the directives, but that I was also willing to be present at whatever task I ordered my men to perform.[313]

Höss here echoes the sentimental opinions and descriptions of John Shipp, John Malcolm, and Tolstoy. He explains that though outwardly he was extremely calm, inwardly he remained a very sensitive person, and did not become desensitized by his experiences in Auschwitz. In the best tradition of Sentimentalism and *Bildung*, Höss is an honorable "man of feeling" *because* of the sensations and emotions he feels inside. That outwardly he was ice cold is irrelevant, because unlike early modern honor, sensibility was above all an "internal" quality.

If anyone was desensitized by Auschwitz, according to Höss, it was only the Jews. Höss writes that he often wondered

> Where did the Jews of the Sonderkommando get the strength to perform this horrible job day and night? Did they hope for some special luck that would save them from the jaws of death? Or had they become too hardened by all the horror, or too weak to commit suicide to escape their existence? I really have watched this closely, but could never get to the bottom of their behavior. The way the Jews lived and died was a puzzle I could not solve.[314]

When outsiders criticized the happenings in Auschwitz, Höss fell back on the argument that those who were not there cannot understand. 'Only someone who had been serving in a concentration camp for years could understand,' he writes.[315] Tom Segev relates an interview he had with Fritz Hensel, Höss's brother-in-law:

> On one of their walks through the camp Höss and Hensel found themselves in front of a truckload of dead bodies. Here, according to Hensel, they again argued about the legal, and particularly the moral aspects of the camp. Höss admitted the atrocious nature of the place [...] "You cannot understand this," he repeated again and again, "because you come from the outside. Here we look at things differently."[316]

Höss's sentimental memoirs were quite characteristic of the general attitude of the SS. It was supremely important for the SS to prove that they remained decent men-of-feeling despite their horrific "job." In his notorious Posen speech (October 4, 1943) Heinrich Himmler spoke openly to the SS leadership about the extermination of the Jews, and addressed the question of sensibility and decency.

> I want to also mention a very difficult subject...I am talking about the evacuation of the Jews, the extermination of the Jewish people. It

is one of those things that is easily said. "The Jewish people is being exterminated", every Party member will tell you, "perfectly clear, it's part of our plans, we're eliminating the Jews, exterminating them, a small matter". And then along they all come, all the 80 million upright Germans, and each one has his decent Jew. They say: all the others are swine, but here is a first-class Jew. And none of them has seen it, has endured it. . . . none of them has seen it, has endured it. Most of you will know what it means when 100 bodies lie together, when 500 are there or when there are 1000. And to have seen this through and – with the exception of human weakness – to have remained decent, has made us hard and is a page of glory never mentioned and never to be mentioned. . . . altogether we can say: We have carried out this most difficult task for the love of our people. And we have suffered no defect within us, in our soul, or in our character.[317]

(Note that Himmler too is appealing to the authority of flesh-witnessing, and ridiculous to the ordinary "upright" Germans who dare to speak about the extermination and even to criticize the SS without having "been there".)

What is disconcerting about this attitude and about Höss's memoirs is that they make it difficult for us to dismiss Höss or Himmler as a "desensitized brute." The thesis of desensitizing tries to explain away cases of people who encountered great suffering and then themselves caused great suffering by arguing that the suffering they had undergone desensitized them and made them blind to the suffering they themselves subsequently inflicted. Höss's example contradicts this reassuring idea. If we believe Höss, then people can cause a tremendous amount of suffering, be fully aware of what they are doing and of their internal sensations and emotions, and yet go on doing it.

For Höss, as for the SS in general, the answer to this dilemma was simple: the Nazi ideals have passed the test of experience. The Sensationist formula says that sensibility × experience = knowledge. The men of the SS have certainly undergone extreme experiences. If they have managed to keep their sensibility intact while undergoing these "experiences," it means that they have gained true knowledge, and that the ideals in whose name they underwent the "experiences" were pure and right.

Hence keeping one's sensibility was for Höss (and Himmler) a question of great epistemological and political importance. On the question of his sensibility depended his image and authority. If he lost his sensibility, he was no more than a coarse brute, and his ideals may well have been dangerous illusions. Readers will read his memoirs only for factual information, and will construct patronizing theories about him, as zoologists do about the behavior of animals. But if he kept his sensibility, he was a privileged flesh-witness and his ideals gained an aura of revelation. Readers will peruse his memoirs with awe, feeling that they lack the ability to judge his actions.

For anyone who rejects the Nazi ideals, there are only two options to deal with Höss's memoirs. One option is to argue that Höss was an insensitive brute after all. He was desensitized during World War I, or during his subsequent career in the SS, or perhaps he was born with a limited sensibility. His attempts to portray himself as a "man of feeling" are only an ingenious fraud. The other option is to argue that people can undergo the most extreme experiences while retaining an acute sensibility, without gaining any wisdom out of it. If so, somewhere in the Sensationist equation there must be a missing variable.

Conclusions: The Things Which Make You Know, 1865–2000

From the late Middle Ages to the early eighteenth century, Western combatants interpreted war in either of two ways: War was an instrument to some greater end (personal or collective), or it was an honorable way of life, worthy in and of itself. With the rise of the state and of military professionalism the instrumental interpretation slowly gained more prestige and power, but the honorary interpretation always remained prestigious and powerful too. During this era, combatants seldom interpreted war as a revelatory experience.

During the "long" Romantic period, stretching from 1740 to 1865, a new interpretation took shape, which saw war above all as "an experience," or even as "the ultimate experience." It narrated and evaluated the events of war in light of their impact on the *Bildung* process of individuals, rather than in light of their utility or honor. Politically, this interpretation remained of limited importance, and culturally too it was still secondary to the instrumental and honorary interpretations, but it was slowly gaining ground.

The immediate forces that shaped this new interpretation were mainly cultural, that is, the culture of sensibility and Romanticism. Other factors also contributed, but this book focused on the cultural factors because I believe they were the most important.

The appearance of the revelatory interpretation cannot be ascribed to any technological changes. The technology of war remained essentially similar from 1700 to the mid-nineteenth century. The material experiences of war – combats, marches, camps, hospitals, diseases, weather conditions, and so on – were also essentially the same.

It might be more tempting to ascribe the rise of the revelatory interpretation to social and political factors. Certainly, the eighteenth century witnessed huge political and social shifts in the way armies were raised and organized. In particular, the social origins and status of the common soldiers changed dramatically. Though these changes contributed significantly to the rise of the revelatory interpretation, they were of secondary importance. It is impossible to argue that the revelatory interpretation of war was a straightforward result of the improvement in soldiers' social status.

First, the revelatory interpretation of war began to rise well before 1789, at a time when the culture of sensibility was already in flowering, but *before* any significant changes in the social composition of armies took place. Some of the earliest manifestations of the new military culture appear in the writing of old regime Prussian soldiers. Even after 1789, it is telling that though amongst major European armies the British army was militarily, socially, and politically the most conservative, it nevertheless led the cultural revolution in the interpretation of war. The largest number of Romantic military memoirs were composed by British common soldiers and subaltern officers, whose social origins in 1815 were largely the same as a century before. It is worth noting that though Western armies are today returning to the model of old regime armies – common soldiers are again "the dregs of society" serving mainly for pay – the revelatory interpretation of war is stronger than ever.

Secondly, if the revelatory interpretation of war was a product of the improvement in soldiers' social status, how can we explain the absence of this interpretation from the writings of early modern *officers*? Early modern officers belonged to the upper strata of society; they came to war voluntarily; and they were literate men with ample opportunities to write and publish their memoirs. The fact that early modern officers did not compose narratives of disillusionment may perhaps be explained by their caste. Unlike the twentieth-century middle-class volunteers, early modern officers belonged to a warrior caste, and had everything to lose if war lost its cultural appeal. Yet how can we explain the fact that early modern officers did not compose narratives of positive revelation? Men such as the marquis de Chouppes or Andrew Melville had a lot to gain from depicting war as a positive revelation. Anyone who argues along Marxist lines that it was all a matter of socio-economic forces should try and explain the complete absence of early modern Ernst Jüngers.

Did the appearance of the new interpretation actually change the experience of combat? This is a question I have avoided in this book, but perhaps now is the time to say a few words about it.

The history of lived experience is to a large extent the history of attention. Humans are bombarded every moment by an overwhelming amount of information: events happening outside, things that people say and do, things that one is saying or doing oneself, thoughts crossing one's mind, emotions swelling and subsiding, a myriad sensations appearing throughout the body. At any given moment, humans are aware only of a tiny fragment of this cascade. What they are aware of – what they actually experience – depends on their attention. One can focus all one's attention on events in the outside world, while ignoring one's sensations and emotions. One can focus so much on an inner sensation or emotional upheaval till one is completely unaware of the surrounding sounds, visions, and smells.

The focus of our attention is to some extent culturally constructed. Each culture "trains" its members to focus attention on different segments of reality. Some attention exercises are fully formalized: Seventeenth-century drill was a formal attention exercise, taking the soldier's attention away from his sensations, emotions, and thoughts, and investing all of it in the movements of his limbs and the commands of his superiors. Till today, the most important command in military drill is "Attention!" Meditation manuals such as Ignatius Loyola's *Spiritual Exercises* were another type of formalized attention exercise. The use of drugs such as alcohol can also be interpreted as an attention exercise, drawing attention away from physical and emotional discomforts.

A culture trains the attention of its members in many informal ways too. When a culture views emotions as an important source for authority, encourages its members to narrate their emotions on different occasions, and supplies them with a rich emotional vocabulary, people are likely to pay more attention to their emotions. When a culture does not view emotions as a source for authority, when the public expression of emotions is rare and inhibited, and when the emotional vocabulary is poor, people are far less likely to pay attention to their emotions.

It is probable that the rise of the revelatory interpretation of war influenced the attention of combatants, and thereby influenced their lived experience in addition to their memories. Fear and cold "in themselves" were perhaps identical in 1450 and 1865. Yet the attention they received was quite different, and hence the *lived* experience of fear and cold was probably different in 1450 than it was in 1865.

***

After 1865 the revelatory interpretation continued to rise. The story of Western war culture in the twentieth century is dominated by the struggle between this rising interpretation and the instrumental and honorary interpretations. This story has been researched and told numerous times, and it suffices to note here that today most personal war stories take the revelatory interpretation for granted, and it has gained great power even in the political sphere.

I would nevertheless like to make a few general comments about twentieth-century war culture from the perspective of the early modern and Romantic era:

(1) All the essential features of the revelatory interpretation of war were already in place *before* 1914, and therefore cannot be construed as the product of twentieth-century developments. In particular, they were not a reaction to the technologization of war.

To cite one last example, in 1903 Rudyard Kipling published 'The Return,' a poem about the return of the British soldiers from the Boer War. In it a British common soldier describes how he returns from war to London, 'but not the same' because 'Things' ave transpired which made me learn/The size and meanin' of the game.' The narrator tries to track the sources of the change war wrought in him: 'I don't know where the change began; / I started as an average kid, / I finished as a thinkin' man.'

First, he notes the impact of "nature." He describes the rivers, the wide plains, the wilderness, and the mountains of South Africa, speculating that 'These may 'ave taught me more or less.' Then come the ravages of war, the burnt towns, the starving stray dogs, the homesick men, the missing comrades. 'They taught me, too,' he says. Finally, he writes about 'the pore dead that look so old / An' was so young an hour ago, / An' legs tied down before they're cold – / These are the things which make you know.'[1]

The entire spectrum of twentieth-century war stories, from Wilfred Owen and Adolf Hitler to *Full Metal Jacket* and *Apocalypse Now*, is encapsulated in Kipling's poem. If this conclusion is correct, it means that the famed late modern revolution in the culture of war should be predated to c.1750 rather than 1914, 1945, or 1968. Nothing essentially new was invented or discovered in the twentieth century itself. What was new is the way in which the revelatory interpretation, which previously was only partially developed and which was still eclipsed by the instrumental and honorary interpretations, spread to become the most popular interpretation of all, and in the process acquired both artistic and political powers that it hitherto lacked.

Twentieth-century stories of martial revelation, and particularly of disillusionment, were certainly far more powerful and moving than anything written in the Romantic period. Yet the increased force of these stories emanated not from some new ingredients, but largely from the fact that they spelled out in full what was only latent in most Romantic memoirs. The basic ideas of twentieth-century war stories remained those of Sensationism, of *Bildung*, and of the sublime. However, twentieth-century memoirists pursued these ideas with far greater devotion than their predecessors, which gave their narratives unprecedented clarity and power.

(2) The honorary interpretation of war, once so prominent, has greatly declined in importance. Even those who still view war as a positive and desirable way of life do so in the name of authenticity rather than honor. Ernst Jünger and his likes love to fight not because it is honorable, but because fighting enables them to get in touch with nature and with themselves, and to discover who they really are.

The main question that the twentieth-century war story deals with is the question of truth and authority – not of courage and heroism. Those who still think that war is a good and recommendable activity ascribe it to war's epistemic delights: War is good because it is conducive to knowledge and self-knowledge.

(3) In the political arena, collective stories of war increasingly imitate the personal stories of military revelation. People speak today about "national trauma," about an entire nation "maturing" or becoming "disillusioned" through war. The history of the United States in Vietnam or of Israel in Lebanon is often told as if the entire nation is a single naïve youth receiving his baptism of fire and learning not to trust the high-blown ideals of his elders.

(4) Perhaps the clearest proof for the unprecedented prestige of the revelatory war story is that some of the harshest struggles within twentieth-century war culture have taken place between different strands of this story, with all sides taking for granted the same underlying assumptions. There are two dominant examples of such internal struggles:

   i. The struggle between narratives of disillusionment and narratives of positive revelation. The "war of the war books" that flared up, for example, in Germany in 1929/30, and which is re-fought today by scholars, is in fact a civil war. All participants, whether pacifist authors such as Erich Maria Remarque or fascists such as Ernst Jünger, share the same Sensationist and Romantic assumptions. They all view war as revelation, they all argue that "those who were not there cannot understand."

Up to World War II it seems that the story of war as a positive revelation was more popular, but from then onward the story of disillusionment became the orthodox war story of Western culture. In many respects, Western war culture today is dominated by disillusioned Materialist Pacifism. Disillusioned veterans have increasingly reduced all human motivation and all human virtues to the pursuit of pleasure and the avoidance of pain, dismissing idealistic talk as so much dangerous humbug. According to this line of (Sensationist) thought, soldiers (and civilians) can be induced to support war and sacrifice their lives and sensory comforts only by mistaken calculation, false belief, and downright deceit. This line of thought reached its apogee in the wake of Hiroshima. Nuclear war is the ultimate proof for the victory of matter over mind in war. No spiritual ideals can redeem nuclear war. No spiritual ideals can even survive it. Any discussion that even for a moment forgets the material realities of nuclear war to speak about spiritual ideals may result in the utter destruction of humanity.

Materialist Pacifism set itself a goal to expose the spiritual deceits that fuel war, assuming that if it only gave a very accurate *sensory* description of the realities of war without covering them up with some shiny spiritual gloss, people would no longer be willing to engage in war. This belief is today so dear to us that it is almost sacrilegious to point out its past failures, or to point out that it shares the same basic logic with the story of war as a positive revelation.

ii. Another internal struggle within the revelatory interpretation of war is between the image of the wise veteran and the image of the crazy veteran. Are veterans made wise by undergoing "the ultimate experience," or are they traumatized and desensitized by undergoing experiences with which they cannot cope? Both approaches share the same Sensationist formula. They merely read it from different angles.

Indeed, the traumatized soldier, who became a stock figure of military culture in the last few decades, is probably the best representation of the double-faced Romantic approach to war. On the one hand, traumatized soldiers represent the revelatory power of war. It is usually believed that soldiers are traumatized due to an encounter with truth, not with error. Traumatized soldiers are not possessed by some evil demon, and nobody argues that what they saw and experienced in war is a lie. Their problem is exactly that they were given a peep behind the curtain of ignorance that shields society from the harsh reality of injury and death.

On the other hand, traumatized soldiers also represent the desensitizing power of war. Most of them are unable to cope with such a large dose of the truth, and consequently develop defense mechanisms to hide that truth and enable them to go on living their lives in ignorance. Alternatively, if they try to live with the new truths they discovered, without developing such defense mechanisms, they become anathema to civilian society, which hospitalizes them in closed departments alongside terminal patients and other uncomfortable truths.

It is notable, however, that Western culture retains a Romantic distinction between traumatized soldiers and other trauma victims. Because they were traumatized by a sublime experience – and not by a merely awful experience such as child abuse – traumatized soldiers often appear in Western culture as "holy fools," bearers of a potent and sacred wisdom.

(5) Though the West is experiencing a period of internal peace with few precedents in human history, and though it has managed to rid itself from positive images of war that have been around for millennia, Western culture still attaches one supremely positive value to war. Deep within late modern Western culture the association between war and truth is hammered again and again. The master narratives of late modern war all agree that war reveals eternal truths – even if weakness prevents people from facing them. Peace, on the other hand, cultivates transient illusions. From here, the road is short to an even more alarming conclusion: War itself is an eternal truth, whereas peace itself is a transient illusion.

Nature – or evolution in present-day parlance – has hardwired uncomfortable realities into the human organism and its environment. Peacetime culture does its best to hide or circumvent these realities. But for a culture that no longer believes in the supremacy of mind over matter, this suppression is only an invitation for a very painful revelation.

By mapping the different war stories of the modern era I hope to have made it a bit easier for people to develop a critical distance from these stories and to navigate their way through today's war culture. Personally, I believe that the formula "sensibility × experience = knowledge" is flawed, and misses at least a variable or two. If this is so, all war stories shaped by this formula are flawed as well, and give a misleading view of war. As to the identity of the missing variables, I have my hypotheses, but since they lack academic credentials, at present I have to leave that to the readers, and perhaps to a future book.

Notes

Introduction: war as revelation, 1865–2000

1. Boswell, *Boswell's Life of Johnson*, April 10, 1778, ed. Hill, 3:265–6.
2. Socrates was himself a veteran of the battles of Spartolus (-429) and Delium (-424).
3. Malcolm, 'Reminiscences,' 248.
4. Tolstoy, *War and Peace*, ed. Edmonds, 2:1153.
5. For a survey of secondary literature on twentieth-century war stories and military memoirs, see Harari, 'Martial Illusions,' 43–8.
6. Cummings, *Moon Dash Warrior*, 86.
7. Fox, *Eyewitness Falklands*, 180–1.
8. Sledge, *With the Old Breed*, 52.
9. Sajer, *Forgotten Soldier*, 495.
10. Leshem, *Beaufort*, 310.
11. Givati, *Three Births*, 155.
12. Compare Bidney, *Patterns of Epiphany*, 1–4.
13. Quoted in Herf, *Reactionary Modernism*, 74.
14. Bowden, *Black Hawk Down*, 301–2.
15. Housman, *War Letters*, 159.
16. See, for example, Jünger, *Storm of Steel*. For Jünger, see Herf, *Reactionary Modernism*, 70–106; Stern, *Ernst Jünger*. For an overview of similar narratives in Germany of the 1920s and 1930s, see Fritz, ' "We are Trying." '
17. For a recent example, see Leshem, *Beaufort*. For twentieth-century military memoirs that evaluate war positively, see in particular Bourke, *Intimate History*. For the idea of "growth through adversity" in contemporary psychology, see Joseph and Linley, 'Positive Adjustment'; Waysman, Schwarzwald, and Solomon, 'Hardiness.'
18. Cru, *War Books*, 8. For disillusionment in twentieth-century military memoirs, see Harari, 'Martial Illusions.'
19. There is an immense literature on trauma and war in the twentieth century. I have relied particularly on Shephard, *War on Nerves*.
20. See, for example, Yost, *Blessings*.
21. For example, the recent Israeli film *Yossi and Jager*. See Bérubé, *Coming Out Under Fire*; Kaplan, *Brothers and Others*.
22. See, for example, Becker, *War and Faith*; Bennett, *Narrative of the Great Revival*; Mahedy, *Out of the Night*; Schweitzer, *Cross and Trenches*.
23. Tolstoy, *War and Peace*, ed. Edmonds, 1:338–40.
24. Bawer, *While Europe Slept*.
25. Bowden, *Black Hawk Down*, 37.
26. For contemporary men regretting the fact that they missed the experience of war, see John Derbyshire, 'How Cheap is Your Manhood?' *National Review Online*, May 5, 2003. See also Yost, *Blessings*, 123.

27. Though see the important and thoughtful work of Edna Lomski-Feder (Lomski-Feder, *As if There Was no War*). On the basis of her interviews with Israeli veterans of the 1973 Arab-Israeli War, Lomski-Feder argues that the late modern interpretation of war as revelation is a cultural ideal that many men do not fulfill. Since having a martial revelation is a source of powerful authority, society allows only some privileged veterans to report such revelations. The rest reconstruct and tell their lifestories, 'as if there was no war.'
28. Loyd, *My War*, 32.
29. Ibid., 67.
30. Ibid., 91.
31. Ibid., 123.
32. Tolstoy, *War and Peace*, ed. Edmonds, 1:162.
33. For the positive experiences of combat, see in particular Bourke, *Intimate History*.
34. Sajer, *The Forgotten Soldier*, 272.
35. Ben-Yehuda, *1948*, 245–6.
36. Ben-Yehuda, *When the State of Israel Broke Out*.
37. Hitler, *Mein Kampf*, 166.
38. Ibid., 163.
39. Jünger, *Storm of Steel*, 1.
40. Ibid., 3.
41. Cooey, 'Experience,' 328–9.
42. Fanning, *Mystics*, 143–4.
43. Cooey, 'Experience,' 327.
44. *Time*, December 20, 2004, vol. 164: 18–19, 25.
45. *Time*, April 17, 2006, vol. 167: 16.
46. Scarry, *Body in Pain*, 30–4. See also Glucklich, *Sacred Pain*, 42; Rey, *History*, 3; Bruhm, *Gothic Bodies*, xx, 6.
47. Ibid., 92.
48. Ibid., 148–9.
49. Caputo, 264–8.
50. Glucklich, *Sacred Pain*, 6.
51. Ibid., 58. See also Ibid., 59–62, 99–100. Glucklich, though, argues that pain does not alter people's beliefs and identity directly. Instead, it only weakens their sense of self and agency, thereby making them more malleable and open to changes and outside influences.
52. Glucklich, *Sacred Pain*, 207. See also Cooey, 'Experience,' 332–3.
53. Please note that this is only a cultural image, not a biological reality.
54. Hitler, *Mein Kampf*, 165.
55. Ibid., 165.
56. Jünger, *Storm of Steel*, 315–16.
57. Yehuda Shaviv, 'A letter to the front line,' appeared in *Alon Shvut* [an internal paper of the "Etzion Mountain" *Yeshiva*], vol. 8 (November 1973). I thank my student, Tzofia Lichtman, for drawing my attention to this passage.
58. Heller, *Catch-22*, 553–4.
59. Ben-Yehuda, *When the State of Israel Broke Out*, 91–2.
60. Livius, *Ab Urbe Condita*, 2.12.
61. Scarry has an explosive explanation for such cases. If by surviving a great amount of suffering an idea is proven to be real – argues Scarry – then

by forcing people to suffer for an idea, one can make that idea real for them. And this, she argues, is the deep basis not only for the phenomenon of war, but also for other human maladies such as social oppression. This argument, however, is not made by any of the war memoirists, partly because it undermines their authority. For it implies that suffering by itself does not guarantee wisdom, and it raises the possibility that the truths memoirists took from war are just more manipulations of the powers-that-be.

62. For an overview of relevant discussions in postmodern and Neo-Marxist thought, see Ireland, 'Appeal to Experience.'
63. For an excellent discussion of related themes, see Lynn, *Battle*, 359–69.
64. See Fussell, *Great War*; Herzog, *Vietnam War Stories*; Hynes, *War Imagined*; Hynes, *Soldiers' Tale*; Leed, *No Man's Land*; Cobley, *Representing War*; Winter, *Sites of Memory*; Linder, *Princes of the Trenches*; Bourke, *Intimate History*; Paris, *Warrior Nation*; Quinn and Trout, *Literature of the Great War*; Bond, *Unquiet Western Front*; Sheffield, *Forgotten Victory*; Watson, *Fighting Different Wars*.
65. See, for example, Hanson, *Hoplites*; Carlton, *Going*; Mortimer, *Eyewitness Accounts*; Brumwell, *Redcoats*; Holmes, *Redcoat*; Forrest, *Napoleon's Men*; Linderman, *Embattled Courage*.
66. In this I followed the example of Charles Taylor in his seminal *Sources of the Self* (Taylor, *Sources*, 202–7).

1 Suffering, death, and revelation in early modern culture

1. For the focus on soldiers in images of the Crucifixion, see for example Hale, *Artists and Warfare*, 228. See also Bynum, 'Blood of Christ,' 685.
2. Groebner, *Defaced*, 111, 121–3. See also Scarry, *Body in Pain*, 215.
3. Ross, ' "She Wept and Cried," ' 45; Perkins, *Suffering Self*, 190, 205–6; Ariès, *Hour*, 370; Morris, *Culture of Pain*, 125–36; Noble and Head, *Soldiers of Christ*, xix; Kolb, *For All the Saints*, 1, 5–15, 19.
4. Kieckhefer, *Unquiet Souls*, 89–98, 102–113; Ross, ' "She Wept and Cried," ' 46; Bynum, 'Blood of Christ,' 685–714; Ariès, *Hour*, 128, 138; Silverman, *Tortured Subjects*, 111–2; Hillman, 'Visceral Knowledge,' 85; Greenblatt, 'Mutilation and Meaning,' 223; Groebner, *Defaced*, 88–101.
5. Cohen, *Metamorphosis*; Ariès, *Hour*, 110–28, 300–4, 327–31; Aberth, *Brink of the Apocalypse*, 181–3, 188–215; Meumann, 'Experience of Violence,' 153–4; Cavalli-Björkman, '*Vanitas* Still Life'; Knauer, 'War as *Memento Mori*.'
6. Kieckhefer, *Unquiet Souls*, 54–5; Glucklich, *Sacred Pain*, 20, 39–42, 83, 127–8; Hawkins, *Archetypes of Conversion*, 21, 156–7; Ross, 'She Wept and Cried,' 47–50, 59; Perkins, *Suffering Self*, 23–4, 34; Evans, *Problems of Authority*, 160; Fanning, *Mystics*, 109, 124–5; Morris, *Culture of Pain*, 125–36; Nugent, *Mysticism*, 10–23; Bynum, 'Why all the Fuss?' 15; Haller, *Rise of Puritanism*, 284–6; Loyola, *Spiritual Exercises*, 137.
7. Watkins, *Puritan Experience*, 65.
8. Ariès, *Hour*, 298, 312.
9. Homer and Tiresias are obvious examples. Longinus, the Roman soldier who pierced Christ's side to relieve him of his misery, was depicted in popular

legends as suffering from impaired eyesight (Hale, *Artists and Warfare*, 229–31). The head of the Nordic–Germanic pantheon, Wotan/Odin, sacrificed an eye to pay for wisdom.

10. Finke, 'Mystical Bodies,' 42; McNamara, 'Rhetoric of Orthodoxy,' 13; Perkins, *Suffering Self*, 114–15, 190; Rey, *History*, 55.

11. Silverman, *Tortured Subjects*, 5, 8–10, 115, 123, 126–9, 133; Greenblatt, 'Mutilation and Meaning,' 223–4, 230; Bynum, 'Why all the Fuss?' 15; Rapley, 'Her Body the Enemy,' 25–35; Scarry, *Body in Pain*, 34; Rey, *History*, 49, 55; Cohn, *Pursuit of the Millennium*, 127–47; Perkins, *Suffering Self*, 205–6; Kieckhefer, *Unquiet Souls*, 67–70, 118–21; Glucklich, *Sacred Pain*, 3–5, 79–82, 104–5; Flynn, 'Spiritual Uses of Pain,' 257–78; Asad, 'Notes on Body Pain,' 307–15, 321–2; Ross, ' "She Wept and Cried," ' 47–50; Fanning, *Mystics*, 107; Kleinberg, *Fra Ginepro's Leg*.

12. Ariès, *Hour*, 14–18, 130–1, 298; Aberth, *Brink of the Apocalypse*, 214–21; Carlton, *Going*, 215–18.

13. Kedar, *Crusade and Mission*.

14. Voragine, *Golden Legend*, 1:97, 99; France, 'War and Sanctity,' 15; Carlton, *Going*, 62–3; Glucklich, *Sacred Pain*, 23; Hawkins, *Archetypes of Conversion*, 49–50, 76; Keen, *Chivalry*, 53; Damon, *Soldier Saints*, 75–81; Watkins, *Puritan Experience*, 12–14, 168–9; Loyola, *Spiritual Exercises*, 16, 146–7, 154–6; Starr, *Defoe*, 48.

15. See also Haller, *Rise of Puritanism*, 158–60, 279–80.

16. Muslim mystics too conceptualized *jihad* as internal spiritual warfare (Glucklich, *Sacred Pain*, 24).

17. Partner, *God of Battles*; Sproxton, *Violence and Religion*; Ulbricht, 'Experience of Violence,' 112; Meumann, 'Experience of Violence,' 153–6; Carlton, *Going*, 62–3; Barker, *Military Intellectual*, 134; Allmand, *Society at War*, 40–3; Strickland, *War and Chivalry*, 58–68; Siberry, *Criticism of Crusading*, 217–18; DeVries, 'God and Defeat,' 87–100. See, for example, Pontis, *Mémoires*, 170; Coxere, *Adventures by Sea*, 64; Contreras, *Discurso*, 153–6; Campion, *Mémoires*, 88; Cavalier, *Memoirs*, 64, 74; Deane, *Journal*, 13, 15; Hodgson, *Memoirs*, 15, 22; Peeke, *Three to One*, E1.

18. Bueil, *Jouvencel*, 2:21. See also Bonet, *Tree of battles*, 157; Vale, *War and Chivalry*, 31; Keen, *Chivalry*, 5–10, 14, 44–63; Barker, *Military Intellectual*, 128; Damon, *Soldier Saints*, 24–5; Siberry, *Criticism of Crusading*, 209–10; Strickland, *War and Chivalry*, 28–9, 55–8, 96–7.

19. Silverman, *Tortured Subjects*, 9.

20. Silverman, *Tortured Subjects*, 62–3; see also 64, 80–2; Cohen, *Crossroads of Justice*, 154–5; Glucklich, *Sacred Pain*, 19, 161–3; DuBois, *Torture and Truth*; Asad, 'Notes on Body Pain,' 287–98; Ruff, *Violence*, 92–6; Peters, *Torture*, 40–73.

21. Groebner, *Defaced*, 108.

22. Hillman, 'Visceral Knowledge,' 82–3, 88; Scholz, *Body Narratives*, 1.

23. See in particular Sawday, *Body Emblazoned*. See also Egmond, 'Execution, Dissection'; Hillman, 'Visceral knowledge,' 83–6; Siraisi, 'Medicine and the Renaissance,' 8–10; Rey, *History*, 57–60; Porter, *Flesh*, 52–4. See also Rembrandt's *The Anatomy Lesson of Dr. Tulp* (1632).

24. See Scarry, *Body in Pain*, 215.

25. Quoted in Van Sant, *Eighteenth-Century Sensibility*, 12.

26. Gwyn, 'Military Memoirs,' 66.
27. Eliade, 'Initiation: An Overview,' 226–7, 231; Eliade, *Rites and Symbols*, 21–40; Van Gennep, *Rites of Passage*, 71–5, 85–7; Perkins, *Suffering Self*, 34; Glucklich, *Sacred Pain*, 3–5, 26, 28, 34–5, 39–42, 150–1; Bloch, *Prey into Hunter*, 6–7; Scarry, *Body in Pain*, 34; Morinis, 'Ritual Experience,' 150–63.
28. Braudy, *Chivalry*, xv.
29. Ehrenreich, *Blood Rites*, 126–8; Eliade, *Rites and Symbols*, 81–5.
30. Shostak, *Nisa*, 84.
31. Kaplan, 'Military'; Lieblich, *Transition to Adulthood*; Sion, *Images of Manhood*.
32. Morinis, 'Ritual Experience,' 166–7.
33. Dewald, *Aristocratic Experience*, 55–6.
34. Ibid., 65–7.

2 The absence of revelation from early modern military memoirs

1. Matthew, 8:5–13; Luke, 7:1–10. This story in its turn resonates with the Old Testament conversion story of the Aramaic general Na'aman (2 Kings, 5:1–19).
2. Voragine, *Golden Legend*, 1:184.
3. Ibid., 1:97–101; Kleinberg, *Fra Ginepro's Leg*, 375–83; Millis, *mystère de Saint Sébastien*; Zupnick, 'Saint Sebastian.'
4. Voragine, *Golden Legend*, 2:266–71; Kleinberg, *Fra Ginepro's Leg*, 364–74.
5. Damon, *Soldier Saints*, 4, 23, 58–9; Hale, *Artists and Warfare*, 234; Vale, *War and Chivalry*, 53–4; Braudy, *Chivalry*, 76–7; Kolb, *For All the Saints*, 66.
6. Felix's *Life of Saint Guthlac*, 80.
7. Ibid., 80–2.
8. Yarom, *Body*, 72–6; Le Goff, *Saint Francis*, 23–4; Fanning, *Mystics*, 85.
9. Yarom, *Body*, 72–6.
10. Thomas of Celano, 'Second Life,' ch. 1.4, ed. Habig, 364; *Legend of the Three Companions*, ch. 2, ed. Habig, 893–5; Voragine, *Golden Legend*, 2:220. See also Thomas of Celano, 'First Life,' ch. 2, ed. Habig, 231–3; St. Bonaventure, 'Major Life of St. Francis,' ch. 1.1–3, ed. Habig, 635–8.
11. Severus, *Vie de Saint Martin*, section 2.4, ed. Fontaine, 1:254.
12. Ibid., 1:254–62. See also Voragine, *Golden Legend*, 2:292–3; Damon, *Soldier Saints*, 1–30; Stancliffe, *Saint Martin*.
13. Maurey, 'Courtly Lover,' 207–8. On Saint Martin see also Maurey, 'Courtly Lover,' 182–5, 204–8; Stancliffe, *Saint Martin*. The story of Saint Maurice and of the martyrs of the Theban Legion similarly tells of conversion preceding combat. The Theban Legion was composed of Christian converts from the city of Thebes in Egypt. They answered the call of Emperor Diocletain to join the army in a campaign against the Barbarians. However, when the emperor discovered that they refused to take part in pagan sacrifices, he turned his army against them and massacred all 6,666 of them (Voragine, *Golden Legend*, 2:188–92).
14. France, 'War and Sanctity,' 16–20. See also Damon, *Soldier Saints*, 293–362.
15. Wright, *Knights*, 14. See also Kaeuper, *Chivalry and Violence*, 60–1.
16. See, for example, Llull, *Book of Knighthood*, 5–6.

17. Lynn, *Giant*, 430–1.
18. Voragine, *Golden Legend*, 1:238–42; Didi-Huberman, *Saint Georges*; Cumont, 'plus ancienne légende de S. Georges'; Kleinberg, *Fra Ginepro's Leg*, 349–63.
19. Goy-Blanquet, *Joan of Arc*; Richey, *Joan of Arc*; Caratini, *Jeanne d'Arc*.
20. Watkins, *Puritan Experience*, 1–3, 9–12, 15; Glucklich, Sacred *Pain*, 163–4; Hawkins, *Archetypes of Conversion*, 80–3, 237–8; Stoeffler, *Rise of Evangelical Pietism*, 157–60, 221–2; Fulbrook, *Piety and Politics*, 33–4; Outram, *Enlightenment*, 44.
21. Watkins, *Puritan Experience*, 1–3, 18–35, 182–207; Hawkins, *Archetypes of Conversion*, 73–4; Haller, *Rise of Puritanism*, 95–101, 113–15; Mascuch, *Origins*, 3–4; Jung, *Frauen des Pietismus*, 61–4; Jung, 'Vorwort,' iv; Bräker, *Life Story*, 3–5; Caldwell, *Puritan Conversion Narrative*, ix, 1–2, 40–1; Starr, *Defoe*, 4–6; Fanning, *Mystics*, 81–2, 85; Swaim, *Pilgrim's Progress*, 132–5; Porter, *Flesh*, 274–8.
22. Haller, *Rise of Puritanism*, 95–101; Kieckhefer, *Unquiet Souls*, 151–65; Hawkins, *Archetypes of Conversion*, 13–14; Fulbrook, *Piety and Politics*, 33–4; Starr, *Defoe*, 38–40; Swain, *Pilgrim's Progress*, 133–9.
23. Watkins, *Puritan Experience*, 65.
24. Fanning, *Mystics*, 144. See also Starr, *Defoe*, 18–21.
25. Watkins, *Puritan Experience*, 161–2; Haller, *Rise of Puritanism*, 115.
26. Starr, *Defoe*, 13–18, 33, 38; Swain, *Pilgrim's Progress*, 132–8.
27. Crichton, *Blackader*, 329. For other Ebenezers, see ibid., 179, 211, 223–4, 248–9, 260, 564.
28. Watkins, *Puritan Experience*, 74.
29. Contreras, *Discurso*, 161.
30. Ibid., 87–8.
31. Herman, *Life*, 3–4.
32. Herman, *Practice*, 'First Conversation.'
33. Lupton, *Obiectorum Reductio*, 57.
34. Ibid., 129–31.
35. Ibid., 49–50.
36. Carlton, *Going*, 344.
37. Guillermou, *Saint Ignace de Loyola*, 18–19.
38. Loyola, *Autobiography*, 21.
39. Ibid., 14, 21.
40. Ibid., 14, 21–2; Guillermou, *Saint Ignace de Loyola*, 20–2.
41. Loyola, *Autobiography*, 22.
42. Ibid., 23.
43. Ibid., 5, 23. These two texts were amongst the most popular religious tracts of the late Middle Ages and the Renaissance. See ibid., 15–24.
44. Loyola, *Autobiography*, 23–4.
45. Ibid., 38.
46. Ibid., 34–6.
47. Loyola, *Spiritual Exercises*, 137.
48. Conversion through reading books has been a dominant theme in Christian writing since Augustine, and spiritual autobiographers often hoped that their readers would be converted by reading these texts (Hawkins, *Archetypes of Conversion*, 26). On the privileged authority of Scriptures and of books in general in the early modern age, see Evans, *Problems of*

Authority, 14–69; Watkins, *Puritan Experience*, 59–61; Fanning, *Mystics*, 139; Mascuch, *Origins*, 40–1; Fulbrook, *Piety and Politics*, 31–2; Starr, *Defoe*, 48; Swain, *Pilgrim's Progress*, 135.

49. Pontis, *Mémoires*, 9–11.
50. Ibid., 212.
51. Ibid., 214–22.
52. Carlton, *Going*, 222.
53. Pontis, *Mémoires*, 476.
54. For example, ibid., 168.
55. Ibid., 16, 190, 327, 414.
56. Ibid., 150–1, 623, 628.
57. Ariès, *Hour*, 10.
58. Pontis, *Mémoires*, 623.
59. Ibid., 627.
60. Ibid., 628.
61. Ibid., 635.
62. Ibid., 170.
63. Bunyan, *Grace Abounding*, section 13, ed. Venables, 300.
64. Ibid., section 14, ed. Venables, 300.
65. Ibid., sections 15–16, ed. Venables, 300–1.
66. For example, Ibid., sections 46–7, ed. Venables, 310.
67. Ibid., sections 245–6, ed. Venables, 370–1.
68. Fussell, *Great War*, 138–44.
69. Martindale, *Life*, 41.
70. Ibid.
71. Ibid., 36.
72. Ibid., 42–4.
73. Crichton, *Blackader*, 218–19.
74. Ibid., 319–20.
75. Ibid., 351.
76. Ibid., 225–6.
77. Ibid., 266.
78. Ibid., 219.
79. Ibid., 224.
80. Ibid., 225–6.
81. Ibid., 154.
82. Ibid., 328.
83. Ibid., 320.
84. Compare Watkins, *Puritan Experience*, 210–12; Caldwell, *Puritan Conversion Narrative*, 12; Fulbrook, *Piety and Politics*, 31–2; Starr, *Defoe*, 48; Swain, *Pilgrim's Progress*, 135.
85. Watkins, *Puritan Experience*, 168. See also the narrative of the Quaker minister and ex-soldier William Edmundson: Edmundson, *Journal*, 2–3.
86. Erasmus, *Praise of Folly*, 30–1.
87. See, for example, Grimmelshausen, *Der abenteurliche Simplicissimus*, book 1.14, 1.16, ed. Meid, 54–8, 60–1. Knauer, 'War as *Memento Mori*'; Kunzle, *From Criminal to Courtier*, 23–4, 167–86, 257–392.
88. Kunzle, *From Criminal to Courtier*, 35–62 and passim.
89. Maarseveen and Kersten, 'Eighty Years' War,' 480–3.

90. Farquhar, 'Recruiting Officer,' Scenes 3.1, 5.5, ed. Myers, 190, 231.
91. Erasmus, *Praise of Folly*, 30–31; Erasmus, 'Military Affairs,' 12–15; Erasmus, 'Soldier and Carthusian,' 128–33; Carlton, *Going*, 41–2; Damon, *Soldier Saints*, 4–5; Dewald, *Aristocratic Experience*, 50–2; Grimmelshausen, *Mother Courage*, 30; Braudy, *Chivalry*, 137–8; Starkey, *War*, 21, 24; Duffy, *Military Experience*, 89–91; Lynn, *Giant*, 435–7; Quilley, 'Duty and Mutiny,' 82.
92. Crichton, *Blackader*, 313. See also ibid., 173, 175, 312.
93. For the exact definition of memoirs as a literary genre, see Harari, *Renaissance*, 1–18; Harari, 'Military Memoirs.' See also Emerson, *Olivier de la Marche*, 33–40; Mascuch, *Origins*; Morgan, 'Memoirs'; Hynes, *Soldiers' Tale*, xi–xvi; Forrest, *Napoleon's Men*, 21–52; Mortimer, *Eyewitness Accounts*, 15–28, 179–98; Kuperty, *Se dire*, 11–31; Hipp, *Mythes et Réalités*, 23–5. For an early modern discussion of the genre, see Loménie, *Mémoires*, 1–50.
94. Harari, *Renaissance*, 21–2, 187–95; Gillingham, 'War and Chivalry,' 231, 236. On early modern memoirs see also Mortimer, *Eyewitness Accounts*; Kuperty, *Se dire*; Hipp, *Mythes et Réalités*; Knecht, 'Sword and Pen'; Knecht, 'Military Autobiography'; Ettinghausen, 'Laconic and Baroque'; Levisi, 'Golden Age Autobiography'; Greyerz, 'Religion'; Dewald, *Aristocratic Experience*, 196–9; Morgan, 'Memoirs'; Harari, 'Military Memoirs,' 293–7.
95. Harari, 'Martial Illusions,' 58; Anderson, *War and Society*, 63–4, 136.
96. Anderson, *War and Society*, 66.
97. Quoted in Herf, *Reactionary Modernism*, 74.
98. Caputo, *Rumor of War*, 127.
99. Carlton, *Going*, 65. See also Dewald, *Aristocratic Experience*, 48.
100. Keen, *Chivalry*, 7–10.
101. Grimmelshausen, *Mother Courage*, 31–2.
102. Commynes, *Mémoires*, 1.4, ed. Mandrot, 1:37–8.
103. Chouppes, *Mémoires*, 73–83.
104. Ibid., 2.
105. Ibid., 3.
106. Other examples of failure to note the revelatory character of one's first campaign and first battle: Lurting, *Fighting Sailor*, 5; Souvigny, *Mémoires*, 13–17; Quincy, *Mémoires*, 1:33–70; La Colonie, *Mémoires*, 60–86; Ludlow, *Memoirs*, 1:42–5; Mortimer, *Eyewitness Accounts*, 142–3, 146–7; Navailles, *Mémoires*, 4–5; Coxere, *Adventures by Sea*, 11; Parker, *Memoirs*, 20; Pontis, *Mémoires*, 87; Contreras, *Discurso*, 76–7; Atkyns, 'Vindication,' 8–9; Cavalier, *Memoirs*, 48; Du Causé, *Mémoires*, 17–19; Hodgson, *Memoirs*, 5–6; Cholmley, *Memoirs*, 67–8; Gledhill, *Memoirs*, 20–1; Kane, *Campaigns*, 2; Kerry, 'Autobiography,' 27; Souvigny, *Mémoires*, 13–17; Puységur, *Mémoires*, 1:1–2; Slingsby, *Memoirs*, 36–42; Poyntz, *Relation*, 45–6; Raymond, *Autobiography*, 35–7.
107. Navailles, *Mémoires*, 3–4.
108. Ibid., 4.
109. Ibid., 5.
110. Ibid., 10.
111. Ibid., 12. For a full discussion, see Harari, *Renaissance*, 72–82. For examples of how memoirists described their own injuries, see Plessis-Besançon, *Mémoires*, 4–5; Ludlow, *Memoirs*, 1:60; Souvigny, *Mémoires*, 310, 314;

Mortimer, *Eyewitness Accounts*, 44, 149; Navailles, *Mémoires*, 15, 17–18, 45–6, 94; Melville, *Mémoires*, 17, 90–1, 231–2; Parker, *Memoirs*, 48; Parker, *Military Memoirs*, 64, 150, 178; Pontis, *Mémoires*, 97–9, 144–5, 165–7, 189–91; Contreras, *Discurso*, 88; Atkyns, 'Vindication,' 9, 24; Du Causé, *Mémoires*, 42, 88; Gwyn, 'Military Memoirs,' 67; Hodgson, *Memoirs*, 6; Gledhill, *Memoirs*, 26; Peeke, *Three to One*, B2, C1; Berlichingen, *Autobiography*, 24–6, 88–90; Monluc, *Commentaires*, 1:78–9, 3:344–5; Poyntz, *Relation*, 45–6, 115; Florange, *Mémoires*, 1:67, 120, 123, 130; Haynin, *Mémoires*, 1:226; Schertlin, *Leben*, 5; Díaz, *Historia Verdadera*, 9–10, 52; Ehingen, *Reisen*, 1:67. See also Harari, *Renaissance*, 48–52; Carlton, *Going*, 225–6.

112. Navailles, *Mémoires*, 215.
113. Saint-Simon, *Mémoires*, 1:37–8.
114. Ibid., 1:56–7.
115. Ibid., 1:249–50.
116. For a detailed discussion, see Harari, *Renaissance*, 141–2.
117. Ibid., 141–2.
118. Remarque, *All Quiet on the Western Front*, ch. 2, ed. Wheen, 20.
119. Raymond, *Autobiography*, 35.
120. Foucault, *Discipline and Punish*, 135–8. See also Taylor, *Sources*, 159. For early modern basic training, see Houlding, *Fit for Service*, 257–87. For a more thorough discussion of drill and training, see Chapter 3.
121. Quoted in Anderson, *War and Society*, 25.
122. See, for example, Ehrenreich, *Blood Rites*, 126–7.
123. Poyntz, *Relation*, 75.
124. Mergey, *Memoires*, 560. For killing performed by others, see also La Colonie, *Mémoires*, 299–300.
125. For other descriptions of killing which are not accompanied by any revelations, see Ludlow, *Memoirs*, 1:112; Parker, *Military Memoirs*, 174–5; Holsten, *Kriegsabenteuer*, 9; Dietz, *Memoirs of a Mercenary*, 48; Du Causé, *Mémoires*, 73–4.
126. Ehingen, *Reisen*, 1:58–60.
127. Peeke, *Three to One*, D1–D4.
128. Melville, *Mémoires*, 24–5; Melville, *Memoirs*, 84–5. For another memoirist who survived an execution without experiencing anything unusual, see Enriquez de Guzmán, *Libro*, 178.
129. Melville, *Mémoires*, 90–5; Melville, *Memoirs*, 123–6.
130. Melville, *Mémoires*, 131–2; Melville, *Memoirs*, 149.
131. Melville, *Mémoires*, 167; Melville, *Memoirs*, 170.
132. *Time*, October 2, 2006, vol. 168:15, 27–9. See also Kovic, *Born on the Fourth of July*.
133. Berlichingen, *Autobiography*, 25–6.
134. Ibid., 24–6.
135. Ibid., 66.
136. Ibid., 44.
137. It should be noted that contemporary culture offered many models of military heroes developing a relationship with inanimate objects, most notably swords.
138. Harari, *Renaissance*, 48–50. For a unique exception, see Carlton, *Going*, 339–40. See also ibid., 84–5; Dewald, *Aristocratic Experience*, 52.

139. Derounian-Stodola, *Indian Captivity Narrative*; Fitzpatrick, 'Figure of Captivity'; Zanger, 'Mary Rowlandson's Captivity Narrative.'
140. Holsten, *Kriegsabenteuer*, 34–5.
141. Quincy, *Mémoires*, 1:33. See also Melville, *Memoirs*, 12–13. For descriptions of the miseries of hunger and disease, see Mortimer, *Eyewitness Accounts*, 32, 42; Chouppes, *Mémoires*, 94; Navailles, *Mémoires*, 18, 162–3, 167; Melville, *Mémoires*, 19–23; Pasek, *Memoirs*, 49; Parker, *Memoirs*, 25; Parker, *Military Memoirs*, 153, 207; Holsten, *Kriegsabenteuer*, 26; Campion, *Mémoires*, 79–88; Cavalier, *Memoirs*, 111, 141; Deane, *Journal*, 6; Poyntz, *Relation*, 120–1; Dietz, *Memoirs of a Mercenary*, 34, 42–3, 56–7; Du Causé, *Mémoires*, 45; Souvigny, *Mémoires*, 79, 240–2. For descriptions of the ravages of the weather, see Campion, *Mémoires*, 111–12; Cavalier, *Memoirs*, 111; Kane, *Campaigns*, 2; Souvigny, *Mémoires*, 302; Puységur, *Mémoires*, 1:66. For descriptions of fatigue, see Parker, *Military Memoirs*, 110, 178; Atkyns, 'Vindication,' 22; Souvigny, *Mémoires*, 16.
142. La Noue, *Discours*, 343–5; Holsten, *Kriegsabenteuer*, 10; Mortimer, *Eyewitness Accounts*, 38; Tallett, *War and Society*, 49–50, 134–6; Duffy, *Military Experience*, 122. For a fuller discussion, see Harari, *Renaissance*, 139–41. See also Farquhar, 'Recruiting Officer,' Scene 3.2, ed. Myers, 199–201.
143. Carlton, *Going*, 76; Mortimer, *Eyewitness Accounts*, 37–8; Allmand, *Society at War*, 28; Braudy, *Chivalry*, 166–7.
144. For a much quoted but unpresentative example, see Bueil, *Jouvencel*, 2:20–1.
145. Monro, *His Expedition*, Epistle, 2. See also ibid., To the reader, 2.
146. Ibid., To the reader, 2.
147. Ibid., 2:156.
148. Mortimer, *Eyewitness Accounts*, 152. For another rare case of a memoirist writing about comrades and comradeship, see Pontis, *Mémoires*, 222.
149. Guyon, *Mémoires*, 90–1.
150. Ibid., 94.
151. Ibid., 135. See also Melville, *Mémoires*, 236–7.
152. See, for example, Navailles, *Mémoires*, 160.
153. Ludlow, *Memoirs*, 1:103. See also ibid., 1:69, 73–4. For examples of how memoirists described the injury or death of other people, see La Colonie, *Mémoires*, 551; Ludlow, *Memoirs*, 1:45; Mortimer, *Eyewitness Accounts*, 149; Chouppes, *Mémoires*, 77; Navailles, *Mémoires*, 32–3; Melville, *Mémoires*, 21, 31, 236–7; Pasek, *Memoirs*, 72–3; Coxere, *Adventures by Sea*, 6–7, 9; Parker, *Memoirs*, 48; Parker, *Military Memoirs*, 64, 150, 175; Atkyns, 'Vindication,' 10–11, 20; Deane, *Journal*, 15, 22; Dietz, *Memoirs of a Mercenary*, 38–43; Du Causé, *Mémoires*, 38; Gwyn, 'Military Memoirs,' 53; Mackay, *Memoirs*, 59; Kane, *Campaigns*, 7; Souvigny, *Mémoires*, 350–1; Peeke, *Three to One*, B1, B4; Slingsby, *Memoirs*, 50–2; Balbi de Correggio, *Verdadera Relación*, 72, 94; Poyntz, *Relation*, 115. See also Murrin, *History and Warfare*, 82–3. Very often there are no detailed descriptions of death and injury, but merely a list of those who were killed or injured. See, for example, Millner, *A Compendious Journal*, 33, 44, 98, 125–8; Puységur, *Mémoires*, 1:6; Saint-Simon, *Mémoires*, 1:252–60.

154. Barker, *Military Intellectual*, 112, 142; Pontis, *Mémoires*, 568; Souvigny, *Mémoires*, 22; Atkyns, 'Vindication,' 8; Poyntz, *Relation*, 58; Lupton, *Warrelike treatise*, 16–17; Defoe, *Memoirs of a Cavalier*, 47–8; Navailles, *Mémoires*, 32; Parrott, *Richelieu's Army*, 43–8; Duffy, *Military Experience*, 96–7.
155. I have dealt with the issue of disillusionment in Renaissance military memoirs quite extensively in previous publications. In the following pages I recapitulate some of the main arguments, and focus on post-1600 memoirs. For a more detailed study of disillusionment in secular military memoirs from the Renaissance, see Harari, *Renaissance*; and Harari, 'Martial Illusions.'
156. Raymond, *Autobiography*, 35.
157. Ibid., 43.
158. See, for example, Melville, *Mémoires*, 5–6; Parker, *Memoirs*, 2; Du Causé, *Mémoires*, 1–4, 71; Puységur, *Mémoires*, 1:1; Florange, *Mémoires*, 1:3; Poyntz, *Relation*, 45. See also Harari, 'Martial Illusions,' 56–7; Duffy, *Military Experience*, 57, 91; Lynn, *Giant*, 252.
159. Ercilla y Zúñiga, *Araucana*, ff. 290v–291v.
160. Ibid., f. 57v.
161. Ibid., ff. 187r–188v.
162. For example, ibid., f. 245v.
163. Thus present-day "action films" – as against "war drama" – very often present realistic and even over-realistic descriptions of death and injury in combat, while simultaneously upholding militaristic ideals.
164. For similarly misplaced beliefs, see also Braudy, *Chivalry*, 177–8; Alker, 'Soldierly Imagination,' 67.
165. Ercilla y Zúñiga, *Araucana*, ff. 318r–319v.
166. Ibid., ff. 327r–328r.
167. Harari, 'Martial Illusions,' 65–6.
168. See *Vida y hechos de Estebanillo Gonzalez*, 288–95.
169. Ibid., 414–15.
170. Ibid., 167. On *Estebanillo*, see also Borque, 'Spanish Literature,' 361.
171. Regarding Grimmelshausen's *Simplicissimus*, see Weinstein, *Fictions of the Self*, 51–9; Schäfer, 'Thirty Years' War.'
172. Grimmelshausen, *Der abenteurliche Simplicissimus*, book 1.4–10, ed. Meid, 25–44.
173. Ibid., book 2.30, ed. Meid, 234–5.
174. Ibid., book 3.14, ed. Meid, pp. 308–13.
175. Caputo, *Rumor of War*, 161.
176. Ibid., 201.
177. Mortimer, *Eyewitness Accounts*, 159.
178. Monro, *His Expedition*, 1:66.
179. Ibid., 1:3.
180. Ibid., 1:5.
181. Ibid., 2:93.
182. Ibid., To the reader, 1.
183. Dietz, *Memoirs of a Mercenary*, 48.
184. Saint-Simon, *Mémoires*, 1:251, 260.
185. Kane, *Campaigns*, 55.
186. Parker, *Memoirs*, 32.

187. Parker, *Military Memoirs*, 43–4.
188. Ibid., 89. See also Navailles, *Mémoires*, 193–4; Quincy, *Mémoires*, 1:239; Defoe, *Memoirs of a Cavalier*, 66.
189. Parker, *Military Memoirs*, 151.
190. Remarque, *All Quiet on the Western Front*, ch. 4, ed. Wheen, 48–53.
191. See, for example, Hale, *Artists and Warfare*, 10, 24, 30–2, 39.
192. For example, Belkin and Depauw, *Images of Death*, 11–12; Paret, *Imagined Battles*, 27–9.
193. Cavalli-Björkman, '*Vanitas* Still Life.'
194. See, for example, Hale, *Artists and Warfare*, 10, 24, 30–2, 39; Auwera, 'Historical Fact,' 466–7. A possible exception is a 1532 anonymous drawing which shows Folly and Death as recruiting officers, tempting men to enlist with their heaps of coins (Hale, *Artists and Warfare*, 24). In this case, it could be argued that the drawing's message is not the typical *memento mori*, but rather a disillusioned warning to young recruits of the dangers of war.
195. For religious artists *not* utilizing the materials provided by war, see also Lavalle, 'Thirty Years' War,' 153–8.
196. See also Cavalli-Björkman, '*Vanitas* Still Life.'
197. Hale, *Artists and Warfare*, 31.
198. Porter, *Medieval Warfare*, 35. See also ibid., 7, 34–8; Smeyers, *Flemish Miniatures*, 256; Prestwich, *Armies*, 79; Keen, *Chivalry*, illustrations number 7, 45; Hale, *Artists and Warfare*, 16, 138; Groebner, *Defaced*, 135; Carlton, *Going*, 18–19.
199. Roeck, 'Atrocities of War,' 129–36; Landwehr, *Romeyn de Hooghe*, 65, 84, 141, 194–5; Richard, 'Jacques Callot'; Kunzle, *From Criminal to Courtier*, 18–20, 24; Paret, *Imagined Battles*, 31–9. Though even in the case of Callot, some scholars have argued that he had no anti-war messages: Thuillier, 'Thirty Years' War,' 22–7; Knauer, 'War as *Memento Mori*,' 509.
200. Bächtiger, 'Marignano,' 31; Paret, *Imagined Battles*, 27.
201. Many veterans who were artists either restricted themselves to painting only "conventional" war scenes, or refrained from painting war scenes at all. For example, Inigo Jones, who survived the storming of Basing House, never sketched the English Civil War (see Carlton, *Going*, 343–4; Hale, *Artists and Warfare*, 55–8, 171).
202. Hale, *Artists and Warfare*, 55–8, 97.
203. Roeck, 'Atrocities of War,' 133. On Graf's *Battlefield* see in particular Bächtiger, 'Marignano.'
204. Hale, *Artists and Warfare*, 175–6; Roeck, 'Atrocities of War,' 133.
205. Kunzle, *From Criminal to Courtier*, 19.
206. Watkins, *Puritan Experience*, 209.
207. For some exceptional early modern uses of these formulas, see Melville, *Memoirs*, 19, 31; Díaz, *Historia Verdadera*, 11, 245–7, 249–50, 337, 349; Carlton, *Going*, 129; Pontis, *Mémoires*, 222; Bueil, *Jouvencel*, 2:21; Holsten, *Kriegsabenteuer*, 34; Defoe, *Memoirs of a Cavalier*, 43–6; Parker, *Military Memoirs*, 108; Harari, *Renaissance*, 69; Groebner, *Defaced*, 126; Mortimer, 'Individual Experience,' 147.
208. Berlichingen, *Autobiography*, 25. See also Cabeza de Vaca, *Naufragios*, 32; Navailles, *Mémoires*, 215; Melville, *Mémoires*, 11–12; Cavalier, *Memoirs*, 145.
209. For a rare exception, see Boyvin, *Mémoires*, 14.

210. Díaz, *Historia Verdadera*, 30–1.
211. Ibid., 26, 37, 48, 61–2, 69, 73, 88, 90, 265–7, 303–4. See also Harari, *Renaissance*, 69–70.
212. Díaz, *Historia Verdadera*, 115.
213. For similar cases when soldiers attacked historians and civilians for factual inaccuracies and favoritism, rather than for experiential inaccuracy, see Parker, *Memoirs*, 20; Tavannes, *Mémoires*, 8, 19; La Colonie, *Mémoires*, 506–7; Quincy, *Mémoires*, 1:308; Monluc, *Commentairres*, 1:337, 2:170, 350, 3:412, 422; Brantôme, *Oeuvres*, 5:336; Peeke, *Three to One*, A.
214. Shakespeare, *Henry V*, Act 4, Scene 3, ed. Taylor, 229–30.

3 Why war revealed nothing

1. Bynum, 'Why all the Fuss?', 13–27; Taylor, *Sources*, 127–42; Aberth, *Brink of Apocalypse*, 221–7; Perkins, *Suffering Self*, 3; Fanning, *Mystics*, 86; Ariès, *Hour*, 300; Watkins, *Puritan Experience*, 6; Le Goff, *Saint Francis*, 26; Michael, 'Renaissance Theories,' 147–50; Porter, *Flesh*, 18. In this, Christianity followed earlier schemes, such as that of Plato (Taylor, *Sources*, 115–26).
2. Quoted in Lozovsky, *Earth*, 142–3.
3. See ibid., 143–5.
4. Erasmus, 'Handbook,' 42–4.
5. Ibid., 44–51.
6. Lupton, *Obiectorum reductio*, 121–3.
7. Crichton, *Blackader*, 153.
8. Ibid., 155–6.
9. Barker, *Military Intellectual*, 130–2.
10. Ibid., 148.
11. On Descartes' military service, see Gaukroger, *Descartes*, 65–7, 102–11; Rodis-Lewis, 'Descartes' Life,' 25, 30–3; Baillet, *Vie*, 23–44; Adam, *Oeuvres de Descartes*, 2:480; Clarke, *Descartes*, 39–65; Sorell, *Descartes*, 7–8; Descartes, *Discours*, part II, ed. Buzon, 83–4.
12. On Descartes see Cottingham, 'Cartesian Dualism'; Rozemond, *Descartes's Dualism*; Sorell, *Descartes*, 71–87; Secada, *Cartesian Metaphysics*; Taylor, *Sources*, 143–58; Rey, *History*, 72–80; Wright and Potter, *Psyche*, 9–11; Voss, 'Descartes,' 175–6; Lennon, 'Bayle,' 198; Wright, 'Substance,' 237; Bynum, 'Why all the Fuss?' 33. For somewhat different interpretations of Descartes' views, see Almog, *What am I?*; Clarke, *Descartes's Theory of Mind*.
13. See Clarke, *Descartes*, 65.
14. Bergman, *History*, 1:147–8.
15. On names and the desire to immortalize them, see Harari, *Renaissance*, 99–100, 117–18, 165–6, 168, 175–60, 194–5.
16. Carlton, *Going*, 219; Prestwich, *Armies*, 333; Beaune, *Birth*, 307–8.
17. Barker, *Military Intellectual*, 132.
18. For criticism of princes who think like that, see Brantôme, *Oeuvres*, 7:278–9. For a modern interpretation of commanders' personal honor in instrumental terms, see Strickland, *War and Chivalry*, 101.
19. For honor and its centrality, see Parrott, *Richelieu's Army*, 71–3; Starkey, *War*, 20–1, 69–78; Duffy, *Military Experience*, 9, 74–80; Anderson, *War and*

Society, 58; Best, *War and Society*, 24; Lynn, *Giant*, 248–54; Neuschel, *Word of Honour*; Vale, *War and Chivalry*, 15–31, 166–7, 174, 249–51; Dewald, *Aristocratic Experience*, 45; Ruff, *Violence*, 75–80; Groebner, *Defaced*, 80–2; Keen, *Chivalry*, 249–51; Kaeuper, *Chivalry*, 153–5; Fallows, 'Knighthood,' 130; Harari, *Renaissance*, 39–40, 98–103, 112–16, 128–9, 159–65, 170–8, 182–3, 194–5; Harari, 'Martial Illusions,' 70–2; Carlton, *Going*, 55–8; Braudy, *Chivalry*, 49–55; Kiernan, *Duel*, 48–9; Hampson, *Cultural History*, 68–9.

20. Quoted in Fallows, 'Knighthood,' 130.

21. Keegan, *History*, 32; Black, 'Introduction,' 1, 4, 11; Black, *Why Wars Happen*, 4; Black, *European Warfare*, 47, 68; Hale, *War and Society*, 17–18, 31–2; Gunn, 'French Wars,' 33–5, 47; Luard, *War*, 330–4; Strickland, *War and Chivalry*, 112–13, 330; Mortimer, *Eyewitness Accounts*, 38; Lynn, *Giant*, 253–4; Machiavelli, *Prince*, ed. Codevilla, xv–xvii. Groebner, *Defaced*, 80–2; Harari, *Renaissance*, 160–4, 171–3.

22. For the dishonor involved in the use of tricks, see Allmand, 'Entre honneur,' 476; Harari, *Special Operations*, 8–9, 29–30.

23. It should be noted, though, that both in the Middle Ages and the early modern period, the dictates of the cult of honor were often bent or ignored on the battlefield. For a discussion, see Vale, *War and Chivalry*, 33, 167; Kaeuper, *Chivalry*, 153–5; Harari, *Special Operations*, 8–9, 13–17, 25–30; Keen, *Chivalry*, 220, 228–37; Contamine, *War*, 284–92; Prestwich, *Armies*, 233–7; Strickland, *War and Chivalry*, 124–31; Showalter, 'Caste,' 417; Gillingham, 'War and Chivalry,' 231–9.

24. Muntaner, *Crònica*, ch. 83, ed. Gustà, 1:127.

25. Ibid., 127–9; Desclot, *Llibre*, 503–4.

26. For a modern account that tries to rationalize Luria's action, see Mott, 'Battle of Malta,' 158–60.

27. See also Harari, *Renaissance*, 161–4.

28. Charny, *Book of Chivalry*, 122. See also Charny, *Book of Chivalry*, 124.

29. For a notable exception, see Brantôme, *Oeuvres*, 7:23. See also La Rochefoucauld, *Maxims*, 215, 219, 221. On the general attitude regarding fear, see also Barker, *Military Intellectual*, 64–6; Melvill, *Mémoires*, 201; Parker, *Military Memoirs*, 178, 184; Raymond, *Autobiography*, 38; Dewald, *Aristocratic Experience*, 59–60; Beaune, *Birth*, 305; Wright, *Knights*, 64; Verbruggen, *Art of Warfare*, 39–52; Contamine, *War*, 250–9; Strickland, *War and Chivalry*, 122–3; Kaeuper, *Chivalry*, 165–6; Parrott, *Richelieu's Army*, 72; Duffy, *Military Experience*, 239–40; Bliese, 'Courage'; Harari, *Renaissance*, 52; Fallows, 'Knighthood,' 123–5.

30. Alker, 'Soldierly Imagination,' 51–52; Carlton, *Going*, 86.

31. Barker, *Military Intellectual*, 113.

32. Monluc, *Commentaires*, 1:41. For honor being an inner quality that must nevertheless be displayed externally, see also Dewald, *Aristocratic Experience*, 59; Starkey, *War*, 70–1; Lynn, *Giant*, 251, 258.

33. Opposite opinions also existed in the early modern age. See, for example, Montaigne's essay "On Glory" (Montaigne, *Complete Essays*, 702–17; See also Taylor, *Sources*, 152). Yet they did not gain much ground in military culture until the eighteenth century.

34. Much of the following discussion is relevant to both the honorary and the instrumental stories of war. The reason I included it here is that it

was more closely connected to the ideal of honor. In the instrumental stories the same dynamics were in place, but there honor was understood as a reward from the state meant to encourage loyal and beneficial behavior.

35. For similar early modern renderings of the scene, see Michelle da Verona, *Mucius Scaevola* (c.1500); Christoph Bockstoffer's *Mucius Scaevola Thrusting His Right Hand into the Flames before Lars Porsenna* (c.1530–40); Hans Baldung Grien's *Mucius Scaevola* (1531); and Abraham Schöpfer, *Mucius Scaevola Burns His Arm before Lars Porsena* (1533).
36. Foxe, *Book of Martyrs*, 386–7.
37. Braudy, *Chivalry*, 191. See also Keen, *Chivalry*, 223; Quevedo, 'Swindler,' 165–6.
38. See, for example, Enriquez de Guzmán, *Libro*, 28–9.
39. For stories of "heroic" criminals, see Mascuch, *Origins*, 162–88; Merback, *Thief*, 126–57; Cohen, 'Die a Criminal,' 288–90, 294–6; Cohen, *Crossroads*, 181–201. See also Pontis, *Mémoires*, 329.
40. Ferguson, *Chivalric Tradition*, 97; Kiernan, *Duel*, 1–2, 14–15, 56–7, 113; Baldick, *Duel*, 84; Billacois, *Duel*, 210–11; Starkey, *War*, 71–8; Duffy, *Military Experience*, 77–8; Lynn, *Giant*, 255–9.
41. Baldick, *Duel*, 34–6; Billacois, *Duel*, 196–8; Stienmetz, *Romance of Duelling*, 1:123.
42. On the adoption of the pistol, see Baldick, *Duel*, 40–2, 73–4, 91; Billacois, *Duel*, 64, 185; Kiernan, *Duel*, 208, 214, 309.
43. Baldick, *Duel*, 41, 102, 139; Kiernan, *Duel*, 79–80, 142, 309; Billacois, *Duel*, 18–19, 28, 217; Steinmetz, *Romance of Duelling*, 1:61.
44. Baldick, *Duel*, 42–6, 74; Kiernan, *Duel*, 142, 144, 259; Billacois, *Duel*, 121; Steinmetz, *Romance of Duelling*, 1:66–73, 76–7, 81, 87, 104–7, 110, 2:152, 175–6, 247–8, 288–9, 303.
45. Quoted in Fallows, 'Knighthood,' 119. See also ibid., 120–1.
46. Ibid., 135.
47. Gwyn, 'Military Memoirs,' 41.
48. Brantôme, *Oeuvres*, 7:53.
49. Ibid., 102–3. See also Brantôme, *Oeuvres*, 7:103–5; Baeça, 'Carta,' 504; Erasmus, 'Soldier and Carthusian,' 132.
50. For example, see Díaz, *Historia Verdadera*, 18, 56.
51. Cerwin, *Bernal Díaz*, 175–6.
52. Muntaner, *Crònica*, ch. 227, ed. Gustà, 2:101.
53. Joinville, *Vie*, section 241, ed. Monfrin, 118.
54. García de Paredes, *Breve Svma*, 167.
55. Schertlin, *Leben*, 23.
56. Bowen, ' "Real Soul" ', 36.
57. Baeça, 'Carta,' 505. Contamine quotes a eulogy for a dead combatant that takes care to note his exact number of wounds (Contamine, 'Mourir,' 26).
58. Pontis, *Mémoires*, 82.
59. Enriquez de Guzmán, *Libro*, 29.
60. Melvill, *Mémoires*, 231.
61. Ercilla y Zúñiga, *Araucana*, f. 179v.
62. Florange, *Mémoires*, 1:127–8. See also Florange, *Mémoires*, 1:67, 120, 123; Berlichingen, *Autobiography*, 88–90; Haynin, *Mémoires*, 1:226; Schertlin,

Leben, 5; Díaz, *Historia Verdadera*, 9–10, 52; Ehingen, *Reisen*, 1:67; Harari, *Renaissance*, 118. On wounds, scars, and their cultural importance, see Fallows, 'Knighthood.'

63. Caputo, *Rumor*, 165.
64. Ibid., 166–7.
65. Quoted in Mortimer, *Eyewitness Accounts*, 146. For a fuller discussion, see Harari, *Renaissance*, 39–42.
66. For a fuller discussion, see Harari, *Renaissance*, 146–55; Harari, 'Martial Illusions,' 67–71. See also Levisi, 'Golden Age,' 99, 106, 114; Watts, 'Self-portrayal,' 265, 274–5; Mortimer, *Eyewitness Accounts*, 145. For memoirists who narrate such a collection of incidents yet insist that this is the story of their lives, see, for example, La Colonie, *Mémoires*, 47; Quincy, *Mémoires*, 1:1–2; Pasek, *Memoirs*, 37, 88.
67. Schertlin, *Leben*, 3–4.
68. Ibid., 16.
69. Ibid., 23.
70. Ibid., 63.
71. Ibid., 100. See also Parker, *Military Memoirs*, 187; Poyntz, *Relation*, 125–30; Navailles, *Mémoires*, 5; Dietz, *Memoirs*, 31, 60. On military entrepreneurs and war as a personal instrument, see also Redlich, *German Military Enterprizer*; Duffy, *Military Experience*, 14–15, 32–4, 71–3; Lynn, *Giant*, 249–50, 417–19; Anderson, *War and Society*, 33–76.
72. Contreras, *Discurso*, 74.
73. For example, see Cerwin, *Bernal Díaz*, 77–83, 94–5; Monluc, *Commentaires*, 3:314–15, 356–67; Roy, *Habsburg-Valois Wars*, 9–10.
74. See, for example, Souvigny, *Mémoires*, 350–1.
75. For the story of war as a collective instrument in medieval and early modern war, see Parrott, *Richelieu's Army*, 77–81, 84, 100–9; Duffy, *Military Experience*, 154–6; Lynn, *Giant*, 275–305; Gillingham, ' "Up with Orthodoxy!" ' 154; Strickland, *War and Chivalry*, 98–131; Black, *Why Wars Happen*, 15–20, 24, 63, 69–70; Black, 'Introduction,' 9–10; Black, *European Warfare, 1494–1660*, 5–6; Howard, *Weapons and Peace*, 7–22; Hale, *War and Society*, 15–16, 22–5, 29; Gunn, 'French Wars,' 28–35; Tallett, *War and Society*, 15–20; Luard, *War*, 24–6, 85–92, 135–44, 187; Wilson, *European Warfare*, passim; Glete, *War and the State*, passim.
76. Dalrymple, *Military Essay*, 79–80.
77. On drill see Van Creveld, *Technology and War*, 92–5; Duffy, *Military Experience*, 96–105, 110–15; Houlding, *Fit for Service*, 153–287; McNeill, *Keeping*, 127–31; Paret, *Yorck*, 13–19, 44; Foucault, *Discipline and Punish*, 135–8, 151–5, 162–4; Rogers, *British Army*, 67–8, 76–7; Holmes, *Redcoat*, 33, 215–16, 275; Anderson, *War and Society*, 25; Roberts, 'Military Revolution,' 14–16; Parker, *Military Revolution*, 20–3; Parker, 'Military Revolution,' 40–1; Parker, *Thirty Years War*, 184–5; Parrott, *Richelieu's Army*, 20–1; Lynn, *Giant*, 481–4, 515–25. I have relied particularly on the following early modern drill manuals: *Maniement d'Armes*; *Military Discipline*; Hexham, *Principles*; Lupton, *Warre-like Treatise*; Kane, *Campaigns*; *The Duke of Marlborough's new exercise*; Bland, *Treatise*; *Regulations for the Prussian infantry*; Dalrymple, *Military Essay*; Frederick II, *Military Instructions*.

78. Maurice's original drill book, illustrated by Jacques de Gheyn, broke down the loading and firing of muskets into 42 different positions, and the handling of a pike into 32 positions (Kunzle, *From Criminal to Courtier*, 206).
79. Hexham, *Principles*, 14–15. For these Pictorial guidebooks, see Knauer, 'War as *Memento Mori*,' 509–10; Kunzle, *From Criminal to Courtier*, 206–7.
80. Quoted in Duffy, *Military Experience*, 103.
81. Paret, *Yorck*, 15; Houlding, *Fit for Service*, 279–80.
82. Quoted in Paret, *Yorck*, 16n. 28.
83. Hexham, *Principles*, 7.
84. *Military Discipline*, 37.
85. Farquhar, 'Recruiting Officer,' Scene 4.1, ed. Myers, 206–7.
86. Duffy, *Military Experience*, 98–103; Duffy, *Army of Maria Theresa*, 56; Anderson, *War and Society*, 64–5; Best, *War and Society*, 32–3, 40–1; McNeill, *Keeping*, 129–30; Foucault, *Discipline and Punish*, 166; Holmes, *Redcoat*, 34–6, 314–26; Büsch, *Military System*, 25–6; Dinwiddy, 'Campaign'; Burroughs, 'Crime.'
87. Harris, *Recollections*, 92. See also Green, *Vicissitudes*, 16.
88. Quoted in Duffy, *Military Experience*, 98–9.
89. Bräker, *Arme Mann*, 75; Bräker, *Life Story*, 122.
90. Bräker, *Arme Mann*, 80; Bräker, *Life Story*, 127–8.
91. See, for example, Barker, *Military Intellectual*, 83.
92. Bishop, *Life*, 161–2.
93. See, for example, Barker, *Military Intellectual*, 73, 112; Souvigny, *Mémoires*, 23. On morale see also Parrott, *Richelieu's Army*, 71–4; Duffy, *Military Experience*, 194–7, 239–40; Lynn, *Giant*, 415–20, 434–50.
94. Navailles, *Mémoires*, 33.
95. For the Great Captain as a thinking machine rather than a brave knight, see, for example, Barker, *Military Intellectual*, 84, 157–8; Dewald, *Aristocratic Experience*, 57; Duffy, *Military Experience*, 140–1.
96. Barker, *Military Intellectual*, 157–8; Pontis, *Mémoires*, 441–2, 448–9, 564–5; Souvigny, *Mémoires*, 311, 350–1; Van Creveld, *Command in War*, 53; Duffy, *Military Experience*, 220–1, 237. Generals were expected to risk themselves only when the military situation – rather than their personal honor – required it (see, for example, Lynn, *Giant*, 314–15).
97. Fernández, 'Hall of Realms,' 122–9; Pfaffenbichler, 'Early Baroque,' 493–5; Paret, *Imagined Battles*, 40–2. Even when the general was not so prominent, most battle and siege paintings gave a panoramic view of battle as a chess-game between precise geometrical formations of pin-men: Auwera, 'Historical Fact'; Maarseveen, 'Eighty Years' War'; Chiarini, 'The Thirty Years' War'; Pfaffenbichler, 'Early Baroque'; Plax, 'Seventeenth-Century French Images of Warfare'; Kunzle, *From Criminal to Courtier*, 441–505; Paret, *Imagined Battles*, 40.
98. See, for example, Chouppes, *Mémoires*, 95–6; Monluc, *Commentaires*, 1:38, 423, 2:164. See also Duffy, *Military Experience*, 10, 14.
99. Parker, *Military Memoirs*, 126–7. See also Mackay, *Memoirs*, 56.
100. Quoted in Rogers, *British Army*, 105.
101. Parker, *Military Memoirs*, 100–1.
102. Ibid., 103–4. See also Barker, *Military Intellectual*, 67–9, 130–8; Machiavelli, *Prince*, ch. 15, ed. Codevilla, 57–8, 67; Dewald, *Aristocratic Experience*, 63–5.

103. It is notable that illness is often blamed for the defeats of those two great military geniuses, Charles XII at Poltava (1709) and Napoleon at Waterloo (1815).

104. See, for example, Monluc, *Commentaires*, 1:47–57, 87–98, 111–19; Verdugo, *Commentario*, 15–18, 161–2; Vere, *Commentaries*, 93–101, 154–9; Mackay, *Memoirs*, 50–5; Navailles, *Mémoires*, 148. See also Harari, *Renaissance*, 76.

105. For the notion of the early modern commander as a chess player, see Brodsky, *Gentlemen of the Blade*, 10–11. For a description of battle as a game of chess, see Gleig, *Subaltern*, 201.

106. Starkey, *War*, 21; Lynn, *Giant*, 275–81, 293–305, 439; Keen, *Chivalry*, 220, 228–37; Keen, 'Changing Scene,' 291; Contamine, *War*, 284–92; Prestwich, *Armies*, 233–4; Strickland, *War and Chivalry*, 124–5; Showalter, 'Caste,' 417; Vale, *War and Chivalry*, 33.

107. See, for example, Pontis, *Mémoires*, 132, 448–9; Defoe, *Memoirs of a Cavalier*, 122–3. See Dewald, *Aristocratic Experience*, 63–4; Adams, *Better*, 144–57. For the debate about the relations between chivalry and military realities, see Keen, 'Chivalry, Nobility'; Keen, 'Huizinga'; Strickland, *War and Chivalry*; Anglo, *Chivalry*; Goodman, *Chivalry and Exploration*; Ferguson, *Chivalric Tradition*; Davis, *Chivalry and Romance*; Day, 'Losing One's Character'; Vale, *War and Chivalry*, 1–10, 174; Keen, *Chivalry*, 1–3; Keen, 'Changing Scene,' 290–1; Gillingham, 'War and Chivalry,' 237–40; Hale, *War and Society*, 37–8; Tallett, *War and Society*, 17–18; Prestwich, *Armies*, 222, 243.

108. Starkey, *War*, 69–71.

109. Whatever "dishonorable" means – and it meant different things in different centuries.

110. On the continuing relevance of the honorary story of war, see Denin, 'Face of Battle'; Anderson, 'Code of Honour'; Tallett, *War and Society*, 17–18; Parrott, *Richelieu's Army*, 71–5; Duffy, *Military Experience*, 75–80; Lynn, *Giant*, 248–52, 439.

4   Bodies begin to think

1. Materialism had a long history predating La Mettrie. Most notably, in the middle of the seventeenth century Thomas Hobbes propagated radical materialist ideas. Nevertheless, full-fledged Materialism remained anathema. For Materialism before La Mettrie, see Yolton, *Locke and French Materialism*; La Mettrie, *Man a Machine*, ed. Bussey, 165–70; Thomson, *Materialism and Society*, 22–30; Rosenthal, *Materialism*, 19–52; Raymond, *Passage*, 43–67; Wellman, *La Mettrie*, 128–32.

2. Holmes, *Redcoat*, 250.

3. Frederick II, 'Eulogy on La Mettrie,' 6.

4. La Mettrie, *Man a Machine*, ed. Lieber, 1–5; Frederick II, 'Eulogy on La Mettrie'; Thomson, *Materialism and Society*, 39–40; O'Neal, *Authority*, 197; Wellman, *La Mettrie*, 5–6.

5. La Mettrie, *L'Homme-machine*, 66–7; La Mettrie, *Man a Machine*, ed. Lieber, 29–30.

6. La Mettrie, *L'Homme-machine*, 73; La Mettrie, *Man a Machine*, ed. Lieber, 36. On La Mettrie arguments against abstract rationalism, see also Wellman, *La Mettrie*, 2, 7–8, 137–49.

7. La Mettrie, *L'Homme-machine*, 64–5; La Mettrie, *Man a Machine*, ed. Lieber, 28–9.

8. La Mettrie, *L'Homme-machine*, 81; La Mettrie, *Man a Machine*, ed. Lieber, 44. See also La Mettrie, *L'Homme-machine*, 87.

9. La Mettrie, *L'Homme-machine*, 97; La Mettrie, *Man a Machine*, ed. Lieber, 58.

10. La Mettrie, *L'Homme-machine*, 98; La Mettrie, *Man a Machine*, ed. Lieber, 59.

11. La Mettrie, *L'Homme-machine*, 67; La Mettrie, *Man a Machine*, ed. Lieber, 31.

12. La Mettrie, *L'Homme-machine*, 68; La Mettrie, *Man a Machine*, ed. Lieber, 31. Other doctors have reached similar conclusions prior to or contemporaneously with La Mettrie, as for example Guillaume Lamy, François Maubec, Moreau de Saint-Elier, Antoine Louis, and Antoine Le Camus (Thomson, *Materialism and Society*, 22–30; Wellman, *La Mettrie*, 128–32).

13. La Mettrie, *L'Homme-machine*, 68; La Mettrie, *Man a Machine*, ed. Lieber, 31.

14. La Mettrie, *L'Homme-machine*, 70–1; La Mettrie, *Man a Machine*, ed. Lieber, 32–4. On La Mettrie's and his philosophy, see also Wellman, *La Mettrie*; Thomson, *Materialism and Society*; McMahon, *Pursuit*, 222–30; O'Neal, *Authority*, 206–7; Vartanian, *La Mettrie's "L'Homme machine"*; Gay, *Enlightenment*, 2:3–27; Israel, *Radical Enlightenment*, 704–9; Callot, *Philosophie*, 195–244; Rosenfield, *From Beast-Machine*, 141–6; Vartanian, *Science and Humanism*, 45–91.

15. On the idea of "thinking matter," see Taylor, *Sources*, 347–9.

16. Thomson, *Materialism and Society*, 18.

17. La Mettrie, *L'Homme-machine*, 104; La Mettrie, *Man a Machine*, ed. Lieber, 64.

18. La Mettrie, *L'Homme-machine*, 107; La Mettrie, *Man a Machine*, ed. Lieber, 67.

19. See also O'Neal, *Authority*, 207–8.

20. Manceron, *Twilight*, 4.

21. See, for example, Vila, *Enlightenment*; Van Sant, *Eighteenth-Century Sensibility*; Ellis, *Politics of Sensibility*; Bruhm, *Gothic Bodies*; Cottom, *Cannibals and Philosophers*; Hunt and Jacob, 'Affective Revolution.'

22. O'Neal, *Authority*, 1, 245. See also Chisick, *Limits*, 6.

23. On the moral-sense school, see Taylor, *Sources*, 258–65, 282–4; Jones, *Radical Sensibility*, 8; Voitle, *Third Earl*; Ellis, *Politics of Sensibility*, 10–14.

24. On eighteenth-century materialism, and particularly on the idea that matter could think, see O'Neal, *Authority*, 197–8, 204, 209–14; Yolton, *Locke and French Materialism*; Yolton, *Thinking Matter*; Richardson, *British Romanticism*; Taylor, *Sources*, 321–54; Outram, *Enlightenment*, 34; Pyenson, *Servants of Nature*, 418–19; Hampson, *Cultural History*, 93–5; Israel, *Radical Enlightenment*, 709.

25. O'Neal, *Authority*, 2, 16–21, 37, 64–7, 84–6, 201, 204–5; Outram, *Enlightenment*, 53; Hampson, *Cultural History*, 39, 75–6, 113, 186–7. Large sections of the medical establishment agreed with the Sensationists, as, for example,

Hermann Boerhaave, the greatest physician and most important medical thinker of the eighteenth century (Wellman, *La Mettrie*, 70, 104).

26. Quoted in O'Neal, *Authority*, 65.
27. Ibid., 81. See also Taylor, *Sources*, 164–7.
28. Ibid., 19, 27, 40, 42, 47–8; Wellman, *La Mettrie*, 167–8.
29. Jones, *Revolution*, 79.
30. O'Neal, *Authority*, 1–2, 89, 94, 175–82; Denby, *Sentimental Narrative*, 170–5; Jones, *Revolution*, 63.
31. My understanding of Sensationist ideas of the nervous system relies primarily on Vila, *Enlightenment*.
32. On the cult of sensibility and its influence on Western culture, see in particular Barker-Benfield, *Culture of Sensibility*; Ellison, *Cato's Tears*; Taylor, *Sources*. I follow Taylor in arguing that the eighteenth century was the most important dividing line in modern cultural history. See also Knott, 'Sensibility'; Bell, *Sentimentalism*, 11–56; O'Neal, *Authority*, 114–18, 128; Hampson, *Cultural History*, 186–7, 200–1; Porter, *Flesh*, 472–3; Breen, *Romantic Literature*, 9–12; Jones, *Revolution*, 105–15; McMahon, *Pursuit*, 197–252.
33. Quoted in O'Neal, *Authority*, 19. See also O'Neal, *Authority*, 69, 84–6, 89–91; Wellman, *La Mettrie*, 124; McGann, *Poetics*, 7.
34. Ibid., 3, 70–4, 84, 89–91; Taylor, *Sources*, 169, 321; McMahon, *Pursuit*, 208–21, 230–1; Wellman, *La Mettrie*, 152–3, 157–60; Van Sant, *Eighteenth-Century Sensibility*, 1–2; Ellis, *Politics of Sensibility*, 10–12; Burke, *Philosophical Enquiry*, xl–xli; Bruhm, *Gothic Bodies*, 2.
35. Quoted in Taylor, *Sources*, 328.
36. See in particular Vila, *Enlightenment*. See also Van Sant, *Eighteenth-Century Sensibility*, 5–14; Ellis, *Politics of Sensibility*, 18–21; Schenk, *Mind*, 4; Bour, 'Sensibility as Epistemology,' 815; Bruhm, *Gothic Bodies*, 4–5, 12–13; Hunt and Jacob, 'Affective Revolution,' 497–8.
37. Quoted in Fischer, *Washington's Crossing*, 107.
38. Gleig, *Subaltern*, 161.
39. Shipp, *Memoirs*, 52–3.
40. Porter, *Greatest Benefit*; McMahon, *Pursuit*, 159; Taylor, *Sources*, 188–91.
41. Taylor, *Sources*, 284.
42. Quoted in Hampson, *Cultural History*, 192–3. For the connection between feeling and knowing, see also Taylor, *Sources*, 294–6, 371–3; Hampson, *Cultural History*, 186–96; Benedict, *Framing Feeling*; Schenk, *Mind*, 4; Richards, *Romantic Conception*, 13–14; Bell, *Sentimentalism*, 2, 110–15, 121–2; McGann, *Poetics*, 7, 13–14; Pinch, *Strange Fits of Passion*, 7–8.
43. Sterne, *Sentimental Journey*, 198–9.
44. Rousseau, *Émile*, 348.
45. Ibid., 353–4.
46. Quoted in Cook, *Thresholds*, 13. See also Cook, *Thresholds*, 3–28; Schenk, *Mind*, 110–15; Menhennet, *Romantic Movement*, 19–21, 27–9; Jones, *Revolution*, 84–92; McGann, *Poetics*, 43; Bour, 'Sensibility as Epistemology,' 820–1; Löwy and Sayre, *Romanticism*, 41, 54–5.
47. Schiller, *Wallenstein*, 'The Piccolomini,' Act 5, Scene 1, trans. Lamport, 313. On Schiller's *Wallenstein*, see Krimmer, 'Transcendental Soldiers,' 105–12.
48. Schiller, *Wallenstein*, 'Wallenstein's Death,' Act 3, Scene 21, trans. Lamport, 410–11.

49. Ibid., Act 4, Scene 8, trans. Lamport, 432.
50. Bruhm, *Gothic Bodies*, 98–9. See also ibid., 21.
51. Ellis, *Politics of Sensibility*, 5.
52. Quoted in Ellis, *Politics of Sensibility*, 35.
53. Knott, 'Sensibility,' 22–3. See also Taylor, *Sources*, 295.
54. Knott, 'Sensibility,' 29–30.
55. O'Neal, *Authority*, 3. See also Ellis, *Politics of Sensibility*, 6; Cook, *Thresholds*, 5–6.
56. Schenk, *Mind*, 168.
57. Van Sant, *Eighteenth-Century Sensibility*, 54. See also ibid., 55–7.
58. Quoted in Van Sant, *Eighteenth-Century Sensibility*, 114. On the connections between the culture of sensibility, travel, and tourism, see also Wilton-Ely, ' "Classic Ground" '; Jones, *Revolution*, 66–7; Cohen, *Fashioning Masculinity*, 54–63.
59. Voltaire, *Candide*, ch. 1, ed. Pomeau, 85–6.
60. Compare Schenk, *Mind*, 164.
61. Vila, *Enlightenment*, 258–92. On the real-life libertine experimentations of Sade, see Manceron, *Twilight*, 132–7. On libertinage and its connection to free-thinking, see Dubost, 'Libertinage'; Goulemot, 'Toward a Definition'; Delon, *Le Savoir-vivre libertin*; Bernier, *Libertinage*; Hunt and Jacob, 'Affective Revolution,' 499–500.
62. For an overview, see Fritz, ' "We are Trying," ' 687–92.
63. Knott, 'Sensibility,' 28.
64. Pinch, *Strange Fits of Passion*, 2; Knott, 'Sensibility,' 34; Bruhm, *Gothic Bodies*, 32.
65. Vila, *Enlightenment*, 1.
66. Pinch, *Strange Fits of Passion*, 2.
67. Jones, *Radical Sensibility*.
68. See Bell, *Sentimentalism*, 120; Jones, *Radical Sensibility*, 64–7; Denby, *Sentimental Narrative*, 48.
69. The following discussion conflates the novel of sensibility and the *Bildungsroman*. For the purposes of the present book the characteristics of the two genres – as well as of other related genres such as the Gothic novel and the libertine novel – are too similar to warrant separate discussions. On the novel of sensibility and the *Bildungsroman*, see Ellis, *Politics of Sensibility*; Shaffner, *Apprenticeship Novel* (particularly on pages 1–27); Denby, *Sentimental Narrative*; Hardin, 'Introduction'; Martini, 'Bildungsroman'; Koepke, '*Bildung* and Transformation'; Sammons, 'Bildungsroman for Nonspecialists'; Mahoney, 'Apprenticeship'; Minden, *German Bildungsroman*; Vila, *Enlightenment*, 111–51; Littlejohns, 'Early Romanticism,' 68–9; Hoffmeister, 'From Goethe's *Wilhelm Meister*,' 80–99; O'Neal, *Authority*, 6–7, 109–29; Trahard, *Maîtres*; Bell, *Sentimentalism*, 11–56; Bruford, *German Tradition*, 29–30; Hampson, *Cultural History*, 108–9; Moretti, *Way of the World*, 3–5, 11; Jones, *Revolution*, 109–14, 233–6; Menhennet, *Romantic Movement*, 152, 158, 182; Beddow, *Fiction of Humanity*, 1–7.
70. Outram, *Enlightenment*, 21. See also Watt, *Rise of the Novel*; Kilgour, *Rise*; Price, *Anthology*; Barney, *Plots*; Ellis, *Politics of Sensibility*, 8–9, 43–6; Taylor, *Sources*, 286–9.
71. Knott, 'Sensibility,' 38.

72. Ellis, *Politics of Sensibility*, 22–3. See also Price, *Anthology*; Barney, *Plots*; Mahoney, 'Apprenticeship.'
73. Dilthey, 'Friedrich Hölderlin,' 335.
74. Quoted in Martini, 'Bildungsroman,' 20.
75. Ibid., 21.
76. Ellis, *Politics of Sensibility*, 16.
77. Van Sant, *Eighteenth-Century Sensibility*, 99–100.
78. Sterne, *Sentimental Journey*, 40–1; Van Sant, *Eighteenth-Century Sensibility*, 100–1.
79. Sterne, *Sentimental Journey*, 39.
80. Van Sant, *Eighteenth-Century Sensibility*, 100.
81. Pyenson, *Servants of Nature*, 410–14.
82. Quoted in Van Sant, *Eighteenth-Century Sensibility*, 50.
83. Schenk, *Mind*, 125–51.
84. Ermarth, *Wilehlm Dilthey*, 97. See also ibid., 97–121, 219, 226–32; Makkreel, *Dilthey*, 8–9, 147–9; Bambach, *Heidegger*, 152–60.
85. Dilthey, *Introduction*, 73.
86. Ibid., 13.
87. Shaffner, *Apprenticeship Novel*, 7–9; Bruford, *German Tradition*, vii; Minden, *German Bildungsroman*, 1; Löwy and Sayre, *Romanticism*, 25; Hardin, 'Introduction,' xii–xiii; Sammons, 'Bildungsroman for Nonspecialists,' 41–2; Mahoney, 'Apprenticeship,' 109–10.
88. Bruford, *German Tradition*, 24.
89. Ibid., 25.
90. Ibid., 24.
91. Thus in Goethe's *Götz von Berlichingen*, the monk Martin is envious of Berlichingen for his way of life. He speaks highly of the exciting life of a warrior compared to the dreary life of a monk (Goethe, 'Goetz von Berlichingen,' Act 1, scene 2, ed. Dole, 242).
92. My understanding of Romanticism is particularly indebted to Taylor, *Sources*; and Löwy and Sayre, *Romanticism*, 1–56.
93. O'Neal, *Authority*, 25.
94. Jones, *Revolution*, 61.
95. Schenk, *Mind*, 162–76; Outram, *Enlightenment*, 50; Hampson, *Cultural History*, 195–6, 206–10; O'Neal, *Authority*, 137, 186–7; Richards, *Romantic Conception*, 13, 201; Jones, *Revolution*, 61–3; Bour, 'Sensibility as Epistemology,' 821–2. On the "noble savage," see Schenk, *Mind*, 130; Menhennet, *Romantic Movement*, 13–14, 20, 102–3. For a critique of the idea of the "noble savage," see Ellington, *Myth*.
96. See Taylor, *Sources*, 297–390.
97. In *A Philosophical Inquiry into our Ideas of the Sublime and the Beautiful* (1756).
98. In *Observations on the Feeling of the Beautiful and Sublime* (1764) and *The Critique of Judgment* (1791).
99. In *On the Sublime: Toward the Further Development of Some Kantian Ideas* (1793) and *Concerning the Sublime* (1801). The following discussion of the sublime and of epiphanies owes a particular debt to Ryan, 'Physiological Sublime.' In addition, it is based on Burke, *Philosophical Enquiry*; Kant, *Critique of Judgement*; Schiller, 'On the Sublime'; Schiller, 'Concerning the Sublime'; Ashfield, *Sublime*; Monk, *Sublime*; Weiskel, *Romantic Sublime*;

Crowther, *Kantian Sublime*; Voller, *Supernatural Sublime*, 3–30; Hinnant, 'Schiller'; Jones, *Radical Sensibility*, 48–9, 56–7; Bidney, *Patterns of Epiphany*, 1–4; Nichols, *Poetics of Epiphany*; Beja, *Epiphany*; Langbaum, 'Epiphanic Mode'; Balfour, 'Torso'; Taylor, *Sources*, 419–34. For theories of the sublime which differ somewhat from those of Burke and Kant, see Crowther, *Kantian Sublime*, 7–18. See Oerlemans, *Romanticism and the Materiality of Nature* for his concept of the "material sublime," which is a sublime routed in material reality rather than in supernatural or transcendent reality.

100. See, for example, Burke, *Philosophical Enquiry*, 39–40, 57–8; Kant, *Critique of Judgement* 2.23, trans. Meredith, 90–1; Schiller, 'On the Sublime,' 28–30.
101. Burke, *Philosophical Enquiry*, 57; Weiskel, *Romantic Sublime*, 87–97.
102. Schiller, 'On the Sublime,' 22; Kant, *Critique of Judgement* 2.28, trans. Meredith, 114. See also Kant, *Critique of Judgement* 2.23–8, trans. Meredith, 90–114; Weiskel, *Romantic Sublime*, 23–4, 38–43.
103. Compare Crowther, *Kantian Sublime*, 2.
104. Ashfield, *Sublime*, 304.
105. Quoted in Manceron, *Twilight*, 362.
106. Voller, *Supernatural Sublime*, 4.
107. Ryan, 'Physiological Sublime,' 277.
108. See Hinnant, 'Schiller,' 127–8; Crowther, *Kantian Sublime*, 115–16.
109. Burke, *Philosophical Enquiry*, 39; Crowther, *Kantian Sublime*, 8; Hinnant, 'Schiller'; Hampson, *Cultural History*, 205; Ashfield, *Sublime*, 276.
110. Shipp, *Memoirs*, 110. See also Gleig, *Subaltern*, 54; *Memoirs of a Sergeant*, 147; Harris, *Recollections*, 26; Perry, *Recollections*, 19.
111. Kant, *Critique of Judgement* 2.28, trans. Meredith, 113.
112. Bowden, *Black Hawk Down*, 301–2.
113. Hampson, *Cultural History*, 186–196; Taylor, *Sources*, 370. On the Romantic concept of the "poetic" soul, see Jones, *Revolution*, 228–60. On the Romantic concept of the intuitive and passionate genius, see Jones, *Revolution*, 261–95; Hampson, *Cultural History*, 199–201; Schenk, *Mind*, 5–6.
114. Quoted in Blanning, *French Revolutionary Wars*, 147.
115. Davidov, *In the Service of the Tsar*, 40.
116. Ibid., 38.

5 The rise of the common soldier

1. Dalrymple, *Military Essay*, 9–11; Anderson, *War and Society*, 28, 46, 120–7, 163; Houlding, *Fit for Service*, 117–19; Best, *War and Society*, 30–2, 40–4; Duffy, *Army of Frederick*, 56–7, 168–9; Duffy, *Military Experience*, 90–4, 285; Duffy, *Army of Maria Theresa*, 47–9; Büsch, *Military System*, 4–5; Rogers, *British Army*, 59–63; Störkel, 'Defenders,' 9; Holmes, *Redcoat*, 34, 75, 144–9; Burroughs, 'Crime,' 548–50. For examples of how soldiers were forced or tricked into the army, see Pearson, *Soldier*, 14–15; Bräker, *Arme Mann*, 72–4; Woelfel, 'Memoirs,' 555–6; Watkins, *Soldiers*, 15–16; Graydon, *Memoirs*, 133–4. (Most of these examples are from the late eighteenth century and nineteenth century, but they illustrate practices which were far more common in earlier centuries. Few examples from earlier centuries survive, because few seventeenth-century common soldiers wrote memoirs, and even when they did, they rarely described the recruiting process.)

2. Frederick II, *Military Instructions*, 1–2; Anderson, *War and Society*, 51–2, 114, 163; Holmes, *Redcoat*, 48–54; Duffy, *Army of Maria Theresa*, 47.
3. Duffy, *Military Experience*, 89.
4. Duffy, *Army of Maria Theresa*, 48–9. See also Dalrymple, *A Military Essay*, 9–11; Frederick II, *Military Instructions*, 5–6; Duffy, *Military Experience*, 90; Starkey, 'War and Culture,' 10; Houlding, *Fit for Service*, 267–8; Quilley, 'Duty and Mutiny,' 82–4; Forrest, *Napoleon's Men*, 59; Forrest, *Conscripts*, 6. The situation in Britain remained largely the same throughout the nineteenth century as well. Wellington observed that 'The French system of conscription [after 1789] brings together a fair sample of all classes; ours is composed of the scum of the earth – the mere scum of the earth.' On another occasion he said that 'the man who enlists into the British army is, in general, the most drunken and probably the worst man of the trade or profession to which he belongs, or of the village or town in which he lives' (quoted in Burroughs, 'Crime,' 548–9. See also Dinwiddy, 'Campaign,' 320; Holmes, *Redcoat*, 148–9).
5. Duffy, *Military Experience*, 101; Duffy, *Prussia's Glory*, 16; Fischer, *Washington's Crossing*, 40.
6. Gat, *Origins*, 35; Anderson, *War and Society*, 88; Kunzle, *From Criminal to Courtier*, 441–505.
7. Paret, *Yorck*, 106.
8. Ibid., 80–1.
9. Desertion was the plague of old regime armies. During the War of Spanish Succession one out of every four French soldiers deserted (Anderson, *War and Society*, 130). It is estimated that during the Seven Years War, 80,000 Prussian soldiers, 70,000 French, and 62,000 Austrians deserted (Blanning, *French Revolutionary Wars*, 13). In the period 1776–80 the British navy lost 1200 sailors in action, whereas over 42,000 deserted (Anderson, *War and Society*, 165). On the problem of desertion, see also Burroughs, 'Crime,' 553–54; Anderson, *War and Society*, 128–31, 165; Holmes, *Redcoat*, 316–17; Best, *War and Society*, 33; Paret, *Yorck*, 16, 26, 30, 96–7; Bräker, *Arme Mann*, 79–80; Forrest, *Conscripts*, 6–8.
10. Paret, *Clausewitz*, 25, 28; Lynn, *Bayonets*, 265; Störkel, 'Defenders,' 11.
11. Anderson, *War and Society*, 130.
12. Frederick II, *Military Instructions*, 3–5. See also Ritter, *Frederick the Great*, 134–5; Büsch, *Military System*, 14, 24–5; Anderson, *War and Society*, 130, 165; Best, *War and Society*, 51; Paret, *Yorck*, 19–20; Duffy, *Army of Maria Theresa*, 141.
13. Frederick II, *Military Instructions*, 112.
14. According to Ulrich Bräker, one of Frederick's unwilling soldiers, the Prussian king had every reason to fear desertion. See in particular Bräker, *Arme Mann*, 87–8, 90–5.
15. Paret, *Yorck*, 20–1.
16. For a fascinating account of guerilla and counter-insurgency warfare in the early eighteenth century, see Cavalier's *Memoirs of the Wars of the Cevennes* (1726). The war of the Camisards was a very different world from the Newtonian science of Vauban's sieges and Marlborough's battles. See also Satterfield, *Princes, Posts, and Partisans*.
17. Blanning, *French Revolutionary Wars*, 119.

18. Palmer, *Improvement of Humanity*, 3, 7; Paret, *Clausewitz*, 36–8; Ezell, 'John Locke's Images of Childhood'; Vila, *Enlightenment*, 35–6, 38, 84–5, 88–93, 141–2, 146–8. For the idea of the *tabula rasa*, see in particular John Locke's *An Essay Concerning Human Understanding* and *Some Thoughts Concerning Education*.
19. Blaze, *Military Life*, 8.
20. Quoted in Paret, *Clausewitz*, 49.
21. Ammon, *Leben Dr. Christian Nagel's*, 165–6; Ammon, *Soldier of Freedom*, 82–3.
22. Paret, *Clausewitz*, 37, 48–9; Stewart, *Progressives*, 3–21; Ezell, 'John Locke's Images of Childhood,' 152–3; Adams, *Evolution*, 94–9.
23. Paret, *Yorck*, 107–8.
24. Paret, *Clausewitz*, 36–8, 46–53; Paret, *Yorck*, 87; Paret, 'Genesis of *On War*,' 8; Duffy, *Army of Maria Theresa*, 58; Gat, *Origins*, 59–66; Gat, *Development*, 17–18; Best, *War and Society*, 26; Chisick, *Limits of Reform*, 25; Duffy, *Army of Maria Theresa*, 29–30; Cuthbertson, *System*, 10.
25. Paret, 'Genesis of *On War*,' 8–9; Paret, *Clausewitz*, 48, 50; Adams, *Evolution*, 96–8.
26. Quoted in Gat, *Origins*, 71.
27. Ibid., 72.
28. Ibid., 150–5.
29. Ibid., 153–4; Gat, *Development*, 13.
30. Paret, *Clausewitz*, 54.
31. Clausewitz, *On War*, 1.1.3, 1.1.22, ed. Howard and Paret, 76, 86; Paret, 'Genesis of *On War*,' 11, 17; Gat, *Origins*, 178–81.
32. Quoted in Gat, *Origins*, 184. In his youth Clausewitz was greatly impressed by Illuminati tracts, which held out the prospect of human perfectibility through education (Paret, 'Genesis of *On War*,' 8; Paret, *Clausewitz*, 39).
33. See also Best, *War and Society*, 52–3, 235; Paret, *Yorck*, 18–19; Duffy, *Army of Maria Theresa*, 61–2; Paret, *Clausewitz*, 49–50; Forrest, *Napoleon's Men*, 65–6.
34. Shipp, *Memoirs*.
35. Knott, 'Sensibility,' 30.
36. The following discussion of light infantry in the eighteenth century and early nineteenth century is based on Gates, *British Light Infantry*; Russell, 'Redcoats'; Paret, *Yorck*, 21–46, 55–6, 253–4, 257–9, 269. Duffy, *Military Experience*, 268–79; Duffy, *Army of Maria Theresa*, 67; Muir, *Tactics*, 51–67; Lynn, *Bayonets*, 217–18, 222, 261–77; Best, *War and Society*, 51–2; Rogers, *British Army*, 70–4, 224; Holmes, *Redcoat*, 39–44, 186, 200; Fischer, *Washington's Crossing*, 35–6; Starkey, *European*, 51–3; Starkey, 'War and Culture,' 3; Dalrymple, *Military Essay*, 297–303; Frederick II, *Military Instructions*, 92, 107–8; Black, *War for America*, 60–5; Blanning, *French Revolutionary Wars*, 18, 123–4. For eighteenth-century treatises on light infantry, see Simcoe, *Journal*; Tarleton, *History*; Emmerich, *Partisan*.

    It should be noted that light infantry were a novel phenomenon only compared to the armies of the previous era. Back in the sixteenth century light infantry and light infantry tactics were common in European warfare. Marshal Blaise de Monluc gives in his memoirs detailed instructions for the use of light infantry, and detailed descriptions of several light infantry actions he commanded. Due to limitations of space, I cannot discuss here the cultural history of light cavalrymen, which is of almost equal importance, but which will have to await a future research.

37. See in particular Lynn, *Bayonets*, 263–4; Paret, *Yorck*, 97; Gates, *British Light Infantry*, 19, 78–85.
38. Rogers, *British Army*, 71; Gates, *British Light Infantry*, 96.
39. Gates, *British Light Infantry*, 96, 138–48; Russell, 'Redcoats,' 645.
40. Quoted in Muir, *Tactics*, 54. On the training of the British light troops, see also Gates, *British Light Infantry*, 95–7; Muir, *Tactics*, 178; Rogers, *British Army*, 64, 70–3; Harris, *Recollections*, vii.
41. Quoted in Gates, *British Light Infantry*, 31.
42. Quoted in Paret, *Yorck*, 200.
43. Paret, *Yorck*, 29–30.
44. Ibid., 106.
45. Ibid., 56.
46. Ibid., 70–1.
47. Quoted in Lynn, *Bayonets*, 268–9.
48. Duffy, *Army of Maria Theresa*, 82–90; Best, *War and Society*, 45; Gates, *British Light Infantry*, 11, 18.
49. Paret, *Yorck*, 29.
50. Duffy, *Russia's Military Way*, 117, 120–1. Rumyantsev, *Dokumenty*, 1:437–9; Suvorov, *Suvorov. Dokumenty*, 1:437–9.
51. Duffy, *Russia's Military Way*, 170, 177, 184.
52. Fischer, *Washington's Crossing*, 35; Duffy, *Military Experience*, 279; Rogers, *British Army*, 70–3.
53. Rogers, *British Army*, 74.
54. Duffy, *Military Experience*, 268.
55. Paret, *Clausewitz*, 26–7.
56. Störkel, 'Defenders,' 5–6, 12.
57. See Blakiston, *Twelve Years*.
58. See Lynn, *Bayonets*, 216–40; Blaze, *Military Life*, 148–9.
59. Paret, *Yorck*, 151, 182.
60. Quoted in Muir, *Tactics*, 74.
61. Ibid., 75.
62. On methods of training in the Napoleonic era, see Lynn, *Bayonets*, 216–40, 282–3; Gates, *British Light Infantry*, 95–7; Duffy, *Military Experience*, 285; Duffy, *Army of Maria Theresa*, 109; Paret, *Yorck*, 18–19.
63. Best, *War and Society*, 53–9, 65–6, 76–87, 95–7, 157–66; Forrest, *Napoleon's Men*, 58–69; Bertaud, *Army*, 133–230; Blanning, *French Revolutionary Wars*, 84–5; Brosman, *Visions of War*, 12–13. It should be emphasized that it was not sufficient to educate only the soldiers. The entire society had to be imbued with republican or patriotic sentiments, so that soldiers would receive positive encouragement from family members, neighbors, and friends to do their duty.
64. Quoted in Duffy, *Military Experience*, 284.
65. Quoted in Starkey, 'War and Culture,' 20–1. For a recent study arguing that the Americans owed their success to their republican ideals see Fischer, *Washington's Crossing*.
66. Lynn, *Bayonets*, 282–3; Paret, *Yorck*, 88–92; Blanning, *French Revolutionary Wars*, 95, 118, 122–3.

67. Quoted in Lynn, *Bayonets*, 265. See also Paret, *Yorck*, 72–5; Esdaile, *Wars of Napoleon*, 57–8.
68. Lynn, *Bayonets*, 273
69. Ibid., 265. For the *tirailleurs* in the revolutionary armies, see in particular Lynn, *Bayonets*, 261–77, 282–3.
70. Quoted in Paret, *Yorck*, 77.
71. Ibid., 78–9.
72. Ibid., 84.
73. Rogers, *British Army*, 70.
74. Paret, *Clausewitz*, 65.
75. Friederich, *Abenteuer*, 28.
76. Ibid., 29. See also Nettelbeck, *Abenteuerliches Lebensbild*, 53–4; Compare Suvorov, *A. V. Suvorov. Dokumenty*, 1:98.
77. Mämpel, *Young Rifleman's Comrade*, 19–20. See also Varnhagen, *Sketches*, 44.
78. On the Prussian reforms of 1807–13, see above all Paret, *Yorck*, 118–90. See also Clark, *Iron Kingdom*, 312–85; Esdaile, *Wars of Napoleon*, 202–15; Best, *War and Society*, 156–67. It is notable that the four-men committee that drafted the new training instructions of the Prussian army was composed of two light infantry officers and two light cavalry officers (Paret, *Yorck*, 140).
79. Paret, *Clausewitz*, 139; Paret, *Yorck*, 161, 164–7.
80. Paret, *Yorck*, 166–7.
81. Ibid., 139–41, 161, 165.
82. Ibid., 219.
83. Paret, *Clausewitz*, 137–46; Muir, *Tactics*, 51–2. For an overview of relevant studies of World War II, see Fritz, ' "We are Trying," ' 683–5.
84. See in particular Bertaud, *Army*.
85. Svetlova, *Art of War*, 2:175.
86. Duffy, *Eagles*, 29, 226–36.
87. Johnson, *Political Writings*, 281.
88. Ibid., 283. For prevailing beliefs in the Napoleonic era that soldiers' effectiveness depends on ideological commitment, see Muir, *Tactics*, 199.
89. Johnson, *Political Writings*, 283–4.
90. Van Creveld, *Fighting Power*. For an overview of relevant studies of World War II, see Fritz, ' "We are Trying," ' 683–5.
91. Duffy, *Army of Frederick the Great*, 58.
92. Duffy, *Military Experience*, 95–6; Muir, *Tactics*, 75.
93. Paret, *Clausewitz*, 25.
94. Paret, *Clausewitz*, 28; Ritter, *Frederick the Great*, 143.
95. Paret, *Yorck*, 209. See also Muir, *Tactics*, 194; Duffy, *Military Experience*, 274.
96. On the *lévee en masse*, see Bertaud, *Army*, 102–32; Blanning, *French Revolutionary Wars*, 101, 120. On mass recruitment and size of armies, see Muir, *Tactics*, 15; Paret, *Yorck*, 133–8; Esdaile, *Wars of Napoleon*, 40–1; Forrest, *Napoleon's Men*, 5–8. For reliance on initiative, see Muir, *Tactics*, 103; Best, *War and Society*, 86–7, 90–1.
97. Best, *War and Society*, 89. It is notable that when in the late twentieth century Western democracies reverted to the use of small professional armies enlisted voluntarily from amongst their poorest members, these armies did not revert back to the Cartesian model, but continued to function along Sensationist lines, co-opting soldiers and delegating to them as

much responsibility as possible. In the U.S. army today there are no longer any common soldiers. The lowest rank is 'specialist.'

98. Quoted in Blanning, *French Revolutionary Wars*, 14.
99. Quoted in Forrest, *Conscripts*, 19. See also Esdaile, *Wars of Napoleon*, 42–3.
100. Muir, *Tactics*, 71–3; Paret, *Yorck*, 65–7, 174, 209; Blanning, *French Revolutionary Wars*, 122–3.
101. French armies in the revolutionary and Napoleonic period were still greatly concerned about desertion, but to a lesser extent than old regime armies. They suffered more from the evasion of recruitment than from post-recruitment desertion. See Forrest, *Conscripts*; Bertaud, *Army*, 259–64.
102. Blaze, *Military Life*, 37.
103. Ibid., 23. See also Blanning, *French Revolutionary Wars*, 159.
104. See Fischer, *Washington's Crossing*, 346–59.
105. Quoted in ibid., 358. On the *Petite Guerre* see also Gates, *British Light Infantry*; Kwasny, *Washington's Partisan War*; Dalrymple, *Military Essay*, 297–303; Starkey, *European*, 46–53; Starkey, 'War and Culture,' 3–4, 16–17; Lynn, *Bayonets*, 271, 279–80; Duffy, *Military Experience*, 269, 287–8; Best, *War and Society*, 265–6; Paret, *Yorck*, 21–3, 176–7; Blanning, *French Revolutionary Wars*, 168–9.
106. See in particular Blanning, *French Revolutionary Wars*, 164–9, 238–48.
107. Friederich, *Abenteuer*, 260.
108. Esdaile, *Wars of Napoleon*, 108–42.
109. For comical representations of common soldiers, see, for example, Farquhar's *Recruiting Officer*.
110. See also Kunzle, *From Criminal to Courtier*.
111. For the rise of the common soldier in the late eighteenth century, see also Quilley, 'Duty and Mutiny'; Best, *War and Society*, 199–202; Forrest, *Napoleon's Men*, 59–70; Blakiston, *Twelve Years*, 2:369–71.
112. *Life and Adventures of Mrs. Christian Davies*, 140.
113. It is interesting to note that the image of commanders being caught off their guard while playing at chess has a long history behind it. Crusader chroniclers depict the Turkish commander Kerbogah being caught off his guard at the battle of Antioch (1098) while playing chess.
114. Bowen, ' "Real Soul," ' 35.
115. Muir, *Tactics*, 208. Compare Durova, *Cavalry Maiden*, 130–1.
116. Forrest, *Napoleon's Men*, 55–6. See also Bell, *Cult*, 103–4.
117. Bell, *Cult*, 78–80, 103–4.
118. Blaze, *Military Life*, 41.
119. Knott, 'Sensibility,' 21.
120. Adye, *Essay*, 272–6; Murashev, *Tituli Chini Nagradi*, 168–9; Dalrymple, *Military Essay*, 339–62; Kutuzov, *Dokumenty*, vol. 4, part 2, 722–3; Starkey, 'War and Culture,' 19–20; Muir, *Tactics*, 195, 272; Holmes, *Redcoat*, 408–9.
121. Best, *War and Society*, 21–7, 75–6; Paret, *Yorck*, 8–9, 130–3, 265–6; Blanning, *French Revolutionary Wars*, 125–6; Esdaile, *Wars of Napoleon*, 56; Scott, *Yorktown to Valmy*, 171, 182. Anderson, *War and Society*, 22–3, 74–5, 132–3; Büsch, *Military System*, 52–61; Rogers, *British Army*, 53. For a classical description of the difficulties of promotion in the early modern period, see Grimmelshausen, *Der abenteurliche Simplicissimus*, book 1.16–17, ed. Meid, 60–7. See also Schiller, *Wallenstein*, 'Wallenstein's Camp,' Act 1, Scene 7,

trans. Lamport, 190–1; Morris, *Recollections*, 50–2; Blaze, *Military Life*, 8, 112–14.

122. Best, *War and Society*, 159–62, 168–83, 187–8, 265–72; Muir, *Tactics*, 199; Paret, *Yorck*, 120, 156, 178–9; Blanning, *French Revolutionary Wars*, 164–9, 238–48.

123. Murashev, *Tituli*, 169–70.

124. Kwasny, *Washington's Partisan War*; Starkey, *European*, 131–5; Duffy, *Military Experience*, 284–6; Holmes, *Redcoat*, 36; Best, *War and Society*, 54–5; Gates, *British Light Infantry*, 16–17.

125. Blanco, 'Attempts to Abolish Branding and Flogging'; Burroughs, 'Crime'; Dinwiddy, 'Campaign'; Steiner, 'Separating the Soldier'; Skelley, *Victorian Army*; Holmes, *Redcoat*, 34, 37–8, 320–6; Paret, *Yorck*, 87, 127–9, 142–3, 202; Best, *War and Society*, 70, 235; Fischer, *Washington's Crossing*, 45; Muir, *Tactics*, 202; Starkey, 'War and Culture,' 20; Adye, *Treatise*; Adye, *Essay*, 276, 283–4; Shipp, *Memoirs*, 12.

126. Quoted in Dinwiddy, 'Campaign,' 317.

127. See also Shipp, *Memoirs*, 140; Morris, *Recollections*, 5, 7, 38, 45–6, 52–3, 95; Perry, *Recollections*, 31–2.

128. Rogers, *British Army*, 97–8; Fischer, *Washington's Crossing*, 420; Anderson, *War and Society*, 107–8; Holmes, *Redcoat*, 95–7, 249–52, 261–2; Forrest, *Conscripts*, 6–7; Blanning, *French Revolutionary Wars*, 208. See, for example, Melville, *Mémoires*, 31; Laukhard, *Magister Laukhards leben*, 2:73–83.

129. See Harari, *Special Operations*, 163–83. For other examples, see Anderson, *War and Society*, 64, 108.

130. Harris, *Recollections*, 72–105, 113–17.

131. The most famous account of this campaign was Caulaincourt's *Mémoires*. But other contemporary accounts, including the memoirs of senior commanders, also focused on the miseries of the common soldiers. See, for example, the memoirs of the duke of Montesquiou-Fezensac; and Vossler, *With Napoleon in Russia*.

132. Holmes, *Redcoat*, 249. See also Best, *War and Society*, 33, 114, 147.

133. Skelley, *Victorian Army*; Hendrickson, 'Kinder, Gentler British Army'; Baly, *Florence Nightingale*; Goldie, *I Have Done My Duty*. See also Holmes, *Redcoat*, 89–90, 95–7; Forrest, *Napoleon's Men*, 63–6; Paret, *Yorck*, 54; Paret, *Clausewitz*, 47; Cuthbertson, *System*, 52–64. See the memoirs of General George Bell (*Soldier's Glory*) for a heart-rending description of the misery of the common soldiers during the siege of Sebastopol. General Bell's narrative is also notable for his attacks on the British government, on the army's 'red tape,' and on apathetic rear-echelon bureaucrats whom he blames for the soldiers' suffering (see, for example, Bell, *Soldier's Glory*, 268).

134. Lynn, *Bayonets*, 282–3; Burroughs, 'Crime,' 548–50, 571; Paret, *Yorck*, 127–9, 134–5, 218–19; Bertaud, *Army*, 127–32. The new magic circle worked unevenly across Europe, and with various fits and starts. In Britain in particular, the old vicious circle continued to function throughout much of the nineteenth century (Burroughs, 'Crime,' 548–50; Dinwiddy, 'Campaign,' 322).

135. Paret, *Imagined Battles*, 114. See also Brosman, *Visions of War*, 41–2.

136. For example, see the narratives of Bernal Díaz del Castillo, Francisco Balbi de Correggio, François de Rabutin, and Elis Gruffydd. See Harari, 'Military Memoirs.'

137. I chose to group the narratives of junior officers together with those of the privates and NCOs because previous to 1750, all of these three groups wrote and published very few memoirs, whereas after 1750 the memoirs published by junior officers resembled those published by their subordinates far more than they resembled those published by their superiors. I chose to term these narratives collectively as 'subaltern narratives' due to the double meaning of the word "subaltern." Today in academe it denotes the lowest ranks in any hierarchy, and connotes the theories of 'subaltern studies.' Around 1800, 'subaltern' was first and foremost a military rank, denoting all officers below the rank of captain (in 1825 Lieutenant George Robert Gleig published his memoirs of service in the Napoleonic Wars, titling the book simply *The Subaltern*). The present book argues that the memoirs of subaltern soldiers – whether subaltern officers, NCOs, or common soldiers – were amongst the first and most successful examples of how a subaltern group can utilize the new importance of feelings and experiences to destabilize hegemonic narratives and thrust its own narratives into the heart of the cultural and political consensus.

138. Denby, *Sentimental Narrative*; Knott, 'Sensibility,' 26.

139. Fabian, *Unvarnished Truth*; Thomas, *Romanticism and Slave Narratives*; Ellis, *Politics of Sensibility*, 44; Knott, 'Sensibility,' 36.

140. Bräker, *Life Story*, 4.

141. Manceron, *Twilight*, 256.

142. Harari, 'Military Memoirs.'

143. Forrest, *Napoleon's Men*, ix–x, 34–40.

144. Fischer, *Washington's Crossing*, 21.

145. Suvorov, *A. V. Suvorov. Dokumenty*, 1:112–13; Duffy, *Army of Maria Theresa*, 58; Cuthbertson, *System*, 6.

146. Cuthbertson, *System*, 10. See also Shipp, *Memoirs*, 80.

147. *Vicissitudes*, v–vi. For contemporary justifications of subalterns writing and publishing their memoirs, see also Mämpel, *Young Rifleman's Comrade*, xiii–xv; Barsewisch, *Von Rossbach bis Freiberg*, 5–12; Küster, *Des Preuß*; Morris, *Recollections*, xiii; Fernyhough, *Military Memoirs*, v–vi; Blakeney, *Boy*, xi–xii; Campbell, *Memoirs*, 1:1–2. On Napoleonic memoirs see also Forrest, *Napoleon's Men*.

6 The rise of the revelatory interpretation of war

1. Küster, *Des Preussischen Staabsfeldpredigers Küster*, xxii–xxiii.

2. Quoted in Krimmer, 'Transcendental Soldiers,' 100.

3. Graydon, *Memoirs*, 146.

4. Blakiston, *Twelve Years*, 1:17.

5. It should again be noted that "nerves," which like "feelings" are today often associated with the mental sphere, were more corporeal phenomena around 1800.

6. Quoted in Holmes, *Redcoat*, 260–1.

7. Muir, *Tactics*, 49.
8. Ibid., 113.
9. Clausewitz, *On War*, 1.3, ed. Howard and Paret, 104.
10. Ibid., 106.
11. Blaze, *Military Life*, 102.
12. Shipp, *Memoirs*, 106–7.
13. See also Gleig, *Subaltern*, 285.
14. Malcolm, 'Reminiscences,' 256–7.
15. Tolstoy, *Sebastopol*, 203.
16. For other analyses of fear and courage see Blaze, *Military Life*, 46–7, 99–100; Muir, *Tactics*, 217; Durova, *Cavalry Maiden*, 41–2, 105; Friederich, *Abenteuer*, 135; La Colonie, *Mémoires*, 274–7.
17. Quoted in Gat, *Development*, 33.
18. Gat, *Development*, 28–34.
19. Bräker, *Arme Mann*, 83; Bräker, *Life Story*, 130.
20. Morris, *Recollections*, 95.
21. Campbell, *Memoirs*, 1:65.
22. Vossler, *With Napoleon in Russia*, 93. See also Marbot, *Memoirs*, 1:90.
23. Thomson, *Memoirs*, v. For sentimental descriptions of misery see, for example, Thomson, *Memoirs*, 9–13.
24. Montesquiou-Fezensac, *Russian Campaign*, 128.
25. Shipp, *Memoirs*, 227.
26. Ibid., 122. See also Ibid., 239, 277, 308, 356–9, 365; Durova, *Cavalry Maiden*, 52; Harris, *Recollections*, 72; Pelet, *French Campaign*, 221.
27. Shipp, *Memoirs*, 277.
28. Ibid., 296.
29. Ibid., 304. See also Ibid., 223–4, 232, 356–7; Gleig, *Subaltern*, 7–19, 253–5; Blaze, *Military Life*, 206–7; Blakiston, *Twelve Years*, 1:146–7; Harris, *Recollections*, 20–1, 62–5, 87–8; *Memoirs of a Sergeant*, 19, 114, 150–1; Butler, *Narrative*, 1st edition, 182; Friederich, *Abenteuer*, 143; Martin, *At the Front*, 76; Montesquiou-Fezensac, *Russian Campaign,* 104–7; Blennie, *Narrative*, 15; Pelet, *French Campaign*, 465–8.
30. Most notably, military memoirs which double as travel memoirs to exotic places, such as Bernal Díaz's history of the conquest of Mexico.
31. Quoted in Blanning, *French Revolutionary Wars*, 91.
32. See also Brosman, *Visions of War*, 37–8.
33. See Gleig, *Subaltern*, 33.
34. Quoted in Paret, *Clausewitz*, 34.
35. Barsewisch, *Von Rossbach bis Freiberg*, 212.
36. Pindar, *Autobiography*, 20–1.
37. Shipp, *Memoirs*, 179–80. See also ibid., 55–6, 169, 176–7; Laverack, *Methodist Soldier*, 47–8, 187–91; Woelfel, 'Memoirs,' 561–2; Pelet, *French Campaign*, 312–13.
38. For other such descriptions see in particular Gleig, *Subaltern*; Malcolm, 'Reminiscences.' Both appear at times to be Romantic tourist guides to the Pyrenees rather than an account of military campaigns.
39. Florange, *Mémoires*, 1:177.
40. Ibid., 2:158–9.
41. McMahon, *Pursuit*, 271–2.

42. See Fischer, *Washington's Crossing*.
43. See, for example, the memoirs of Montesquiou-Fezensac (e.g., Montesquiou-Fezensac, *Russian Campaign*, 104–5).
44. See also Brosman, *Visions of War*, 73–4.
45. Campbell, *Memoirs*, 1:47. Compare Marbot, *Memoirs*, 1:4.
46. Bourgogne, *Memoirs*, 92–3.
47. Ibid., 273.
48. Shipp, *Memoirs*, 34–5.
49. Bräker, *Arme Mann*, 72–84.
50. *Memoirs of a Sergeant*, 13–14.
51. See also Hülsen, *Unter Friedrich dem Grossen*, 11–21; Blaze, *Military Life*, 8–18; Woelfel, 'Memoirs,' 555–61; Holmes, *Redcoat*, 275–8; Marbot, *Memoirs*, 1:38–43.
52. Compare Burke's thoughts on the power of "novel" experiences: Burke, *Philosophical Enquiry*, 31.
53. Pindar, *Autobiography*, 26–7.
54. Ibid., 27–8.
55. Bell, *Soldier's Glory*, 12.
56. Blakiston, *Twelve Years*, 1:130. See also Malcolm, 'Reminiscences,' 247, 258; Morris, *Recollections*, 13.
57. Durova, *Cavalry Maiden*, 38. See also Blakeney, *Boy*, 9; Campbell, *Memoirs*, 1:24–8; *Memoirs of a Sergeant*, 28; Friederich, *Abenteuer*, 135; Cavalier, *Memoirs*, 45; Gleig, *Subaltern*, 5, 33–4; Mämpel, *Young Rifleman's Comrade*, 39; Forrest, *Napoleon's Men*, 112–14; Perry, *Recollections*, 9–11; Martin, *At the Front*, 56.
58. On Stendhal's *Charterhouse of Parma* see Brosman, *Visions of War*, 94–8.
59. Stendhal, *Charterhouse of Parma*, 49.
60. Ibid., 58.
61. Ibid., 67.
62. Ibid., 78.
63. Schiller, *Wallenstein*, 'Wallenstein's Death,' Act 2, Scene 3, trans. Lamport, 354.
64. Gleig, *Subaltern*, 50–1. See also Malcolm, 'Reminiscences,' 249–50, 255–6; Blakiston, *Twelve Years*, 2:202–5.
65. Bruford, *German Tradition*, 25.
66. Shipp, *Memoirs*, 106–7.
67. Blaze, *Military Life*, 103.
68. Pelet, *French Campaign*, 190.
69. Malz, 'Kriegs- und Friedensbilder,' 36–7. See also Marbot, *Memoirs*, 1:265–9; Malz, 'Kriegs- und Friedensbilder,' 28–9; Barsewisch, *Von Rossbach bis Freiberg*, 45–7; Shipp, *Memoirs*, 123–4; Malcolm, 'Reminiscences,' 297–8; Campbell, *Memoirs*, 1:63–6.
70. Tolstoy, *War and Peace*, ed. Edmonds, 1:215–17.
71. Collins, *Revolutionary Soldier*, 55–6.
72. Marbot, *Memoirs*, 2:327–8.
73. Durova, *Cavalry Maiden*, 141. See also *Memoirs of a Sergeant*, 127; Roberts, *Memoirs*, 58; Harris, *Recollections*, 38; Heath, *Life*, 14; Blatchford, *My Life*, 111; Muir, *Tactics*, 164–5.
74. Malcolm, 'Reminiscences,' 297.

75. Blennie, *Narrative*, 44. See also Green, *Vicissitudes*, 3.
76. Blakeney, *Boy*, 1–2.
77. Tolstoy, *War and Peace*, ed. Edmonds, 1:163.
78. The macabre was still a vibrant cultural stream in the eighteenth century, but within civilian culture it had a far less prominent position than in previous centuries (Jones, *Revolution*, 92–7).
79. Melville, *Mémoires*, 90–5; Melville, *Memoirs*, 123–6.
80. Bourgogne, *Memoirs*, 142.
81. On the pathetically sublime see Schiller, 'On the Sublime,' 42–4.
82. *Memoirs of a Sergeant*, 29.
83. Vossler, *With Napoleon in Russia*, 67.
84. Malcolm, 'Reminiscences,' 252.
85. Majendie, *Up Among the Pandies*, 111.
86. Bell, *Soldier's Glory*, 248. See also ibid., 239–40.
87. Martin, *At the Front*, 67.
88. Mason, *Primitive Methodist Soldier*, 156. For other wake-of-battle descriptions see also Campbell, *Memoirs*, 29; Collins, *Revolutionary Soldier*, 52–4; Gleig, *Subaltern*, 85–9, 184–5; Blennie, *Narrative*, 49; Deane, *Journal*, 15; *Journal of an Officer*, 157–8; *Memoirs of a Sergeant*, 72; Morris, *Recollections*, 82; Barrès, *Souvenirs*, 51, 80; Ammon, *Leben Dr. Christian Nagel's*, 158–9; Forrest, *Napoleon's Men*, 116–17; Durova, *Cavalry Maiden*, 44; Malcolm, 'Reminiscences,' 279; Blakiston, *Twelve Years*, 1:110, 178–9; Bishop, *Life*, 214–15; Pearson, *Soldier*, 71–2.
89. See, for example, Shaw, 'Introduction,' 3–5.
90. Forrest, *Napoleon's Men*, 19.
91. O'Brien, 'Propaganda and the Republic of Arts.'
92. Cru, *War Books*, 18.
93. Similar in many respects to the wake-of-battle scenes were the military hospital scenes. They too gave Romantic memoirists ample opportunities to describe pathetic and sublime events, and to comment on the nature of war from an authoritative position. See, for example, Blennie, *Narrative*, 110–19; Blakiston, *Twelve Years*, 2:257–61; Brandt, *In the Legions of Napoleon*, 51–2; Malz, 'Kriegs- und Friedensbilder,' 38–9; *Memoirs of a Sergeant*, 170–3; Blaze, *Military Life*, 98–9; Green, *Vicissitudes*, 39–40, 75–7, 194–9; Malcolm, 'Reminiscences,' 300–5.
94. See in particular Haggerty, *Men in Love*. See also Hunt and Jacob, 'Affective Revolution'; Schenk, *Mind*, 158–62.
95. On comradeship see also Knott, 'Sensibility,' 31–2, 35; Muir, *Tactics*, 200; Duffy, *Military Experience*, 97, 122, 131.
96. Muir, *Tactics*, 57.
97. Schiller, *Wallenstein*, 'Wallenstein's Death,' Act 3, Scene 10, trans. Lamport, 386. See also Pelet, *French Campaign*, 113–14, 313, 370.
98. Stendhal, *Charterhouse of Parma*, 54.
99. This was an ancient trope, going back to the story of Joseph and Jacob. It was occasionally employed even by early modern memoirists (see, for example, Coxere, *Adventures by Sea*, 28; Contreras, *Discurso*, 133).
100. Bräker, *Arme Mann*, 98; Bräker, *Life Story*, 146.
101. Laverack, *Methodist Soldier*, 27–8. See also *Memoirs of a Sergeant*, 177–8; Holmes, *Redcoat*, 415–16; Harris, *Recollections*, 120–1; Fox, *Adventures*, 228.

102. For an illuminating discussion of such language, see Lamb, 'Sterne.'
103. Fischer, *Washington's Crossing*, 208.
104. Butler, *Narrative*, 1st edition, 171.
105. Ibid., 192.
106. Nettelbeck, *Abenteuerliches Lebensbild*, 324–5.
107. Quoted in Faust, 'Christian Soldiers,' 84. See also Ammon, *Leben Dr. Christian Nagel's*, 266; Shipp, *Memoirs*, 54, 88, 119; Gleig, *Subaltern*, 14, 177; Green, *Vicissitudes*, 77–8, 193; Harris, *Recollections*, 24; Barrès, *Souvenirs*, 26, 96; Bräker, *Arme Mann*, 83; Thomson, *Memoirs*, 20; Fox, *Adventures*, 119; Blaze, *Military Life*, 8, 22; Gleig, *Subaltern*, 49; Pearson, *Soldier*, 26; Montesquiou-Fezensac, *Russian Campaign*, 86, 104, 127; Roberts, *Memoirs*, 74.
108. Deane, *Journal*, 20–1.
109. Bishop, *Life*, 232–3. See also Bishop, *Life*, 274.
110. *Memoirs of a Sergeant*, 215–16. See also Blakeney, *Boy*, xi–xii.
111. See Blaze, *Military Life*, 49, 111–12.
112. Ibid., 94.
113. Ibid., 94–5.
114. Ibid., 56.
115. Brandt, *In the Legions of Napoleon*, 41.
116. Coleridge, "Fears in Solitude," lines 104–121, in *Poetical Works*, ed. Campbell, 129.
117. Clausewitz, *On War*, 1.4, ed. Howard and Paret, 113–14.
118. Clausewitz, *On War*, 1.5, ed. Howard and Paret, 115.
119. On the "Newtonian" approach to war see Gat, *Origins*, 13–135. In particular 25–53, 80–3; Paret, 'Genesis of *On War*,' 10–11. On the reaction to this approach see Gat, *Origins*, 139–55.
120. On Clausewitz's aversion to "Newtonian" war theories, see Clausewitz, *On War*, 'Author's Preface,' ed. Howard and Paret, 61–2; Clausewitz, *On War*, 1.1.6, 1.1.21–2, ed. Howard and Paret, 78, 86; Paret, 'Genesis of *On War*,' 6, 14. On Clausewitz as a Romantic thinker, see Gat, *Origins*, 156–250; Paret, *Clausewitz*, 84; Paret, 'Genesis of *On War*,' 14–15.
121. On Clausewitz's friction, see Clausewitz, *On War*, 1.1.18–21, 1.4–1.7, ed. Howard and Paret, 84–6, 113–22; Paret, 'Genesis of *On War*,' 16–18; Paret, *Yorck*, 213, 316; Houlding, *Fit for Service*, 2–3. Compare Blaze, *Military Life*, 109.
122. Paret, *Yorck*, 213–16.
123. Clausewitz, *On War*, 1.7, ed. Howard and Paret, 119.
124. Romantics in general feared and deplored the boredom of everyday life. Sublime experiences were often sought as an antidote to this boredom: Weiskel, *Romantic Sublime*, 18.
125. See also Brosman, *Visions of War*, 3–5.
126. Pindar, *Autobiography*, 9.
127. Durova, *Cavalry Maiden*, 125–6. Compare the scene in *Wallenstein's Camp* where a young bourgeois enlists in the army: Schiller, *Wallenstein*, "Wallenstein's Camp," Act 1, Scene 7, trans. Lamport, 189–192. See also Malcolm, 'Reminiscences,' 235, 261; Woelfel, 'Memoirs,' 569. For the development of this attitude in the twentieth century, see Herf, *Reactionary Modernism*, 70–106.

128. Ammon, *Leben Dr. Christian Nagel's*, 54–5; Ammon, *Soldier of Freedom*, 23–4.
129. Ammon, *Leben Dr. Christian Nagel's*, 67; Ammon, *Soldier of Freedom*, 28–31.
130. Ammon, *Leben Dr. Christian Nagel's*, 68–89; Ammon, *Soldier of Freedom*, 31.
131. Ammon, *Leben Dr. Christian Nagel's*, 71; Ammon, *Soldier of Freedom*, 32.
132. Ammon, *Leben Dr. Christian Nagel's*, 74–6; Ammon, *Soldier of Freedom*, 33–4.
133. Ammon, *Leben Dr. Christian Nagel's*, 77; Ammon, *Soldier of Freedom*, 35.
134. Ammon, *Leben Dr. Christian Nagel's*, 78; Ammon, *Soldier of Freedom*, 35.
135. Ammon, *Leben Dr. Christian Nagel's*, 80–1.
136. Ibid., 83.
137. Ammon, *Leben Dr. Christian Nagel's*, 87; Ammon, *Soldier of Freedom*, 40–1.
138. Ammon, *Leben Dr. Christian Nagel's*, 91–2; Ammon, *Soldier of Freedom*, 43.
139. Ammon, *Leben Dr. Christian Nagel's*, 92–3; Ammon, *Soldier of Freedom*, 44.
140. Ammon, *Leben Dr. Christian Nagel's*, 98; Ammon, *Soldier of Freedom*, 46.
141. Ammon, *Leben Dr. Christian Nagel's*, 101; Ammon, *Soldier of Freedom*, 49.
142. Ammon, *Leben Dr. Christian Nagel's*, 106; Ammon, *Soldier of Freedom*, 51.
143. Schiller, *Wallenstein*, "Wallenstein's Camp." Act 1, Scene 6, trans. Lamport, p. 184.
144. Ammon, *Leben Dr. Christian Nagel's*, 120; Ammon, *Soldier of Freedom*, 59.
145. Ammon, *Leben Dr. Christian Nagel's*, 124–5; Ammon, *Soldier of Freedom*, 61.
146. Ammon, *Leben Dr. Christian Nagel's*, 137–8; Ammon, *Soldier of Freedom*, 67–8.
147. Ammon, *Leben Dr. Christian Nagel's*, 143; Ammon, *Soldier of Freedom*, 72.
148. Ammon, *Leben Dr. Christian Nagel's*, 166–9; Ammon, *Soldier of Freedom*, 84–5.
149. Ammon, *Leben Dr. Christian Nagel's*, 173; Ammon, *Soldier of Freedom*, 85–6.
150. Ammon, *Leben Dr. Christian Nagel's*, 180; Ammon, *Soldier of Freedom*, 89.
151. Ammon, *Leben Dr. Christian Nagel's*, 198; Ammon, *Soldier of Freedom*, 100. On his introduction of gymnastics to Cleve, see Ammon, *Leben Dr. Christian Nagel's*, 198–208.
152. See Brewer, *Greek War*, 137–9, 153.
153. Ammon, *Leben Dr. Christian Nagel's*, 310; Ammon, *Soldier of Freedom*, 143.
154. Brewer, *Greek War*, 149–51.
155. Ammon, *Leben Dr. Christian Nagel's*, 316; Ammon, *Soldier of Freedom*, 145.
156. Ammon, *Leben Dr. Christian Nagel's*, 320; Ammon, *Soldier of Freedom*, 147.
157. Ammon, *Leben Dr. Christian Nagel's*, 318; Ammon, *Soldier of Freedom*, 146.
158. Ammon, *Leben Dr. Christian Nagel's*, 323; Ammon, *Soldier of Freedom*, 148.
159. See, for example, Ben-Yehuda, *1948*, 358–9.
160. Pelet, *French Campaign*, 249.
161. Harris, *Recollections*, 106.
162. Bishop, *Life*, 273.
163. Fischer, *Washington's Crossing*, 334.
164. Martin, *At the Front*, 122. See also Pindar, *Autobiography*, 168; Marbot, *Memoirs*, 2:267; Muir, *Tactics*, 274; Forrest, *Napoleon's Men*, 133–4.
165. For the notion that such reactions are natural and universal, see Faust, 'Christian Soldiers.'
166. Winter, *Sites of Memory*, 2–5, 54–69, 161–5, 217–21; Schweitzer, *Cross and Trenches*, xix–xx; Becker, *War and Faith*, 2.
167. The following paragraphs also rely on Juster, ' "In a Different Voice." '

168. Davies, *Methodism*, 97–8.
169. See in particular Taves, *Fits, Trances, & Visions*. See also Outram, *Enlightenment*, 34; Jones, *Revolution*, 88–90; Watson, 'Religion,' 38–40.
170. Watkins, *Soldiers*, 14. For the interest Methodism showed in converting soldiers, and for the central role soldiers played in the spread of Methodism around the world, see Watkins, *Soldiers*, 1–194; Male, *Scenes*.
171. Haime, *Short Account*, 15–23; Watkins, *Soldiers*, 26–46.
172. Watkins, *Soldiers*, 23.
173. Butler, *Narrative*, 4th edition, vii–viii.
174. Haime, *Short Account*, 6–9.
175. Ibid., 11–12.
176. Ibid., 25.
177. Figley, *Stress Disorders*, 4–5.
178. Haime, *Short Account*, 27–8.
179. Downing, *Narrative*, 44–5. See also Downing, *Narrative*, 31–2.
180. Downing, *Narrative*, 78. See also Downing, *Narrative*, 7–8.
181. Ibid., 100–4.
182. *Memoirs of a Sergeant*, 35.
183. Ibid., 179, 184, 223–5, 248–57.
184. Ibid., 35–37. See also Ibid., 106.
185. Blennie, *Narrative*, 1.
186. Ibid., 38. For more examples of this cycle, see Blennie, *Narrative*, 31, 46–48, 53–54, 59, 67, 86–88, 92–93, 110, 140–41. For a similar account of promising to mend one's ways under the influence of immanent danger, and forgetting the promises later on, see Roberts, *Memoirs*, 94–96.
187. Blennie, *Narrative*, 98–100.
188. Ibid., 106.
189. Ibid., 143–4.
190. Ibid., 118.
191. Ibid., 146.
192. Ibid., 141.
193. For other narratives that display similar characteristics, see Laverack, *Methodist Soldier*; Mason, *Primitive Methodist Soldier*; Butler, *Narrative*. Watkins's *Soldiers* contain dozens of short conversion narratives of soldiers. The conversion is almost always attributed to preaching and reading, and never to combat. See also Dobbs, *Recollections*, 70–2.
194. Some stories of soldiers converting due to the experiences and pressures of battle appeared before 1850, but these seem to be the exception rather than the rule. See, for example, Shipp, *Memoirs*, 106, 114–15, 121.
195. Watkins, *Soldiers*, 6–7; Laverack, *Methodist Soldier*, vii; *Memoirs of a Sergeant*, 219; Faust, 'Christian Soldiers,' 68.
196. Tolstoy, *War and Peace*, ed. Edmonds, 2:1088–90.
197. Watson, 'Religion,' 51–3; Faust, 'Christian Soldiers,' 71–2. Faust's 'Christian Soldiers' is the best scholarly account of these revivals. For contemporary accounts see Jones, *Christ in Camp*; Bennett, *Narrative of the Great Revival*.
198. Watson, 'Religion,' 47–8.
199. Jones, *Christ in Camp*, 390. Whether there is any truth in this claim is irrelevant. The main point is that it was believed that war converted men.
200. Quoted in Watson, 'Religion,' 30.

201. Faust, 'Christian Soldiers,' 67. See also Muir, *Tactics*, 220.
202. Schweitzer, *Cross and Trenches*, xviii. See also Becker, *War and Faith*, 4.
203. Billingsley, *From the Flag to Cross*, 51–2, 179, 235, 227, 253.
204. Ibid., 51.
205. Ibid., 235. See also Billingsley, *From the Flag to Cross*, 224, 234.
206. See, for example, Billingsley, *From the Flag to Cross*, 184, 188, 239–40.
207. Ibid., 179.
208. Male, *Scenes*, 115–16.
209. See Schweitzer, *Cross and Trenches*, and Becker, *War and Faith*, for balanced researches of these claims. They quote not only numerous stories of men who were converted to various faiths by battle, but also a number of stories of men converted to humanism, agnosticism, atheism, and socialism. The latter stories illustrate the expectation that war would result in conversion just as much as the former.
210. Quoted in Becker, *War and Faith*, 23.
211. Voltaire, *Candide*, ch. 3, ed. Pomeau, 91.
212. Voltaire, *Candide*, ch. 4, ed. Pomeau, 96.
213. See also Shaffner, *Apprenticeship Novel*, 50–2; Hoffmeister, 'From Goethe's *Wilhelm Meister*,' 81–2.
214. Koepke, '*Bildung* and Transformation,' 231. See also Minden, *German Bildungsroman*, 5.
215. Schiller, *Robbers*, Act 3, Scene 2, trans. Lamport, 103.
216. Brewer, *Greek War*, 145–53.
217. Byron, *Don Juan*, canto 8:42, ed. Kroneneberger, 287.
218. Byron, *Don Juan*, canto 7:21, ed. Kroneneberger, 260.
219. Schenk, *Mind*, 8–14.
220. Hazlitt, *Complete Works*, 3:156.
221. Ibid., 12:135. See also Jones, *Radical Sensibility*, 14–15.
222. Löwy and Sayre, *Romanticism Against the Tide*, 19, 29–35.
223. Lermontov, *A Hero of Our Time*, 36.
224. Ibid., 37.
225. Another central example of military disillusionment narratives is Alfred de Vigny's *Servitude et grandeur militaries* (1835), which Vigny described as 'a sort of epic poem about disillusionment' (Brosman, *Visions of War*, 17).
226. Jones, *Revolution*, 79.
227. Compare Winter, *Sites of Memory*, 184.
228. Durova, *Cavalry Maiden*, 143–4.
229. Mämpel, *Young Rifleman's Comrade*, 17.
230. Ibid., 18–19.
231. Ibid., 19.
232. Ibid., 22.
233. Ibid., 22–3.
234. Ibid., 82–3.
235. Compare Fox, *Adventures*, 142–8.
236. Mämpel, *Young Rifleman's Comrade*, 135–6. For other examples of soldiers shooting themselves and committing suicide, see Durova, *Cavalry Maiden*, 89, 99.
237. Mämpel, *Young Rifleman's Comrade*, 287–8.

238. Blaze, *Military Life*, 203. For other disillusioned statements, see Durova, *Cavalry Maiden*, 32; Harris, *Recollections*, 110, 123–4; Fox, *Adventures*, 55; Vossler, *With Napoleon in Russia*, 24, 32–4, 44; Marbot, *Memoirs*, 1:76; Green, *Vicissitudes*, 49.
239. Majendie, *Up Among the Pandies*, 168–9. See also Gleig, *Subaltern*, 63–4.
240. Barrès, *Souvenirs*, 43; Barrès, *Memoirs*, 55.
241. Laukhard, *Magister Laukhards leben*, 2:49–50; Laukhard, *Allemand en France*, 85.
242. Eksteins, 'All Quiet on the Western Front,' 355–6.
243. Laukhard, *Magister Laukhards leben*, 2:73.
244. Ibid., 2:73–80. For other descriptions centering on material sensory miseries, see Forrest, *Napoleon's Men*, 148–53.
245. Graydon, *Memoirs*, 154, 211–12.
246. Parquin, *Napoleon's Army*, 126.
247. Marbot, *Memoirs*, 1:246. See also Ibid., 2:143.
248. Ibid., 1:315.
249. Stendhal, *Charterhouse of Parma*, 54.
250. Ibid., 75.
251. Friederich, *Abenteuer*, 119.
252. Ibid., 397.
253. Ibid., 546.
254. Ibid., 78.
255. Barrès, *Souvenirs*, 48–9; Barrès, *Memoirs*, 62. See also Laukhard, *Magister Laukhards leben*, 2:28–9, 32–3.
256. Bräker, *Arme Mann*, 85.
257. Ibid., 87; Bräker, *Life Story*, 134.
258. Bräker, *Arme Mann*, 90–5; Bräker, *Life Story*, 138–42.
259. Varnhagen, *Sketches*, 68.
260. Ibid., 72.
261. Ibid., 100.
262. Ibid., 100–1.
263. Ibid., 102–3.
264. Compare Leed, *No Man's Land*, 75–96. For recent narratives that express disillusionment primarily with the ideal of comradeship, see Lahav, *Go to Gaza*; Spivak, *Whose Golani?*; Neumann, *Good Soldier*; and the film *One of Us*.
265. Bourgogne, *Memoirs*, 80–1.
266. Ibid., 81.
267. Ibid., 86.
268. Ibid., 92.
269. Ibid., 130–1.
270. Faber du Faur, *With Napoleon*, plate 89.
271. Montesquiou-Fezensac, *Russian Campaign*, 104.
272. Vossler, *With Napoleon in Russia*, 93.
273. Ibid., 169.
274. Best, *War and Society*, 202.
275. In one respect, though, twentieth-century disillusioned memoirs were less extreme than their predecessors. Quite a few eighteenth-century and nineteenth-century memoirists took their disillusionment to its logical

conclusion, and deserted the army. Twentieth-century memoirists, even when expressing extreme disillusionment with the military effort, never took this step. A few, such as Siegfried Sassoon or Heller's Yossarian, contemplated desertion, but recoiled from the actual deed. Indeed, in most disillusioned twentieth-century memoirs, showing one's loyalty to the military effort was a necessary precondition for gaining the right to criticize it in theory.

276. See also Harari, 'Martial Illusions.'
277. Hitler, *Mein Kampf*, 165. Compare Crowther, *Kantian Sublime*, 20, 30.
278. Tolstoy, *Sebastopol*, 27.
279. Ibid., 26.
280. Ibid., 29–30.
281. Ibid., 90–3.
282. Ibid., 109–10.
283. Ibid., 139–40.
284. Ibid., 140–1.
285. Ibid., 148–9.
286. Ibid., 154.
287. Ibid., 162–3.
288. Ibid., 184.
289. Ibid., 197.
290. Ibid., 211.
291. Ibid., 223.
292. Ibid., 228.
293. The present chapter relies heavily on Bruhm, Gothic Bodies.
294. The following arguments are based mainly on Bruhm, *Gothic Bodies*, and O'Neal, *Authority of Experience*, 239–44.
295. Burke, *Philosophical Enquiry*, 40; Ryan, 'Physiological Sublime,' 275–7.
296. Kant, *Critique of Judgement* 2.28, trans. Meredith, 110–11. See also Crowther, *Kantian Sublime*, 8; Bruhm, *Gothic Bodies*, 17–18, 57.
297. Schiller, 'On the Sublime,' 29.
298. Ammon, *Leben Dr. Christian Nagel's*, 138.
299. Blaze, *Military Life*, 97. See also Barrès, *Souvenirs*, 150–1.
300. Harris, *Recollections*, 16–17.
301. Ibid., 41. See also Harris, *Recollections*, 49.
302. Marbot, *Memoirs*, 1:203.
303. Graydon, *Memoirs*, 269.
304. Gleig, *Subaltern*, 89.
305. Ibid., 114. See also Gleig, *Subaltern*, 194–5, 224–5.
306. Tolstoy, *Sebastopol*, 182. See also Tolstoy, *Sebastopol*, 15–16; Stendhal, *Charterhouse of Parma*, 50; Malcolm, 'Reminiscences,' 275, 279; Shipp, *Memoirs*, 58–9; Vossler, *With Napoleon in Russia*, 93; Durova, *Cavalry Maiden*, 125, 149.
307. Höss, *Death Dealer*, 48.
308. Ibid., 54.
309. Ibid., 55–6.
310. Ibid., 58.
311. Ibid., 82.
312. Ibid., 100.

313. Ibid., 162.
314. Ibid., 161.
315. Ibid., 126.
316. Ibid., 198.
317. See: http://www.nizkor.org/hweb/people/h/himmler-heinrich/posen/oct-04-43/ ausrottung-transl-nizkor.html

Conclusions: The things which make you know, 1865–2000

1. Kipling, *Five Nations*, 210–13.

Works Cited

Primary sources

Adam, Charles, and Paul Tannery (eds), *Oeuvres de Descartes*, 30 vols (Paris, 1969).

Adye, Stephen Payne, *A Treatise on Courts Martial* (London, 1785).

Adye, Stephen Payne, *An Essay on Military Punishments and Rewards* (London, 1785).

Ammon, Friedrich von, and Theodor Herold, *Das Leben Dr. Christian Samuel Gottlieb Ludwig Nagel's* (Cleve, 1829).

Ammon, Friedrich von, and Theodor Herold, *Soldier of Freedom: The Life of Dr. Christian Nagel 1787–1827*, trans. Gunther W. Nagel (San Francisco, 1968).

Atkyns, Richard, 'The Vindication of Richard Atkyns,' in: Peter Young and Norman Tucker (eds), *Richard Atkyns and John Gwyn* (Hamden, 1968).

The Autobiography of a Private Soldier, Showing the Danger of Rashly Enlisting (Sunderland, 1838).

Baeça, Pedro de, 'Carta que Pedro de Baeça escrivio a el marques de Villena sobre que le pidio un memorial de lo que por el avia fecho,' in: Real academia de la historia (ed.), *Memorial Historico Espanol: Coleccion de documentos, opusculos y antiguedades*, vol. 5 (Madrid, 1853), pp. 485–510.

Baillet, Adrien, *Vie de Monsieur Descartes*. Collection 'Grandeurs,' vol. 1 (Paris, 1946).

Balbi de Correggio, Francisco, *La Verdadera Relación de todo lo que el anno de M.D.LXV. ha succedido en la isla de Malta...* (Barcelona, 1568).

Barker, Thomas M., *The Military Intellectual and Battle: Raimondo Montecuccoli and the Thirty Years War* (Albany, 1975).

Barrès, Jean-Baptiste, *Memoirs of a French Napoleonic Officer*, ed. Maurice Barrès, trans. Bernard Miall (London, 1988 [1925]).

Barrès, Jean-Baptiste, *Souvenirs d'un officier de la Grande Armée*, ed. Maurice Barrès (Paris, 2004).

Barsewisch, Ernst-Friedrich Rudolf von, *Von Rossbach bis Freiberg 1757–1763: Meine Kriegs-Erlebnisse während des Siebenjährigen Krieges 1757–1763* (Krefeld, 1959 [1863]).

Bell, George, *Soldier's Glory; Being Rough Notes of an Old Soldier* (London, 1991 [1867]).

Bellay, Martin du, and Guillaume du Bellay, *Mémoires (1513–47)*, ed. V.-L. Bourrilly and F. Vindry, 4 vols (Paris, 1908–19).

Bennett, William W., *A Narrative of the Great Revival in the Southern Armies* (Philadelphia, 1877).

Ben-Yehuda, Netiva, *1948 – Between Calendars* (Jerusalem, 1981).

Ben-Yehuda, Netiva, *When the State of Israel Broke Out: A DocuNovel* (Jerusalem, 1991).

Berlichingen, Götz von, *The Autobiography of Götz von Berlichingen*, ed. H. S. M. Stuart (London, 1956).

Billingsley, A. S., *From the Flag to the Cross; or, Scenes and Incidents of Christianity in the War* (Philadelphia, 1872).

Bishop, Matthew, *The life and adventures of Matthew Bishop of Deddington in Oxfordshire. Containing an account of several actions by sea, battles and sieges by land,...from 1701 to 1711,...Written by himself* (London, 1744).

Blakeney, Robert, *A boy in the Peninsular war; the services, adventures and experiences of Robert Blakeney, subaltern in the 28th regiment; an autobiography*, ed. J. Sturgis (London, 1899).

Blakiston, John, *Twelve Years' Military Adventure in Three Quarters of the Globe, 1813–14 with the Portugese Caçadores*, 2 vols (London, 1829).

Bland, Humphrey, *A Treatise of Military Discipline; in which is laid down and explained the duty of the officer and soldier* (London, 1727).

Blatchford, Robert, *My Life in the Army* (London, 1915?).

Blaze, Elzéar, *Military Life under Napoleon*, trans. John R. Elting (Chicago, 1995).

Blennie, George, *Narrative of a Private Soldier in one of his Majesty's Regiments of Foot, Written by Himself* (Glasgow, 1820).

Bräker, Ulrich, *Der Arme Mann im Tockenburg* (Dortmund, 1985).

Bräker, Ulrich, *The Life Story and Real Adventures of the Poor Man of Toggenburg*, trans. Derek Bowman (Edinburgh, 1970).

Brandt, Heinrich von, *In the Legions of Napoleon: The Memoirs of a Polish Officer in Spain and Russia, 1808–1813*, ed. and trans. Jonathan North (London, 1999).

Bonet, Honoré, *The Tree of Battles of Honoré Bonet: An English version with introduction by G. W. Coopland; with a hitherto unpublished historical interpolation* (Liverpool, 1949).

Boswell, James, *Boswell's Life of Johnson*, ed. George Birkbeck Hill, 6 vols (Oxford, 1934).

Bourgogne, Adrien Jean Baptiste, *Memoirs of Sergeant Bourgogne (1812–1813)*, ed. J. W. Fortescue (London, 1930).

Boyvin, François de, *Mémoires*, in Michaud, *Nouvelle Collection*, ser. I, vol. 10, pp. 1–390.

Brantôme, Pierre de Bourdeille, seigneur de, *Oeuvres complètes de Pierre de Bourdeille, seigneur de Brantôme*, ed. Ludovic Lalanne, 10 vols (Paris, 1864–82).

Bueil, Jean de, *Le Jouvencel par Jean de Bueil suivi du commentaire de Guillaume Tringant*, ed. Camille Favre and Léon Lecestre, 2 vols (Paris, 1889).

Bunyan, John, 'Grace Abounding to the Chief of Sinners,' *The Pilgrim's Progress; Grace Abounding; and, A Relation of His Imprisonment*, ed. Edmund Venables, revised by Mabel Peacock, 2nd edition (Oxford, 1900).

Burke, Edmund, *A Philosophical Enquiry into the Origin of our Ideas of the Sublime and Beautiful*, ed. James T. Boulton (London, 1967).

Butler, Robert, *Narrative of the Life and Travels of Serjeant B____. Written by Himself*, 1st edition (Edinburgh & London, 1823).

Butler, Robert, *Narrative of the Life and Travels of Serjeant Butler. Written by Himself*, 4th edition (Edinburgh, 1855).

Byron, George Gordon Lord, *Don Juan*, ed. Louis Kroneneberger (New York, 1949).

Cabeza de Vaca, Alvar Núñez, *Naufragios y Comentarios* (Madrid, 1922).

Campbell, Sir James of Ardkinglass, *Memoirs*, 2 vols (London, 1832).

Campion, Henri de, *Mémoires*, ed. Marc Fumaroli (Paris, 1967).

Caputo, Philip, *A Rumor of War* (London, 1977).

Caulaincourt, Armand-Augustin-Louis de, duc de Vicence, *Mémoires du general de Caulaincourt Duc de Vicenza*, ed. Jean Hanoteau, 3 vols (Paris, 1933).

Cavalier, Jean, *Memoirs of the Wars of the Cevennes...* (Dublin, 1726).

Charny, Geoffroi de, The "Book of Chivalry" of Geoffroi de Charny: Text, Context, and Translation, ed. and trans. Richard W. Kaeuper and Elspeth Kennedy (Philadelphia, 1996).

Cholmley, Hugh, The Memoirs of Sir Hugh Cholmley (London, 1787).

Chouppes, Aymar, marquis de, Mémoires, ed. M.C. Moreau (Paris, 1861).

Clausewitz, Carl von, On War, ed. and trans. Michael Howard and Peter Paret (Princeton, 1989).

Coleridge, Samuel Taylor, Poetical Works, ed. James Dykes Campbell (London, 1903).

Collins, James Potter, A Revolutionary Soldier, ed. John M. Roberts (New York, 1979 [1859]).

Commynes, Philippe de, Mémoires, ed. B. de Mandrot, 2 vols (Paris, 1901–3).

Contreras, Alonso de, Discurso de mi vida, ed. Henri Ettinghausen (Madrid, 1988).

Coxere, Edward, Adventures by Sea, ed. E. H. W. Meyerstein (New York, 1946).

Crichton, Andrew, The Life and Diary of Lieut. Col. J. Blackader (Edinburgh, 1824).

Cummings, Delano, Moon Dash Warrior: The Story of an American Indian in Vietnam, a Marine from the Land of the Lumbee, ed. Mariana Novak and David Novak (Livermore, 1998).

Cuthbertson, Bennett, A System for the Complete Interior Management and Oeconomy of a Battalion of Infantry (Dublin, 1768).

Dalrymple, Campbell, A Military Essay Containing Reflections on the Raising, Arming, Cloathing [sic!] and Discipline of British Infantry and Cavalry (London, 1761).

Davidov, Denis, In the Service of the Tsar against Napoleon. The Memoirs of Denis Davidov, 1806–1814, ed. and trans. Gregory Troubetzkoy (London, 1999).

Davies, M. Bryn, 'Suffolk's Expedition to Montdidier 1523,' Bulletin of the Faculty of Arts. Fouad I University, 7 (1944), pp. 33–43.

Deane, John Marshall, A Journal of The Campaign in Flanders... 1708, ed. J. B. Deane ([n.p.], 1846).

Defoe, Daniel, Memoirs of a Cavalier (London, 1926).

Descartes, René, Discours de la méthode, ed. Frédéric de Buzon (Paris, 1991).

Desclot, Bernard, Llibre del rei en pere, in: Ferran Soldevila (ed.), Les Quatre Grans Cròniques (Barcelona, 1971), pp. 403–664.

Díaz del Castillo, Bernal, Historia Verdadera de la Conquista de la Nueva España, ed. Joaquín Ramírez Cabañas, 10th edition (Mexico, 1974 [1955]).

Didi-Huberman, Georges, Riccardo Garbetta, and Manuela Morgaine, Saint Georges et la dragon: Version d'une légende (Paris, 1994).

Dietz, Johann, Memoirs of a Mercenary, Being the Memoirs of Master Johann Dietz, Surgeon in the Army of the Great Elector and Barber to the Royal Court, ed. Mervyn Horder, trans. Bernard Miall (London, 1987).

Dilthey, Wilhelm, Introduction to the Human Sciences: An Attempt to Lay a Foundation for the Study of Society and History, trans. Ramon J. Betanzos (London, 1988).

Dilthey, Wilhelm, 'Friedrich Hölderlin,' in Poetry and Experience, ed. Rudolf A. Makkreel and Frithjof Rudi (Princeton, 1985), pp. 303–384.

Dobbs, John, Recollections of an Old 52nd Man (Staplehurst, 2000 [1863]).

Downing, James, A Narrative of the Life of James Downing, a Blind Man, Late a Private in His majesty's 20th Regiment of Foot, 3rd edition (London, 1815).

Du Causé de Nazelle, Jean Charles, Mémoires du temps de Louis XIV, ed. Ernest Daudet (Paris, 1899).

The Duke of Marlborough's new exercise of firelocks and bayonets... With instructions to preform [sic] *every motion by body foot and hand* (London, 1708).

Durova, Nadezhda Andreevna, *The Cavalry Maiden: Journals of a Russian Officer in the Napoleonic Wars*, ed. and trans. Mary Fleming Zirin (Bloomington and Indianapolis, 1988).

Edmundson, William, *A Journal of the Life, Travels, Sufferings and Labour of Love in the work of the ministry, of that worthy elder and faithful servant of Jesus Christ, William Edmundson, who departed this life...* (Dublin, 1820 [1715]).

Ehingen, Jörg von, *Reisen nach der Ritterschaft*, ed. Gabriele Ehrmann, 2 vols (Göppingen, 1979).

Emmerich, Andrew, *The Partisan in War: Or the Use of a Corps of Light Trops to an Army* ([s.l.]: 1789).

Enriquez de Guzmán, Alonso, *Libro de la vida y costumbres de Alonso Enriquez de Guzman*, ed. Hayward Keniston, *Biblioteca de autores españoles* 126 (Madrid, 1960).

Erasmus, Desiderius, 'The Handbook of the Militant Christian,' in: Desiderius Erasmus, *The Essential Erasmus*, ed. and trans. John P. Dolan (New York, 1983).

Erasmus, Desiderius, *In Praise of Folly* (London, 1951).

Erasmus, Desiderius, 'Military Affairs,' in: Desiderius Erasmus, *The Colloquies of Erasmus*, trans. N. Bailey (Glasgow, 1877).

Erasmus, Desiderius, 'The Soldier and the Carthusian,' in: Desiderius Erasmus, *The Colloquies of Erasmus*, trans. N. Bailey (Glasgow, 1877).

Ercilla y Zúñiga, Alonso de, *Primera, segunda, y tercera partes de la Araucana de don Alonso de Ercilla y çuñiga...* (Barcelona, 1592).

Faber du Faur, Christian Wilhelm von, *With Napoleon in Russia; The Illustrated Memoirs of Faber du Faur, 1812*, ed. and trans. Jonathan North (London, 2001).

Farquhar, George, 'The Recruiting Officer,' *The Recruiting Officer and Other Plays*, ed. William Myers (Oxford, 1995), pp. 159–242.

Felix's *Life of Saint Guthlac*, ed. and trans. Bertram Colgrave (Cambridge, 1985).

Fernyhough, Thomas, *Military Memoirs of Four Brothers, by the survivor* (London, 1829).

Florange, Robert III de la Marck, lord of, *Mémoires du Maréchal de Florange dit le Jeune Adventureux*, ed. Robert Goubaux and P.-André Lemoisne, 2 vols (Paris, 1913–24).

Fox, Ebenezer, *The Adventures of Ebenezer Fox in the Revolutionary War* (Boston, 1847).

Fox, Robert, *Eyewitness Falklands. A Personal Account of the Falklands Campaign* (London, 1982).

Foxe, John, *Foxe's Book of Martyrs*, ed. W. Grinton-Berry (New York, 1932).

Frederick II, King of Prussia, 'Eulogy on Julian Offray de la Mettrie,' in: Julian Offray de la Mettrie, *Man a Machine*, ed. Gertrude Carman Bussey (La Salle, Illinois, 1961), pp. 1–9.

Frederick II, King of Prussia, *Military Instructions from the Late King of Prussia to his Generals to which is added, Particular Instructions to the Officers of his Army, and especially those of the Cavalry*, trans. T. Foster, 3rd edition (London, 1797?).

Friederich, Johann Konrad, *Abenteuer unter fremden Fahnen. Erinnerungen eines deutschen Offiziers im Dienste Napoleons* (Berlin, 1990).

García de Paredes, Diego, *Breve Svma dela Vida y Hechos de Diego Garcia de Paredes la qual el mismo escriuio...*, in: Hernando Perez del Pulgar, *Chronica del gran capitan Gonçalo Hernandez de Cordova y Aguilar* (Alcala, 1584), pp. 165–67.

Givati, Moshe, *Three Births in September* (Tel Aviv, 1990 [Hebrew]).

Gledhill, Samuel, *Memoirs of Samuel Gledhill, 1719 to 1727. To which is prefixed a narrative of his life, by W.H. Chippindall* (Kendal, 1910).

Gleig, George Robert, *The Subaltern: A Chronicle of the Peninsular War* (London, 1825).

Goethe, J. W. von, 'Goetz von Berlichingen,' in: J. W. Goethe, *Ephigenia in Tauris; Torquato Tasso; Goetz von Berlichingen*, ed. Nathan Haskell Dole, trans. Anna Swanwick and Walter Scott (Boston, 1902), pp. 227–356.

Graydon, Alexander, *Memoirs of His Own Time. With Reminiscences of the Men and Events of the Revolution*, ed. John Stockton Littell (New York, 1969 [1846]).

Green, John, *Vicissitudes in a Soldier's life, by John Green, late of the 68th Durham Light Infantry* (Louth, 1827).

Grimmelshausen, Jacob Christoph von, *Mother Courage*, trans. Walter Wallich (London, 1965).

Grimmelshausen, Jacob Christoph von, *Der abenteurliche Simplicissimus Teutsch*, ed. Volker Meid (Stuttgart, 1996).

Guyon, Fery de, *Mémoires de Fery de Guyon*, ed. A.-P.-L. de Robaulx de Soumoy (Brussells, 1858).

Gwyn, John, 'The Military Memoirs of John Gwyn,' in: Peter Young and Norman Tucker (eds), *Richard Atkyns and John Gwyn* (Hamden, 1968).

Habig, Marion A. (ed.), *St. Francis of Assisi. Writings and Early Biographies. English Omnibus of the Sources for the Life of St. Francis* (Quincy, Ill., 1991).

Haime, John, *A Short Account of God's Dealings with Mr. John Haime* (London, 1785).

Harris, John, *Recollections of Rifleman Harris*, ed. Christopher Hibbert (Hamden, Connecticut, 1970).

Haynin, Jean de, *Mémoires de Jean, Sire de Haynin et de Louvignies, 1465–1477*, ed. D. D. Brouwers, 2 vols (Liège, 1905–1906).

Hazlitt, William, *The Complete Works*, ed. P. P. Howe, 21 vols (London, 1930–34).

Heath, William, *The Life of a Soldier; a poem, with 18 engravings* (London, 1823).

Heller, Joseph, *Catch-22* (New York, 1961).

Herman, Nicholas, *The Life of Nicolas Herman, a Native of Lorrain ...* (Edinburgh, 1727).

Herman, Nicholas, *The Practice of the Presence of God* (London, 1887).

Hexham, Henry, *The Principles of the Art Militarie; Practised in the Warres of the United Netherlands* (London, 1637).

Hitler, Adolf, *Mein Kampf*, trans. Ralph Manheim (Houghton, 1943).

Hodgson, John, *Memoirs of Captain John Hodgson, of Coalley-Hall, near Halifax* (Upton, 1994).

Hölderlin, Friedrich, *Hyperion, or, the Hermit in Greece*, trans. Willard R. Trask (New York, 1970).

Holsten, Hieronymus Christian von, *Kriegsabenteuer des Rittmeisters Hieronymus Christian von Holsten, 1655–1666*, ed. Helmut Lahrkamp (Wiesbaden, 1971).

Höss, Rudolph, *Death Dealer: The Memoirs of the SS Kommandant of Auschwitz*, ed. Steven Paskuly, trans. Andrew Pollinger (New York, 1992).

Housman, Laurence (ed.), *War Letters of Fallen Englishmen* (Philadelphia, PA, 2002).

Hülsen, Carl Wilhelm, *Unter Friedrich dem Grossen. Aus den Memoiren des Aeltervaters 1752–1773*, ed. H. Hülsen (Berlin, 1890).

Johnson, Samuel, *Political Writings*, ed. Donald J. Greene (New Haven, 1977).

Joinville, Jean de, *Vie de Saint Louis*, ed. J. Monfrin (Paris, 1995).

Jones, J. William, *Christ in Camp, or, Religion in Lee's Army* (Richmond, 1887).

Journal of an Officer of the King's German Legion, 1803–16 (London, 1827).

Jünger, Ernst, *The Storm of Steel: From the Diary of a German Storm-Troop Officer on the Western Front* (London, 1993).

Kane, Richard, *Campaigns of King William and Queen Anne; from 1689, to 1712. Also, a new system of military discipline...* (London, 1745).

Kant, Immanuel, *The Critique of Judgement*, trans. James Creed Meredith (Oxford, 1986).

Kerry, Charles (ed.), 'The Autobiography of Leonard Wheatcroft,' *Journal of the Derbyshire Archeological and Natural History Society* XXI (1899), 26–60.

Kipling, Rudyard, *The Five Nations* (London, 1923).

Kovic, Ron, *Born on the Fourth of July* (New York, 1976).

Küster, Carl Daniel, *Des Preussischen Staabsfeldpredigers Küster, Bruchstück seines Campagnelebens im siebenjährigen Kriege* (Braunschweig, 1998 [1791]).

Kutuzov, Mihail, *Dokumenty*, ed. L. G. Beskrovnyi, 5 vols (Moscow, 1950–1956).

La Colonie, Jean Martin de, *Mémoires*, ed. Anne-Marie Cocula (Paris, 1992).

La Mettrie, Julian Offray de, *Histoire naturelle de l'âme, traduite de l'anglais de M. Charp, par feu M. H** de l'académie des sciences* (La Haye, 1745).

La Mettrie, Julian Offray de, *Man a Machine*, ed. Gertrude Carman Bussey (La Salle, Ill., 1961).

La Mettrie, Julian Offray de, *Man a Machine and Man a Plant*, ed. Justin Lieber, trans. Richard A. Watson and Maya Rybalka (Cambridge, 1994).

La Mettrie, Julian Offray de, *L'Homme-machine*, in *Oeuvres Philosophiques*, ed. Francine Markovitz, 2 vols (Paris, 1987 [1751]), 1:63–118.

La Noue, François de, *Discours politiques et militaires*, ed. F. E. Sutcliffe (Geneva, 1967).

La Rochefoucauld, François de, *Maxims*, trans. Leonard Tancock (Harmondsworth, 1959).

Lahav, Shay, *Go to Gaza* (Tel Aviv, 2005 [Hebrew]).

Laukhard, Friedrich Christian, *Un Allemand en France sous la terreur: souvenirs de Frédéric-Christian Laukhard, 1792–1794*, ed. and trans. Wilhelm Bauer (Paris, 1915).

Laukhard, Friedrich Christian, *Magister F. Ch. Laukhards leben und schicksale von ihm selbst beschrieben*, ed. Viktor Petersen, 2 vols (Stuttgart, 1908).

Laverack, Alfred, *A Methodist Soldier in the Indian Army: His Personal Adventures and Christian Experience* (London, [s.d.]).

'Legend of the Three Companions,' in Habig, *St. Francis of Assisi*, pp. 853–956.

Lermontov, Mikhail, *A Hero of Our Time*, trans. Marian Schwartz (New York, 2004).

Leshem, Ron, *Beaufort* (Tel Aviv, 2005 [Hebrew]).

The Life and Adventures of Mrs. Christian Davies, commonly called Mother Ross (London, 1740).

Livius, Titus, *Ab Urbe Condita*, ed. Robert Seymour Conway and Charles Flamstead Walters, 5 vols (Oxford, 1960).

Llull, Ramon, *Ramon Lull's Book of Knighthood and Chivalry*, trans. William Caxton, rendered into modern English by Brian R. Price (Union City, 2002).

Loménie, Louis-Henri de, comte de Brienne, *Mémoires de Louis-Henri de Loménie, comte de Brienne, dit le jeune Brienne*, ed. Paul Bonnefon (Paris, 1916–19).

Loyd, Anthony, *My War Gone By, I Miss It So* (London, 1999).

Loyola, Saint Ignatius of, *The Autobiography of St. Ignatius Loyola*, ed. John C. Olin, trans. Joseph F. O'Callaghan (New York, 1974).

Loyola, Saint Ignatius of, *The Spiritual Exercises and Selected Works*, ed. George E. Ganss (New York, 1991).

Ludlow, Edmund, *The Memoirs of Edmund Ludlow, Lieutenant-General of the Horse in the Army of the Commonwealth of England, 1625–1672*, ed. C. H. Firth, 2 vols (Oxford, 1894).

Lupton, Donald, *Obiectorum Reductio or, Daily Imployment for the Soule. In Occasionall maditations upon severall Subjects* (London, 1634).

Lupton, Donald, *A Warre-like Treatise of the Pike* (London, 1642).

Lurting, Thomas, *The fighting sailor turn'd peaceable Christian: manifested in the convincement and conversion of Thomas Lurting* (London, 1766).

Machiavelli, Niccolò, *The Prince*, ed. and trans. Angelo M. Codevilla (New Haven, 1997).

Mackay, Hugh, *Memoirs of the war carried on in Scotland and Ireland, M.DC.LXXXIX.–M.DC.XCI.* (Edinburgh, 1833).

Majendie, Vivian Dering, *Up among the Pandies: or, A year's service in India* (Allahabad, 1974 [1859]).

Malcolm, John, 'Reminiscences of a Campaign in the Pyrenees and South of France,' in *Constable's Miscellany of Original and Selected Publications ....*, Memorials of the Late War, 2 vols (Edinburgh, 1828), 1:233–307.

Male, Arthur, *Scenes Through the Battle Smoke* (London [n.d.]).

Malz, R. (ed.), 'Kriegs- und Friedensbilder aus den Jahren 1754–1759. Nach dem Tagebuch des Leutnants Jakob Friedrich v. Lemcke 1738–1810,' *Preussische Jahrbücher*, CXXXVIII (Berlin, 1909), pp. 20–43.

Mämpel, Johan Christian, *The Young Rifleman's Comrade – A Narrative of his Military Adventures, Captivity and Shipwreck* (Philadelphia, 1827).

Maniement d'armes d'arquebuses, mousquetz, et piques En conformite de l'ordre de Monseigneur le Prince Maurice, Prince d'Orange ... Represente par figures par Jaques de Gheyn (Amsterdam, 1608).

Marbot, Jean-Baptiste-Antoine-Marcelin, Baron de, *The Memoirs of Baron de Marbot*, trans. Arthur John Butler, 2 vols (London, 1892).

Martin, William, *At the Front: A Record of a Soldier's Experiences in the Crimean War and Indian Mutiny, by One Who Was There* (Paisley, 1915 [1893]).

Martindale, Adam, *The Life of Adam Martindale, Written by Himself*, ed. Richard Parkinson, in: The Chetham Society (ed.), *Remains, Historical and Literary, Connected with the Palatine Counties of Lancaster and Chester*, vol. 4 ([s.l.], 1845).

Mason, William, *A Primitive Methodist Soldier in the British Army* (Leeds, 1877).

Melville, Andrew, *Mémoires* (Amsterdam, 1704).

Melville, Andrew, *Memoirs*, trans. Torick Ameer-Ali (London, 1918).

Memoirs of a Sergeant Late of the 43rd Light Infantry, previously to and during the Peninsular war, including an account of his conversion from Popery to the Protestant Religion (London, 1835).

Mergey, Jean de, *Mémoires militaires du Sieur de Mergey*, in: Michaud, *Nouvelle collection*, series 1, vol. 9 (1836).

Michaud, Joseph François and Jean Joseph Poujoulat (eds), *Nouvelle collection des mémoires pour servir à l'histoire de France, depuis le XIIIe siècle jusqu'à la fin du XVIIIe*, 3 series, 32 vols (Paris, 1836–1839).

Millner, John, *A compendious journal of all the marches [&c.] ... of the triumphant armies, of the ... confederate high allies, in their ... war against... France* (London, 1733).

The Military Discipline, wherein is most Martially shone the order of Drilling for the Musket and Pike (London? 1623 [1622]).

Monluc, Blaise de, *Commentaires de Blaise de Monluc, Maréchal de France*, ed. Paul Courteault, 3 vols (Paris, 1911–25).

Monro, Robert, *Monro his Expedition Vvith the Vvorthy Scots Regiment...* (London, 1637).

Montaigne, Michel De, *The Complete Essays*, ed. and trans. M. A. Screech (London, 1991).

Montesquiou-Fezensac, Raimond-Emery-Philippe-Josephe, Duc de, *The Russian Campaign, 1812*, trans. Lee Kennett (Athens, GA, 1970).

Morris, Thomas, *The Recollections of Sergeant Morris*, ed. John Selby (Moreton-in-Marsh, 1998 [1845]).

Muntaner, Ramon, *Crònica*, ed. Marina Gustà, 2 vols (Barcelona: Edicions 62, 1979).

Navailles, Montault de Bénac, Philippe de, duc de, *Mémoires du duc de Navailles et de La Valette, pair et marechal de France, et gouverneur de monseigneur le duc de Chartes* (Amsterdam, 1701).

Nettelbeck, Joachim, *Ein abenteuerliches Lebensbild von ihm selbst erzählt* (Greifswald zu Rudolstadt, 1953).

Neumann, Boaz, *Good Soldier* (Lod, 2001 [Hebrew]).

Parker, Robert, *Memoirs of the most Remarkable Military Transactions from the year 1683 to 1718* (Dublin, 1746).

Parker, Robert, *Military Memoirs of Marlborough's Campaigns, 1702–1712*, ed. David Chandler (London, 1998).

Parquin, Charles, *Napoleon's Army*, ed. and trans. B. T. Jones (London, 1969).

Pasek, Jan Chrystozom, *Memoirs of the Polish Baroque: The Writings of Jan Chrystozom Pasek, a Squire of the Commonwealth of Poland and Lithuania*, ed. and trans. Catherine S. Leach (Berkeley, 1976).

Pearson, Andrew, *The Soldier Who Walked Away: The Autobiography of Andrew Pearson, a Peninsular War Veteran*, ed. Arthur H. Haley (Woolton, 1987).

Peeke, Richard, *Three to One: being, an English-Spanish combat, performed by a western gentleman...* (London, 1626).

Pelet, Jean-Jacques, *The French Campaign in Portugal, 1810–1811*, ed. and trans. Donald D. Horward (Minneapolis, 1973).

Perry, David, *Recollections of an Old Soldier. The Life of Captain David Perry, a Soldier of the French and Revolutionary Wars* (Windsor, Vermont, 1822).

Pindar, John [Pseud. for Peter Leslie], *Autobiography of a Private Soldier* (Cupar-Fife, 1877).

Plessis-Besançon, Bernard du, *Mémoires de Du Plessis-Besançon*, ed. Horric de Beaucaire (Paris, 1892).

Pontis, Louis de, *Mémoires*, ed. Andrée Villard (Paris, 2000).

Poyntz, Sydenham, *The Relation of Sydnam Poyntz*, ed. A. T. S. Goodrick (London, 1908).

Puységur, Jacques de Chastenet, vicomte de Buzancy, seigneur de, *Les Mémoires de Jacques De Chastenet, Sr de Puysegur, donnez au public par Duchesne*, 2 vols (Paris, 1690).

Quevedo, Francisco de, *The Swindler*, in: Michael Alpert (ed. and trans.), *Two Spanish Picaresque Novels* (Harmondsworth, 1969).

Quincy, Joseph Sevin, comte de, *Mémoires du Chevalier de Quincy*, ed. Léon Lecestre, 3 vols (Paris, 1898–1901).

Raymond, Thomas, *The Autobiography of Thomas Raymond and Memoirs of the family of Guise of Elmore, Gloucestershire*, ed. G. Davies. *Camden Third Series*, vol. 28 (London, 1917).

Regulations for the Prussian infantry. Translated from the German original (London, 1754).

Remarque, Erich Maria, *All Quiet on the Western Front*, trans. A. W. Wheen (London, 1963).

Roberts, Lemuel, *Memoirs of Captain Lemuel Roberts* (Bennington, Vermont, 1809).

Rousseau, Jean-Jacques, *Émile, ou de l'éducation* (Paris, 1967).

Roy, Ian (ed.), *The Habsburg-Valois Wars and the French Wars of Religion* (London, 1971).

Rumyantsev, Piotr, *P. A. Rumyantsev, Dokumenty*, ed. P. K. Fortunatov, 2 vols, (Moscow, 1953–1959).

Saint-Simon, Louis de Rouvroy, Duke of, *Mémoires de Saint-Simon*, ed. A. de Boislisle, 45 vols (Paris, 1923–28).

Sajer, Guy, *The Forgotten Soldier. War on the Russian Front – A True Story*, trans. Lily Emmet (London: 2000).

Schertlin, Sebastian von Burtenbach, *Leben und Thaten des weiland wohledlen und gestrengen Herrn Sebastian Schertlin von Burtenbach*, ed. Ottmar F. H. Schönhuth (Münster, 1858).

Schiller, Friedrich, 'Concerning the Sublime,' in: Friedrich Schiller, *Essays*, ed. Walter Hinderer, trans. Daniel O. Dahlstrom (New York, 2001), pp. 70–85.

Schiller, Friedrich, 'On the Sublime,' in: Friedrich Schiller, *Essays*, ed. Walter Hinderer, trans. Daniel O. Dahlstrom (New York, 2001), pp. 22–44.

Schiller, Friedrich, 'The Robbers,' *The Robbers and Wallenstein*, trans. F. J. Lamport (Harmondsworth, 1979), pp. 21–160.

Schiller, Friedrich, 'Wallenstein,' *The Robbers and Wallenstein*, trans. F. J. Lamport (Harmondsworth, 1979), pp. 161–472.

Sterne, Laurence, *A Sentimental Journey through France and Italy* (London, 1941).

Severus, Sulpicius, *Vie de Saint Martin*, ed. Jacques Fontaine, 3 vols (Paris, 1967).

Shakespeare, William, *Henry V*, ed. Gary Taylor (Oxford, 1982).

Shipp, John, *Memoirs of the Extraordinary Military Career of John Shipp* (London, 1890 [1829]).

Simcoe, J. G., *A Journal of the Operations of the Queen's Rangers from the End of the Year 1777, to the Conclusion of the Late American War* (Exeter, 1787).

Sledge, Eugene B., *With the Old Breed At Peleliu and Okinawa* (Annapolis, Maryland, 1996 [1981]).

Slingsby, Henry, *Original memoirs written during the great Civil war, the life of sir H. Slingsby [written by himself] and memoirs of capt. Hodgson, with notes [by sir W. Scott. Followed by] Relations of the campaigns of Oliver Cromwell in Scotland, 1650* (Edinburgh, 1806).

Souvigny, Jean Gangnières, comte de, *Mémoires du Comte de Souvigny, Lieutenant Général des Armées du Roi*, ed. Ludovic de Contenson, 3 vols (Paris, 1906–09).

Spivak, Or, *Whose Golani?* (Jerusalem, 2001 [Hebrew]).

St. Bonaventure, 'Major Life of St. Francis,' in Habig, *St. Francis of Assisi*, pp. 627–787.

Stendhal, Marie-Henri Beyle, *The Charterhouse of Parma*, trans. C. K. Scott-Moncrieff (New York, 1962).

Suvorov, Aleksandr, *A. V. Suvorov. Dokumenty*, ed. G. P. Meshcheryakov, 4 vols (Moscow, 1949–1953).

Svetlova, R. V. (ed.), *Art of War – An Anthology of Military Thinking*, 2 vols (St. Petersburg, 2000 [Russian]).

Tarleton, Banastre, *A History of the Campaigns of 1780 and 1781, in the Southern Provinces of North America* (London, 1787).

Tavannes, Jean de Saulx, Viscount of, *Mémoires de tres-noble et tres-illustre Gaspard de Saulx, seigneur de Tavannes,* in: Michaud, *Nouvelle collection*, ser. 1, vol. 8 (1836), pp. 1–504.

Thomas of Celano, 'First Life of St. Francis,' in Habig, *St. Francis of Assisi*, pp. 225–355.

Thomas of Celano, 'Second Life of St. Francis,' in Habig, *St. Francis of Assisi*, pp. 357–543.

Thomson, William, *Memoirs of the late war in Asia: With a narrative of the imprisonment and sufferings of our officers and soldiers: by an officer of Colonel Baillie's detachment* (London, 1788).

Tolstoy, Leo, *Sebastopol*, ed. and trans. Frank D. Millet (Ann Arbor, 1961).

Tolstoy, Leo, *War and Peace*, trans. Rosemary Edmonds, 2 vols (Harmondsworth, 1957).

Verdugo, Francisco, *Commentario del coronel Francisco Verdugo de la guerra de Frisa*, ed. H. Lonchay (Brussels, 1899).

Vere, Francis, *The Commentaries of Sir Francis Vere*, in: Charles Harding Firth (ed.), *An English Garner. Stuart Tracts, 1603–1693* (Westminster, 1903), pp. 83–210.

Varnhagen von Ense, Karl August, *Sketches of German life, and Scenes from the War of Liberation in Germany*, trans. Alexander Duff Gordon (London, 1847).

La vida y hechos de Estebanillo de González, hombre de buen humor. Compuesto por él mismo (Antwerp, 1646).

Vicissitudes in the Life of a Scottish Soldier. Written by Himself (London, 1827).

Voltaire, *Candide, ou L'Optimisme*, ed. René Pomeau (Paris, 1959).

Voragine, Jacobus de, *The Golden Legend: Readings on the Saints*, trans. William Granger Ryan, 2 vols (Princeton, 1993).

Vossler, Heinrich August, *With Napoleon in Russia 1812: The Diary of Lt H. A. Vossler, a Soldier of the Grand Army 1812–1813*, trans. Walter Wallich (London, 1998).

Woelfel, Margarete (ed. and trans.), 'Memoirs of a Hessian Conscript: J. G. Seume's Reluctant Voyage to America,' *The William and Mary Quarterly*, 3rd series, 5:4 (1948), 553–70.

Yost, Don, *Blessings: Transforming my Vietnam Experience* (Kansas City, 1995).

Secondary sources

Aberth, John, *From the Brink of the Apocalypse: Confronting Famine, War, Plague, and Death in the Later Middle Ages* (New York, 2000).

Adams, John, *The Evolution of Educational Theory* (London, 1928).

Adams, Robert P., *The Better Part of Valor: More, Erasmus, Colet, and Vives, on Humanism, War, and Peace, 1496–1535* (Seattle, 1962).

Alker, Sharon, 'The Soldierly Imagination: Narrating Fear in Defoe's *Memoirs of a Cavalier*,' *Eighteenth-Century Fiction*, 19:1–2 (2006/7), 43–68.

Allmand, Christopher T., 'Entre honneur et bien commun: le témoignage du *Jouvencel* au XVe siècle,' *Revue Historique* 301:3 (1999), 463–81.

Allmand, Christopher (ed.), *Society at War: The Experience of England and France during the Hundred Years War*, 2nd edition (Rochester, 1998).

Almog, Joseph, *What am I? Descartes and the Mind-Body Problem* (Oxford, 2002).

Anderson, D. R., 'The Code of Honour and its Critics: The Opposition to Duelling in England, 1700–1850,' *Social History* 5:3 (Oxford, 1980), 409–34.

Anderson, M. S., *War and Society in Europe of the Old Regime 1618–1789* (Phoenix Hill, 1998 [1988]).

Anglo, Sydney (ed.), *Chivalry in the Renaissance* (Woodbridge, 1990).

Ariès, Philippe, *The Hour of Our Death*, trans. Helen Weaver (New York, 1981).

Asad, Talal, 'Notes on Body Pain and Truth in Medieval Christian Ritual,' *Economy and Society* 12 (1983), 287–327.

Ashfield, Andrew and Peter de Bolla (eds), *The Sublime: A Reader in British Eighteenth-Century Aesthetic Theory* (Cambridge, 1996).

Auwera, January Vander, 'Historical Fact and Artistic Fiction: The Face of the Eighty Years' War in Southern Netherlandish Paintings,' in: Bussmann and Schilling (eds), *1648*, 2:461–68.

Bächtiger, Franz, 'Marignano: Zum *Schlachtfeld* von Urs Graf,' *Zeitschrift fuer schweizerische Archaeologie und Kunstgeschichte*, 31 (1974), 31–54.

Baldick, Robert, *The Duel: A History of Duelling* (London, 1965).

Balfour, Ian, 'Torso: (The) Sublime Sex, Beautiful Bodies, and the Matter of the Text,' *Eighteenth-Century Studies*, 39:3 (2006), 323–36.

Baly, Monica E., *Florence Nightingale and the Nursing Legacy* (London, 1988).

Bambach, Charles R., *Heidegger, Dilthey, and the Crisis of Historicism* (Ithaca, 1995).

Barker-Benfield, G. J., *The Culture of Sensibility: Sex and Society in Eighteenth-Century Britain* (Chicago, 1992).

Barney, Richard A., *Plots of Enlightenment: Education and the Novel in Eighteenth-Century England* (Stanford, 1999).

Bawer, Bruce, *While Europe Slept: How Radical Islam is Destroying the West from Within* (New York, 2006).

Beaune, Colette, *The Birth of an Ideology: Myths and Symbols of Nation in Late-Medieval France*, ed. Fredric L. Cheyette, trans. Susan Ross Huston (Berkeley, 1991).

Becker, Anette, *War and Faith: The Religious Imagination in France, 1914–1930*, trans. Helen McPhail (Oxford, 1998).

Beddow, Michael, *The Fiction of Humanity: Studies in the Bildungsroman from Wieland to Thomas Mann* (Cambridge, 1982).

Beja, Morris, *Epiphany in the Modern Novel* (London, 1971).

Belkin, Kristin Lohse, and Carl Depauw, *Images of Death: Rubens Copies Holbein* (Antwerp, 2000).

Bell, David A., *The Cult of the Nation in France: Inventing Nationalism, 1680–1800* (Cambridge, MA, 2001).

Bell, Michael, *Sentimentalism, Ethics and the Culture of Feeling* (Houndmills, 2000).

Benedict, Barbara M., *Framing Feeling: Sentiment and Style in English Prose Fiction, 1745–1800* (New York, 1994).

Bergman, Samuel Hugo, *History of Philosophy*, 4 vols (Jerusalem, 1990 [Hebrew]).

Bernier, Marc André, *Libertinage et figure du savoir: Rhétorique et roman libertin dans la France des Lumières (1734–1751)* (Paris, 2001).

Bertaud, Jean-Paul, *The Army of the French Revolution*, trans. R. R. Palmer (Princeton, 1988).

Bérubé, Allan, *Coming Out Under Fire: The History of Gay Men and Women in World War Two* (New York, 1990).

Best, Geoffrey, *War and Society in Revolutionary Europe, 1770–1870* (London, 1982).

Bidney, Martin, *Patterns of Epiphany: From Wordsworth to Tolstoy, Pater, and Barrett Browning* (Carbondale, Illinois, 1997).

Billacois, Francois, *The Duel: Its Rise and Fall in Early Modern France*, ed. and trans. Trista Selous (New Haven, 1990).

Black, Jeremy, *European Warfare, 1494–1660* (London, 2002).

Black, Jeremy, 'Introduction,' in: Jeremy Black (ed.), *The Origins of War in Early Modern Europe* (Edinburgh, 1987), pp. 1–27.

Black, Jeremy, *War for America: The Fight for Independence, 1775–1783* (New York, 1994).

Black, Jeremy, *Why Wars Happen* (New York, 1998).

Blanco, Richard L., 'Attempts to Abolish Branding and Flogging in the Army of Victorian England before 1881,' *Journal of the Society for Army Research* xlvi (1968), 137–45.

Blanning, T. C. W., *The French Revolutionary Wars, 1787–1802* (London, 1996).

Bliese, John R. E., 'The Courage of the Normans: A Comparative Study of Battle Rhetoric,' *Nottingham Medieval Studies* 35 (1991), 1–26.

Bloch, Maurice, *Prey into Hunter: The Politics of Religious Experience* (Cambridge, 1992).

Bond, Brian, *The Unquiet Western Front. Britain's Role in Literature and History* (Cambridge, 2002).

Borque, José María Díez, 'Spanish Literature during the Thirty Years' War (1618–1648),' in: Bussmann and Schilling (eds), *1648*, 2:359–68.

Bour, Isabelle, 'Sensibility as Epistemology in *Caleb Williams*, *Waverley*, and *Frankenstein*,' *Studies in English Literature 1500–1900*, 45:4 (2005), 813–27.

Bourke, Joanna, *An Intimate History of Killing: Face-to-Face Killing in Twentieth-Century Warfare* (London, 1999).

Bowden, Mark, *Black Hawk Down: A Story of Modern War* (New York, 2001).

Bowen, Scarlet, ' "The Real Soul of a Man in her Breast": Popular Opposition and British Nationalism in Memoirs of Female Soldiers, 1740–1750,' *Eighteenth-Century Life*, 28:3 (2004), 20–45.

Braudy, Leo, *From Chivalry to Terrorism: War and the Changing Nature of Masculinity* (New York, 2003).

Breen, Jennifer and Mary Noble, *Romantic Literature* (London, 2002).

Brewer, David, *The Greek War of Independence* (Woodstock, 2001).

Brodsky, G. W. Stephen, *Gentlemen of the Blade: A Social and Literary History of the British Army Since 1660* (New York, 1988).

Brosman, Catharine Savage, *Visions of War in France: Fiction, Art, Ideology* (Baton Rouge, 1999).

Bruford, W. H., *The German Tradition of Self-Cultivation: 'Bildung' from Humboldt to Thomas Mann* (Cambridge, 1975).

Bruhm, Steven, *Gothic Bodies: The Politics of Pain in Romantic Fiction* (Philadelphia, 1994).

Brumwell, Stephen, *Redcoats: The British Soldier and War in the Americas, 1755–1763* (Cambridge, 2001).

Burroughs, Peter, 'Crime and Punishment in the British Army, 1815-1870,' *English Historical Review* 100:396 (1985), 545–71.

Büsch, Otto, *Military System and Social Life in Old Regime Prussia, 1713–1807*, trans. John G. Gagliardo (Atlantic Highlands, N. J., 1996).

Bussmann, Klaus and Heinz Schilling (eds), *1648: War and Peace in Europe*, 3 vols (Munster, 1999).

Bynum, Caroline Walker, 'The Blood of Christ in the Later Middle Ages,' *Church History* 71:4 (2002), 685–714.

Bynum, Caroline Walker, 'Why All the Fuss about the Body? A Medievalist's Perspective,' *Critical Inquiry* 22:1 (1995), 1–33.

Caldwell, Patricia, *The Puritan Conversion Narrative: The Beginnings of American Expression* (Cambridge, 1985).

Callot, Emile, *La philosophie de la vie au XVIIIe siecle: etudiee chez Fontenelle, Montesquieu, Maupertuis, La Mettrie, Diderot, d'Holbach, Linne* (Paris, 1965).

Caratini, Roger, *Jeanne d'Arc: de Domremy a Orleans et du bucher a la legende* (Paris, 1999).

Carlton, Charles, *Going to the Wars: The Experience of the British Civil Wars, 1638–1651* (London, 1992).

Cavalli-Björkman, Görel, 'The *Vanitas* Still Life: A Phenomenon of the Crisis of Consciousness,' in: Bussmann and Schilling (eds), *1648*, 2:501–507.

Cerwin, Herbert, *Bernal Díaz: Historian of the Conquest* (Norman, 1963).

Chiarini, Marco, 'The Thirty Years' War and its Influence on Battle Painting in the Seventeenth and Eighteenth Century,' in: Bussmann and Schilling (eds), *1648*, 2:485–92.

Chisick, Harvey, *The Limits of Reform in the Enlightenment: Attitudes towards the Education of the Lower Classes in Eighteenth-Century France* (Princeton, 1981).

Clark, Christopher, *Iron Kingdom: The Rise and Downfall of Prussia, 1600–1947* (London, 2006).

Clarke, Desmond, *Descartes: A Biography* (Cambridge, 2006).

Clarke, Desmond, *Descartes's Theory of Mind* (Oxford, 2005).

Cobley, Evelyn, *Representing War: Form and Ideology in First World War Narratives* (Toronto, 1993).

Cohen, Esther, 'To Die a Criminal for the Public Good: The Execution Ritual in Later Medieval Paris,' in: Bernard S. Bachrach and David Nicholas (eds), *Law, Custom and the Social Fabric in Medieval Europe: Essays in Honor of Bruce Lyon*, Studies in Medieval Culture 28 (Kalamazoo, 1990), pp. 285–304.

Cohen, Esther, *The Crossroads of Justice* (Leiden, 1993).

Cohen, Kathleen, *Metamorphosis of a Death Symbol: The Transi Tomb in the Late Middle Ages and the Renaissance* (Berkeley, 1973).

Cohen, Michèle, *Fashioning Masculinity: National Identity and Language in the Eighteenth Century* (London, 1996).

Cohn, Norman R. C., *The Pursuit of the Millennium: Revolutionary Millenarianism and Mystical Anarchists of the Middle Ages*, Rev. edition (New York, 1970).

Contamine, Philippe, 'Mourir pour la patrie,' in: Pierre Nora (ed.), *Les Lieux de Mémoire. II. La Nation*, 3 vols (Paris, 1986), vol. 2, pp. 12–43.

Contamine, Philippe, *War in the Middle Ages*, trans. Michael Jones (New York, 1984).

Cooey, Paula M., 'Experience, Body, and Authority,' *Harvard Theological Review* 82:3 (1989), pp. 325–342.

Cook, Albert, *Thresholds: Studies in the Romantic Experience* (Madison, 1985).

Cottingham, John, 'Cartesian Dualism: Theology, Metaphysics, and Science', in: John Cottingham (ed.), *The Cambridge Companion to Descartes* (Cambridge, 1992), 236–57.

Cottom, Daniel, *Cannibals and Philosophers. Bodies of Enlightenment* (Baltimore, 2001).

Crowther, Paul, *The Kantian Sublime: From Morality to Art* (Oxford, 1991).

Cru, Jean N., *War Books: A Study in Historical Criticism*, trans. S. J. Pincetl and E. Marchand (San Diego, 1976).

Cumont, Franz, 'La plus ancienne légende de S. Georges,' *Revue de l'Histoire des Religions* 114 (1936), 5–51.

Damon, John Edward, *Soldier Saints and Holy Warriors: Warfare and Sanctity in the Literature of Early England* (Aldershot, 2003).

Davies, Rupert E., *Methodism* (Harmondsworth, 1963).

Davis, Alex, *Chivalry and Romance in the English Renaissance. Studies in Renaissance Literature*, vol. 11 (Cambridge, 2003).

Day, J. F. R., 'Losing One's Character: Heralds and the Decline of English Knighthood from the Later Middle Ages to James I,' in: Susan J. Ridyard (ed.), *Chivalry, Knighthood, and War in the Middle Ages* (Sewanee, 1999), pp. 97–116.

Delon, Michel, *Le Savoir-vivre libertin* (Paris, 2000).

Denby, David J., *Sentimental Narrative and the Social Order in France, 1760–1820* (Cambridge, 1994).

Denin, Greg, 'The Face of Battle: Valparaiso, 1814,' *War and Society* 1 (1983), 25–42.

Derounian-Stodola, Kathryn Zabelle, and James A. Levernier. *The Indian Captivity Narrative, 1550–1900* (New York, 1993).

DeVries, Kelly, 'God and Defeat in Medieval Warfare: Some Preliminary Thoughts,' in: Donald J. Kagay and L. J. Andrew Villalon (eds), *The Circle of War in the Middle Ages: Essays on Medieval Military and Naval History* (Woodbridge, 1999), pp. 87–97.

Dewald, Jonathan, *Aristocratic Experience and the Origins of Modern Culture: France, 1570–1715* (Berkeley, 1993).

DuBois, Page, *Torture and Truth* (New York, 1991).

Dubost, Jean-Pierre, 'Libertinage and Rationality: From the "Will to Knowledge" to Libertine Textuality,' in: Catherine Cusset (ed.), *Libertinage and Modernity*, *Yale French Studies*, vol. 94 (New Haven, 1999), pp. 52–78.

Duffy, Christopher, *The Army of Frederick the Great* (New York, 1974).

Duffy, Christopher, *The Army of Maria Theresa: The Armed Forces of Imperial Austria, 1740–1780* (New York, 1977).

Duffy, Christopher, *Russia's Military Way to the West: Origins and Nature of Russian Military Power 1700–1800* (London, 1981).

Duffy, Christopher, *The Military Experience in the Age of Reason* (London, 1987).

Duffy, Christopher, *Eagles over the Alps – Suvorov in Italy and Switzerland, 1799* (Chicago, 1999).

Duffy, Christopher, *Prussia's Glory: Rossbach and Leuthen 1757* (Chicago, 2003).

Dinwiddy, J. R., 'The Early Nineteenth-Century Campaign Against Flogging in the Army,' *English Historical Review* 97:383 (1982), 308–31.

Egmond, Florike, 'Execution, Dissection, Pain and Infamy: A Morphological Investigation,' in: Florike Egmond and Robert Zwijnenberg (eds), *Bodily Extremities. Preoccupations with the Human Body in Early Modern European Culture* (Aldershot, 2003), pp. 92–127.

Ehrenreich, Barbara, *Blood Rites: Origins and History of the Passions of War* (New York, 1997).

Eksteins, Modris, 'All Quiet on the Western Front and the Fate of a War,' *Journal of Contemporary History* 15 (1980), 345–66.

Eliade, Mircea, 'Initiation: An Overview,' *Encyclopedia of Religion*, vol. 7 (New York, 1995), pp. 224–9.

Eliade, Mircea, *Rites and Symbols of Initiation: The Mysteries of Birth and Rebirth* (New York, 1958).

Ellington, Ter, *The Myth of the Noble Savage* (Berkeley, 2001).

Ellis, Markman, *The Politics of Sensibility: Race, Gender and Commerce in the Sentimental Novel* (New York, 1996).

Ellison, Julie, *Cato's Tears and the Making of Anglo-American Emotion* (Chicago, 1999).

Emerson, Catherine, *Olivier de la Marche and the Rhetoric of 15th-Century Historiography* (Woodbridge, 2004).

Encyclopedia of the Romantic Era, 1760–1850, Christopher John Murray (ed.), 2 vols (New York, 2003).

Ermarth, Michael, *Wilehlm Dilthey: The Critique of Historical Reason* (Chicago, 1978).

Esdaile, Charles J., *The Wars of Napoleon* (London, 1995).

Ettinghausen, Henry, 'The Laconic and the Baroque: Two 17th-Century Spanish Soldier Autobiographers (Alonso de Contreras and Diego Duque de Estrada),' *Forum for Modern Language Studies* 26:3 (1990), 204–11.

Evans, Gillian Rosemary, *Problems of Authority in the Reformation Debates* (Cambridge, 1992).

Ezell, Margaret J. M., 'John Locke's Images of Childhood: Early Eighteenth Century Response to *Some Thoughts Concerning Education*,' *Eighteenth-Century Studies* 17:2 (1983–84), 139–55.

Fabian, Ann, *The Unvarnished Truth: Personal Narratives in Nineteenth-Century America* (Berkeley, 2000)

Fallows, Noel, 'Knighthood, Wounds, and the Chivalric Ideal,' in: Susan J. Ridyard (ed.), *Chivalry, Knighthood, and War in the Middle Ages* (Sewanee, 1999), pp. 117–136.

Fanning, Steven, *Mystics of the Christian Tradition* (London, 2001).

Faust, Drew Gilpin, 'Christian Soldiers: The Meaning of Revivalism in the Confederate Army,' *The Journal of Southern History*, 53:1 (1987), 63–90.

Ferguson, Arthur B., *The Chivalric Tradition in Renaissance England* (Washington, 1986).

Fernández, Jouan José Luna, 'The Hall of Realms of the *Buen Retiro* Palace in Madrid,' in: Bussmann and Schilling (eds), *1648*, 2:121–9.

Figley, Charles R. (ed.), *Stress Disorders among Vietnam Veterans: Theory, Research, and Treatment* (New York, 1978).

Finke, Laurie A., 'Mystical Bodies and the Dialogics of Vision,' in: Ulrike Wiethaus (ed.), *Maps of Flesh and Light: The Religious Experience of Medieval Women Mystics* (Syracuse, 1993), pp. 28–44.

Fischer, David Hackett, *Washington's Crossing* (Oxford, 2004).

Fitzpatrick, Tara, 'The Figure of Captivity: The Cultural Work of the Puritan Captivity Narrative,' *American Literary History* 3:1 (1991), 1–26.

Flynn, Maureen, 'The Spiritual Uses of Pain in Spanish Mysticism,' *Journal of the American Academy of Religion* 64:2 (1999), 257–78.

Forrest, Alan I., *Conscripts and Deserters: The Army and French Society during the Revolution and Empire* (Oxford, 1989).

Forrest, Alan I., *Napoleon's Men: The Soldiers of the Revolution and Empire* (London, 2002).

Foucault, Michel, *Discipline and Punish: The Birth of a Prison* (New York, 1995).

France, John, 'War and Sanctity: Saints' Lives as Sources for Early Medieval Warfare,' *Journal of Medieval Military History* 3 (2005), 14–22.

Fritz, Stephen G., ' "We are Trying... to Change the Face of the World" – Ideology and Motivation in the Wehrmacht on the Eastern Front: The View from Below,' *The Journal of Military History* 60:4 (1996), 683–710.

Fulbrook, Mary, *Piety and Politics: Religion and the Rise of Absolutism in England, Wuerttemberg, and Prussia* (Cambridge, 1983).

Fussell, Paul, *The Great War and Modern Memory* (Oxford, 1975).

Gat, Azar, *The Origins of Military Thought: From the Enlightenment to Clausewitz* (Oxford, 1989).

Gat, Azar, *The Development of Military Thought: The Nineteenth Century* (Oxford, 1992).

Gates, David, *The British Light Infantry Arm c. 1790–1815* (London, 1987).

Gaukroger, Stephen, *Descartes: An Intellectual Biography* (Oxford, 1995).

Gay, Peter, *The Enlightenment: An Interpretation*, 2 vols (New York, 1969).

Gillingham, John, ' "Up with Orthodoxy!": In Defense of Vegetian Warfare,' *Journal of Medieval Military History* 2 (2004), 149–58.

Gillingham, John, 'War and Chivalry in the History of William the Marhsal,' *Richard Coeur de Lion: Kingship, Chivalry and War in the Twelfth Century* (London, 1994), pp. 227–42.

Glete, Jan, *War and the State in Early Modern Europe: Spain, the Dutch Republic and Sweden as Fiscal-Military States, 1500–1660* (London, 2002).

Glucklich, Ariel, *Sacred Pain: Hurting the Body for the Sake of the Soul* (Oxford, 2001).

Goldie, Sue M. (ed.), *I Have Done My Duty: Florence Nightingale in the Crimean War, 1854–56* (Iowa City, 1987).

Goodman, Jennifer R., *Chivalry and Exploration, 1298–1630* (Woodbridge, 1998).

Goulemot, Jean-Marie, 'Toward a Definition of Libertine Fiction and Pornographic Novels,' in: *Libertinage and Modernity*, ed. Catherine Cusset, *Yale French Studies*, vol. 94 (New Haven, 1999).

Goy-Blanquet, Dominique (ed.), *Joan of Arc, a Saint for All Reasons: Studies in Myth and Politics* (Aldershot, 2003).

Greenblatt, Stephen, 'Mutilation and Meaning,' in: David Hillman and Carla Mazzio (eds), *The Body in Parts: Fantasies of Corporeality in Early Modern Europe* (New York, 1997), pp. 221–42.

Greyerz, Kaspar von, 'Religion in the Life of German and Swiss Autobiographers (Sixteenth and Early Seventeenth Centuries),' in: Kaspar von Greyerz (ed.), *Religion and Society in Early Modern Europe, 1500–1800* (London, 1984), pp. 223–41.

Groebner, Valentin, *Defaced: The Visual Culture of Violence in the Late Middle Ages*, trans. Pamela Selwyn (New York, 2004).

Guillermou, Alain, *Saint Ignace de Loyola: Suivi de Ignace de Loyola: pages choisies* (Paris, 1957).

Gunn, Steven, 'The French Wars of Henry VIII,' in: Jeremy Black (ed.), *The Origins of War in Early Modern Europe* (Edinburgh, 1987), pp. 28–51.

Haggerty, George E., *Men in Love: Masculinity and Sexuality in the Eighteenth Century* (New York, 1999).

Hale, John Rigby, *Artists and Warfare in the Renaissance* (New Haven, 1990).

Hale, John Rigby, *War and Society in Renaissance Europe*, 2nd edition (Guernsey, 1998).

Haller, William, *The Rise of Puritanism* (New York, 1957).

Hampson, Norman, *A Cultural History of the Enlightenment* (New York, 1968).

Hanson, Victor Davis, *Hoplites: The Classical Greek Battle Experience* (London, 1991).

Harari, Yuval Noah, 'Martial Illusions: War and Disillusionment in Twentieth-Century and Renaissance Military Memoirs,' *Journal of Military History* 69:1 (2005), 43–72.

Harari, Yuval Noah, 'Military Memoirs: A Historical Overview of the Genre from the Middle Ages to the Late Modern Era,' *War in History* 14:3 (2007), 289–309.

Harari, Yuval Noah, *Renaissance Military Memoirs: War, History and Identity, 1450–1600* (Woodbridge, 2004).

Harari, Yuval Noah, *Special Operations in the Age of Chivalry, 1100–1550* (Woodbridge, 2007).

Hardin, James (ed.), *Reflection and Action: Essays on the Bildungsroman* (Columbia, SC, 1991).

Hardin, James (ed.), 'Introduction,' *Reflection and Action*, i–xxvii.

Hawkins, Anne Hunsaker, *Archetypes of Conversion: The Autobiographies of Augustine, Bunyan and Merton* (London, 1985).

Hendrickson, Ken, 'A Kinder, Gentler British Army: Mid-Victorian Experiments in the Management of Army Vice at Gibraltar and Aldershot,' *War and Society* 14:2 (1996), 21–33.

Herf, Jeffrey, *Reactionary Modernism: Technology, Culture, and Politics in Weimar and the Third Reich* (Cambridge, 1984).

Herzog, Tobey C., *Vietnam War Stories: Innocence Lost* (London, 1992).

Hillman, David, 'Visceral Knowledge,' in: David Hillman and Carla Mazzio (eds), *The Body in Parts: Fantasies of Corporeality in Early Modern Europe* (New York, 1997), pp. 81–106.

Hinnant, Charles H., 'Schiller and the Political Sublime: Two Perspectives,' *Criticism* 44:2 (2002), 121–38.

Hipp, Marie-Thérèse, *Mythes et Réalités: Enquête sur le roman et les mémoires (1660–1700)* (Paris, 1976).

Hoffmeister, Gerhart, 'From Goethe's *Wilhelm Meister* to anti-*Meister* Novels: The Romantic Novel between Tieck's *William Lovell* and Hoffmann's *Kater Murr*,' in: Mahoney, *Literature of German Romanticism*, pp. 79–100.

Holmes, Richard, *Redcoat: The British Soldier in the Age of Horse and Musket* (London, 2002).

Houlding, J. A., *Fit for Service: The Training of the British Army, 1715–1795* (Oxford, 1981).

Howard, Michael, *Weapons and Peace* (London, 1983).

Hunt, Lynn and Margaret Jacob, 'The Affective Revolution in 1790s Britain,' *Eighteenth-Century Studies* 34:4 (2001), 491–521.

Hynes, Samuel, *The Soldiers' Tale. Bearing Witness to Modern War* (London, 1998).

Hynes, Samuel Lynn, *A War Imagined: The First World War and English Culture* (London, 1990).

Ireland, Craig, 'The Appeal to Experience and its Consequences: Variations on a Persistent Thompsonian Theme,' *Cultural Critique* 52 (2002), 86–107.

Israel, Jonathan I., *Radical Enlightenment: Philosophy and the Making of Modernity 1650–1750* (Oxford, 2001).

Jones, Chris, *Radical Sensibility: Literature and Ideas in the 1790s* (London, 1993).

Jones, Howard Mumford, *Revolution and Romanticism* (Cambridge, MA, 1974).

Joseph, Stephen and P. Alex Linley, 'Positive Adjustment to Threatening Events: An Organismic Valuing Theory of Growth through Adversity,' *Review of General Psychology* 9:3 (2005), 262–280.

Jung, Martin H., *Frauen des Pietismus* (Gütersloh, 1998).

Jung, Martin H. (ed.), 'Vorwort,' *"Mein Herz brannte richtig in der Liebe Jesu": Autobiographien frommer Frauen aus Pietismus und Erweckungsbewegung* (Aachen, 1999).

Juster, Susan, ' "In a Different Voice": Male and Female Narratives of Religious Conversion in Post-Revolutionary America,' *American Quarterly* 41:1 (1989), 34–62.

Kaeuper, Richard W., *Chivalry and Violence in Medieval Europe* (Oxford, 1999).

Kaplan, Danny, 'The Military as a Second Bar Mitzvah: Combat Service as an Initiation-Rite to Zionist Masculinity,' in: Mai Ghoussoub and Emma Sinclair-Webb (eds), *Imagined Masculinities: Male Identity and Culture in the Modern Middle East* (London, 2000), pp. 127–44.

Kaplan, Danny, *Brothers and Others in Arms: The Making of Love and War in Israeli Combat Units* (New York, 2003).

Kedar, Benjamin Z., *Crusade and Mission: European Approaches Towards the Muslims* (Princeton, NJ, 1984).

Keegan, John, *A History of Warfare* (New York, 1993).

Keen, Maurice (ed.), 'The Changing Scene: Guns, Gunpowder, and Permanent Armies,' *Medieval Warfare: A History* (Oxford: Oxford University Press, 1999), pp. 273–92.

Keen, Maurice, *Chivalry* (New Haven, 1984).

Keen, Maurice, 'Chivalry, Nobility and the Man-at-Arms,' in: Christopher T. Allmand (ed.), *War, Literature and Politics in the Late Middle Ages* (Liverpool, 1976), pp. 32–45.

Keen, Maurice, 'Huizinga, Kilgour and the Decline of Chivalry,' *Medievalia et Humanistica*, new ser., 8 (1977), pp. 1–20.

Kieckhefer, Richard, *Unquiet Souls: Fourteenth-Century Saints and Their Religious Milieu* (Chicago, 1984).

Kiernan, V. G., *The Duel in European History* (Oxford, 1988).

Kilgour, Maggie, *The Rise of the Gothic Novel* (London, 1995).

Kleinberg, Aviad, *Fra Ginepro's Leg of Pork. Christian Saints' Stories and Their Cultural Role* (Tel Aviv, 2000 [Hebrew]).

Knauer, Martin, 'War as *Memento Mori*: The Function and Significance of the Series of Engravings in the Thirty Years' War,' in: Bussmann and Schilling (eds), *1648*, 2:509–15.

Knecht, Robert J., 'Military Autobiography in Sixteenth-Century France,' in: J. R. Mulryne and Margaret Shewring (eds), *War, Literature and the Arts in Sixteenth-Century Europe* (London, 1989), pp. 3–21.

Knecht, Robert J., 'The Sword and the Pen: Blaise de Monluc and his *Commentaires*,' *Renaissance Studies* 9:1 (1995), 104–18.

Knott, Sarah, 'Sensibility and the American War for Independence,' *American Historical Review* 109 (February 2004), 19–41.

Koepke, Wulf, '*Bildung* and the Transformation of Society: Jean Paul's *Titan* and *Flegeljahre*,' in: Hardin (ed.), *Reflection and Action*, pp. 228–53.

Kolb, Robert, *For All the Saints: Changing Perceptions of Martyrdom and Sainthood in the Lutheran Reformation* (Macon, 1987).

Krimmer, Elisabeth, 'Transcendental Soldiers: Warfare in Schiller's *Wallenstein* and *Die Jungfrau von Orleans*,' *Eighteenth-Century Fiction* 19:1–2 (2006/7), 99–121.

Kunzle, David, *From Criminal to Courtier: The Soldier in Netherlandish Art 1550–1672* (Leiden, 2002).

Kuperty, Nadine, *Se dire à la Renaissance: les mémoires au XVIe siècle* (Paris, 1997).

Kwasny, Mark V., *Washington's Partisan War, 1775–1783* (Kent, Ohio, 1996).

Lamb, Jonathan, 'Sterne, Sebald, and Siege Archirecture,' *Eighteenth-Century Fiction* 19:1–2 (2006/7), 21–41.

Landwehr, John, *Romeyn de Hooghe the Etcher: Contemporary Portrayal of Europe, 1662–1707* (Leiden, 1973).

Langbaum, Robert, 'The Epiphanic Mode in Wordsworth and Modern Literature,' *New Literary History* 14 (1983), 335–58.

Lavalle, Denis, 'The Thirty Years' War, Artists and Great Religious Painting,' in: Bussmann and Schilling (eds), *1648*, 2:153–59.

Le Goff, Jacques, *Saint Francis of Assisi*, trans. Christine Rhone (London, 2004).

Leed, Eric J., *No Man's Land: Combat and Identity in World War I* (Cambridge, 1979).

Lennon, Thomas M., 'Bayle and Late Seventeenth-Century Thought,' in: John P. Wright and Paul Potter (eds), *Psyche and Soma: Physicians and Metaphysicians on the Mind-Body Problem from Antiquity to Enlightenment* (Oxford, 2000), pp. 197–216.

Levisi, Margarita, 'Golden Age Autobiography: The Soldiers,' in: Nicholas Spadaccini and Jenaro Taléns (ed.), *Autobiography in Early Modern Spain* (Minneapolis, 1988), pp. 97–118.

Lieblich, Amia, *Transition to Adulthood during Military Service: The Israeli Case* (Albany, 1989).

Linder, Ann P., *Princes of the Trenches: Narrating the German Experience of the First World War* (Columbia, 1996).

Linderman, Gerald F., *Embattled Courage: The Experience of Combat in the American Civil War* (London, 1987).

Littlejohns, Richard, 'Early Romanticism,' in: Mahoney (ed.), *Literature of German Romanticism*, pp. 61–78.

Lomski-Feder, Edna, *As if There Was no War* (Jerusalem, 1998 [Hebrew]).

Löwy, Michael and Robert Sayre, *Romanticism against the Tide of Modernity* (London, 2001).

Lozovsky, Natalia, *The Earth is Our Book: Geographical Knowledge in the Latin West ca. 400–1000* (Ann Arbor, 2000).

Luard, Evan, *War in International Society* (London, 1986).

Lynn, John A., *Bayonets of the Republic: Motivation and Tactics in the Army of Revolutionary France, 1791–94* (Boulder, Colo., 1996).

Lynn, John A., *Giant of the Grand Siècle: The French Army, 1610–1715* (Cambridge, 1997).

Lynn, John A., *Battle: A History of Combat and Culture* (Boulder, Colo., 2003).

Maarseveen, Michel P. van, 'The Eighty Years' War in Northern Netherlandish Painting of the Seventeenth Century: Siege Scenes,' in: Bussmann and Schilling (eds), *1648*, 2:469–76.

Maarseveen, Michel P. van, and Michiel Kersten, 'The Eighty Years' War in Northern Netherlandish Painting of the Seventeenth Century: Cavalry Skirmishes and Guardroom Scenes,' in: Bussmann and Schilling (eds), *1648*, 2:477–84.

Mahedy, William P., *Out of the Night: The Spiritual Journey of Vietnam Vets* (New York, 1986).

Mahoney, Dennis F., 'The Apprenticeship of the Reader: The Bildungsroman of the "Age of Goethe," ' in: Hardin, *Reflection and Action*, 97–117.

Mahoney, Dennis F. (ed.), *The Literature of German Romanticism* (Rochester, 2004).

Makkreel, Rudolf A., *Dilthey: Philosopher of the Human Studies* (Princeton, 1977).

Manceron, Claude, *Twilight of the Old Order 1774–1778*, trans. Patricia Wolf (New York, 1977).

Martini, Fritz, 'Bildungsroman – Term and Theory,' in: Hardin, *Reflection and Action*, pp. 1–25.

Mascuch, Michael, *Origins of the Individualist Self: Autobiography and Self-Identity in England, 1591–1791* (Stanford, 1996).

Maurey, Yossi, 'A Courtly Lover and an Earthly Knight Turned Soldiers of Christ in Machaut's Motet 5,' *Early Music History* 24 (2005), 169–212.

McGann, Jerome, *The Poetics of Sensibility: A Revolution in Literary Style* (Oxford, 1996).

McMahon, Darrin M., *The Pursuit of Happiness: A History from the Greeks to the Present* (London, 2006).

McNamara, Jo-Ann, 'The Rhetoric of Orthodoxy: Clerical Authority and Female Innovation in the Struggle with Heresy,' in: Ulrike Wiethaus (ed.), *Maps of Flesh and Light: The Religious Experience of Medieval Women Mystics* (Syracuse, 1993), pp. 9–27.

McNeill, William H., *Keeping Together in Time: Dance and Drill in Human History* (Cambridge, MA, 1995).

Menhennet, Alan, *The Romantic Movement* (London, 1981).

Merback, Mitchell B., *The Thief, the Cross, and the Wheel: Pain and the Spectacle of Punishment in Medieval and Renaissance Europe* (Chicago, 1998).

Meumann, Markus, 'The Experience of Violence and the Expectation of the End of the World in Seventeenth Century Europe,' in: Joseph Canning, Hartmut Lehmann, and Jay Winter (eds), *Power, Violence and Mass Death in Pre-Modern and Modern Times* (Aldershot, 2004), pp. 141–62.

Michael, Emily, 'Renaissance Theories of Body, Soul, and Mind,' in: John P. Wright and Paul Potter (eds), *Psyche and Soma: Physicians and Metaphysicians on the Mind-Body Problem from Antiquity to Enlightenment* (Oxford, 2000), pp. 147–72.

Millis, Léonard R. (ed.), *Le mystére de Saint Sébastien* (Geneva, 1965).

Minden, Michael, *The German Bildungsroman: Incest and Inheritance* (Cambridge, 1997).

Monk, S. H., *The Sublime: A Study of Critical Theories in 18th Century England* (New York, 1935).

Moretti, Franco, *The Way of the World: The Bildungsroman in European Culture* (London, 1987).

Morgan, D. A. L., 'Memoirs and the Self-Consciousness of the Court: The Birth of a Genre,' in: Steven Gunn and Antheun Janse (eds), *The Court as a Stage: England and the Low Countries in the Later Middle Ages* (Woodbridge, 2006), pp. 118–31.

Morinis, Alan, 'The Ritual Experience of Pain and the Transformation of Consciousness,' *Ethos* 13 (1985), 150–74.

Morris, David, B., *The Culture of Pain* (Berkeley, 1991).

Mortimer, Geoffrey, 'Individual Experience and Perception of the Thirty Years War in Eyewitness Personal Accounts,' *German History* 20:2 (2002), 141–60.

Mortimer, Geoffrey, *Eyewitness Accounts of the Thirty Years War, 1618–48* (Houndmills, 2002).

Mott, Lawrence V., 'The Battle of Malta, 1283: Prelude to a Disaster,' in: Donald J. Kagay and L. J. Andrew Villalon (eds), *The Circle of War in the Middle Ages: Essays on Medieval Military and Naval History* (Woodbridge, 1999), pp. 145–72.

Muir, Rory, *Tactics and the Experience of Battle in the Age of Napoleon* (New Haven, 1998).

Murashev, Gennady A., *Tituli Chini Nagradi* (St. Petersburg, 2000).

Murrin, Michael, *History and Warfare in Renaissance Epic* (Chicago, 1994).

Neuschel, Kristen B., *Word of Honor: Interpreting Noble Culture in Sixteenth-Century France* (Ithaca, 1989).

Nichols, Austin, *The Poetics of Epiphany* (Tuscaloosa, 1987).

Noble, Thomas F. X. and Head, Thomas (eds), *Soldiers of Christ: Saints and Saints' Lives from Late Antiquity and the Early Middle Ages* (University Park, 1995).

Nugent, Christopher, *Mysticism, Death and Dying* (Albany, 1994).

O'Brien, David, 'Propaganda and the Republic of Arts in Antoine-Jean Gros's *Napoleon Visiting the Battlefield of Eylau the Morning after the Battle*', *French Historical Studies* 26:2 (2003), 281–314.

Oerlemans, Onno, *Romanticism and the Materiality of Nature* (Toronto, 2002).

O'Neal, John C., *The Authority of Experience: Sensationist Theory in the French Enlightenment* (University Park, Pennsylvania, 1996).

Outram, Dorinda, *The Enlightenment* (Cambridge, 1995).

Palmer, R. R., *The Improvement of Humanity: Education and the French Revolution* (Princeton, 1985).

Paret, Peter, *Clausewitz and the State* (Oxford, 1976).

Paret, Peter, 'The Genesis of *On War*,' in: Clausewitz, *On War*, ed. Howard and Paret, pp. 3–25.

Paret, Peter, *Imagined Battles* (Chapel Hill, 1997).

Paret, Peter, *Yorck and the Era of Prussian Reform, 1807–1815* (Princeton, 1966).

Paris, Michael, *Warrior Nation: Images of War in British Popular Culture, 1850–2000* (London, 2000).

Parker, Geoffrey, 'The Military Revolution, 1560–1660 – A Myth?' in: Clifford J. Rogers (ed.), *The Military Revolution Debate: Readings in the Military Transformation of Early Modern Europe* (Boulder, 1995), pp. 37–54.

Parker, Geoffrey, *The Military Revolution: Military Innovation and the Rise of the West, 1500–1800*, 2nd edition (New York, 1996).

Parker, Geoffrey (ed.), *The Thirty Years War*, 2nd edition (London, 1997).

Parrott, David, *Richelieu's Army: War, Government and Society in France, 1624–1642* (Cambridge, 2001).

Partner, Peter, *God of Battles: Holy Wars of Christianity and Islam* (Princeton, 1998).

Perkins, Judith, *The Suffering Self: Pain and Narrative Representation in the Early Christian Era* (London, 1995).

Peters, Edward, *Torture* (Oxford, 1985).

Pfaffenbichler, Matthias, 'The Early Baroque Battle Scene,' in: Bussmann and Schilling (eds), *1648*, 2:493–500.

Pinch, Adela, *Strange Fits of Passion: Epistemologies of Emotion, Hume to Austen* (Stanford, 1996).

Plax, Julie Anne, 'Seventeenth-Century French Images of Warfare,' in: Pia Cuneo (ed.), *Artful Armies, Beautiful Battles: Art and Warfare in Early Modern Europe* (Leiden, 2002), pp. 131–58.

Porter, Pamela, *Medieval Warfare in Manuscripts* (Toronto, 2000).

Porter, Roy, *Flesh in the Age of Reason* (New York, 2004).

Porter, Roy, *The Greatest Benefit to Mankind: A Medical History of Humanity* (New York, 1997).

Prestwich, Michael, *Armies and Warfare in the Middle Ages: The English Experience* (New Haven, 1996).

Price, Leah, *The Anthology and the Rise of the Novel: From Richardson to George Eliot* (Cambridge, 2000).

Pyenson, Lewis and Susan Sheets-Pyenson, *Servants of Nature: A History of Scientific Institutions, Enterprises and Sensibilities* (New York, 1999).

Quilley, Geoff, 'Duty and Mutiny: The Aesthetics of Loyalty and the Representation of the British Sailor c.1798–1800,' in: Shaw, *Romantic Wars* (Aldershot, 2000), 80–109.

Quinn, Patrick J. and Steven Trout (eds), *The Literature of the Great War Reconsidered: Beyond Modern Memory* (New York, 2001).

Rapley, Elizabeth, 'Her Body the Enemy: Self-Mortification in Seventeenth-Century Convents,' *Proceedings of the Annual Meeting of the Western Society for French History* 21 (1994), 25–35.

Raymond, Pierre, *Le passage au materialisme: idealisme et materialisme dans l'histoire de la Philosophie, mathematiques et materialisme* (Paris, 1973).

Redlich, Fritz, *The German Military Enterpriser and His Work Force: A Study in European Economic and Social History*, 2 vols (Wiesbaden, 1964–65).

Rey, Roselyne, *History of Pain*, trans. Louise Elliott Wallace, J. A. Cadden and S. W. Cadden (Cambridge, MA, 1995).

Richard, Marie, 'Jacques Callot (1592–1635) *Les Miseres et les Malheurs de la Guerre* (1633): A Work and its Context,' in: Bussmann and Schilling (eds), *1648*, 2:517–23.

Richards, Robert J., *The Romantic Conception of Life: Science and Philosophy in the Age of Goethe* (Chicago, 2002).

Richardson, Alan, *British Romanticism and the Science of the Mind* (Cambridge, 2001).

Richey, Stephen W., *Joan of Arc: The Warrior Saint* (Westport, Conn., 2003).

Ritter, Gerhard, *Frederick the Great*, trans. Peter Paret (Berkeley, 1974).

Roberts, Michael, 'The Military Revolution, 1560–1660,' in: Clifford J. Rogers (ed.), *The Military Revolution Debate: Readings in the Military Transformation of Early Modern Europe* (Boulder, 1995), pp. 13–36.

Rodis-Lewis, Geneviève, 'Descartes' Life and the Development of his Philosophy,' in: John Cottingham (ed.), *The Cambridge Companion to Descartes* (Cambridge, 1992), pp. 21–57.

Roeck, Bernd, 'The Atrocities of War in Early Modern Art,' in: Joseph Canning, Hartmut Lehmann, and Jay Winter (eds), *Power, Violence and Mass Death in Pre-Modern and Modern Times* (Aldershot, 2004), pp. 129–140.

Rogers, H. C. B., *The British Army of the Eighteenth Century* (London, 1977).

Rosenfield, Leonora Cohen, *From Beast-Machine to Man-Machine* (New York, 1968).

Rosenthal, David M., *Materialism and the Mind-Body Problem* (Engelwood Cliffs, NJ, 1971).

Ross, Ellen, ' "She Wept and Cried Right Loud for Sorrow and for Pain": Suffering, the Spiritual Journey, and Women's Experience in Late Medieval Mysticism,' in: Ulrike Wiethaus (ed.), *Maps of Flesh and Light: The Religious Experience of Medieval Women Mystics* (Syracuse, 1993), pp. 45–59.

Rozemond, Marleen, *Descartes's Dualism* (Cambridge, MA, 1998).

Ruff, Julius, *Violence in Early Modern Europe* (Cambridge, 2001).

Russell, Peter E., 'Redcoats in the Wilderness: British Officers and Irregular Warfare in Europe, 1740 to 1760," *William and Mary Quarterly*, 3rd series, 35 (October 1978), 629–52.

Ryan, Vanessa L., 'The Physiological Sublime: Burke's Critique of Reason,' *Journal of the History of Ideas*, 62:2 (2001), 265–79.

Sammons, Jeffrey L., 'The Bildungsroman for Nonspecialists: An Attempt at a Clarification,' in: Hardin, *Reflection and Action*, pp. 26–45.

Satterfield, George, *Princes, Posts, and Partisans: The Army of Louis XIV and Partisan Warfare in the Netherlands (1673–1678)* (Leiden, 2003).

Sawday, Jonathan, *The Body Emblazoned: Dissection and the Human Body in Renaissance Culture* (London, 1995).

Scarry, Elaine, *The Body in Pain: The Making and Unmaking of the World* (Oxford, 1985).

Schäfer, Walter Ernst, 'The Thirty Years' War in Moscherosch's "A Soldier's Life" and the Simplician Tales of Grimmelshausen,' in: Bussmann and Schilling (eds), *1648*, 2:339–45.

Schenk, H. G., *The Mind of the European Romantics* (Oxford, 1979).

Scholz, Susanne, *Body Narratives: Writing the Nation and Fashioning the Subject in Early Modern England* (Houndmills, 2000).

Schweitzer, Richard, *The Cross and the Trenches: Religious Faith and Doubt among British and American Great War Soldiers* (Westport, 2003).

Scott, Samuel F., *From Yorktown to Valmy: The Transformation of the French Army in the Age of Revolution* (Niwot, Colo., 1998).

Secada, Jorge, *Cartesian Metaphysics: The Late Scholastic Origins of Modern Philosophy* (Cambridge, 2000).

Shaffner, Randolph P., *The Apprenticeship Novel: A Study of the* Bildungsroman *as a Regulative Type in Western Literature with a Focus on Three Classic Representatives by Goethe, Maugham, and Mann* (New York, 1984).

Shaw, Philip (ed.), *Romantic Wars: Studies in Culture and Conflict, 1793–1822* (Aldershot, 2000).

Shaw, Philip, 'Introduction,' in: Shaw, *Romantic Wars*, pp. 1–12.

Sheffield, Gary, *Forgotten Victory: The First World War: Myths and Realities* (London, 2002).

Shephard, Ben, *War on Nerves: Soldiers and Psychiatrists in the Twentieth Century* (Cambridge, MA, 2001).

Shostak, Marjorie, *Nisa: The Life and Words of a !Kung Woman* (New York, 1983).

Showalter, Dennis E., 'Caste, Skill, and Training: The Evolution of Cohesion in European Armies from the Middle Ages to the Sixteenth Century', *Journal of Military History* 57:3 (1993), 407–30.

Siberry, Elizabeth, *Criticism of Crusading: 1095–1274* (Oxford, 1985).

Silverman, Lisa, *Tortured Subjects: Pain, Truth, and the Body in Early Modern France* (Chicago, 2001).

Siraisi, Nancy G., 'Medicine and the Renaissance World of Learning,' *Bulletin of the History of Medicine* 78:1 (2004), 1–36.

Skelley, Alan Ramsey, *The Victorian Army at Home: The Recruitment, Terms and Conditions of the British Regular, 1859–1889* (London, 1977).

Smeyers, Maurits, *Flemish Miniatures from the 8th to the Mid-16th Century: The Medieval World on Parchment* (Turnhout, 1999).

Sorell, Tom, *Descartes: A Very Short Introduction* (Oxford, 2000 [1987]).

Sproxton, Judy, *Violence and Religion: Attitudes towards Militancy in the French Civil Wars and the English Revolution* (London, 1995).

Stancliffe, Clare, *Saint Martin and His Hagiographer: History and Miracle in Sulpicius Severus* (Oxford, 1983).

Starkey, Armstrong, 'War and Culture, a Case Study: The Enlightenment and the conduct of the British Army in America, 1755–1781,' *War and Society* 8:1 (1990), pp. 1–28.

Starkey, Armstrong, *War in the Age of Enlightenment, 1700–1789* (London, 2003).

Starkey, Armstrong, *European and Native American Warfare 1675–1815* (London, 1998).

Starr, G. A., *Defoe and Spiritual Autobiography* (New York, 1971).

Steiner, E. E., 'Separating the Soldier from the Citizen: Ideology and Criticism of Corporal Punishment in the British Armies, 1790–1815,' *Social History* 8 (1983), 19–35.

Steinmetz, Andrew, *The Romance of Duelling, in All Times and Countries*, 2 vols (Richmond, 1971 [1868]).

Stern, J. P., *Ernst Jünger: A Writer of Our Times* (Cambridge, 1953).

Stewart, W. A. C., *Progressives and Radicals in English Education 1750–1970* (London, 1972).

Stoeffler, Fred Ernest, *The Rise of Evangelical Pietism* (Leiden, 1971).

Störkel, Arno, 'The Defenders of Mayence in 1792: A Portrait of a Small European Army at the Outbreak of the French Revolutionary Wars,' *War in History* 12:2 (1994), 1–21.

Strickland, Matthew, *War and Chivalry: The Conduct and Perception of War in England and Normandy, 1066–1217* (Cambridge, 1996).

Swaim, Kathleen M., *Pilgrim's Progress, Puritan Progress: Discourses and Contexts* (Urbana, 1993).

Tallett, Frank, *War and Society in Early Modern Europe, 1495–1715* (London, 1992).

Taves, Ann, *Fits, Trances, & Visions: Experiencing Religion and Explaining Experience from Wesley to James* (Princeton, NJ, 1999).

Taylor, Charles, *Sources of the Self: The Making of Modern Identity* (Cambridge, MA, 1989).

Thomas, Helen, *Romanticism and Slave Narratives: Transatlantic Testimonies* (Cambridge, 2000).

Thomson, Ann, *Materialism and Society in the Mid-Eighteenth Century: La Mettrie's Discours Préliminaire* (Geneva, 1981).

Thuillier, Jacques, 'The Thirty Years' War and the Arts,' in: Bussmann and Schilling (eds), *1648*, 2:15–28.

Trahard, Pierre, *Les Maîtres de la sensibilité française au XVIIIe siècle (1715–1789)*, 4 vols (Paris, 1931–33).

Ulbricht, Otto, 'The Experience of Violence during the Thirty Years War: A Look at the Civilian Victims,' in: Joseph Canning, Hartmut Lehmann, and Jay Winter (eds), *Power, Violence and Mass Death in Pre-Modern and Modern Times* (Aldershot, 2004), pp. 97–128.

Vale, Malcolm, *War and Chivalry: Warfare and Aristocratic Culture in England, France, and Burgundy at the End of the Middle Ages* (Athens, GA, 1981).

Van Creveld, Martin, *Command in War* (Cambridge, MA, 1985).

Van Creveld, Martin, *Fighting Power: German and US Army Performance, 1939–1945* (London, 1983).

Van Creveld, Martin, *Technology and War: From 2000 B.C. to the Present* (New York, 1989).

Van Gennep, A., *The Rites of Passage*, trans. Monika B. Vizedom and Gabrielle L. Caffee, with an introduction by Solon T. Kimball (Chicago, 1960).

Van Sant, Ann Jessie, *Eighteenth-Century Sensibility and the Novel* (Cambridge, 1994).

Vartanian, Aram, *La Mettrie's "L'Homme machine": A Study in the Origins of an Idea* (Princeton, 1960).

Vartanian, Aram, *Science and Humanism in the French Enlightenment* (Charlottesville, 1999).

Verbruggen, Jan Frans, *The Art of Warfare in Western Europe during the Middle Ages: From the Eighth Century to 1340*, trans. Sumner Willard and S. C. M. Southern, 2nd edition (Woodbridge, 1997).

Vila, Anne C., *Enlightenment and Pathology: Sensibility in the Literature and Medicine of Eighteenth-Century France* (Baltimore, 1998).

Voitle, R., *The Third Earl of Shaftesbury* (Baton Rouge, 1984).

Voller, Jack G., *The Supernatural Sublime: The Metaphysics of Terror in Anglo-American Romanticism* (DeKalb, Ill., 1994).

Voss, Stephen, 'Descartes: Heart and Soul,' in: John P. Wright and Paul Potter (eds), *Psyche and Soma: Physicians and Metaphysicians on the Mind-Body Problem from Antiquity to Enlightenment* (Oxford, 2000), pp. 173–96.

Watkins, Owen C., *The Puritan Experience* (London, 1972).

Watkins, Owen Spencer, *Soldiers and Preachers Too* (Royal Navy, Army and Royal Air Force Board of the Methodist Church [s.l.], 1981).

Watson, Janet S. K., *Fighting Different Wars: Experience, Memory, and the First World War in Britain* (Cambridge, 2004).

Watson, Samuel J., 'Religion and Combat Motivation in the Confederate Armies,' *The Journal of Military History*, 58:1 (1994), 29–55.

Watt, Ian, *The Rise of the Novel: Studies in Defoe, Richardson, and Fielding* (Harmondsworth, 1963).

Watts, Derek A., 'Self-Portrayal in Seventeenth-Century French Memoirs,' *Australian Journal of French Studies* 12 (1975), 263–86.

Waysman, M., J. Schwarzwald, and Z. Solomon, 'Hardiness: An Examination of its Relationship with Positive and Negative Long Term Changes Following Trauma,' *Journal of Traumatic Stress* 14 (2001), 531–548.

Weinstein, Arnold L., *Fictions of the Self: 1550–1800* (Princeton, 1981).

Weiskel, Thomas, *The Romantic Sublime: Studies in the Structure and Psychology of Transcendence* (Baltimore, 1976).

Wellman, Kathleen, *La Mettrie: Medicine, Philosophy, and Enlightenment* (Durham, 1992).

Wilson, Peter, 'European Warfare 1450–1815,' in: Jeremy Black (ed.), *War in the Early Modern World* (Boulder, 1999), pp. 177–206.

Wilton-Ely, John, '"Classic Ground": Britain, Italy, and the Grand Tour,' *Eighteenth-Century Life* 28:1 (2004), 136–65.

Winter, Jay, *Sites of Memory, Sites of Mourning: The Great War in European Cultural History* (Cambridge, 1995).

Wright, John P., 'Substance versus Function Dualism in Eighteenth-Century Medicine,' in: John P. Wright and Paul Potter (eds), *Psyche and Soma: Physicians and Metaphysicians on the Mind-Body Problem from Antiquity to Enlightenment* (Oxford, 2000), pp. 237–54.

Wright, John P. and Potter, Paul (eds), *Psyche and Soma: Physicians and Metaphysicians on the Mind-Body Problem from Antiquity to Enlightenment* (Oxford, 2000).

Wright, Nicholas, *Knights and Peasants: The Hundred Years War in the French Countryside* (Woodbridge, 1998).

Yarom, Niza, *Body, Blood and Sexuality*, trans. Irith Miller (Lod, 2001 [Hebrew]).

Yolton, John W., *Thinking Matter: Materialism in Eighteenth-Century Britain* (Oxford, 1983).

Yolton, John W., *Locke and French Materialism* (Oxford, 1991).

Zanger, Jules. 'Mary Rowlandson's Captivity Narrative as Confessional Literature: "After Such Knowledge, What Forgiveness?" ' *American Studies in Scandinavia* 27.2 (1995), 142–52.

Zupnick, Irving L., 'Saint Sebastian: The Vicissitudes of the Hero as Martyr,' in Norman T. Burns and C. J. Reagan (eds), *Concepts of the Hero in the Middle Ages and Renaissance* (Albany, 1975), pp. 239–67.

Movies

Apocalypse Now, directed by Francis Ford Coppala (USA, 1979).

Black Hawk Down, directed by Ridley Scott (USA, 2001).

Born on the Fourth of July, directed by Oliver Stone (USA, 1989).

Full Metal Jacket, directed by Stanley Kubrick (USA, 1987).

One of Us, directed by Uri and Beni Barabash (Tel Aviv, 1989).

Platoon, directed by Oliver Stone (USA, 1986).

Saving Private Ryan, directed by Steven Spielberg (USA, 1998).

Yossi & Jager, directed by Eytan Fox (Israel, 2002).

Index

References to material in the endnotes are presented in the following format: page number followed by the abbreviation n. and the number of the endnote in question. Words in foreign languages, and the names of books, plays, poems, and movies are italicized.